BIG TECH AND THE DIGITAL ECONOMY

BIG TECH AND THE DIGITAL ECONOMY

THE MOLIGOPOLY SCENARIO

NICOLAS PETIT

Professor of Competition Law,
European University Institute (EUI)

OXFORD
UNIVERSITY PRESS

OXFORD
UNIVERSITY PRESS

Great Clarendon Street, Oxford, OX2 6DP,
United Kingdom

Oxford University Press is a department of the University of Oxford.
It furthers the University's objective of excellence in research, scholarship,
and education by publishing worldwide. Oxford is a registered trade mark of
Oxford University Press in the UK and in certain other countries

First Edition published in 2020

Impression: 1

Published in the United States of America by Oxford University Press
198 Madison Avenue, New York, NY 10016, United States of America

British Library Cataloguing in Publication Data

Data available

Library of Congress Control Number: 2020932774

ISBN 978-0-19-883770-1

Printed and bound by
CPI Group (UK) Ltd, Croydon, CR0 4YY

Acknowledgments

This book is the product of cooperation, not competition. I owe first an imprescriptible debt to my former research assistant at the University of Liege, Jérôme De Cooman who helped me from the early background research until the final stage of proofreading. This book would not exist without his tireless work. My other research assistants and former PhD students Sandrine Matthieu, Jorge Marcos Ramos, and Dirk Auer provided welcome support at critical times. I am also their *obligé*.

Some people have played a key role in relation to specific chapters. My work on textual analysis in Chapter 2 benefited from the invaluable advice of my former colleague Ashwin Ittoo and from assistance of Dr. Xiaoxia Ye at the University of Liverpool Management School. Paul Belleflamme, Alex Galetovic, Axel Gautier, Lowie Knockaert, Alexis Walckiers, Greg Werden and Luigi Zingales offered great comments on Chapter 3. My friends Bo Heiden and Richard Sousa gave me the confidence to write Chapter 4, helping me improve my analytical focus. Lapo Fillistrucci confirmed my intuitions about the policy power of multisided market theory in Chapter 5.

My sabbatical at Stanford University in 2018 was foremost an opportunity for discussions with phenomenally thoughtful colleagues. In no particular order, I want to thank Steve Haber, Mark Lemley, Russ Roberts, Lew Zaretski, Christos Makridis, John Taylor, Paul Goldstein, and Manny Rincon Cruz for the time and attention they gave me.

Since I started this project in 2017, I interacted with many other peers. My pen sharpened upon discussion with Adi Ayal, Max Berre, Diane Coyle, Jacques Crémer, Ariel Ezrachi, Michal Gal, Jason Furman, Pablo Ibanez, Pierre Larouche, Philip Marsden, Frédéric Marty, Julian Nowag, Jorge Padilla and Alexandre de Streel. Lots of other unnamed academics, intellectuals as well as creative artists, also inhabit the pages of this book.

Many lost interactions in the form of unanswered calls and emails made the progress of this book possible. I apologize for the frustration that my lack of responsiveness created towards colleagues, friends and family.

Last, but not least, I had the privilege of submitting my final manuscript to an oligopoly of demanding reviewers. In a non-collusive way, Doug Melamed, Thibault Schrepel, Laurent Blavier, and Norman Neyrinck supplied an unrestricted quantity of challenging comments. I will never find enough words to thank them for the opportunity cost they incurred in committing time to review my work.

This book is dedicated to the three princesses of my life, Prescillia, Rachel, and Margot, who kept me spinning along the way.

Table of Contents

Table of Cases

GERMAN CASE

UK CASES AND DECISIONS

US CASES AND DECISIONS

Table of Legislation

Introduction

> There are these two young fish swimming along, and they happen to
> meet an older fish swimming the other way, who nods at them and says,
> "Morning, boys, how's the water?" And the two young fish swim on for
> a bit, and then eventually one of them looks over at the other and goes,
> "What the hell is water?"
>
> David Foster Wallace[1]

This book owes its existence to a series of articles that appeared in Slate in
2013. In "WarGames: Google vs. Apple," columnists Farhad Manjoo and
Matthew Yglesias imagine "what if Google and Apple went to (actual) war."[2] In
the fictional war-game, hostilities start when Apple decides to remove Google
as the default search engine on the iPhone and iPad. Google reciprocates with
operation "GhostFruit," a complete delisting of Apple from the search engine.
The tit for tat between Google and Apple escalates into an all-out war. Each
player leverages its installed base of customers, network of suppliers, and distinct
technological capabilities to harm the other. Google's engineers write a software that shut downs Apple's Chinese factory. Apple recruits an "Army" of loy-
alist customers to attack Google's data centers and snatch Android phones out
of people's hands. Eventually, the Obama administration, lobbied by Google,
steps in. It adds Apple to the State Department's list of international terror-
ist organizations. Apple's next move is brutal. Exiled on a Caribbean island,

---

1. David Foster Wallace, "This is Water" (2005) Commencement speech to the graduating class
at Kenyon College <https://fs.blog/2012/04/david-foster-wallace-this-is-water/> accessed
December 19, 2019.
2. See Farhad Manjoo and Matthew Yglesias, "WarGames: Google vs. Apple" (*Slate*, July 29,
2013) <http://www.slate.com/articles/technology/low_concept/features/2013/wargames/
what_if_google_and_apple_went_to_war_in_real_life.html> accessed December 10, 2019
(Manjoo plays Google. Yglesias plays Apple).

Big Tech and the Digital Economy. Nicolas Petit, Oxford University Press (2020). © Nicolas Petit.
DOI: 10.1093/oso/9780198837701.001.0001

Apple CEO Tim Cook instructs Air Force One's pilot, a secret member of the "Apple Army," to crash the Presidential plane (in exchange for his sacrifice, the pilot's wife and kids have been promised unlimited App Store downloads …). In the end, no clear winner emerges. But Amazon, Facebook, Walmart, and Elon Musk are rubbing their hands with glee.

Why does this matter? The Slate war-game hints at the possibility of intense levels of competition amongst big tech and other firms.[3] The implicit assumption underlying the Slate stories draws on a rich body of economic observations, made as early as 1942 by Joseph Schumpeter,[4] popularized by James Moore in the 1980s under the concept of "ecosystems" competition,[5] and more recently developed by scholars like David Teece in works on "dynamic competition."[6]

And yet, in more mainstream debates about tech firms, little attention is given to the bigger game of competition. The press seems obsessed by metrics suggestive of tech bigness: nine out of ten searches in the United States are done through Google or its subsidiary YouTube;[7] 67 percent of the US population uses Facebook;[8] Amazon controls 52.4 percent of online retail sales.[9] In turn, a current shibboleth is to employ monopoly rhetoric to discuss Google, Apple, or other tech firms like Facebook, Amazon, Microsoft, and Netflix. The assumption seems to be that the holding of a dominant share of a product without substitutes is evidence of low rivalry and weakened competition.

In the same spirit, one fashionable idea is that the monopoly of big tech is unprecedented. To many, the durability of big tech firms' monopoly

---

3. At the flick of a switch, Google and Apple substitute "nuclear" competition to "cold war" cooperation.

4. Joseph A Schumpeter, *Capitalism, Socialism and Democracy* (Harper and Brothers 1942) 85 "the businessman feels himself to be in a competitive situation even if he is alone in his field or if, though not alone, he holds a position such that investigating government experts fail to see any effective competition between him and any other firms in the same or a neighboring field and in consequence conclude that his talk, under examination, about his competitive sorrows is all make-believe."

5. James F Moore, "Predators and Prey: A New Ecology of Competition" (1993) 71(3) *Harvard Business Review* 75.

6. David J Teece, "Next-Generation Competition: New Concepts for Understanding How Innovation Shapes Competition and Policy in the Digital Economy" (2012) 9(4) *Journal of Law, Economics & Policy* 97.

7. Jeff Cockrell, "Does America Have an Antitrust Problem?" (2019) *Chicago Booth Review* <https://review.chicagobooth.edu/economics/2019/article/does-america-have-antitrust-problem> accessed December 10, 2019.

8. J Clement, "Facebook: Online Reach in the United States 2017–2023" (2019) *Statista* <https://www.statista.com/statistics/183460/share-of-the-us-population-using-facebook/> accessed December 10, 2019.

9. Andrew Lipsman, "The Future of Retail 2019" (*eMarketer*, December 5, 2018) <https://www.emarketer.com/content/the-future-of-retail-in-2019> accessed December 12, 2019.

positions allows an inference of qualitatively stronger incumbency advantages compared to the former generation of Internet giants like AOL, MySpace, or Yahoo!. Big tech's durability is interpreted as a sign of stasis and little effort is invested to seriously understand if these monopoly firms have competitively evolved through time.

Equally missing from this monopoly discussion is a consideration of how tech firms perform under standard measures of consumer welfare. Historical inhospitality to monopoly invites skepticism toward the benefits that consumers derive from big tech firms—including free services[10]—and suspicion toward novel consumer harms like privacy reductions, fake news, or hate speech. Worse, despite a stated interest in the promotion of innovation, most observers treat tech firms' colossal R&D expenditures—an aggregate of USD 111 billion in 2018—as water under the bridge.

Now let us return to the Slate war-game. The hint is that big tech firms are at war, just not a military one. With this, we should reconsider knee jerk monopoly reasoning and ask: why should there be only one form of competition in which *rivalry* is what imposes competitive pressure on firms? Can other forces like *technology* plausibly impose on firms—including firms with a dominant share of a product—a degree of uncertainty equivalent to the pressure of oligopoly competition.

This book is based on the intuition that an understanding of these other channels of competitive pressure is of great importance to any public policy committed to evidence-based decision-making. And the object of this book is to supply such an understanding. In particular, it represents an attempt to provide an analytical framework that gives a full account of firm behavior under the coexistent forces of monopoly due to relaxed rivalry and oligopoly competition induced by digital technology.

Our practical motivation is limited. We hope to refine the application of the tools of public policy used to promote competition in markets,

---

10. A more accurate way to describe them is to talk of unpriced services. Allcott, Braghieri, Eichmeyer, and Gentzkow estimate the median user surplus of Facebook to represent about USD 100 per month. And in another study, Brynjolfsson, Eggers, and Gannamaneni find that the median user surplus of Facebook for a year is USD 322. See Hunt Allcott, Luca Braghieri, Sarah Eichmeyer, and Matthew Gentzkow, "The Welfare Effects of Social Media" (2019) SSRN Working Paper <https://papers.ssrn.com/sol3/papers.cfm?abstract_id=3308640> accessed 10 December 10, 2019. See also Erik Brynjolfsson, Felix Eggers, and Avinash Gannamaneni, "Using Massive Online Choice Experiments to Measure Changes in Well-Being" (2018) NBER Working Paper Series <https://www.nber.org/papers/w24514.pdf> accessed 10 December 10, 2019.

that is antitrust and economic regulation. The point is not to formulate a new Schumpeterian theory of monopoly efficiency. Instead, the point is to illuminate the heterogeneity of business organizations and strategies under coexistence of monopoly and oligopoly, and allow policymakers to separate the wheat of procompetitive outcomes from the chaff of anticompetitive situations. This is a timely ambition. In recent years, big tech's entry into new markets like entertainment, banking, or healthcare has aroused monopoly complaints from established players. Both in the European Union ("EU") and the United States, congressional institutions, antitrust agencies, and market regulators appear to be increasingly concerned. Whilst US antitrust authorities are yet to act,[11] the European Union has adopted aggressive competition decisions against big tech.[12] In addition, regulatory reform is on the tables of European lawmakers with proposals to limit tech firms' acquisitions of startups or mandate data sharing with competitors.

The structure of this book is as follows. Chapter I sets the scene by describing the polarization observed in the contemporary policy conversation about big tech. In an attempt to overcome this deadlock, Chapter II examines the empirical validity of the *moligopoly* hypothesis, that is the idea—implicit in the Slate stories—that big tech monopolies (or some of them) might be exposed to a degree of oligopoly competition across markets. On this basis, Chapter III reconsiders the economics of big tech and finds that models of increasing returns to adoption, network effects, and uncertainty provide a better explanatory framework than the textbook monopoly model. Chapter IV then formulates a concrete theory of moligopoly competition in which big tech firms compete by a process of indirect entry. Chapter V draws the consequences of this analysis: sound antitrust policy requires to limit big tech's monopoly rents in markets that have *tipped*, and only oppose carefully defined legal restrictions to big tech oligopoly competition in *untipped* markets. Chapter VI then considers policy options for novel harms like privacy, fake news, or hate speech in digital

---

11. In September 2019, Attorneys General of fifty US states have opened antitrust investigations into Google's monopolization of online search and search advertising. See Kiran Stacey, "Google Targeted in New Investigation from 50 Attorneys-General" *Financial Times* (September 9, 2019). <https://www.ft.com/content/01144058-d334-11e9-8367-807ebd53ab77> accessed December 12, 2019.
12. See Chapters I and V for references.

markets, suggesting that some sort of regulation, not competition enforcement, is the appropriate tool.

The questions discussed in this book are of interest to economists and lawyers, theorists and practitioners, in the United States, the European Union, and beyond. To accommodate readership diversity, we have kept the focus on substantive issues of law, economics, and policy, and avoided issues of procedure and institutional design. For the same reasons, we do not discuss big tech's alleged monopsony power in labor markets due to major regulatory differences across and within the United States and the European Union .

Some words about methodology. This book covers the six following tech firms: Amazon, Apple, Facebook, Google, Microsoft, and Netflix.[13] We did not select them. The European and North American press did, by lumping them in two acronyms that connote their gang power, namely GAFAM and FANGs. For convenience of exposition, we refer to them as "big tech" or the "tech giants." These are figurative terms. As will be clear below, the arguments made in this book do not apply equally to the six tech firms covered in this book, even less so to the wide diversity of firms active in digital industries. For obvious informational constraints, we do not discuss Chinese tech giants like Alibaba, Baidu, Tencent, or Xiaomi, though the analysis might be applicable to them as well.

In this book, we rely in as much as possible on empirical—though not necessarily quantitative—data. As a trained lawyer and autodidact economist, we have privileged a non-technical discussion of issues. In every case though, readers with a technical background will find ample references to economic authorities. The computer assisted textual analysis in Chapter II was conducted with assistance of two natural language processing experts.

With this said, let us now look at the contemporary policy conversation about big tech.

★

★   ★

---

13. We use here "Google" for ease of understanding, but we cover the entire set of activities of its holding structure Alphabet.

I

Policy Conversation on Big Tech

April 10, 2018, Washington DC. Facebook CEO Mark Zuckerberg labors before the US Senate to explain that his firm competes with the "other tech platforms—… Google, Apple, Amazon, Microsoft."[1] Somewhat impatient, Senator Lindsey Graham interrupts Zuckerberg: "If I buy a Ford, and it doesn't work well, and I don't like it, I can buy a Chevy. If I'm upset with Facebook, what's the equivalent product?" This dialogue trails until it hits a wall. Senator Graham asks: "You don't think you have a monopoly?" Zuckerberg replies: "It certainly doesn't feel like that to me."

This exchange reflects a wider gulf between two groups of views on big tech. According to one group—which we call "neo-structuralism"—each tech company must be regarded as a structural monopoly in one product or service area: Facebook in social networks, Apple in smartphones, Amazon in online retail, Netflix in digital content distribution, and Google in Internet search. The neo-structuralists' concern with tech giants' monopolies is as much political as it is economic. Big tech threatens the ideal of a democracy where power is distributed not centralized, benevolent not captured. Lawmakers should thus pass statutory legislation to dismember the tech giants, ban mergers and acquisitions ("M&A") transactions, and adopt entry and pricing regulation. And government agencies should step up enforcement against big tech.

According to another group—which we call consumer welfarism—no categorical inference of monopoly can be drawn from tech giants' single supplier positions. Monopoly power, if any, is to be feared for its adverse

---

1. "Transcript of Mark Zuckerberg's Senate Hearings" (2018) *The Washington Post (Transcript courtesy of Bloomberg Government)* <https://www.washingtonpost.com/news/the-switch/wp/2018/04/10/transcript-of-mark-zuckerbergs-senate-hearing/?utm_term=.54a601e376f9> accessed April 12, 2019.

Big Tech and the Digital Economy. Nicolas Petit, Oxford University Press (2020). © Nicolas Petit.
DOI: 10.1093/oso/9780198837701.001.0001

economic consequences and potential for abuse. This, in turn, requires serious factual evaluation of tech companies' market power and business conduct under the antitrust laws. In the United States a discussion currently
exists on whether adjustments to antitrust doctrine are required to unlock
enforcement from existing substantive constraints.[2] This discussion is relevant to the tech giants to the extent that they might hold forms of market
power that create idiosyncratic harms, and that adaptations might be needed
to avoid under-enforcement (known as false acquittals or type-2 errors).
Beyond this, however, existing antitrust laws must remain the primary rules
for the protection of market competition and no radical reform is needed.

The difference between both groups is as much normative as it is methodological.[3] This chapter discusses neo-structuralism (A) and consumer welfarism (B). It shows that both frameworks have limitations and concludes that
additional inquiry is needed to understand the competition issues raised by
tech giants (C).

A. Neo-Structuralism

To many neo-structuralists, "technologically dominant large corporations" are
the robber barons of the digital age.[4] Let us discuss the origins (1), claims (2),
policies (3), and limitations (4) of neo-structuralism.

1. Origins

The intellectual ground work of neo-structuralism has been laid by Barry
C Lynn in a 2010 book titled *Cornered: the New Monopoly Capitalism and the
Economics of Destruction*.[5] Lynn writes: "Commerce on the Internet tends to

---

2. Jonathan B Baker, *The Antitrust Paradigm: Restoring a Competitive Economy* (Harvard University
   Press 2019). Jonathan B Baker, Jonathan Sallet, and Fiona Scott Morton, "Unlocking Antitrust
   Enforcement" (2018) 127(7) *The Yale Law Journal*, 1916.
3. Little known is that Bernie Sanders and Donald Trump are quite aligned on antitrust. Neo-
   structuralism appeals both to the radical left and right. And the press, a net loser of advertisement revenue in the digital era, predominantly sides with them. Besides, consumer welfarism
   cuts across the center left and right. When it comes to antitrust, Clinton, Bush, and Obama's
   policies mostly quibbled on details.
4. Barry C Lynn, "Estates of Mind" *Washington Monthly* (July–August 2013).
5. Barry C Lynn, *Cornered: The New Monopoly Capitalism and the Economics of Destruction* (John
   Wiley & Sons 2010) (hereafter Lynn, *Cornered*); much of his work has also appeared in a series

collapse into near monopoly even faster than commerce in the real world … The result is consolidation beyond anything we have ever seen in the physical world, often in the form of a super dominant entity—Netflix, Amazon, iTunes—that also tends to enjoy real cost advantages over real-world rivals."[6] But the historical roots of neo-structuralism are much older.

Neo-structuralism draws inspiration from Supreme Court Justice Louis Brandeis' "political economic model."[7] Brandeis' vision is one of a decentralized economy, where ownership is distributed, not concentrated, and where small businesses and workers are independent, not coerced into economic exchange by firms with wealth and power. Brandeis' main objection to economic concentration is political. The "monopolization" of "public markets" leads to the reestablishment of "private government."[8] Brandeis captures this in his 1933 dissent in *Liggett v Lee*:

> Through size, corporations, once merely an efficient tool employed by individuals in the conduct of private business, have become an institution—an institution which has brought such concentration of economic power that so-called private corporations are sometimes able to dominate the state. The typical business corporation of the last century, owned by a small group of individuals, managed by their owners, and limited in size by their personal wealth, is being supplanted by huge concerns in which the lives of tens or hundreds of thousands of employees and the property of tens or hundreds of thousands of investors are subjected, through the corporate mechanism, to the control of a few men.[9]

Brandeis' vision was implemented during the second New Deal.[10] After a first phase characterized by economic planning, business-friendly policies,

---

of publications of a think tank named the Open Markets Institute ("OMI"). <https://open-marketsinstitute.org/>.

6. Lynn, *Cornered* (n 5) 54.
7. Louis D Brandeis, "A Curse of Bigness" *Harper's Weekly* (January 10, 1914).
8. Barry C Lynn, "Killing the Competition, How the New Monopolies are Destroying Open Markets" *Harper's Magazine* (February 2012).
9. *Louis K. Liggett Co v Lee* [1993] 288 US 517 Dissent.
10. Barry C Lynn and Phillip Longman, "Who Broke America's Jobs Machine" (*Washington Monthly*, March/April 2010) <https://washingtonmonthly.com/magazine/marchapril-2010/who-broke-americas-jobs-machine-3/> accessed February 17, 2020. This date seems to coincide with the year in which the Supreme Court adopted its decision in *ALA Schechter Poultry Corp v United States* [1935] 295 US 495. In this Opinion, the Supreme Court declared unconstitutional the National Industrial Recovery Act ("NIRA")'s presidentially sanctioned industrial "codes of fair competition."

and Government-supported cartelization,[11] Franklin D Roosevelt reverses course.[12] In a message to Congress on April 29, 1938, Roosevelt says that a "concentration of private power without equal in history is growing" and that the "American economy is becoming a concealed cartel system like Europe."[13] A Temporary National Economic Committee ("TNEC") is created to perform a "full-dress study of the economy."[14] And a "revival of antitrust prosecution" is introduced, with a growth in appropriations for enforcement, and the appointment of Thurman Arnold as head of the Antitrust Division of the Department of Justice ("DoJ").

This, however, is a far cry from Brandeis' vision.[15] Roosevelt's main concern is dismal price competition.[16] Arnold's vision is aligned. The "golden age" of antitrust enforcement dies in 1940, with the conversion of the United States to a war economy.[17]

To a European eye, neo-structuralism shares analogies with 1930s German ordo-liberalism.[18] But the resemblance is superficial at best. Ordo-liberalism is essentially an *anti-political* movement concerned with the tendency of Governments to adopt concentration-prone policies.[19] A political

---

11. Lynn writes that after his second election Roosevelt was "forced to abandon his flirtations with corporatism." See Lynn, *Cornered* (n 5) 170.

12. After the recession of 1937. Ellis W Hawley, *The New Deal and the Problem of Monopoly* (Fordham University Press 1995) (hereafter Hawley, *The New Deal*).

13. Franklin D Roosevelt, "Message to Congress on the Concentration of Economic Power" April 29, 1938 (hereafter Roosevelt, "Message to Congress").

14. Hawley, *The New Deal* (n 12) 419.

15. ibid at 360 noting that the Brandeisian were "unable to get much in the way of administrative or legislative action" yet "their activities did help to shape the content, scope, and rationale of the antitrust campaign that got underway in 1938." He identifies some "skirmishes" on the antitrust front, with actions taken against basing point pricing practices, block booking, and blind selling in the motion picture industry and against the use and abuse of lax incorporation laws adopted by a number of the state legislatures.

16. Roosevelt "Message to Congress" (n 13): "One of the primary causes of our present difficulties lies in the disappearance of price competition in many industrial fields, particularly in basic manufacture where concentrated economic power is most evident—and where rigid prices and fluctuating payrolls are general." Political threats of private government or of captured democracy seem irrelevant.

17. Hawley, *The New Deal* (n 12) 442–43 writing that "the antitrust campaign became a casualty of the war effort. The conduct of a war, so it was argued, called for a carefully planned, highly controlled, and well-coordinated economy."

18. Thomas Biebricher and Frieder S Vogelmann (eds), *The Birth of Austerity: German Ordoliberalism and Contemporary Neoliberalism* (Rowman & Littlefield 2017) (hereafter Biebricher and Vogelmann, *The Birth of Austerity*).

19. Walter Eucken, "Competition as the Basic Principle of the Economic Constitution" in Biebricher and Vogelmann, *The Birth of Austerity* (n 18) 86. Ordoliberalism goes beyond

theory known as distributism may be thought to offer a better parallel.[20] Distributism emerges in the United Kingdom in the early twentieth century as a third way between capitalism and socialism.[21] It claims that economic freedom requires a system in which ownership of capital is local, individuals control productive resources (ie, land), and economic concentration is dispersed.[22] Interestingly, distributism warns against the harmful consequences of industrialization and technology.[23]

2. Claims against Big Tech

Neo-structuralism assails big tech companies on several grounds. We go through them in rough logical order.

structuralism at the normative level. Besides its commitment to protect individual freedom, it is also concerned with safeguarding the proper functioning of the "price system." See generally, Thomas Biebricher and Frieder Vogelmann, "Introduction" in Biebricher and Vogelmann, *The Birth of Austerity*. And at the methodological level, ordoliberals strongly believe in the "power of science" to unearth empirical truth and inform decision-making. See Franz Böhm, Walter Eucken, and Hans Großmann-Doerth, "The Ordo Manifesto of 1936" in Biebricher and Vogelmann, *The Birth of Austerity* 27–40 ("Men of science, by virtue of their profession and position being independent of economic interests, are the only objective, independent advisers capable of providing true insight into the intricate interrelationships of economic activity and therefore also providing the basis upon which economic judgments can be made." And "whether competition is efficient or obstructive, whether or not price-cutting contradicts the principle of the system—all these issues can only be decided by investigations conducted by economists into the various states of the market").

20. Marcus Epstein, Walter Block, and Thomas E Woods. "Chesterton and Belloc: A Critique" (2007) 11(4) *The Independent Review*, 579–94.

21. Unlike socialism, distributism believes in private property. Unlike capitalism, it does not believe in the accumulation of property. The distributist movement is also steeped in Catholicism and in particular the principle of subsidiarity found in Pius XI encyclical Quadragesimo Anno of 1931 (it is "an injustice and at the same time a grave evil and disturbance of right order to assign to a greater and higher association what lesser and subordinate organizations can do").

22. Belloc and Chesterton praise pre-industrialist ages (and in particular the middle ages). This is very close to Brandeis' idea that public and private institutions should be built to human scale. See Tim Wu, *The Curse of Bigness: Antitrust in the New Gilded Age* (Columbia Global Reports 2018) 43 (hereafter Wu, *The Curse*).

23. The distributists' concern is with industrialization, held guilty of transforming nations of small landowners into wage earners. The parallel with neo-structuralism's concern is obvious, in that digitalization is said to transform a vibrant economy of entrepreneurs into one of precarious temporary contractors, workers, and freelancers. Note moreover, that like neo-structuralism, distributism claims that small businesses are exposed to predatory pricing and M&A from big business. Barry C Lynn and Lina Khan, "The Slow-Motion Collapse of American Entrepreneurship" *Washington Monthly* (July–August 2012).

a) Structural Dominance

Neo-structuralism maintains that tech giants enjoy "structural dominance."[24] Structural dominance means control of a large share of industry output, but also large corporate size, product portfolio, or market capitalization.[25] Amazon's "sheer scale and breadth" is for example described as an unmistakable sign of structural dominance.

Neo-structuralism singles out the role of data in tech giants' structural dominance. Lina Khan argues that "control over data" can (i) "entrench" a dominant position in a market by improving the platform's service and its understanding of demand; but also (ii) leverage a dominant position across markets by permitting to "use data gleaned from one market to benefit another business line."[26] Maurice Stucke goes a step further, writing that "Facebook, Google, Amazon, and similar companies are data-opolies," that are "more dangerous than traditional monopolies."[27]

b) Predatory Pricing

According to neo-structuralists, one of tech giants' preferred tactics to achieve structural dominance is predatory pricing. A common example is Amazon. Until 2013, Amazon's retail operations have made low profits.[28] And yet, year over year, investors have backed Amazon's expansion. Neo-structuralists believe that this unique deviation from capital markets' short termism has enabled Amazon to suppress competition. With investors' implicit license to spend, Amazon can "deeply" cut prices and eliminate rivals.[29] Amazon allegedly used this strategy against book publishers when it introduced a USD 9.99 reference price for bestseller eBooks. Khan writes that Amazon's end game is to "forego profits to establish dominance."[30]

---

24. Lina Khan, "Amazon's Antitrust Paradox" (2016) 126(3) *Yale Law Journal* 710–805 (hereafter Khan, "Amazon's Antitrust Paradox") (writing at footnote 191 "I am using 'dominance' to connote that the company controls a significant share of market activity in a sector").
25. For instance, see Julie E Cohen, "Law for the Platform Economy" (2017) 51 *UC Davis Law Review* 133, 142 (hereafter Cohen, "Law for the Platform Economy"): "The dominant platform firms—Alphabet (Google), Amazon, Apple, Facebook, and Microsoft—have a combined market capitalization that (as of this writing) exceeds $3.5 trillion."
26. Khan, "Amazon's Antitrust Paradox" (n 24) 785–86.
27. Maurice E Stucke, "Here Are All the Reasons It's a Bad Idea to Let a Few Tech Companies Monopolize Our Data" (*Harvard Business Review*, March 27, 2018) <https://hbr.org/2018/03/here-are-all-the-reasons-its-a-bad-idea-to-let-a-few-tech-companies-monopolize-our-data> accessed February 17, 2020.
28. On some segments, like international, losses have been substantial.
29. Khan, "Amazon's Antitrust Paradox" (n 24) 753.
30. ibid 747.

How to explain investors' tolerance to long-term loss? Neo-structuralists consider that the "winner take all" effects typical of "platform markets" drive investors to preference growth and scale over revenue and profits.[31] This arguably "incentivizes and permits predatory pricing," even though *recoupment* through exercise of market power is not as clearly predictable.[32] Moreover, data may enable an "incumbent platform to recoup losses in ways less obviously connected to the initial form of below-cost pricing."[33] Khan concludes that there is an "anticompetitive nature of platform markets."[34]

c) Leveraging

A third objection against big tech involves the leveraging of their "monopoly" toward other business segments. Tech giants use diverse methods to achieve leveraging. Some are common business practices, like tying or bundling. Others are more specific to tech firms like self-preferencing or copycat expropriation. In all cases, neo-structuralism challenges both offensive and defensive leveraging. Leveraging is offensive when a tech company uses its monopoly position in a market to gain a monopoly position in another market. A common example is Amazon's inducement of sellers to use its Fulfillment By Amazon ("FBA") service in exchange for higher placement

---

31. ibid 785.
32. Recall that predatory pricing is a two-stage strategy where after a first phase of below-cost prices, the predatory firm uses its newly acquired market power in a second phase to raise prices above costs and recoup its losses. Khan writes (ibid 803) that predatory pricing is "highly rational," in platform markets cutting against the *dicta* that "predatory pricing schemes are rarely tried, and even more rarely successful." Khan, "Amazon's Antitrust Paradox" (n 24) 717.
33. Khan, "Amazon's Antitrust Paradox" (n 24) 788–89.
34. ibid 790. Other firms like Uber, and even before Microsoft might also be, or have already been, hit by similar versions of predatory pricing allegations. US District Court, Northern District of California (San Francisco), *Desoto Cab Company, Inc, d/b/a Flywheel Taxi v Uber Technologies, Inc* Case No: 3:16-cv-06385, §70: "Uber has been able to maintain below-cost pricing for its UberX and UberXL services in the San Francisco Ride-Hail Market due to vast reserves of capital invested with the expectation of reaping extraordinary future returns." Kartikay Mehrotra, "Uber Accused of Predatory Pricing by San Francisco Cab Firm" (*Bloomberg*, November 2, 2016) <https://www.bloomberg.com/news/articles/2016-11-02/uber-accused-by-san-francisco-taxi-company-of-predatory-pricing> accessed December 12, 2019. In the past, Microsoft has also been subject of predatory pricing allegations when it included Internet Explorer in Windows at no separate or extra charge. However, the US Court of Appeals did not uphold any finding of predatory pricing noting: "the rare case of price predation aside, the antitrust laws do not condemn even a monopolist for offering its product at an attractive price, and we therefore have no warrant to condemn Microsoft for offering either IE or the IEAK free of charge or even at a negative price." US Court of Appeals, *USA v Microsoft Corp*, No 00-5212 (DC Cir 2001).

in search results.[35] Leveraging is defensive when a tech company protects its monopoly position by suppressing competition in another market. A common example is Microsoft's efforts to eliminate middleware platform threats like Java and Netscape to protect its monopoly in operating systems.[36]

Neo-structuralism considers that a strong case against leveraging can be made in tech markets. In addition to other advantages like scale, networks effects, and reputation, big tech firms can distinctly cross-leverage data to tilt a market in their favor.[37] Facebook allegedly uses proprietary app Onavo Protect VPN for iOS and Android to carry out market research, and possibly to "monitor potentially competitive applications."[38] And Amazon is suspected of using rival merchants' data to redesign or reprice its own private label offerings so as to outcompete them.[39] Khan writes that "involvement across markets ... may permit a company to use data gleaned from one market to benefit another business line."[40]

d) Killer M&A

Another class of objections alleged against the tech giants involves killer M&A. Neo-structuralism characterizes killer M&A as a constructive form of predatory conduct. Big tech, it is said, uses "sell or be ruined" threats to coerce smaller rivals into acquisition.[41] Amazon's acquisition of growing

---

35. Khan, "Amazon's Antitrust Paradox" (n 24).
36. Lynn, *Cornered* (n 5) 19.
37. Khan, "Amazon's Antitrust Paradox" (n 24) 782–85.
38. Senate Commerce Committee, November 6, 2018, Questions from Senator Udall to Facebook, replies to questions 16 and 17 <https://www.judiciary.senate.gov/imo/media/doc/Zuckerberg%20Responses%20to%20Commerce%20Committee%20QFRs.pdf>. Khan, "Amazon's Antitrust Paradox" (n 24) 781 makes a similar allegation in relation to Amazon ("Amazon seems to use its Marketplace 'as a vast laboratory to spot new products to sell, test sales of potential new goods, and exert more control *over pricing*'").
39. Foo Yun Chee, "Amazon's Use of Merchant Data under EU Microscope" (*Reuters*, September 19, 2018) <https://www.reuters.com/article/us-eu-amazon-com-antitrust/amazons-use-of-merchant-data-under-eu-microscope-idUSKCN1LZ1UV> accessed April 12, 2019.
40. Khan, "Amazon's Antitrust Paradox" (n 24) 783 (and multiple other statements to the effect that online platforms "collect swaths of data that they can then use to build up other lines of business"; "data make it easier for dominant platforms to enter new markets with greater ease"; data "acts as an entry barrier"; and "control over data ... heightens the anticompetitive potential" of leveraging).
41. Unlike in the leveraging scenario, the tech firm here does not use its monopoly power to exclude the prey, but its financial resources. Those practices belong to the folklore of US antitrust, and have been already reported in the late nineteenth and early twentieth centuries in the oil refining and slaughterhouses industries. See, for a good discussion of the historical context, Ernest Gellhorn, William Kovacic, and Stephen Calkins, *Antitrust Law and Economics in a Nutshell* (5th edn, West Academic Publishing 2004) 20.

e-commerce rival Quidsi is the classic example.[42] As Quidsi turned down Amazon's takeover offers, Amazon cut prices in selected markets to force it to sell out. Amazon subsequently bought Quidsi and its operations were shut down. The concern of neo-structuralism with killer M&A lies in the disappearance of small firms and disincentives to small firm creation.[43]

e) Gatekeeping

The neo-structuralist critique of tech giants also attacks their position as "gatekeepers." The difference from the structural dominance argument is a matter of focus. While structural dominance is a way to criticize tech firms' positions of "bigness," the gatekeeping allegation challenges their situation as intermediaries. Tech companies that mediate many communications and transactions use their power to "coer[ce]," 'tax,' 'squeeze," or expropriate suppliers.[44] In the media industry, Google and Facebook have allegedly captured all the profits of the press, without bearing the financial burden of news production.[45] In entertainment, big tech's "blatant disregard for the artist's intellectual property" has caused substantial harm to creative artists.[46]

Tech companies also inefficiently replace direct economic exchange with mediated transactions. This outcome is deemed worse than marketplaces

---

42. Another example is Amazon's Zappos acquisition. See, on this, Carl T Bogus, "The New Road to Serfdom: The Curse of Bigness and the Failure of Antitrust" (2015) 49 *University of Michigan Journal of Law Reform* 1.

43. Frank Pasquale observes that venture capitalists and innovators "are loath to enter online markets knowing that a dominant firm could effectively cut off their air supply on a whim." Frank Pasquale, "Privacy, Antitrust, and Power" (2013) 20(4) *George Mason Law Review*, 1009–24. See also Lynn, *Cornered* (n 5) 169 (reporting the words of a famous investment banker at a Senate hearing "companies subject to, or potentially subject to, anti–competitive practices ... will not be funded by venture capital. As a result, many of their innovations will die, even if they offer a dramatic improvement over an existing solution.").

44. Lynn, *Cornered* (n 5) 56 and Khan, "Amazon's Antitrust Paradox" (n 24) 743.

45. Jonathan Tepper, *The Myth of Capitalism: Monopolies and the Death of Competition* (John Wiley & Sons 2018) 99: "Facebook and Google's fabulous profitability and complete power over the internet is due to the greatest arbitrage in media history. The traditional media and online publishers bear the financial burdens of analyzing, reporting, fact checking, writing, and publishing the news. Songwriters and musicians bear the burden of composing, recording, and producing their music, yet get paid nothing by the tech monopolies. Almost all of the economics flow to the two companies."

46. Jonathan Taplin, *Move Fast and Break Things: How Facebook, Google, and Amazon Cornered Culture and Undermined Democracy* (Little, Brown and Company 2017) 83 (hereafter Taplin, *Move Fast and Break Things*). See Andrew Orlowski, "'Break up Google and Facebook if you ever Want Innovation Again' Jonathan Taplin against the Tech Giants" (*The Register*, November 28, 2017) <https://www.theregister.co.uk/2017/11/28/break_up_google_and_facebook_if_you_want_tech_innovation_ever_again/> accessed April 12, 2019 (on the cloning of Snapchat features by Facebook).

where consumers, citizens, workers, and producers engage in economic exchange with each other directly.[47]

In addition to friction, mediated transactions "accelerate the centripetal movement" toward monopoly.[48] Users' expectations are indeed that tech firms provide "legibility" in an environment awash with an "enormous number and variety of information sources," raising tech firms' returns to scale.[49]

f) Political Harms

Neo-structuralism claims that tech giants threaten democracy at several levels. To start, tech monopolies restrict free speech. Tim Wu provides the argument. In information industries, market structure is "what determines the freedom of expression in the underlying medium" or, more simply, "who gets heard."[50]

Besides, users of tech companies' services are subject to pervasive surveillance.[51] Tech firms' surveillance allegedly cuts deeper than communications data, a point popularized in Shoshana Zuboff's book *The Age of Surveillance Capitalism.*[52] For tech firms, what people say to each other matters far less than what they do."[53] This is a problem because unlike government actors, tech firms are not limited by constitutional safeguards.[54]

Last, tech giants subvert the political process. Though we know little of the link between industry concentration and political influence, Tim Wu argues that when economies of scale wear out, firms turn to politics for protection.[55] Google, which spends relatively little on lobbying, has been

---

47. Julia Cohen stresses that "platforms represent infrastructure-based strategies for introducing friction into networks." Cohen, "Law of the Platform Economy" (n 25) 143. She adds: "Internet is not 'open' as we often hear."
48. ibid. A platform's goal is "to become and remain the indispensable point of intermediation for parties in its target markets."
49. ibid.
50. Tim Wu, *The Master Switch: The Rise and Fall of Information Empires* (Vintage 2011) 155. Compared to previous monopolistic industries like the telegraph, radio, or wireless communications, the Internet does not display competitive singularity.
51. On what follows, see generally Cohen, "Law of the Platform Economy" (n 25) 198–99.
52. Shoshana Zuboff, *The Age of Surveillance Capitalism* (PublicAffairs 2019). Note that Zuboff is not a neo structuralist though.
53. Cohen, "Law of the Platform Economy" (n 25) 198.
54. ibid 193–94: "Concern about the unaccountability of private economic power is a longstanding theme within human rights scholarship and activism." But some academic commentators consider that platforms "fulfill an important separation of powers function without which the potential for surveillance abuses by the state would be far greater."
55. This is a central point of Tim Wu's book *The Curse of Bigness.* Wu, *The Curse* (n 22) 71. See also Biebricher and Vogelmann, *The Birth of Austerity* (n 18).

under attack for the frequent visits of its employees to the White House.[56] Moreover, tech firms' business models might be turned against democracy by third parties, as seen with the Russian interference in the 2016 Brexit referendum or the 2016 US presidential election.

3. Policy Proposals

a) Abrogation of the Consumer Welfare Standard

Neo-structuralism wants to abrogate the "consumer welfare" ("CW") standard that governs the application of US and EU antitrust laws. CW expresses a policy preference for consumers over producers in the assessment of business conduct and transactions by displaying a relatively superior concern for allocative efficiency over productive and dynamic efficiency. Allocative efficiency is achieved when price is as low as the marginal cost ("MC") incurred by producers. In this situation, output is said to be maximized.[57] By contrast, output is presumptively not maximized under monopoly where firms have ability and incentive to restrict output.

Neo-structuralism thinks that an abrogation of the CW standard is justified, because its perceived "price fixation" creates a zone of *de facto* immunity. Often, tech companies supply goods and services at low prices, if not for free.[58] And predatory pricing, leveraging, discrimination, or gatekeeping do not produce the bad short-term prices or output effects allegedly required to challenge business conduct or transactions under antitrust laws.[59]

Neo-structuralism believes that the adoption of a broader "protection of competition" or "competitive process" standard[60] would allow for the consideration of "non-economic" and "political" harms in antitrust enforcement.[61]

---

56. Luigi Zingales, "Towards a Political Theory of the Firm" (2017) 31(3) *Journal of Economic Perspectives* 113.

57. In pure economic terms, this is not entirely true. Allocative efficiency may also be maximized with prices above marginal costs, for instance in situations of perfect price discrimination.

58. Tim Wu, "After Consumer Welfare, now What? The 'Protection of Competition' Standard in Practice" *Competition Policy International Antitrust Chronicle* (April 18, 2018) <https://www.competitionpolicyinternational.com/after-consumer-welfare-now-what-the-protection-of-competition-standard-in-practice/> accessed February 17, 2020 (hereafter Wu, "After Consumer Welfare").

59. Khan, "Amazon's Antitrust Paradox" (n 24) 722.

60. Wu, "After Consumer Welfare" (n 58).

61. ibid.

b) Breakup

Neo-structuralism recommends adoption of measures designed to dissolve tech firms found to have structural dominance. Breaking up tech companies would disperse their economic and political power, improve quality, and promote innovation.[62] Support for this position is essentially based on the evidence supplied by past antitrust cases.[63] Wu argues that the dissolution of AT&T's monopoly triggered a dramatic reboot of the communications industry,[64] which has become a centerpiece of the US economy.[65]

Another motivation that underlies the dissolution proposals of tech firms is to address vertical concerns of gatekeeping bias "inherent in controlling market access for one's competitors,"[66] or lateral ownership of properties that allows the leveraging of data advantages across business segments.[67] Obvious targets for separation appear to be Amazon's retail and cloud computing activities, Google's search and advertisement, or Facebook's social network and messaging applications.[68]

---

62. Wu, *The Curse* (n 22) 132. Wu writes that breakups "can completely realign an industry's incentives, and can at their best, transform a stagnant industry into a dynamic one."

63. Stoller, eg, suggests a dissolution of Amazon "into regional players a la Standard Oil break-up." Matt Stoller, "Why We Need to Break Up Amazon … And How to Do It" (*Medium*, October 16, 2014) <https://medium.com/@matthewstoller/how-to-break-up-amazon-fe947c15cb61> accessed April 12, 2019. See also in relation to Facebook: Eric Wilson, "It's Time to Break Up Facebook" (*Politico*, March 21, 2018) <https://www.politico.com/magazine/story/2018/03/21/its-time-to-break-up-facebook-217665> accessed April 12, 2019 ("the government should begin looking into breaking Facebook into smaller entities to allow for greater competition and more consumer-friendly practices in the online advertising, publishing and communications spaces").

64. *Standard Oil* is another case that is praised by neo-structuralists, often to stress that breakups may be beneficial to the dismembered firm.

65. Wu, *The Curse* (n 22) 110 and 97. This stands in contrast with Europe, which did not dismember incumbent telecommunications companies, and finds its computing industries perpetually lagging behind. Weirdly, however, Wu fails to consider that price and quality competition in telecommunications is higher in Europe than in the United States.

66. Stacy Mitchell, "Amazon Doesn't Just Want to Dominate the Market—It Wants to Become the Market" (*The Nation*, February 15, 2018) <https://www.thenation.com/article/amazon-doesnt-just-want-to-dominate-the-market-it-wants-to-become-the-market/> accessed April 12, 2019.

67. Taplin wants to force Google to sell DoubleClick and Facebook to sell WhatsApp and Instagram. Taplin, *Move Fast and Break Things* (n 46).

68. Neo-structuralism concedes, however, that concentration may be "desirable" or even "necessary" in heavy industry or utilities, and no reason is apparent why network effects industries should be treated differently. Philipp Longman and Lina M Khan, "Terminal Sickness" *Washington Monthly* (March–April 2012).

c) Public Utilities Regulation

Proponents of neo-structuralism are prepared to regulate tech companies as public utilities."[69] They wish to place tech firms under a duty to share their customer base, technical infrastructure, or data with third parties,[70] as well as additional nondiscrimination duties,[71] must carry obligations, interoperability requirements, or line of business restrictions.[72] The evidence needed to support the proposal is again found in the history of antitrust. In 1913, the placement of AT&T under "common carrier" obligations led to substantial innovation in telecommunications markets.[73]

d) M&A Ban

A straightforward proposal of neo-structuralism recommends adoption of a prophylactic ban on tech companies' M&A. This means, to use the example of social networks, that Facebook would not have been able to buy Instagram or WhatsApp. A prophylactic ban is expected to limit small firm destruction. But it is also considered in support of small firm creation, as venture capital allegedly flows more readily to businesses protected from big tech acquisition (and shutdown).

4. Summation

The main beliefs of neo-structuralism are four: (i) economic concentration is a political issue;[74] (ii) a concern for small business protection, not

---

69. See Elizabeth Warren, "Here's How We Can Break Up Big Tech" (March, 8, 2019) Medium <https://medium.com/@teamwarren/heres-how-we   -can-break-up-big-tech   - 9ad9e0da324c> accessed April 22, 2020 (talking of platform "utilities"). For a more thorough analogy, see Lina M Khan "The separation of platforms and commerce" (2019) 119(4) Columbia Law Review 973.
70. Possibly in exchange for a fee. Taplin, *Move Fast and Break Things* (n 46).
71. For example, some would like to require Amazon to treat its clients neutrally regardless of whether they use its fulfillment services or those of competitors. Khan, "Amazon's Antitrust Paradox" (n 24).
72. Luigi Zingales and Guy Rolnik, "A Way to Own Your Social-Media Data" *The New York Times* (June 30, 2017) <https://www.nytimes.com/2017/06/30/opinion/social-data-google-facebook-europe.html?_r=1&mtrref=www.aei.org&gwh=9548B05E4B7FACF-812B51619635EC9C1&gwt=pay&assetType=opinion> accessed April 12, 2019.
73. See Wu, *The Master Switch* (n 50) 55–57.
74. A consequence of this is that neo-structuralism manifests no interest in starting a consensus-building conversation with the other side. Its motivation is to create a political power struggle and win it. This comes with a sophisticated public advocacy strategy and political positioning. Neo-structuralism addresses the media structure, much less the academia (only to the extent needed to provide a veneer of credibility). Both the mainstream press and social networks are its preferred channels to rally influencers and move the goalposts in antitrust discussion.

efficiency, undergirds antitrust law; (iii) the design of antitrust law is the role of legislative assemblies, not of courts or agencies; (iv) economics constrain the development of a normative critique of tech companies' dominance.[75]

B. Consumer Welfarism

1. Origins

CW is a method for the conduct of antitrust policy, more than as a movement. In the United States, CW has been applied in all areas of antitrust laws since the late 1970s.[76] In *Reiter v Sonotone*, the Supreme Court characterized the Sherman Act as a "consumer welfare prescription."[77] In the European Union, the recognition of CW as the goal of antitrust law has been slower, but the tendency to rely on the CW standard is undisputable.[78] Admittedly,

---

Because neo-structuralism talks directly to the broadest base in the public opinion and not to antitrust experts, it has been characterized as a form of grassroots movement. Its opponents actually derided it under the label "antitrust populism." Note though that populism in antitrust refers to the People's party. See Eleanor M Fox, "Modernization of Antitrust: A New Equilibrium" (1981) 66(6) *Cornell Law Review* 1140 at footnote 12.

75. Pasquale writes in 2010 that: "It is now time for scholars and activists to move beyond the crabbed vocabulary of competition law to develop a richer normative critique of search engine dominance." See Frank Pasquale, "Dominant Search Engines: An Essential Cultural & Political Facility" in Berin Szoka and Adam Marcus (eds), *The Next Digital Decade: Essays on the Future of the Internet* (Tech Freedom 2010) 402. Neo-structuralism does not feel constrained by the strictures of terms of art or rules of evidence that have become central to antitrust and regulatory policy discussion. Lina Khan's abundantly quoted note in the Yale Law Journal is a case in point. In her Note, Khan implicates Amazon's dominance at least two dozen times. Yet, in two footnotes, she explains that she "does not mean to attach the legal significance that sometimes attends 'dominance'." See Khan, "Amazon's Antitrust Paradox" (n 24) footnote 191. More generally, neo-structuralists resort to the well-known legal and economic term of "dominance" all the time to implicate large tech firms. But they do not use this term in the conventional sense. They use it as a "catchall" for size (in market capitalization or employment terms), political influence, or any degree of oligopoly concentration. See Zephyr Teachout and Lina Khan, "Market Structure and Political Law: A Taxonomy of Power" (2014) 9(1) *Duke Journal of Constitutional Law & Public Policy* 40 ("Throughout, we discuss size and concentration, which we take to be connected. Our concern with size is with regard to size relative to the total economy"; we use dominance as a "catchall").

76. Today, US doctrine conditions a finding of liability under the Sherman Act to either (i) direct proof of supra-competitive prices or output restrictions or (ii) indirect proof of acquisition, maintenance, or consolidation of market power.

77. *Reiter v Sonotone Corp* [1979] 442 US 330.

78. Note though that already in 1977, the Court of Justice talked of preserving competition "in the interests of consumers." See *Metro v Commission* [1977] ECLI:EU:C:1977:167, para 21. For a modern restatement, see Guidelines on Article 101(3), §13 ("The objective of Article [101] is to protect competition on the market as a means of enhancing consumer welfare and of ensuring

additional welfare goals inform antitrust policy like the achievement of a European-wide single market.[79]

In essence, the CW standard serves two very different and important functions. First, the CW standard makes clear that the proscriptions enunciated in the antitrust rules are about conduct that reduces or is likely to reduce economic welfare and are not intended to prevent noneconomic harms such as harm to the political process or to serve other social objectives. Second, the CW standard provides a criterion to guide the formulation and case-by-case application of the specific rules that are used to identify prohibited, anticompetitive conduct.

It remains unsettled today whether antitrust policy is concerned with CW literally or with total welfare. Some believe that the CW standard requires to weigh social losses to buyers more heavily than gains to sellers.[80] But economists have challenged the distributional and efficiency justifications behind a literal application of the CW standard.[81] In 1968, Oliver Williamson asked: why treat as anticompetitive a merger to monopoly that makes consumers worse off—say they lose USD 2 to a post-merger price increase—regardless of whether it can make sellers disproportionately better off—say they gain USD 2 on the post-merger price increase + USD 1 in post-merger efficiencies? Unless one considers that income is more valuable to buyers than to sellers—and disregards that all economic agents are at some point one or the other—there is no economic reason for public policy to discriminate against sellers.[82]

2. Implications for Big Tech

CW does not define a set of antitrust recommendations toward big tech companies. In effect, both lax (a) and strict (b) antitrust policies might be

---

an efficient allocation of resources"). In *Intel v Commission* [2017] ECLI:EU:C:2017:632, the EU upper court has indirectly embraced efficiency as the goal of EU competition law, thus broadly supporting the CW standard (see paras 133 and 134).

79. Even if the single market objective has some welfare blood, inconsistencies arise. Critics say that cars, drugs, or alcohols reimports are promoted in pursuit of the single market amidst ambiguous evidence that this pushes consumption prices down.

80. See Richard S Markovits, "Limits to Simplifying Antitrust: A Reply to Professor Easterbrook" (1984) 63 *Texas Law Review* 41. Note, however, that this is a topic of considerable controversy.

81. Oliver E. Williamson, "Economies as an Antitrust Defense: The Welfare Tradeoffs" (1968) 58(1) American Economic Review, 18.

82. Unless one introduces additional social optimum criterion like for instance, Rawlsian fairness or Kaldor Hicks efficiency.

conducted against tech firms based on CW. Recently, several expert reports have proposed a modern formulation of the principles that should guide application of antitrust law to tech companies under the CW standard (c).

a) Tech Firms without Markets?

When tech firms give away services for free to users,[83] a claim might be made that there is no market in the standard economic sense.[84] To date, antitrust courts and agencies have disposed of this problem by considering that users transfer valuable resources to tech firms: time, attention, and personal data (search queries, social graph, sentiment information).[85] A widely accepted view today is that "online search"[86] or "social network services"[87] constitute antitrust markets, if not economic ones.

But more problematic is the litigation rule under which a plaintiff must demonstrate *actual* anticompetitive harm at the onset of antitrust cases.[88] The hard question for antitrust agencies and courts operating under the CW framework is this: absent a price, where is the harm? It is now understood that harm might be manifest in "non price-product attributes, such as consumer privacy protections or service quality."[89] And yet, because non-price harms are knowingly hard to estimate, the litigation rule might not give plaintiffs the right amount of incentives to start antitrust proceedings, leading to under enforcement.[90]

---

83. Tech firms charge prices elsewhere. Google and Facebook charge online advertisers. Amazon charges for its cloud service, and cross-subsidizes free online retail services like Prime. Microsoft offers email service outlook.com for free, but makes profits on operating system software and productivity applications.
84. In *Kinderstart v Google*, the Northern District of California noted "Providing search functionality may lead to revenue from other sources, but KinderStart has not alleged that anyone pays Google to search. Thus, the Search Market is not a "market" for purposes of antitrust law." See Case Number C 06-2057 JF (RS). (ND Cal March 16, 2007).
85. Commission Decision of 18 July 2018 relating to a proceeding under Article 102 of the Treaty of the Functioning of the European Union (the Treaty) and Article 54 of the EEA Agreement (2018) C(2018)4761 final (Google Android Case AT.40099), §326–27.
86. In its review of allegations of abuse of dominance against Google, the Competition Bureau of Canada has characterized an "online search market" distinct from search advertising markets.
87. See Commission, Case M.8228 Facebook/WhatsApp Regulation (EC) no 139/2004 Merger Procedure, para 68; Commission, Case M.8124 Microsoft/LinkedIn, Regulation (EC) no 139/2004 Merger Procedure, para 116.
88. Geoffrey A Manne and Joshua D Wright "If Search Neutrality is the Answer, What's the Question?" (2012) 1 *Columbia Business Law Review* 151, 185–86.
89. *Google/DoubleClick*, FTC File No 071-0170.
90. A Douglas Melamed and Nicolas Petit, "Before 'After Consumer Welfare'—A Response to Professor Wu" *Competition Policy International* (July 1, 2018) <https://www.competitionpolicyinternational.com/before-after-consumer-welfare-a-response-to-professor-wu/> accessed February 17, 2020.

b) Tech Firms without Competitors?

Application of CW-driven methods of market definition might give rise to antitrust over-enforcement against tech companies. The standard procedure in an antitrust case in which market power is at issue "is first to define a relevant market, then to compute the defendant's market share."[91] Market definition focuses on demand substitution: identifying the alternative products and services that are available to buyers and constrain seller's behavior.[92] An antitrust market comprises all the products or groups of product to which consumers would switch in response to a small but significant and non-transitory increase in price ("SSNIP").

But the standard SSNIP test is unworkable in markets in which tech firms charge no nominal prices to users. Antitrust agencies and courts have thus fallen back on qualitative methods to assess demand substitution, often with focus on similarities in product characteristics. But this method is conducive to insoluble problems. In particular, market definition might underestimate functional substitutions that cut across product dissimilarities. For example, a credible argument might be made that Facebook and Netflix compete in a market for users' attention. This defect is nowhere better seen than in the *Facebook/WhatsApp* decision of the European Commission ("EC"), in which traditional communications services like SMS were not really considered in the assessment of the competitive constraints bearing on WhatsApp.[93]

c) Proposals for more CW Antitrust in Tech Markets

In 2019, three reports prepared for the UK Government, the European Commission, and the Stigler Center at Chicago Booth Business School have advanced recommendations on the future of CW-driven competition policy in digital industries (hereafter referred to as "the UK," "the European," and "the Stigler" reports or, together, "the reports").[94] The

---

91. William M Landes and Richard A Posner, "Market Power in Antitrust Cases" (1981) 94(5) *Harvard Law Review*, 960.

92. William J Kolasky and Andrew R Dick, "The Merger Guidelines and the Integration of Efficiencies into Antitrust Review of Horizontal Megers" (US Department of Justice 2010) <https://www.justice.gov/sites/default/files/atr/legacy/2007/07/11/11254.pdf> accessed February 17, 2020.

93. See Commission, Case M.8228—Facebook/WhatsApp—Regulation (EC) no 139/2004 Merger Procedure. Note, however, that this blunder had little if no bearing on the outcome of the case.

94. The authors of the reports are interdisciplinary teams of independent lawyers, economists, and data scientists.

reports are representative of a trend of thinking worried about big tech monopoly power.

A common view in the reports is that tech firms' entrenched market power results from a unique combination of network effects, economies of scale and scope (especially in relation to data), and behavioral biases.[95] But, the reports note, conventional assumptions of market self-correction do not hold due to incumbency advantages and winner take all effects.[96] This means that CW is best served by antitrust intervention. To that end, the reports recommend burden-shifting rules,[97] and lower burdens of production and proof on plaintiffs.[98] They call attention to a wide range of harms like quality reduction, privacy loss, or reduced choice, and warn against the false CW appeal of zero price markets.

We need not discuss the universe of other proposals made in the reports to see that all recommend more antitrust.[99] But it may clarify discussion to stress that the reports do not call for "no fault" legislation designed to

---

95. Jason Furman et al, "Unlocking Digital Competition: Report of the Digital Competition Expert Panel" (*HM Treasury* 2019) §2.25 <https://www.gov.uk/government/publications/unlocking-digital-competition-report-of-the-digital-competition-expert-panel>.

96. As a result, users of digital platforms incur switching costs and end up single homing. Fiona Scott Morton et al, "Report of the Committee for the Study of Digital Platforms, Market structure and Antitrust Subcommittee" (George J Stigler Center for the Study of the Economy and the State 2019), 9.

97. The European report supports development of a quick look rule (also known as the truncated rule of reason) under which harm to competition from challenged conduct is presumed, so that agencies and courts can shift the burden of proof to the defendant to justify its conduct.

98. The Stigler report invites expansive revisions of antitrust doctrine and the introduction of less demanding proof requirements on plaintiffs.

99. Note though that the three reports also envision a significant role for institutional innovation, and possibly some regulation beyond antitrust. However, the reports differ on models of regulation. The UK report supports a co-regulation model in which digital firms with "strategic market status," stakeholders, and a newly appointed regulator (called Digital Markets Units) anticipatively collaborate toward the formulation of binding codes of pro-competitive conduct. The Stigler report recommends an institutional approach. Congress should establish a "digital authority" tasked with rule-making, law enforcement, and remediation functions. The Stigler report also proposes the establishment of a "specialized antitrust court," in an attempt to sidestep the narrow intellectual interpretation of antitrust law prevalent in the conservative US courts system (and, to a lesser extent, in federal antitrust enforcement agencies). The European report suggests a more classic division of labor between antitrust and regulation. The European view is one in which antitrust enforcement serves as a "background regime" and guides complementary "sector specific regulation" initiatives to promote horizontal policies on data access, sharing, and interoperability. No institutional or procedural reform is called for in the European report.

dismember or regulate tech companies. Rather, the reports propose to adjust existing antitrust doctrine, but in significant ways.[100]

3. A New Consensus?

Can the reports achieve a new consensus on big tech? The answer is uncertain. To begin, neo-structuralists will see no merits in the reports. Excepting the case of the EC report where an analogy is drawn between tech companies and "Nation States," the political harms central to neo-structuralism are conspicuously absent from the reports.

More important, the reports might split adherents to the CW standard. This is plausible in the United States, where beyond the rhetoric of CW, progressive[101] and conservative[102] antitrust and regulatory experts are deeply divided. In particular, the reports' acknowledgement of a "pro competition" perspective, means a pro-competition *enforcement* philosophy that is no less questioning than someone declaring that he is unconditionally pro-medicine, pro-military, or pro-guns.[103] Conservatives might be right to

---

100. The reports are also concerned that antitrust enforcement is not fast enough. A variety of (otherwise legitimate) procedural and evidentiary requirements limit antitrust laws' ability to keep pace with fast-moving market developments typical of the digital economy, including anticompetitive ones. See Stigler report (n 96), 66; UK Report (n 95), §3.118–20.

101. Progressives consider that the simplistic Chicago School premises about the efficiency of markets and sweeping justifications to business conduct continue to exert excessive influence in the application and formulation of contemporary antitrust policy and doctrine. They demand a recalibration of antitrust rules similar to what happened with the post-Chicago movement in the 1980s, when theories of strategic entry deterrence were used in vertical restraints law; with the 1990s introduction of behavioral economics concepts for the analysis of aftermarkets (see *Eastman Kodak Co v Image Technical Services, Inc et al*, [1992] 504 US 451); or with the introduction of raising rivals' costs theory in the assessment of exclusive dealing (see *McWane, Inc, v Federal Trade Commission* [2015] 11th Cir No 14-11363). Mark R Patterson, "Antitrust, Consumer Protection, and the New Information Platforms (2017) 31(3) *Antitrust*, 97-103; Kevin W Caves and Hal J Singer, "When the Econometrician Shrugged: Identifying and Plugging Gaps in the Consumer Welfare Standard" (2018) 26(2) *Georges Mason Law Review* 395; Adam Candeub, "Behavioral Economics, Internet Search and Antitrust" (2014) 9(3) *A Journal of Law and Policy*, 407. Progressives do not dismiss the role of CW as a principle, but are critical of the mainstream doctrinal and policy implementation of CW.

102. Conservatives believe in a strict application of the CW guideline. They consider that antitrust enforcement is mostly about empirically observable anticompetitive effects. Hence, empirical observation or estimation of price, output, and investment should guide antitrust analysis.

103. Because the intensity of enforcement does not correlate with improvements in economic performance. Bill Kovacic makes this point well, in discussing how antitrust agencies often signal quality by stressing high enforcement levels ("to say that an agency is bringing lots of cases, or collecting substantial fines, does not establish that its program is improving economic performance—the genuine test of effectiveness. Activity is not a synonym for

suspect antitrust overreach, as when the reports inconsistently pretend that big tech's market power is distinctively greater, yet move to recommend a relaxation of the traditional threshold rules on dominance or monopoly in order to apply antitrust or regulatory remedies to bottleneck firms," firms with "strategic market status," or platforms with "intermediation power."[104]

In Europe, no more optimism is warranted. A case might be made that a further increase in Government intervention will irk the practicing bar, given the already intrusive oversight of antitrust agencies on markets, and the discretionary treatment of the evidence inherent in Europe's administrative enforcement culture.

To be sure, the reports might produce an indirect impact on the future of antitrust by stimulating research and discussion. And a new era of antitrust expansion might occur from the outside of the antitrust community as a result of the swinging mood toward big tech. While the evidence is clear that tech firms remain popular in the public opinion,[105] the press systematically favors a pessimistic coverage of big tech.[106] Given that large gaps between press coverage and actual antitrust policy are increasingly hard to sustain, the press might thus be a bellwether for future shifts in antitrust policy.

C. Neo-Structuralism or Consumer Welfarism?

1. Methodological Issues

At this stage, one might ask: who's right?

At a high analytical level, each group of views makes acceptable propositions. Neo-structuralists' insistence that the tech giants are structurally big

accomplishment"). See William E Kovacic, "Creating a Respected Brand: How Regulatory Agencies Signal Quality" (2014) 22 *George Mason Law Review* 237.

104. Jacques Crémer, Yves-Alexandre de Montjoye, and Heike Schweitzer, "Competition Policy for the Digital Era (Final Report)" (2019) *Publication Office of the European Union*, <https://ec.europa.eu/competition/publications/reports/kd0419345enn.pdf>. ("'intermediation power'—and hence regulatory power—can exist even where the market share, however measured, is significantly below 40 %.") The UK and Stigler reports offer to place these firms under a specific status and designation procedure. By contrast, the European report identifies flexibility in antitrust doctrine, reserving the fallback possibility of antitrust enforcement.

105. Statista, "Tech Giants in the U.S. 2019 Report" (April 2019) Statista Global Consumer Survey <https://www.statista.com/page/techgiants> accessed December 12, 2019.

106. Dirk Auer and Nicolas Petit, "Two Systems of Belief about Monopoly: The Press vs. Antitrust" (2019) 39(1) *Cato Journal* 99.

firms is unquestionably right. And consumer welfarists correctly advise that performance, and not just structure, must inform antitrust decision-making and policy formulation.

And yet, several fundamental methodological errors affect both groups of views. Neo-structuralism has an "is-ought" problem. As soon as the descriptive *fact* that tech firms are "monopolies" is stated, neo-structuralism moves to derive the *normative* policy principle that big tech ought to be bad.[107] Philosophers stress that moving from "is" to "ought" can only be done with the addition "of at least one evaluative premise."[108] But neo-structuralism does not provide that additional premise. Granted, neo-structuralism adds that a monopoly structure is incompatible with competitive markets, workers' welfare, and democracy. But that premise is neither reasoned nor evidenced. Though this problem might be one of maturity and articulation, this leaves neo-structuralism prone to faith-based "big is bad" claims and a disinterest for empirically observable market facts. On closer look, counter-evidence inconsistent with monopoly harms is rarely, if ever, discussed in neo-structuralism scholarship.

Consumer welfarism, in its two variants, is far from defect-free. Conservative scholarship, to start with, falls prey to the fallacy of "argument from ignorance." A common attitude of conservatives consists in dismissing antitrust concerns in tech markets on grounds of empirically observed low prices, growing output, or substantial R&D investments. But a tenet of science is that absence of evidence is not evidence of absence, and this logic should apply to consumer harms too.

Progressive scholarship makes the exact opposite mistake. It falls prey to the "Nirvana fallacy," whereby low prices, increasing output, or high R&D investments could always reach more optimal levels.[109] Economist Harold Demsetz warned against using idealized, unrealistic benchmarks to assess firm conduct.[110] In tech markets, this may lead to the introduction of

---

107. Max Black, "The Gap Between 'Is' and 'Should'" (1964) 73(2) *The Philosophical Review* 165.
108. John R Searle, "How to Derive 'Ought' From 'Is'" (1964) 73(1) *The Philosophical Review* 43.
109. This fallacious belief builds on the hidden premise that consumer welfare driven antitrust is about maximizing something, and not about identifying conduct that causes markets to deliver less economic welfare than would otherwise be the case absent said conduct. For an overview of that fallacy, see Douglas A Melamed and Nicolas Petit "The Misguided Assault on the Consumer Welfare Standard in the Age of Platform Markets" (2019) 54(4) Review of Industrial Organization 741.
110. Harold Demsetz, "Information and Efficiency: Another Viewpoint" (1969) 12(1) *The Journal of Law and Economics* 1.

a winner's curse, where firms at the head of the innovation race are sanctioned because they could do better.[111]

2. Overcoming Bias

What, then, can we do to situate ourselves in this discussion of big tech without just picking sides on the basis of ideological, political, or psychological priors?[112] To start, the truth is more likely to come out under a rigorous application of the CW standard. The reason for this is simple. CW, as opposed to neo-structuralism, offers a multitude of criteria for evaluation. Neo-structuralism provides none beyond "bigness."[113] As Thurman Arnold wrote, the bigness discussion is "like arguing whether tall buildings are better than low ones."[114] The result of neo-structuralism is to leave what Robert Bork called an impression of "complete subjectivism."[115] And the only way to overcome it might be the creation of new distinctions without any reality.[116]

Besides, if the hypothesis that big tech has emergent properties is taken seriously, we may place higher confidence in CW's commitments to advance the law by recourse to expertise on the basis of hard facts, than by reliance on political perceptions shaped by the press. There is nothing shocking to this statement. Modern societies are based on democratic decisions to

---

111. With dramatic counter-effects on incentives to innovation in the first place.
112. As seen previously, ideological lines do not hold well in the policy discussion on big tech. Right-wing libertarians and thinkers from the radical left are amongst the most forceful critiques of large tech platforms. And the CW school's commitment to a limited purpose antitrust federates both traditional Republicans and progressive Democrats.
113. To address this criticism, neo-structuralists have attempted to clarify the changes that they would like to bring to doctrine. Their suggested modifications are to reverse precedent in several areas of antitrust. But neo-structuralists do not really say what substantive legal rules or standards should then apply in areas where precedent is reversed. See Tim Wu, "The Utah Statement: Reviving Antimonopoly Traditions for the Era of Big Tech" (*Medium,* November 5, 2019) <https://onezero.medium.com/the-utah-statement-reviving-antimonopoly-traditions-for-the-era-of-big-tech-e6be198012d7> accessed December 13, 2019.
114. Arnold Thurman, *The Bottlenecks of Business* (Reynal & Hitchcock 1940) 122. See also at 263 and 296.
115. See Robert Bork, *The Antitrust Paradox: A Policy at War with Itself* (Basic Books, 1978) (hereafter Bork, *The Antitrust Paradox*) 85. Similarly, in a 1987 paper, Donald Turner (hardly a conservative) maintained that "the use of 'populist' goals in developing antitrust standards would increase vagueness in the law and could discourage conduct that promotes efficiency in the market." See Donald F Turner, "The Durability, Relevance, and Future of American Antitrust Policy" (1987) 75(3) *California Law Review,* 798.
116. Bork, *The Antitrust Paradox* (n 115) 85.

insulate fields of public policies like antitrust, monetary policy, or defense from direct majoritarian control, and subject them to an expert process because majoritarian bodies have limited ability to generate optimal policies when preferences are incoherent and time inconsistent.[117]

This leaves us with the divide amongst consumer welfarists. A tentative way to overcome the deadlock between them might be to stray from what is common to both antitrust conservatives and progressives: the method of assessment of monopoly power itself. This is the path that we explore in the next chapter.

★

★   ★

---

117. This wisdom is often loosely referred to as the Tinbergen principle. Jan Tinbergen, *On the Theory of Economic Policy* (North-Holland Publishing 1952). It may also be linked to the Arrow impossibility theorem whereby a rational social planner will fail to optimize inconsistent, heterogeneous, and intransitive preferences from the public opinion. See Kenneth J Arrow, *Social Choice and Individual Values* (Wiley 1951); Kenneth J Arrow, "A Difficulty in the Concept of Social Welfare" (1950) 58(4) *Journal of Political Economy* 328.

II

The "Moligopoly" Hypothesis

Nietzsche once wrote that "truths are illusions about which one has forgotten that this is what they are."[1] As adept of healthy skepticism, we now try to stress test the mainstream idea that big tech are unassailable monopolists. To that end, we develop a theory (A), that we test with firm level decontextualized data (B) and market research produced by financial data vendors (C). This leads us to identify the rudimentary components of an alternative model of big tech competition (D).

A. Study Design

We start with issues of methods. This section frames our basic research question (1), formulates a theory (2), and specifies a test (3) amenable to empirical verification (4).

1. Research Question

Could antitrust and regulatory experts be wrong to view big tech firms as "monopolies" that deserve to be regulated? The question is not just the product of Nietschzean elucubrations. Instead, it arises because the mainstream big tech monopolization narrative built by antitrust and regulatory decision-makers, the press, and public intellectuals (a) displays significant deviations from accepted principles of evidence, reason, and science (b).

---

1. Friedrich Nietzsche, *On Truth and Lies in a Nonmoral Sense* (1896).

Big Tech and the Digital Economy. Nicolas Petit, Oxford University Press (2020). © Nicolas Petit.
DOI: 10.1093/oso/9780198837701.001.0001

a) Mainstream Narrative on Big Tech Monopolies

Through an antitrust or regulatory lens, it is tempting to find that each big tech firm enjoys a monopoly position in a market: Google in Internet search, Facebook in personal social networks, Amazon in online retail, Microsoft in operating systems for PC, Netflix in video streaming, and Apple in high end smartphones. Applying that logic, official declarations of big tech monopolies have followed each other like night the day.[2] Across the world, antitrust agencies have been racing to expose the next digital monopolist. Statements of tech monopolies are not the preserve of interventionist (or protectionist) jurisdictions. In the United States, home to the tech giants, the Federal Trade Commission ("FTC") declared Google a monopolist in 2012.[3]

In the press, the picture is the same. The term "monopoly" is the buzzword, including in pro-market publications like *The Economist*. Amazon, Apple, Facebook, Google, and other tech firms, young (Uber) or old (Yahoo!) are all described in figurative terms like "big tech," "behemoths," "gatekeepers," "giants," "goldilocks," or "titans."[4] Analogies to historical monopolies like Standard Oil, AT&T, Microsoft, or AOL are commonplace. Often, articles underline the perils posed by these "monopolists" by adding cartoon representations—of the kind found in Howard P Lovecraft imagery—that are reminiscent of the famous Standard Oil octopus. In academic publishing, a similar trend is observed. Books, essays, and novels that put tech firms in the monopoly camp sell like hotcakes. Public intellectuals with diverse background—business gurus, historians, philosophers, or audiovisual producers—have joined the big tech monopoly bandwagon.[5]

Law reviews do not fare differently. Student editors seem to follow a simple selection rule: in case of doubt, take the big tech monopoly paper. Lina Khan's 2017 Note in the Yale Law Journal on "Amazon's Antitrust Paradox" is a case in point.[6] The press reports that it attracted 146,255

---

2. With exception of Netflix.

3. In a 2012 report, the staff of the US Federal Trade Commission ("FTC") concluded its investigation noting that Google enjoyed "monopoly power in the markets for search and search advertising." See FTC, Memorandum, August 8, 2012, Google Inc, File No 111-01631.

4. Dirk Auer and Nicolas Petit, "Two Systems of Belief about Monopoly: The Press vs. Antitrust" (2019) 39(1) *Cato Journal* 99.

5. Scott Galloway, *The Four: The Hidden DNA of Amazon, Apple, Facebook and Google* (Bantam Press 2017); Niall Ferguson, *Square and Tower: Networks and Power, from the Freemasons to Facebook* (Penguin Press 2018); Jonathan Taplin, *Move Fast and Break Things: How Facebook, Google, and Amazon Cornered Culture and Undermined Democracy* (Little, Brown and Company 2017).

6. Lina M Khan, "Amazon's Antitrust Paradox" (2017) 126(3) *The Yale Law Journal* 710.

downloads.[7] The *New York Times* even credits the Note as the stepping stone of a new antitrust movement (and perhaps of a scholarly genre of its own).[8] Since then, demand for antitrust law papers railing against big tech has grown unabated.[9]

b) Limitations

This new mainstream narrative is a sufficient justification to motivate a critical inquiry. But there is more to justify the investigation. In environments distant from public policy circles, big tech companies seem more often than not described as rival firms. It is actually not uncommon to see business analysts, journalists and bloggers, tech evangelists, or Silicon Valley investors discuss big tech firms with anecdotal reference—and often times hyperbolical—to cut-throat competition.[10]

Whilst part of this may be due to technology hype,[11] this calls into question whether the mainstream is right. And when one starts to think about it, the possibility of antitrust and regulatory groupthink is not unattractive. To

---

7. Tiffany Cullen, "Amazon Is at the Forefront of Antitrust Criticism" (*Sludgefeed*, September 12, 2018) <https://sludgefeed.com/amazon-at-the-forefront-of-antitrust-criticism/> accessed December 13, 2019.

8. David Streifield, "Amazon's Antitrust Antagonist Has a Breakthrough Idea" (*New York Times*, September 7, 2018) <https://www.nytimes.com/2018/09/07/technology/monopoly-antitrust-lina-khan-amazon.html> accessed December 13, 2019. On this phenomenon, see Thibault Schrepel, "Antitrust Without Romance" (2020) 13 *NYU Journal of Law & Liberty* 326.

9. Lina M Khan, "Sources of Tech Platform Power" (2018) 2(2) *Georgetown Law Technology Review* 325.

10. Benedict Evans, "Platform Wars: The Final Score" (*Benedict Evans' Blog,* July 25, 2016) <https://www.ben-evans.com/benedictevans/2016/7/25/platform-wars-final-score> accessed December 13, 2019. Jeff Reeves, "Opinion: The FAANG Companies Are Starting to Turn against One Another" (*Marketwatch*, September 18, 2017) <https://www.marketwatch.com/story/the-faang-companies-are-starting-to-turn-against-one-another-2017-09-18> accessed December 13, 2019; Investopedia, "Why Facebook Is The Biggest Threat To Google's Ad-Revenue Throne" (*Investopedia*, October 10, 2018) <https://www.investopedia.com/articles/investing/060315/why-facebook-biggest-threat-googles-adrevenue-throne.asp> accessed December 13, 2019; CNBC Live, "Fierce Competition in Silicon Valley" (*CNBC*, April 3, 2014) <https://www.cnbc.com/video/2014/04/03/fierce-competition-in-silicon-valley.html> accessed December 13, 2019; Rhiannon Williams, "Why Competition between Apple and Google Is More Brutal than Ever" (*The Telegraph*, September 19, 2014) <https://www.telegraph.co.uk/technology/google/11127694/Why-competition-between-Apple-and-Google-is-more-brutal-than-ever.html> accessed December 13, 2019. Note than some analysts have changed views (Eric Johnson, "We Have to Rewrite Antitrust Law to Deal with Tech Monopolies, Says 'Positive Populism' Author Steve Hilton" (*Recode*, October 24, 2018) <https://www.recode.net/2018/10/24/18016832/steve-hilton-positive-populism-book-fox-news-monopoly-antitrust-kara-swisher-recode-decode-podcast> accessed December 13, 2019).

11. Evgeny Morozov, *The Net Delusion: The Dark Side of Internet Freedom* (Public Affairs 2012) xiii.

start, why should we place confidence in antitrust and regulatory decision-makers' findings of big tech monopoly? In spite of its commitments to the scientific method, antitrust law lacks one of its key tenets: falsification. Antitrust law provides no procedure to establish the existence of big tech competition. This is because it is a sort of proscriptive law enforcement. As a result, antitrust law is never required to provide, and thus never makes, dispositive findings of competition (even appeals do not provide this).[12] By extension antitrust law never specifies what it would need to find competition.[13] Like it or not, this limitation means that antitrust law cannot be considered "scientific."

Moreover, we cannot trust the press in its discussion of big tech firms as monopolies. In 1974, Nobel Prize economist Ronald Coase noted that the press had spent decades defending its sacrosanct freedom to provide news against government regulation, meanwhile spending large resources to ensure that competing technologies like broadcasting would be strictly regulated.[14] In today's digital age, the situation has hardly changed. The publishing industry is a net loser of revenue to Facebook, Google, and Amazon with whom it competes and purchases Internet advertising services.[15] This creates is a strong conflict of interest.[16] Public intellectual Steve Pinker discusses it as follows:

> the tirades in the mainstream media don't disclose a conflict of interest. Social media, by siphoning off ad dollars, are the biggest threat to newspapers'

12. When it does, it says that there is no reason to believe that a particular business conduct or transaction has led to an antitrust violation.

13. In standard operation, an antitrust fact finder either declares a market failure or says that there is nothing to see. It is rare to witness an antitrust agency declare a market to be effectively competitive.

14. Ronald H Coase, "The Market for Goods and the Market for Ideas" (1974) 54(2) *The American Economic Review* 384.

15. See Statista Research Department, "Digital and Print Advertising Revenue of U.S. Newspapers from 2003 to 2014 (in Billion U.S. Dollars)" (*Statista*, April 28, 2015) <https://www.statista.com/statistics/189844/online-and-print-advertising-revenue-of-us-newspapers-since-2003/> accessed December 13, 2019; Kurt Wagner, "Digital Advertising in the US is Finally Bigger than Print and Television" (*Vox*, February 20, 2019) <https://www.vox.com/2019/2/20/18232433/digital-advertising-facebook-google-growth-tv-print-emarketer-2019> accessed December 13, 2019. See Jonathan Tepper, *The Myth of Capitalism: Monopolies and the Death of Competition* (Wiley 2018) 99 (hereafter Tepper, *The Myth of Capitalism*).

16. See Ramsi Woodcock, "When Writers Are a Special Interest: The Press and the Movement to Break Up Big Tech" (*What Am I Missing?*, July 15, 2019) <https://zephyranth.pw/2019/07/15/when-writers-are-a-special-interest-the-press-and-the-movement-to-break-up-big-tech/> accessed January 10, 2020.

revenue since Craigslist, which means that those outlets have much to gain if social media companies are broken up, regulated, or otherwise crippled.[17]

Granted, this does not explain the press's adverse position to other big tech firms that do not participate in online advertising markets. At the same time, it is rational for the press to put all tech companies in the same box, if only to create bigger buzz, more sensational coverage, and longer negative news cycles.

Last, relative to other fields of science, legal scholarship in the United States and the European Union ("EU") has been criticized for its loose publication standards.[18] In the United States, most law journals are "student edited." Referees are not a common practice. Richard Posner writes that the selection process thus reflects "congeniality of the author's politics to the editor."[19] In the European Union, peer review in law journals is only a recent innovation. Most legal scholarship is produced on demand. Add to this that the tech giants have been lambasted for buying academic research.[20] This does not provide much confidence toward what appears in law journals.

2. Hypothesis

Seventy years ago, Schumpeter wrote about the possibility of competition without competitors.[21] This section builds on his idea to elaborate the following hypothesis: big tech firms, or perhaps just some of them, may simultaneously be monopolists and competitive firms. The competition that bears on tech firms is a form of pressure. It originates from firms outside of the product and service markets that they serve alone. It also stems from indeterminate firms, markets, or industries. The reason why antitrust

17. Sean Illing, Kurt Wagner, and Karen Turner, "Has Facebook Been Good for the World? (*Vox*, February 4, 2019) <https://www.vox.com/technology/2019/2/4/18205138/facebook-15-anniversary-social-network-founded-date-2004> accessed February 5, 2019.
18. Eric J Segall, "The Law Review Follies" (2018) 50(2) *Loyola University of Chicago Law Journal* 385. See also, Lawrence J Trautman, "The Value of Legal Writing, Law Review, and Publications" (2018) 51(3) *Indiana Law Review* 693.
19. Richard A Posner, "The Future of the Student-Edited Law Review" (1995) 47 *Stanford Law review* 1134.
20. Luigi Zingales, "Towards a Political Economy of the Firm" (2017) 31(3) *Journal of Economic Perspectives* 113.
21. See our reference to the relevant Schumpeter quote in Chapter I.

and regulatory decision-makers, as well as public intellectuals and scholars, do not—and cannot be expected to—observe that competitive pressure is due to methodology. Even in their most refined analysis, applied antitrust and regulatory economics rely on structural assumptions, models, and tools to draw inferences on firm behavior. This leads antitrust and regulatory decision-makers to reach crude monopoly findings against big tech firms and to discount evidence of competitive constraints outside of relevant markets and of heterogeneity at firm level.

The problem has little to do with ideology, as is sometimes heard. Many scholars and practitioners skeptical about antitrust enforcement also concede that big tech are monopolies and instead challenge enforcement on grounds of incentive effects or efficiency considerations.

Our hypothesis draws on several implicit assumptions that deserve to be uncovered. *First*, we consider that it is a common practice of antitrust and regulatory decision-makers to infer evidence of monopoly from absence of competitors.[22] This assumption reflects the rivalry premise of antitrust, according to which there cannot be competition without competitors.[23] Of course, disagreement occurs in scholarship and practice over the criteria that should guide identification of what counts as competitors (actual rival or potential entrants).

Second, antitrust and regulatory decision-makers infer harm to competition from evidence of monopoly. The point here is not that antitrust and regulation proscribe monopoly *per se*. They do not.[24] Instead, the point is that antitrust and regulatory decision-makers might infer that a monopoly

22. Such inferences are reached after case-specific empirical observations of markets, rigorous application of analytical tools over a significant period of time, across a wide array of distinct situations.
23. See Andrew Gavil, "Exclusionary Distribution Strategies by Dominant Firms: Striking a Better Balance" (2004) 72(1) *Antitrust Law Journal* 3 ("the mantra that the antitrust laws are designed to protect competition, not competitors is an empty slogan. There can be no competition without competitor").
24. Across the world, an additional element of bad conduct is required to apply antitrust law and it is measured through an inquiry of purpose or effects. See Chapter V. In the bad conduct inquiry, suppression of competition understood as rivalry is key. See Jonathan B Baker, *The Antitrust Paradigm: Restoring a Competitive Economy* (Harvard University Press 2019) 178 ("As in all antitrust cases, restrictions on competition are a predicate for finding harm; harm to suppliers matters only when it results from conduct limiting competition, not from any other sources").

position excludes a finding of competition by some significant levels,[25] allowing further inquiry into, and remediation of, suspicious business conduct.[26]

Third, we assume that antitrust and regulatory decision-makers—and officials that work with them—seek exclusively to maximize the public interest. We exclude regulatory competition and public choice theories of self-interested behavior by civil servants and judges.[27]

The scope of our inquiry is still uncertain at this stage. The set of circumstances in which we speculate that antitrust and regulatory decision-makers might be wrong in their monopoly findings essentially concerns six US information technology firms. Our hypothesis is thus distinct from, and probably more restricted than, the pre-digital industries that Schumpeter was observing in 1946.

3. Test

Let us try to assess whether our methodological theory of antitrust and regulatory blindness to big tech competition is supported. One possible approach is to derive the following test. If our hypothesis is true, we should expect to observe that experts unconstrained by the methods of applied antitrust and regulatory economics do not, on average, characterize big tech firms as monopolies. Or, put differently, an observable implication of our hypothesis should be that non-antitrust and regulatory decision-makers more often (than not) contemplate big tech oligopoly competition.

$$\pm \text{ monopoly} \leftarrow + \text{ methodology}$$

Let us call this the "moligopoly" hypothesis.

25. There are several possible rationales for such an inference. A monopoly finding might imply that (i) there are no sufficient competitive constraints on the dominant firm to prevent *actual* harm; (ii) there has been *past* harm to competition leading to a monopoly position; or (iii) there will be *future* harm as the monopoly will inevitably be used to prevent competition.
26. Within this structural paradigm, the social welfare implications of monopoly, and the optimal policy response, are intensely debated.
27. If opportunistic behavior was occurring at any level of significance in the real world, we would likely observe a higher degree of heterogeneity amongst authorities in their findings of big tech monopolies.

4. Data and Observable Indicators

It is not instantly clear how we can operationalize the concept of an "expert stranger to the antitrust or regulatory system," and understand his or her view of big tech's competitive environment with a high level of confidence. On further thought, however, we can identify two sets of indicators to measure the average perceptions of the non-antitrust world on big tech competition and test our hypothesis.

First, the yearly filings ("10-K") of tech firms with the US Securities and Exchange Commission ("SEC") provide decontextualized data on the nature of competition at firm level.[28]

Second, market research, business analysis, and competitive intelligence produced by financial data providers on tech firms can be used to build measurable indicators. Experts trained in strategic and managerial analysis indeed typically rely on qualitative and quantitative frameworks distinct from those applied in antitrust and regulatory contexts.[29] In particular, their frame of reference is not one influenced by social performance considerations, unlike antitrust and regulatory decision-makers.[30]

Let us now review the data, keeping in mind that we claim neither empirical nor statistical significance.

B. SEC 10-K Filings

1. Why 10-Ks are Helpful

The US Securities Exchange Act of 1934 ("Exchange Act" or "1934 Act") requires companies whose securities are listed to file an annual report with the SEC on Form 10-K. The purpose of 10-Ks is to give a comprehensive

28. For each firm, we have consulted the document titled "Report pursuant to Section 13 or 15(d) of the Securities Exchange Act of 1934," with the code "10-K" on the SEC website, using the EDGAR search tool. See <http://www.sec.gov/Archives/edgar/data>.
29. Furkan Amil Gur and Thomas Greckhamer, "Know Thy Enemy: A Review and Agenda for Research on Competitor Identification" (2019) 45(5) *Journal of Management* 2072 (hereafter Gur et al, "Know Thy Enemy").
30. Michael Porter made this point in 1981, and there is little reason to believe this has significantly changed. See Michael Porter, "The Contributions of Industrial Organization to Strategic Management" (1981) 6(4) *The Academy of Management Review* 609.

overview of the firm's business and financial condition as well as audited statements.[31]

10-Ks provide insights on how reporting firms perceive their competitive environment. Disclosure rules require reporting firms to specifically provide a "narrative description of their business," including specifically a discussion of "competitive conditions," an "estimate of the number of competitors," possible existence of "dominant" competitors in the industry, "principal methods of competition," and registrant's "competitive position."[32] Reporting firms must disclose the most significant "risk factors" that affect their business.[33] And 10-Ks must include a "Management Discussion and Analysis" ("MD&A") where the top-level management discusses with greater specificity "known trends or uncertainties" that have had or can "reasonably" be expected to have a "material favorable or unfavorable impact on net sales or revenues or income,"[34] including possibly a "loss in competitive position and market share."[35]

As previously hinted at, tech firms' 10-Ks are useful because disclosure occurs in a context that is distinct from antitrust and regulatory proceedings.[36] Admittedly, many actors including corporate counsels, and perhaps antitrust lawyers, draft 10-K submissions. However, even if executive officers and directors do not write the 10-Ks themselves, they must sign and certify them.[37] This makes them personally liable for false or misleading statements.[38] Penalties for willful breach

---

31. The technical purpose of 10-Ks is to update the information contained in the securities registration statements initially filed by firms when they want to sell shares to the public on US stock markets.

32. Regulation S-K [17 CFR 229], Item 101.

33. ibid, Item 503(c).

34. ibid, Item 303.

35. See Commission Guidance Regarding Management's Discussion and Analysis of Financial Condition and Results of Operations, Securities and Exchange Commission, 17 CFR Parts 211, 231 and 241, Release Nos 33-8350; 34-48960; FR-72.

36. 10-Ks convey the business perspective of the reporting firm's top level management and of its directors whose frame of reference differ from antitrust experts.

37. The report must be signed by the registrant, and on behalf of the registrant by its principal executive officer or officers, its principal financial officer or officers, its controller or principal accounting officer, and by at least the majority of the board of directors or persons performing similar functions. See US SEC, "Form 10-K: Annual Report Pursuant to Section 13 or 15(d) of the securities Exchange Act of 1934—General Instructions" <https://www.sec.gov/files/form10-k.pdf> accessed April 20, 2020.

38. Executives and directors incur liability under the Securities Exchange Act of 1934, at Sec 18 (the act declares them liable for statements made knowingly. Good faith is a valid defense). Moreover, the CEO and CFO incur additional liability under Sec 906 of the Sarbanes-Oxley

include fines up to USD 5 million or imprisonment up to twenty years.[39]

Moreover firms' financial reporting may be biased against competition (and skewed toward market power), as evidenced by empirical studies showing "earnings management."[40] Firms tend to overstate profits, hide debt, or more generally paint a rosy picture of key performance indicators (Enron is a well-known example) and competitive position.[41] In the literature, studies from non-competition scholars have empirically established a general relationship between a firm representation of intense competition in the whole text of 10-Ks and diminishing marginal returns on investment.[42]

Last, we owe an answer to an economist colleague who wrote to us "I never heard a business not claim it faced intense competition, even when there were only two in the market." In our sample, there is anecdotal evidence of firms discussing low levels of competition.[43]

2. Sample and Tests

Our focus is on the 10-Ks of Microsoft, Apple, Google, Netflix, Amazon, and Facebook ("MAGNAF"). All MAGNAFs' common stock is publicly traded on US exchanges. MAGNAF thus all fall under the scrutiny of the SEC, and are subject to 10-K reporting duties.

To make the sample representative, we have tried to collect longitudinal data. Unfortunately, however, the historical collection of 10-K reports of MAGNAF is restricted by their availability. The EDGAR database contains few filings before 1995. Moreover, some MAGNAF filings are older than

---

Act under their duty to issue certification of periodic firms reports. In most cases, the SEC can obtain injunctive relief or a civil penalty. Third parties' victims can seek damages by suing at law or in equity.

39. See Sec 32(a).
40. In order to reassure investors and regulators. See Paul M Healy and Krishna G Palepu, "The Fall of Enron" (2003) 17(2) *The Journal of Economic Perspectives* 3.
41. Robert A Prentice, "The Inevitability of a Strong SEC" (2006) 91(4) *Cornell Law Review.* 775.
42. Feng Li, Russel Lundholm, and Michael Minnis, "A Measure of Competition Based on 10-K Filings" (2013) 51(2) *Journal of Accounting Research* 399 (hereafter Li, Lundholm, and Minnis, "Measure of Competition").
43. In 2004, Netflix reported in its 10-K that it had historically "faced limited direct competition." And in 2009, it declared: "We have achieved a level of scale in our business that provides many operational and competitive advantages ... Such scale economies also have contributed over time to expanding operating margins which has made it possible for Netflix to aggressively price its service offering at levels difficult for competition to meet."

Table 2.1 Key Specifications of our Corpus of Data

Total number of words	10,325,222
Total number of docs (incl non–MAGNAF firms)	308
Number of docs per firm	8
Average number of words per doc	33,523
Average number of words per firm	258,130

others. Apple and Microsoft's reports go as far back as 1994. Facebook only started to report in 2012. Where appropriate, we have restricted comparison to the time periods common to all MAGNAF. To allow comparison, we have enriched our dataset with 10-K reports from firms in other industries that have been characterized as weakly competitive (non-MAGNAF firms).

The above table (Table 2.1) provides the key specifications of our corpus of data.

We run three main tests on the sample data.

a) Risk Factor Analysis

To start, we try to assess whether MAGNAF consider competition a business risk. In 2005, the SEC introduced an obligation on reporting firms to disclose the "most significant factors that make the offering speculative or risky."[44] Risks listed must be firm specific, not generic. Applicable regulations require the discussion to be concise and organized logically. On average, firms disclose twenty-two risk factors.[45]

In the first subsection, we document whether MAGNAF rank competition as a "risk factor," and the position of "competition" as a risk factor ("RFPComp"). Typical disclosures of competition include statements like: "we face intense competition," "our industry is fiercely competitive," "Increased competitive pressures may reduce our revenues or increase our costs," "Competition and industry consolidation may erode our profit."

We then compare MAGNAF with firms said to operate in industries subject to limited competition. To compose this control group without bias, we have used third parties' lists of monopoly and/or oligopoly industries

---

44. See "How to read a 10-K <https://www.sec.gov/answers/reada10k.htm> accessed December 13, 2019.

45. See Concept Release, "Business and Financial Disclosure Required by Regulation S–K" (2016) 81(78) *Federal Register* 23955 (hereafter Concept Release).

allegedly subject to weak competition.[46] Within these lists, we have retrieved the 10-Ks of all firms that operate in the following industries: airlines, telecoms and Internet Service Providers ("ISPs"), pharmaceuticals, media, credit reporting, and drug wholesaling. We have also excluded industries with fewer than two reporting firms.[47] The full list of the firms covered in the dataset can be found in Appendix 1.

b) Frequency Analysis: Competition

The second set of tests measures MAGNAF's managements perceived intensity of their competition using computer assisted textual analysis of firms' 10-K filings. To that end, we have conducted a frequency of occurrence analysis of the word "competition" in the 10-Ks of each MAGNAF over 2012–17; of Apple and Microsoft over 1995–2017; and compared that with firms in other industry groups over the same period. Within the 10-K reports, the sample is restricted to Business Item1 and MD&A Item 5.[48]

In line with the approach followed by Li, Lundholm, and Minnis,[49] we have considered that occurrences of word "competition" include the synonyms or near synonyms "competitor," "competitive," "compete," "competing," "rival," "rivalry." We have integrated plural forms (words with an s), excluded "competitiveness,"[50] and removed any case where "not," "less," "few," or "limited," "weak," "little," "moderate," "low" appears by three of fewer words.[51] The point was to exclude statements like "we face a low degree of competition" from our results.

Once this had been done, occurrences of competition were searched by reference to the above mentioned lexicon. However, since the lexicon is limited, we augmented it by using the Word2Vec model for the original

---

46. They are based on the lists established by Tim Wu and Jonathan Tepper in their two books; Tim Wu, *The Curse of Bigness: Antitrust in the New Gilded Age* (Columbia Global Reports 2018) and Tepper, *Myth of Capitalism* (n 15).

47. This has led us to eliminate Ticketmaster (no comparator) and the agricultural sector (only ADM reports in ways comparable to other industries: Bunge has a different exposition of risk factors, Dreyfus does not issue 10-K reports as a foreign firm, and Cargill is a private company). In addition, we have eliminated some firms from specific industries for expositional reasons (the structuring of their risk factors made the comparison impossible).

48. Note that for 20-F reports, risk factors are found in Item 3D.

49. Li, Lundholm, and Minnis, "Measure of Competition" (n 42).

50. Competitiveness has a distinct meaning as competition, and may be related to a discussion of country competitiveness.

51. To remove stopwords in the initial text, we apply a stemmer (eliminate s at end of a word) and/or a lemmatizer (transform "bought" in "buy"). We also exclude the numbers that appear in the document (eg, 1990 (year), 382.5 (share price), etc).

words based on the Jena Organization Corpus ("JOCo").[52] JOCo corpus is an openly licensed corpus of annual and corporate social responsibility reports of US American, British, and German business organizations intended to help improve natural language processing techniques for the economic language domain.[53] The aim of this augmented approach was to find synonyms or near synonyms.

This has led to the identification of 145 similar words. Following inspection of the list (ignoring the scores), we have restricted the sample to those that we found most relevant based on our domain-knowledge expertise. We have removed from the corpus words which are not domain specific, like intensify ("the regulatory pressure intensifies"), "intense" ("there is intense regulatory scrutiny of our reporting by investors"), or ambiguous ("face" or "edge"), but kept industry specific references to competition like "generic" (in pharma) or "liberalization" (in network industries); qualifiers and nouns like "entrant," "fierce," "pressure," or "peers" that almost always appear in reference to competition. We added "rival" and "rivalry." This resulted in a final list of nineteen basewords that are competition-related (Table 2.2).

With all this, we have been able to compute three series of metrics. First, we have obtained word counts of competition-related terms for each MAGNAF over the period 2012 to 2018.[54] Second, we have been able to measure the word count ratio of competition-related words to the total number of words in the sections Business Item1 and MD&A Item 5.[55] Third, we have calculated document frequency ("DF") and term frequency ("TF") measures. The DF score is the average firm level percentage of the number of documents that contain a given competition-related word. And the TF score is the average number of times each competition-related term

52. In line with Thomas Mikolov, Ilya Sutskever, Kai Chen, Greg Corrado, and Jeffrey Dean, "Distributed Representations of Words and Phrases and their Compositionality" in Christopher JC Burges, Léon Bottou, Max Welling, Zoubin Ghahramani, and Kilian Q Weinberger (eds), *Advances in Neural Information Processing Systems* (MIT Press 2013) 3111–19.
53. For full information on JOCo, see here <https://www.orga.uni-jena.de/en/Jena+Organization+Corpus+%28JOCo%29.html> accessed December 13, 2019.
54. Word count for individual companies are the total word counts of the basewords (augmented) in Item 1. Business and Item 5 MD&A of each year's 10-K (or 20-F, for foreign private companies). The total word count is defined as the sum of the word counts of each word in the basewords list. Unlike Li, Lundholm, and Minnis we did not produce pure word count per 10 thousand words/year or ratio per 10 thousand words/year, as we thought these two would be just word count/ratio divided by 10 thousand.
55. Word count ratio is equal to total word counts divided by total number of words in Item 1. Business and Item 5. MD&A. Along the lines of Li, Lundholm, and Minnis, our ratio RCOMP is thus equal to NCOMP/NWORDS.

Table 2.2 Final List of Similar Words "Competition"

Alternatives
Compete
Competes
Competing
Competition
Competitive
Competitively
Competitor
Competitors
Entrants
Fierce
Fragmented
Innovate
Liberalization
Peers
Pressure
Pressures
Rival
Rivalry

occurs in each document. For each firm, we have added all TFs for each word, and divided by the total word count of 10-Ks in the sections Business Item1 and MD&A Item 5.

Note that in line with the approach followed for risk factors, we have compared MAGNAF results with firms said to operate in industries subject to limited competition.

c) Collocation Analysis

The third set of tests estimates the degree of collocation of the word competition with other words in the same sentence within the same sample data.[56] Collocation tests provide the following estimate: probability that two words A and B (for instance, innovation and competitors) appear together, divided by probability of single appearance of word A (innovation).[57]

Against this background, the approach that has been followed here consisted in localizing the nineteen competition basewords in MAGNAF

---

56. Again, we relied on Item 1 Business and Item 5. MD&A.
57. Technically, collocation tests estimate the degree to which two (or more words) tend to co-occur (ie, appear together), and whether their co-occurrence is statistically significant or

10-Ks, and then in finding words collocated with statistical significance.[58] Furthermore, we have derived the part of speech ("POS") of words in our documents and focus only on nouns and adjectives. Words of other classes (eg verbs, adverbs) were discarded. The POS information was obtained using the standard Matlab tagger in order to isolate and focus on nouns and adjectives. Once this was done, we have removed stopwords,[59] and calculated Pointwise Mutual Information ("PMI") scores to measure the frequency of appearance of each baseword with another within a five words' distance (both left and right).[60] We have not restricted the collocation words to predefined sets and let the language processing tool retrieve all nouns and adjectives. The expected output are MAGNAF-level tables that give colocation scores for all and for each of the nineteen basewords.

3. Descriptive Statistics and Discussion

a) Risk Factor Analysis: MAGNAF v Other Industries?

Table 2.3 reports the risk factor position for each MAGNAF ("RFPComp"). We can see that Google, Amazon, and Microsoft rank competition first, and Apple and Netflix second. Facebook places competition at a lower level. In addition, we observe that RFPComp does not vary much through time here.

For all or most MAGNAF, this first measure of RFPComp thus points out to competition as an existential threat, not a trivial one.

Now, if RFPComp does not vary significantly across firms in the digital industry, let us compare this with firms in six other industries said to be subject to low competition, ie airlines, telecom and ISPs, pharmaceuticals,

---

spurious. A common metric for collocation estimate is the Pointwise Mutual Information ("PMI"). Given two words, A and B (for instance, "innovation" and "competitors"), their PMI score is calculated as the ratio of their joint probability (ie, probability of A and B co-occurring) to their individual probabilities (ie, probability of A and of B individually). Probabilities are estimated via the maximum likelihood estimate ("MLE"), obtained from frequency counts. See Ashwin Ittoo and Bouma Gosse, "Minimally-Supervised Extraction of Domain-Specific Part–Whole Relations Using Wikipedia as Knowledge-Base" [2013] 85 *Data & Knowledge Engineering* 57.

58. For each MAGNAF, we pooled documents in all years to do the analysis.

59. We used "stopwords.txt" from Long Stopword List at <https://www.ranks.nl/stopwords>.

60. PMI between two words x and y = $f(x,y)/f(y)$, where f is the probability (ie, frequency with which x and y co-occur over frequency of y occurring alone). Y can be any of our competition-related words. The word x can be any word found to the right or left of y (known as the context of y).

Table 2.3 Competition—Risk Factor Position, 2012–19

	2012	2013	2014	2015	2016	2017
Microsoft	1	1	1	1	1	1
Apple	2	2	2	2	2	2
Google	1	1	1	1	1	1
Netflix	2	2	2	2	2	2
Amazon	1	1	1	1	1	1
Facebook	5	5	5	4	4	4

media, credit reporting and drug wholesaling. Figure 2.1 shows boxplots of the RFPComp for each industry over the period 2012–17. Lines extending vertically from the boxes indicate variability outside the upper and lower quartile. For example, in 2012, in the credit reporting category, Transunion ranks competition eighteenth in its list of risk factors.

This suggests that MAGNAF's lowest RFPComp ranking (in particular, Facebook) remains significantly higher than the bottom value of most other industries supposed to be little competitive. One exception to this is the industry group Telecom and ISPs which references similar RFPComps as MAGNAF.

Besides, we observe more homogeneity in the MAGNAF industry group than in other industry groups. Put differently, there is higher variance between firms belonging to other industry groups (RFPComps between

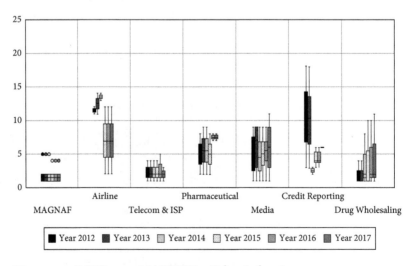

Figure 2.1 RFPComp: MAGNAF v Other Industries

one and eighteen) than for MAGNAF (RFPComps between one and five). This is significant in light of the fact that there are more firms in the MAGNAF industry group than in each of the other control groups.

Last, there seems to be more significant longitudinal change in other industry groups, be it toward higher reporting of competition as a risk factor (credit reporting) or less (media).

The results shown here are subject to discussion. In 2016, the SEC issued a communication in which it expressed concerns about the proliferation of risk factors and an increase in generic risks not specific to the firm. The SEC observed that firms "use risk factors that are similar to those used by others in their industry or circumstances as the starting point for risk disclosure."[61] Some authors have also talked of a problem of "disclosure overload."[62]

Further, the literature considers that no formal framework exists to assist companies "when it comes to deciding which risks they should report, how these risks should be quantified and where they should be presented."[63]

On top of this, researchers have stressed that reporting firms behave strategically and manipulate disclosures to minimize costs. A high RFComp may be a strategy to raise entry barriers. Abraham and Strives consider that the "disclosure of 'bad news' prevents potential competitors entering the market or a particular subsection of the market," so that "future cash flows may increase as a result." [64] At the same time, if this strategy is followed, we can infer that entry is a credible risk and that the industry is competitive.

We believe these critics do not invalidate our analysis. Many pieces of academic research consider that risk factor disclosure remains informative.[65]

61. Concept Release (n 45) 23955. See also, Santhosh Abraham and Philip J Shrives, "Improving the Relevance of Risk Factor Disclosure in Corporate Annual Reports" (2014) 46 *The British Accounting Review* 93 (hereafter Abraham and Shrives, "Improving the Relevance of Risk Factor") ("Observed homogeneity may also mean managers may consider mimicking other companies' disclosures, particularly companies with good reputations" and "Writing of either generalised risk disclosures or repeating risk disclosures from previous years may be akin to cargo cult science").

62. Sarah Johnson, "SEC Pushes Companies for more Risk Information" (*CFO Magazine*, August 2, 2010) <https://www.cfo.com/risk-compliance/2010/08/sec-pushes-companies-for-more-risk-information/> accessed December 13, 2019.

63. J David Cabedo and José Miguel Tirado, "The Disclosure of Risk in Financial Statements" (2004) 28(2) *Accounting Forum* 197.

64. Abraham and Shrives, "Improving the Relevance of Risk Factor" (n 61) 93.

65. See eg, John Campbell et al, "The Information Content of Mandatory Risk Factor Disclosures in Corporate Filings" (2014) 19(1) *Review of Accounting Studies* 396; Anne Beatty, Lin Cheng, and Haiwen Zhang, "Are Risk Factor Disclosures Still Relevant? Evidence from Market Reactions to Risk Factor Disclosures Before and After the Financial Crisis" (2018) 36 *Contemporary Accounting Research* 2.

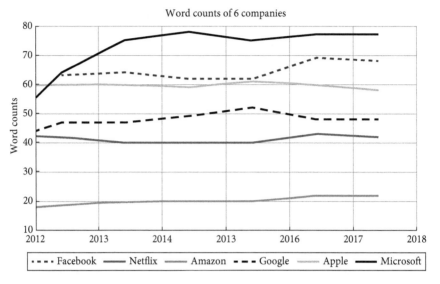

Figure 2.2 Word Count MAGNAF

Even more importantly, most if not all criticism concerns the unspecific content and excessive length of risk factor disclosures, not their ranking. And if reporting firms are admittedly not required to follow a strict hierarchical order in the classification of their risk factors, both SEC guidance and firm practice makes clear that they are listed by order of importance.[66]

b) Frequency Analysis: Firm and Industry-Level Heterogeneity

Our evidence provides interesting insights at firm and industry level. Let us start with MAGNAF. Figure 2.2 above and Figure 2.3 below record MAGNAF's competition-related word count and word count ratios. We see that Microsoft, Facebook, and Apple discuss competition the most in their 10-K. By contrast, competition seems to be a less significant topic for Amazon.

Comparison with the other industry groups on Figures 2.4 and 2.5 below (mean and median) shows that MAGNAF discuss competition more frequently than a majority of other industries. Only the credit reporting, pharmaceutical, and payment systems industries discuss

---

66. Concept Release (n 45).

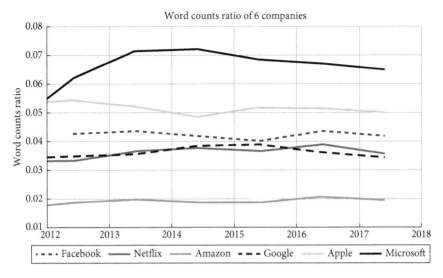

Figure 2.3 Word Count Ratio MAGNAF

competition more frequently. Both figures also show that MAGNAF discuss competition steadily over the sample period, while other industries' frequency measures tend to be more volatile. For instance, we can see that the number of competition words for the credit reporting industry has decreased over the sample period, while it has increased for the pharmaceutical industry.

Let us now move to document frequency ("DF") and term frequency ("TF") scores on Figures 2.6 and 2.7.[67] At a high level, we can see that all firms talk about competition and their competitors. At a finer level, DF scores show that Apple, Microsoft, and Amazon use more competition generic terms than Facebook and Google. This may be indicative of older MAGNAF's higher competition concerns than younger ones. We can also see that diversified MAGNAF like Amazon, Apple, and Microsoft have higher DF scores than more specialized firms like Facebook or Netflix. This suggests that MAGNAF conglomerates take more competition than single product ones. Last, if we look at the graphs

---

67. The queue terms (these with value looking close to zero) appear in a distinct order for each firm, because we have sorted the words first by average TF or DF (ascend) then by alphabetic (descend).

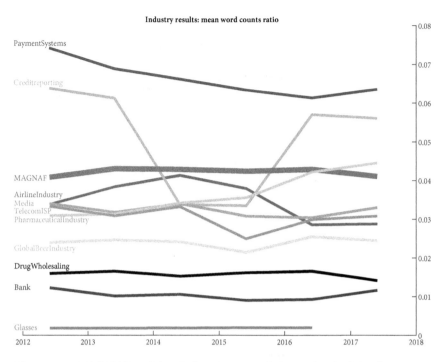

Figure 2.4 MAGNAF v Other Industries—Word Count Ratio (Mean)

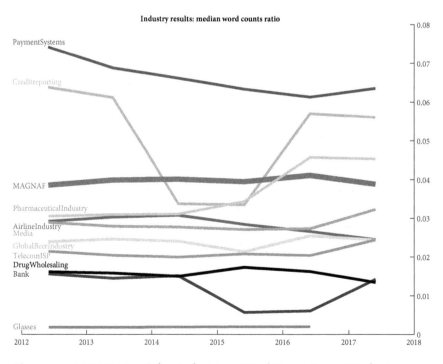

Figure 2.5 MAGNAF v Other Industries—Word Count Ratio (Median)

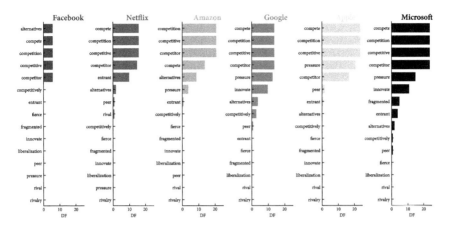

Figure 2.6 DF—MAGNAF

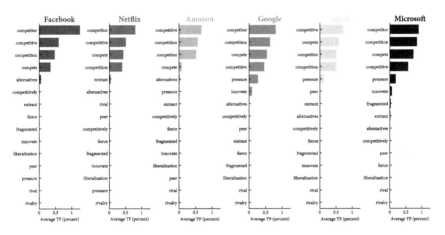

Figure 2.7 Average TF—MAGNAF

vertically, it appears that Microsoft and Google display more documents with competition-related words than Facebook and Apple (though we cannot exclude that this is a by-product of their exposure to antitrust and regulatory investigations).

Joint analysis of TF scores provide further information. DF and TF graphs suggest that Google, Apple, and Microsoft (and to a lesser extent Amazon) discuss to a certain extent the "pressure" bearing on them. Relatedly, the term "innovate" appears as a specific issue for both Google and Microsoft.

c) Collocation Analysis

Linguist John Firth said: "You shall know a word by the company it keeps."[68] This is what we study now. Collocation measures provide clues on the *semantical* similarity of the competition words that MAGNAF use in their 10-K disclosures. We discuss results for each MAGNAF.[69]

Amazon's competition discussion is often linked to "retail," and possibly of "potential" competition, or "longer" or "traditional" players from "industries" with "histories." This hints at competition from non-digital players in legacy industries. The word entrant gives cues as to "narrow," "niche," and "specialty" entry competition.

Apple appears to put emphasis on "aggressive," "rapid," "intense" competition on "price," "prices," or "margins" "cutting" competition. This hints at direct rivalry and zero sum game competition. Apple talks also about "platforms" (or "platform") when it discusses competition.

Google discusses the "intense" nature of competition, in particular in relation to "announcements." There is also significant reference to "pressure" and "innovation." One possible interpretation is to infer from this a forward-looking concern for competition in new products and services. A noticeable result for Google is also the widespread distribution of terms like "laws," "government," "orders," "unlawful," "authorities," "tort," and "investigations" in relation to competition.

Microsoft talks of "intense" competition and "pressure," insisting on "price" and "pricing," like Apple. Across our lists, Microsoft singles out many firms in relation to competition basewords, like Sun, Oracle, IBM, Apple, Borland, AOL, Sybase, Intuit and CompuServe, and Prodigy. Microsoft also makes extensive discussion of "government," "proceedings," "laws," and "scrutiny."

Netflix discusses competition in terms of "pricing," "appropriation," or its "rapid" nature. There is also collocational reference to Amazon and to retail.

Facebook has a lesser range of collocated words overall and they are quite bland.

---

68. John R. Firth, "A Synopsis of Linguistic Theory 1930–1955" in John R. Firth (ed), *Studies in Linguistic Analysis* (Basil Blackwell, 1957).
69. Note that we have discarded the collocation of competitor with competitors.

4. Summation

Some MAGNAF appear to live in a "cognitive oligopoly," consistent with the moligopoly hypothesis[70] Most of them report that they face intense, rapid, fierce, or formidable competition.[71] By contrast, others like Netflix, or even more Facebook, discuss competition abstractly, and seemingly with less risk concern. Diversified firms more frequently refer to competition as a risk factor. And firms with strong software positions like Google or Microsoft relate competition to innovation (and to litigation). Last, even though the discussion of competition by MAGNAF is not an industry specific feature, MAGNAF display more observations of competition-related words than many other industries.

C. Market Research, Business Analysis, and Competitive Intelligence

We now turn to third party data. This will allow us to complete, and objectivize, the data treatment of our inquiry.

1. Sample and Tests

Our dataset aggregates information on MAGNAF "competitors" produced by firms specialized in market research, business analysis, or competitive intelligence (hereafter, "market research firms").[72] We have selected all sources which provide a competitor identification. This includes "competitor," "comparable," or "related"-firm search tools or analysis as well as "company profiles." As a result, the sample data comprises input from seventeen market research firms: Bloomberg, CapitalIQ, CB Insights, D&B

---

70. Joseph F Porac, Howard Thomas, and Charles Baden-Fuller, "Competitive Groups as Cognitive Communities: The Case of the Scottish Knitwear Manufacturers" (1989) 26(4) *Journal of Management Studies* 397 (observing that "... the existence of cognitive oligopolies turns standard economic dogma around completely by suggesting that interfirm monitoring and co-ordination create rather than result from oligopolistic situation").

71. For example, Microsoft's 10-Ks have referred to formidable competition. Amazon, Google, and Netflix's 10-Ks have historically contained numerous mentions of intense competition. And Apple's 10-Ks has talked of fierce competition and rapid technological change.

72. We have accessed these resources between August 15 and 17, 2018 from a local IP address based at the Graduate School of Business at Stanford University.

Hoovers, Factiva, Faulkner Advisory for IT Studies (FAITS), Google Finance, ICD Research Reports,[73] LexisNexis Corporate Affiliations, MarketLine (through Business Source Complete), Matlab, Mattermark, Morningstar, MSN Money, Plunkett Corporate Benchmarking Reports, Reuters Finance and Thomson One.

These raw data were subject to limited preprocessing. We have applied the following conservative rules: we have counted as relevant all observations of a MAGNAF competitor, without taking ranking order or relevancy scores into consideration;[74] we have included sources that do not report on all MAGNAF (eg, ICD returned no data for Facebook and Netflix; Reuters Finance did not cover Google) or that shortlist a lower number of competitors than others (eg, MorningStar reports two competitors by firm only); we have excluded from the dataset all sample firms that are reported as competitors, but that are not considered comparable.[75]

Once this was done, we have subjected the sample data to three sets of tests. First, we have counted the number of competitor and competitor observations for each MAGNAF and computed a variety of competitive scores based on these numbers.[76]

Second, we have isolated MAGNAF in the data sample, and excluded non-MAGNAF firms from results, in order to understand if and to what extent market research firms consider that MAGNAF compete against each other, and which MAGNAFs are each others' closest competitors.[77] This analysis includes data on "related firms" in which MAGNAF enjoy ownership or controlling interests.

---

73. ICD did not cover Amazon and Netflix.
74. Some market research firms give top *n* competitors lists (eg, Plunkett Research and Factiva). Others do not. Some use distinct ranking criterion like "strong" and "moderate" (eg, Mattermark), "true" or "false" competitors (eg, D&B Hoovers) or "major competitors" (eg, Faulkner). Moreover, we did not have access to proprietary data gathering collection processes. We sent an email to LexisNexis asking clarifications about the method used to establish their rankings. We received the following reply: "our Competitor information is collected through our proprietary data gathering collection processes which includes publically facing documents such as company websites and annual reports along with direct phone calls to companies."
75. For example, S&P Capital IQ reports a total of 266 entries for Amazon's competitors, but considers that only eleven of these are "comparable" with Amazon.
76. For example, the company 1-800 flowers is only mentioned once as a competitor to Amazon, so it receives a score of 1. In contrast, Adobe is mentioned eight times for Microsoft, so it receives a higher score.
77. For Google, we use the ticker GOOG and not ALPH for the holding group Alphabet in order to be as conservative as possible in findings of competition. ALPH is relevant only to the extent that it can be counted as a related firm.

Table 2.4 MAGNAF v MAGNAF

Competitor ID	GOOG	AMZN	FB	AAPL	MSFT	NFLX
GOOG	1	4	8	6	7	2
AMZN	9	2	2	5	6	9
FB	9	0	3	1	4	0
AAPL	8	6	3	3	11	6
MSFT	10	6	7	13	2	0
NFLX	2	4	3	2	0	2
Total	39	22	26	30	30	19
Related firm	9	4	17	3	3	4

Third, we have crossed competitor observations of US non-MAGNAFs firms with Standard Industrial Classification ("SIC") codes.[78] Through this, we have attempted to better visualize the existence, and extent, of levels of inter-industry competition with MAGNAF.

For expositional simplicity, charts and tables sometimes use ticker numbers to denominate MAGNAF competitors (see list in Appendix 1).[79]

2. Descriptive Statistics

a) MAGNAF v MAGNAF Competition

Let us focus on MAGNAF v MAGNAF competition first. The values mentioned in Table 2.4 record how many times a MAGNAF is considered to compete with another MAGNAF. The table can be read as follows: if we look at Apple's column, we see that thirteen market research firms consider that Apple has Microsoft as a competitor. By contrast, if we look at the Amazon column, we see that no market research firm categorizes Facebook as one of Amazon's competitors.

What do we learn? At a high level, Table 2.4 suggests that some firms face more aggregate MAGNAF competition than others. For example, Google attracts a significantly higher total number of MAGNAF competitor observations than others (thirty-nine). By contrast, Amazon (twenty-two) and Netflix register fewer competitor observations within MAGNAF (nineteen).

At a finer grained level, we see that some tech giants seem exposed to competition from multiple MAGNAF, while others face less diverse sources

---

78. See <https://siccode.com/>.
79. They were also retrieved from <https://finance.yahoo.com/>.

of MAGNAF competition. Google has four significant MAGNAF competitors, namely Microsoft, Facebook, Amazon, and Apple. By contrast, Apple essentially takes competition from Microsoft. In some cases, we witness an absence of competitive relationship between certain MAGNAF firms. Netflix is reported to face no competition from Facebook or Microsoft. Figure 2.8 illustrates this. Firms with a spread-out spider chart like Google or Amazon are exposed to competition from a relatively higher number of MAGNAF companies. By contrast, firms with a less spread-out spider chart like Apple or Netflix face lower competition from other MAGNAF.

The data also suggests that MAGNAF competition is *not bilateral*. For example, when market research firms consider Facebook's competitive environment, they identify Amazon (or Netflix) as a competitor. By contrast, when they look at Amazon (or Netflix), they do not list Facebook as a competitor. Besides these extreme cases, the sample data suggests that MAGNAF do not operate in balanced one to one competitive relationships (with the exception of Apple and Microsoft). For example, Amazon seems to represent a bigger competitive threat on Netflix and Google (nine citations for each) than the other way around (four citations for each).

Another interesting result is that market research firms appear to identify as competitors firms that are related to MAGNAF through ownership links or controlling interests. For example, Amazon's property of gaming

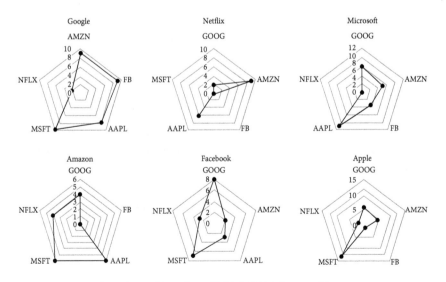

Figure 2.8 Spider Chart: Diversity of MAGNAF Competition

platform Twitch Interactive makes it a competitor to Facebook and Google. The last line in Table 2.4 computes the amount of observations of related firms that compete with MAGNAF.[80]

More striking, perhaps, is the result in Table 2.4 whereby Facebook and Google attract "related firm" competition from their respective subsidiaries Instagram and YouTube. Similarly, Amazon is reported to be competing with its subsidiary Zappos. In other words, market research firms accept to treat as competitors entities operating within, and owned by, the firm subject to analysis. Overall, these crude statistics suggest existence of an additional channel of MAGNAF competition through ownership or control.

b) Beyond MAGNAF Competition

When we look beyond MAGNAF six players' competition, we can see that market research firms consider that a total of 371 firms compete with MAGNAF. With 115 reported competitors, Amazon has more non-MAGNAF rivals than any other MAGNAF. By contrast, with fifty-nine reported competitors, Google has fewer non-MAGNAF rivals than other MAGNAF. Facebook, Apple, Netflix, and Microsoft respectively have 106, 84, 78, and 76 rivals. Those findings hold when we look at the number of competitor *observations* for each MAGNAF (recall that one competitor can be subject to multiple observations).[81]

To make sense of the data, we structured tech giants competitor observations under three heads, which we call: (1) other MAGNAF firms; (2) US non-MAGNAF firms; (3) foreign firms.[82] Figure 2.9 records the distribution of MAGNAF competitor observations along those three categories. For all MAGNAF, we see that most competitor observations relate to US non-MAGNAF firms. Amazon, Microsoft, and Netflix are in particular exposed to much competition from US non-MAGNAF firms. Google, by contrast, registers the lowest number of competitor observations for the US non-MAGNAF category. Another surprising finding is that all firms but

---

80. Unfortunately, the available data on firm ownership is poor. There is no structured record of ownership or controlling interests held by MAGNAF. We therefore performed discrete online researches to see whether each listed MAGNAF competitor was under an ownership or controlling interest by a MAGNAF. The implication of this approach is that our test probably understates the number of related firms that compete with MAGNAF.
81. One competitor to a MAGNAF can generate more than one competitor observation.
82. We determine the geographical origin of firms using data found on Yahoo! Finance. The data reflects the location of the company's corporate HQ (see <https://finance.yahoo.com/>).

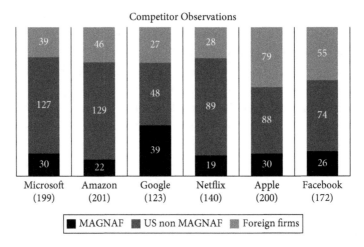

Figure 2.9 Competitor Observations Graph

Google register more competitor observations from foreign firms than from other MAGNAF firms.

A further refinement consists in using competitor observations to construct a list of MAGNAF top ten competitors (see Table 2.5 below).[83] Consistent with the previous findings, we see again that MAGNAF take competition from firms in distinct product and geographic markets. Chinese or Russian tech companies Alibaba, Baidu, Tencent, or Yandex are obvious examples.

The table also presents information relating to the closeness of competitors for each MAGNAF. To see it, one possible approach consists in looking at competitor observations on which a majority of analysts converge. Following this method, we can classify as a close competitor any observation equal or superior to 7 (above the median of 6.5, considering that no single firm identified as a competitor to MAGNAF attracts more than thirteen observations).[84] The shaded area in Table 2.5 represents the set of closest competitors for each MAGNAF.

This procedure (again) yields consistent results. With the exception of Google who exclusively has MAGNAF firms as its closest competitors,

---

83. The literature on competitor identification suggests that the set of firms that managers typically consider ranges between 1.3 and 10.6. See Bruce H Clark and David B Montgomery "Managerial Identification of Competitors" (1999) 63(3) *Journal of Marketing* 67.
84. In our dataset, no competitor exceeds thirteen references, hence seven is just above median.

Table 2.5 MAGNAF Top 10 and Closest Competitors (Obs)

Microsoft Competitor	Obs	Amazon Competitor	Obs	Google Competitor	Obs	Netflix Competitor	Obs	Apple Competitor	Obs	Facebook Competitor	Obs
ORCL	13	EBAY	13	MSFT	10	AMZN	9	MSFT	13	TWTR	13
AAPL	11	WMT	10	AMZN	9	CMCSA	7	HPQ	11	GOOG	8
CRM	9	BABA	9	FB	9	AAPL	6	Samsung	11	MSFT	7
VMW	9	BBY	7	AAPL	8	BBY	5	6758.T	9	GOOG.L	6
ADBE	8	TGT	7	TWTR	6	Hulu	5	DVMT	7	SNAP	4
HPQ	8	AAPL	6	BIDU	6	WMT	5	IBM	7	Mixi, Inc.	4
IBM	8	MSFT	6	EBAY	4	T	4	GOOG	6	RENN	4
SONY	8	RKUNNY	5	YNDX	4	HBO	4	CSCO	5	LNKD.N	4
SAP	7	COST	4	AABA	3	VZ	4	LG Electronics	5	MySpace	3
GOOG	7	OSTK	4	LNKD.N	3			NOK	5	Pinterest	3
		GOOG	4					AMZN	5	Tencent	3
		NFLX	4							AAPL	3
										FB	3
										NFLX	3
										YouTube	3

Note: Reference to Samsung and Sony company names, not to ticker numbers (005930.KS and 6758.T)

the other tech giants' closest competitors are essentially non-MAGNAF firms. This is particularly clear in the case of Amazon, Microsoft, and Apple. Facebook and Netflix's closest competitors are both MAGNAF and non-MAGNAF firms.

To finish, we can draw one final clue from the observation of significant non-MAGNAF competition by screening the competitor identifications of our dataset through the North American Industry Classification System ("NAICS"). NAICS codes segment US firms by industry.[85] They are based on product characteristics, but may also take account of production methods.[86] NAIC codes are coarse because they are binary.[87] Firms that fall within distinct industries might compete against each other through secondary segments. Yet, these measures help appreciate the distribution of inter- versus intra-industry competition exerted on MAGNAF by other US firms.[88] Table 2.6 records the number of US competitors and of competitors observations that MAGNAF attract from within

85. Charles O Kile and Mary E Phillips, "Using Industry Classification Codes to Sample High-Technology Firms: Analysis and Recommendations" (2009) 24(1) *Journal of Accounting, Auditing & Finance* 35. In the 1930s, industry codes were known as SIC when the focus of the US economy was manufacturing. In 1997, NAICS codes were introduced to put "emphasis on the service sector and emerging industries."

86. Executive Office of the US President—Office of Management and Budget, "North American Industry Classification System" (2017) <https://www.census.gov/eos/www/naics/2017NAICS/2017_NAICS_Manual.pdf>: "NAICS uses a six-digit coding system to identify particular industries and their placement in this hierarchical structure of the classification system. The first two digits of the code designate the sector, the third digit designates the subsector, the fourth digit designates the industry group, the fifth digit designates the NAICS industry, and the sixth digit designates the national industry. A zero as the sixth digit generally indicates that the NAICS industry and the U.S. industry are the same. The subsectors, industry groups, and NAICS industries, in accord with the conceptual principle of NAICS, are production-oriented combinations of establishments."

87. Fang Fang, Kaushik Dutta, and Anindya Datta, "LDA-Based Industry Classification" (2013) *ICIS 2013 Proceedings, Research-in-Progress* <https://aisel.aisnet.org/icis2013/proceedings/ResearchInProgress/36/> accessed December 13, 2019 ("There exist a number of Industry Classification schemes such as the Standard Industrial Classification (SIC) and the North American Industry Classification System (NAICS). However, these schemes have two major limitations. Firstly, they are all static and assume that the industry structure is stable ... Secondly, these schemes assume binary relationship—two firms either in the same industry or from different industries—and do not measure the degree of similarity. This is particularly important when identifying rivals for a target firm").

88. MAGNAF operate in the following five industries: MSFT: 511210—Software publishers; AMZN: 454110—Electronic shopping and mail-order houses; GOOG: 518210—Data processing, hosting and related services; NFLX: 532282—Video tape and disc rental; AAPL: 334111—Computer and office machine repair and maintenance; FB: 518210—Data processing, hosting and services.

Table 2.6 MAGNAF Competitors NAICS Codes

	NAIC Code	Legend	Total number of US competitors	Total observations of US competitors	Number of US competitors in same industry	Number of US competitors in different industry	Observations of US competitors in same industry	Observations of US competitors in different industry
MSFT	511210	Software publishers	58	159	10	48	17	142
AMZN	454110	Electronic shopping and mail-order houses	87	158	7	80	14	144
GOOG	518210	Data processing, hosting, and related services	42	95	7	35	20	75
NFLX	532282	Video tape and disc rental	50	109	2	48	5	104
AAPL	334111	Computer and office machine repair and maintenance	50	121	3	47	15	106
FB	518210	Data processing, hosting, and related services	61	115	9	52	34	81

and outside their industry. We see again that Facebook and Google attract more intra-industry competition than others. Netflix, by contrast, and most other MAGNAF, take mostly inter-industry competition.

3. Analysis

Three implications can be drawn from the above. First, market research firms do not identify MAGNAF as firms without competitors. Table 2.5 on closest competitors suggests that we are in oligopoly, not in monopoly, territory. This oligopoly competition comes from large MAGNAF and non-MAGNAF firms, and the risk factors suggest that the resulting pressure does not seem trivial.

Second, there is significant *heterogeneity* amongst MAGNAF. Some firms like Google essentially take competition from other MAGNAF. Others like Apple, Amazon, and Microsoft have non-MAGNAF firms as their closest competitors. Amongst them, some MAGNAF are reported to compete with foreign firms like Baidu or Alibaba, in spite of the absence of any competitive interaction in an existing market.

Third, we can observe *non-reciprocity* in MAGNAF competition. Compared to others, Amazon and Netflix face less competitive risk from other MAGNAF than others in the group. In their relation with other MAGNAF, both companies seem to benefit from what Warren Buffet calls a "moat," or a stronger defensive position. Another interesting finding is that Microsoft, Apple, and Amazon enjoy stronger offensive positions than others. Comparatively, Netflix or Facebook represent a lesser attack potential. This hints at the possibility that either diversified or older MAGNAF have higher capabilities to credibly enter new markets. At the same time, firms with widespread product or service portfolios are exposed to more competition than less diversified ones like Facebook or Netflix.

Beyond this, the important lesson of the above analysis is this. The tech giants appear to be exposed to a degree of competition that originates outside of relevant markets where antitrust and regulatory experts attempt to evaluate monopoly power. To some extent, the above data supports the moligopoly hypothesis.

And yet, diagnosing the existence of moligopoly competition might be looked down upon with neglect. Whilst our dataset certainly reports the existence of competition on tech giants, it fails to produce any operational measurement of competition. However, we want to stress that the purpose of this section was to localize competition relationships, not to give a metric of their intensity.

More importantly, an obvious weakness of our analysis is captured in the wisdom known as Wittgenstein's ruler: "Unless you have confidence in the ruler's reliability, if you use a ruler to measure a table you may also be using the table to measure the ruler."[89] Put differently, different tools produce different outcomes, and the choice of different tools reflects different motivations.

Admittedly, we do not know the motivations of the market research firms composing our dataset.[90] Our best assumption, however, is that analysts, managers, and strategists want to avoid "myopia" in identifying competitive threats that might destroy shareholder value.[91] Hence the selection of an "extensive" method for competitor identification, captured in Michael Porter's five competitive forces of "extended rivalry."[92] This ought to be contrasted with antitrust and regulatory decision-makers' motivation. In antitrust and economic regulation, the point of the market power analysis is to avoid false negatives that might hurt consumer welfare. Hence it is legitimate for antitrust and regulatory decision-makers to use a somewhat "restrictive" method of competitive assessment, focused on the identification of substitute products and services deemed rival in a relevant market.

These methodological differences should, however, not be overstated. In a meta review of competitor identification techniques used in industrial

89. Nassim N Taleb, *Fooled by Randomness: The Hidden Role of Chance in Life and in the Markets* (Random House 2001).

90. Sanjeev Bhojraj, Charles MC Lee, and Derek K Oler, "What's My Line? A Comparison of Industry Classification Schemes for Capital Market Research" (2003) 41(5) *Journal of Accounting Research* 745 ("While financial analysts and professional asset managers use many proprietary industry classification schemes, most of these are not available to academic researchers at a reasonable cost"). Our data sample brings together many potential groups of experts, like financial analysts, credit analysts, marketing experts, strategy analysts, investors, and managers. What we can conjecture is that they most likely apply the theory, cases and methods learned in higher educational curriculums, and in particular in business schools. We may therefore assume that most, if not all, have been exposed to the basic tools and methods of competitive analysis.

91. Mark Bergen and Margaret A Peteraf, "Competitor Identification and Competitor Analysis: A Broad-Based Managerial Approach" (2003) 23(4–5) *Managerial and Decision Economics* 157. Other studies talk of "blind spots." See Shaker A Zahra and Sherry S Chaples, "Blind Spots in Competitive Analysis" (1993) 7(2) *Academy of Management Perspectives* 7.

92. Michael Porter, *Competitive Strategy: Techniques for Analyzing Industries and Competitors* (The Free Press 1998) vi. ("… competition in an industry goes well beyond the established players. Customers, suppliers, substitutes, and potential entrants are all 'competitors' to firms in the industry and may be more or less prominent depending on the particular circumstances. Competition in this broader sense might be termed extended rivalry").

organization ("IO") economics, marketing research, and management papers, Furkan Gur and Thomas Greckhamer show that in spite of distinct intellectual commitments, each discipline follows not one, but a *variety* of overlapping perspectives on competitor identification.[93] IO economics use "industry oriented" and "strategic group" perspectives, like marketing and management studies.[94] Even more, Gur and Greckhamer report that a "large majority of articles is informed by positivism."[95] That point is critical. It means that there is no, and there should not be any, methodological bias or preference in competitor identification toward fulfilment of a specific goal, be it maximization of shareholder value or consumer welfare. Antitrust and regulatory decision-makers' commitment to evidence-based policy requires descriptive realism and empiricism above and beyond disciplinary boundaries.[96]

D. Conclusion: Unaccounted Big Tech Competition?

Proof of the moligopoly hypothesis confirms the coexistence of structural monopoly with cognitive oligopoly. It calls attention to the possibility of latent and complementary levels of competition in big tech that antitrust and regulatory decision-makers fail to observe. Put differently, while there is an undisputable trend toward industry concentration in the digital economy, there is also a competitive force behind it. This force is real, as evidenced by the regularities displayed in 10-Ks and market research competitor analysis. And this competition does not seem to originate from substitute products or services.

---

93. Gur et al, "Know Thy Enemy" (n 29). See also Edward J Zajac and Max H Bazerman, "Blind Spots in Industry and Competitor Analysis: Implications of Interfirm (Mis) Perceptions for Strategic Decisions" (1991) 16(1) *Academy of Management Review* 37, 38 recalling that competitive decision-making—what antitrust and regulatory economics study—seats indeed in the middle of the behavioral literature on strategic decision-making and the economics literature on industry and competitor analysis.
94. Gur et al, "Know Thy Enemy" (n 29) 2079 and 2083.
95. ibid 2077.
96. One more reason justifies consideration of market research on competitor identification, and it is that analysts are well placed to understand business motivation and behavior.

A key and related finding is that there is significant heterogeneity amongst big tech firms. Levels of oligopoly competition currently unaccounted for may therefore vary at firm level.

At this stage, skeptics will say that we have not proven conclusively that there is competition. Perhaps. But our analysis allows us to entertain doubts that big tech firms deserve to be considered as monopolies. Given the deep implications this may have, we cannot dispense with a more thorough inquiry of what received economic theory has to say about monopolies, and how this fits—or not—with big tech. This is what we now do.

★

★   ★

III

Economics of Big Tech: Monopoly v Uncertainty

A. Introduction

Are big tech firms monopolists? As when he discusses football, the man in the street appears to entertain no uncertainties that they are. But as Franklin Fisher wrote "words which are in common use and whose everyday meanings are not in fact the same as their technical definitions."[1] And monopoly is one of them. Surely the world would be a simpler place if "one could decide that some firm has a monopoly by observing that it has one hundred percent of whatever it is that the firm is selling."[2] But economics has developed a much subtler definition of monopoly.

In this chapter, we return to the drawing board. We try to establish whether received economic theory supports a discussion of big tech in terms of monopoly. The question is important. The monopoly model underpins antitrust and regulatory policy frameworks. It is the framework used to evaluate anticompetitive conduct and transactions, including in big tech.

We shall entertain no certainties about this question. Economic models on which laws are arrayed may lose relevance as a result of technological change.[3] This can be understood with a mythological metaphor. Daedalus assumed that the sun was just a shining star. His model for flying logically underestimated the risk that wax wings would burn as his son Icarus would

---

1. Franklin M Fisher, "Diagnosing Monopoly" (1975) *MIT Working Paper Department of Economics* 226, 1.
2. ibid 2.
3. The problem exists in other areas of antitrust law. The rules that prohibit cartels rely on models of competition with and without agreement, making it uneasy to fight welfare-reducing tacit collusion or intra group conspiracies. See Louis Kaplow, *Competition Policy and Price Fixing* (Princeton University Press 2013).

Big Tech and the Digital Economy. Nicolas Petit, Oxford University Press (2020). © Nicolas Petit.
DOI: 10.1093/oso/9780198837701.001.0001

get closer to it.[4] Nobel prize economist Sir John Hicks generalized the point: "since it is a changing world that we are studying, a theory which illumines the right things at one time may illumine the wrong things at another ... There is, there can be, no economic theory which will do for us everything we want all the time."[5]

With an open mind, this chapter attempts to determine whether the standard monopoly model is the appropriate framework to analyze big tech firms. Our analysis suggests that the average tendencies of big tech do not fit the textbook monopoly model (B). Instead, observed properties of big tech such as increasing returns to adoption, network externalities, and tipping effects hint at the applicability of a distinct economic model of competition under uncertainty (C).

Before we turn to the discussion, two additional remarks are in order. First, model validation and theory formulation require careful observation. We thus ground our analysis in empirical data taken from big tech's 10-K filings with the Securities and Exchange Commission ("SEC"), well aware of their limitations. Second, we use the term monopoly throughout the chapter in its strict economic sense. But we take this opportunity to recall the reader about the importance of the concept for the purposes of establishing dominance or market power under antitrust law and regulation.

B. Big Tech and the Textbook Monopoly Model

Using monopoly terminology to refer to big tech firms is not necessarily wrong to the extent that each of them is a single supplier that holds a large share of output in a market where entry is limited.[6] Moreover, the fact that high prices, low output, and reduced innovation are not manifest in big tech is irrelevant, because absence of evidence is not evidence of absence.

---

4. Though in real life, we know that temperature gets colder as one moves closer to the sun. See Kyle Hill, "Forget Icarus, Fly As Close To The Sun As You Want!" *Discover Magazine* (April 22, 2014) <http://blogs.discovermagazine.com/but-not-simpler/2014/04/22/forget-icarus-fly-close-sun-want/> accessed December 17, 2019.

5. John R Hicks, "The Scope and Status of Welfare Economics" (1975) 27(3) *Oxford Economic Papers, New Series* 307–26. Hicks added that revolutions in economy are changes in "attention," not of the science itself as in physics.

6. Note that this is sensitive to how the market is defined. For example, Amazon is dominant only to the extent that the relevant market is defined as online retail, not retail in general.

What is, however, more problematic, is that big tech firms display significant motivational differences from the textbook equilibrium model where the monopolist equalizes marginal revenue and costs (1). It is precisely this feature that makes the traditional monopoly model a poor framework to discuss big tech firms (2), and that justifies the search of an alternative model.

1. Standard Monopoly Model

a) *Theory*

In the pure world of economics, a monopolist is a dictator with absolute power.[7] No rival, entrant, input seller, or buyer can influence its decisions. But how, then, does the lone monopolist set an output and price level combination?

The standard monopoly model gives a response to this decision-making problem. Monopoly output and price setting is a "marginalist" process. Assuming profit maximization, the monopolist grows output and lowers price up to the level where marginal revenue ("MR") equals marginal cost ("MC").[8] Put differently, the monopolist decides to produce an extra quantity of output if (and only if) this yields a revenue greater than the costs incurred to produce a marginal unit.[9] In practice, marginalism is not literally followed by monopolists.[10] Yet the model matters in that it emphasizes the high-level constraints of falling revenue and increasing (or constant) costs that structure a monopolist's decisional context.

In the standard monopoly model, MR declines as the quantity of output rises. This is because the monopolist faces a falling demand curve for its

---

7. Abba Lerner gives the following description "the power of the monopolist—as distinguished from a seller in a competitive market—arbitrarily to decide the price of the commodity, leaving it to the buyers to decide how much they will buy at that price, or, alternatively, to decide the quantity he will sell, by so fixing the price as to induce buyers to purchase just this quantity." See Abba Lerner, "The Concept of Monopoly and the Measurement of Monopoly Power" (1934) 1(3) *Review of Economic Studies* 157 (hereafter Lerner, "Concept of Monopoly").

8. This is not true for a firm in a competitive market, which sets price equal to marginal cost without considering marginal revenue. The firm in a competitive market is said to be a "price taker." By contrast, the firm in a monopoly market is said to be a "price setter."

9. Here is an untechnical example to help the non-economist understand the monopolist's thinking: do marginal returns on producing ten additional pages in a long working paper compensate the marginal costs of writing them? In this example, marginal returns are reader's attention, downloads, or citations to the paper. And in both the metaphor and the model, marginal returns tend to decrease at some point when more pages are added to the paper.

10. To be more accurate, what we mean is that firms do not undertake the marginal computation that is described here. But firms may iteratively discover the profit maximizing price.

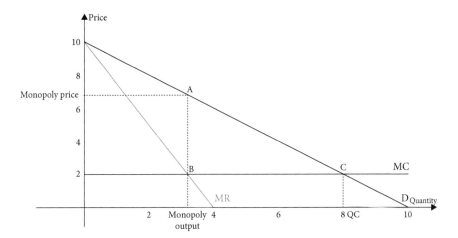

Figure 3.1 Standard Monopoly Model

product.[11] To sell more output, the monopolist must lower the price to get (all) people to buy more units of output.[12] As served buyers experience satisfaction through consumption, they derive marginally fewer benefits from extra units, and are thus willing to pay less for them. Moreover, MR is lower than price at each level of output, because all previous units must be sold at a lower price too.

A logical implication is that the monopolist's marginal profit ("MP") decreases up to the point of equality between MR and MC (see point B on Figure 3.1 above). At the output level where MR=MC, the monopolist's total profits are maximized. MP is 0. This is a stable *equilibrium* because no other output level can make the monopolist better off: one more unit produced, and the monopolist registers a loss; one less unit produced, and it misses a profit opportunity.

From a social welfare standpoint, the profit maximizing equilibrium level of output leads to a monopoly price level greater than MC, a situation referred to as "monopoly power" or "market power." The monopoly equilibrium imposes a loss on society because some customers ready to pay a price lower than the monopoly price but higher than MC are not served (see triangle ABC on Figure 3.1 above). They either do without,[13] buy

---

11. Lerner, "Concept of Monopoly" (n 7).
12. John Taylor, *Principles of Microeconomics* (Cengage Learning 2011) 255.
13. Lerner, "Concept of Monopoly" (n 7) 157.

non-substitute goods or services that give them lower utility, or purchase substitutes that are more costly to produce.[14] This allocative inefficiency of the monopoly is coupled with a variety of other harms stemming from insulation from competition. In the conventional theory, these are cost inefficiencies, reduced innovation, and rent seeking.

b) Two Monopoly Decision-Making Properties that Matter

The textbook monopoly model theorizes an equilibrium tendency. Besides the key assumption of profit maximization, a critical condition for a monopoly equilibrium is that MR and MC converge and eventually intersect in the short run. In turn, this means that only industries with two properties can move toward the socially inefficient monopoly equilibrium. One is decreasing MR (even if total revenue increases with output).[15] The other is decreasing MP (because MC are constant or increasing).[16] This last condition also holds in the natural monopoly model with increasing returns to scale.[17]

Both properties are linked to external factors. These are factors on which no firm has direct control, even a monopolist. Decreasing MR is the consequence of the falling demand curve.[18] And decreasing MP is the consequence of the decreasing marginal product of labor.[19] As output expands, workers are less productive.[20] Monopolists must take these for granted, like dictators must accept to be overthrown by uprisings when citizens are left starving.

---

14. Richard A Posner, *Antitrust Law* (2nd edn, University of Chicago Press 2001) 12.
15. Note that a monopolist may experience an increase in MR if he reduces output after having wrongly set its initial production level too high, so that MR<MC and MP is negative.
16. Even though there can be convergence when MC decrease slower than MR, though this seems to be a rare scenario.
17. In a natural monopoly, long-run average costs decline with output, because MC is lower than average costs. However, even in a natural monopoly situation, MP decreases because MC and MR intersect at some point. See Richard A Posner, "Natural Monopoly and its Regulation" (1968) 21 *Stanford Law Review* 548.
18. As seen before, when customers increase their consumption, they derive less marginal benefits from additional units, and are willing to pay less.
19. Note that in an extreme case, MP can be decreasing even with a zero production cost simply because MR is decreasing.
20. And more costly. Additional workers, overtime plans, or additional compensation may be needed. But note that even if wages are constant, there is still decreasing marginal product of labor.

2. Are Big Tech Firms Decision-Making Monopolists?

When we discuss big tech firms amongst antitrust and regulation experts, we seldom think about the decision-making properties of monopolies. Instead, the discussion invariably focuses on either structural factors or welfare outcomes. Yet, the two properties of decreasing MR and decreasing MP provide useful testable hypotheses. In particular, we may be tempted to use firm-level data to get a better understanding of big tech firms' decision-making universe, and try to infer whether they behave like textbook monopolists.

This is what we try to do in the following sections. We test the properties and results of the textbook monopoly model against a dataset covering Facebook, Amazon, Netflix, and Google's SEC 10-K filings.[21] The basic finding is that big tech firms seem to operate in a manner inconsistent with the textbook monopoly model (c). Let us see why this is the case, first by setting out our approach to measurement (a), and then by showing our results (b).

a) Evaluating Big Tech Decision-Making

Saying that big tech firms are monopolies should be a way to suggest that as they increase output, they experience a decrease in MR, and move society one step closer to the stable and inefficient equilibrium level where MR intersects with MC, in turn justifying antitrust or regulatory intervention. If the textbook monopoly model appropriately applies to big tech firms, we should thus be able to observe decreasing MR and MP at firm-level.

To assess this, we need to know big tech firms' year-over-year revenues, costs, and profits. We can retrieve this from the accounting data reported in their 10-Ks. However, SEC reporting firms are not required to disclose information about output or quantities sold.[22] While some companies like Amazon acknowledge "increased sales,"[23] we have no readily available quantitative measure of output that entitles us to compute revenues, costs, and profits on a marginal basis, as would be required to estimate MR and MP.

Information found in the "Statista premium" database provides useful data points that help overcome this difficulty. In particular, we can retrieve

---

21. We do not use Microsoft and Apple data, because their 10-K forms are not disaggregated enough to allow us to compute proxies for MR, MC, and MP.
22. Reporting on output is actually complicated in industries that supply intangibles services.
23. Amazon Inc, Form 10-K, US SEC, 2011.

Amazon's number of active customer accounts worldwide from 1997 to 2015; Facebook's number of daily active users worldwide from 2011 to 2017; and Netflix streaming subscribers in the United States from third quarter 2011 to fourth quarter 2017. As to Google, its flagship search product has no clear, publicly available output metric. Search does not require an account or subscription. Yet, the Statista premium database gives data on "explicit core search queries" on Google sites in the United States over 2008 to 2016. For all firms, except for Google since 2014, output measures have grown.

By crossing SEC data and Statista premium data, we can estimate "approximate" MR, MC, and MP. We use the term "approximate" because what we actually calculate is the incremental evolution of the average revenue, costs, and profits made by each big tech firm on each customer account, user, subscriber, or core search query as output grew on a year-over-year basis. We can however take those estimates as proxy for marginal measures on the basis of two considerations. The first is not extreme, but deserves explanation: it is not our purpose to define what the *level* of MR and MC is, but essentially if both metrics follow a decreasing or increasing *tendency*.[24] In this context, average measures are informative because a property of averaging is that a group average moves in the direction of the contribution of the latest additions to the group.

The second is that we equate reported measures of "costs of goods sold" ("COGS" or costs of revenue/sales) to variable costs.[25] COGS include all costs associated or allocated to products sold, and include labor costs, input and material costs, and other costs required for the sale of products. COGS may be more inclusive than variable costs. We believe this is not a problem, for COGS can only bias our MC estimates upward and our MP estimates downwards. Using COGS is a conservative choice because this biases our results towards a textbook monopoly explanation.[26]

---

24. When average revenue falls, this implies that MR is below average (and that when average variable costs fall, MC is below average).

25. This is also the approach followed by De Loecker, Eeckhout, and Unger who estimate markup by using cost of goods sold ("COGS") as a proxy for all of a firm's costs that are directly traceable to a unit of output. See Jan De Loecker, Jan Eeckhout, and Gabriel Unger, "The Rise of Market Power and the Macroeconomic Implications" (2019) Working Paper <http://www.janeeckhout.com/wp-content/uploads/RMP.pdf> accessed December 17, 2019.

26. At the same time, one might counter-argue that COGS might be under inclusive, because they exclude Selling, General and Administrative Expenses ("SGA"), which measure indirect costs of sales such as marketing and management.

One last remark is in order. We had to tweak the data for Google. While Google provides indirect data on US revenue from 2008 to 2017, costs of sales are not broken down for individual countries. To overcome this problem, we applied Google's reported ratio of United States to global revenue to costs figures. For example, when Google reported that 49 percent of its total revenue was generated in the United States, we decided that 49 percent of Google's total costs of sales could be allocated to the United States.[27]

All the data used for the analysis can be found in Appendix 2.

b) Results

According to the prediction of the textbook monopoly model, as output grows we should observe a dual decline in big tech firms approximate MR and MP. Let us see to what extent this is the case.

With our data, we can estimate, with more or less accuracy, big tech's approximate MR and MP on a year-over-year basis. Figure 3.2 represents big tech firms' MR (in grey), MP (in black), and MC (in dots). The resulting diffusion curves show two regularities. First, the MR of all big tech firms rises—albeit with heterogeneity at firm level. Second, and perhaps most important, MP is increasing too. Tech firms thus seem to violate two essential conditions of the textbook monopoly model.

These observations raise an intriguing question: if both MR and MP increase, is there a possibility of short-term equilibrium? A logical implication of a simultaneous increase in MR and MP is indeed that MC remains close to constant (as can be seen for Facebook), decreases or rises more slowly than MR (as can be seen for Google). In all four cases, this means that there is no convergence between MR and MC. The wedge between both curves increases, and short-term equilibrium is unlikely.[28]

---

27. A more extreme approach could have been to think of Google producing in the United States, and exporting elsewhere. On that basis, we could have allocated all COGS to Google's US revenue. We show the result of this in Appendix 3. This scenario does not affect our analysis significantly.

28. The profit maximization rule says that output should be expanded as long as MR > MC. Because here MR > MC occurs over a period that exceeds the short term, then the short-term optimum consists in continuing to produce. This is distinct from the short-term optimum in a monopoly where output is fixed.

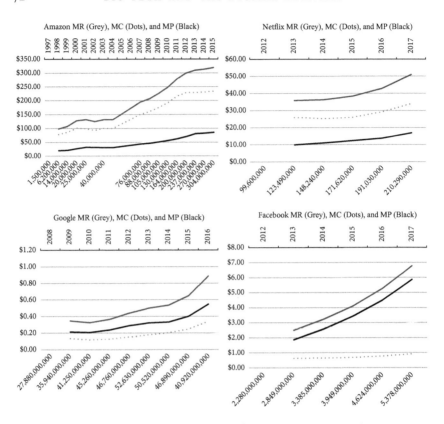

Figure 3.2 Big Tech's Approximate MR and MP (moving averages)

c) Discussion

The big tech monopoly hypothesis appears to fail the test of evidence. Unlike a profit maximizing monopoly, the decision-making of a big tech firm cannot seek to set short-term output so that MR=MC, absent a foreseeable perspective that both curves will intersect. This has two logical implications. First, assuming that MR=MC remains a valid profit maximization proposition for big tech firms, it must be a long term perspective.[29] Second, big tech firms' short-term profit maximization approach must be about something else.

29. If we consider it a reasonable proposition to think that there are income constraints and decreasing marginal product of labor.

But what is it? Let us look again at our data, and think of further differences with the textbook monopoly model. In standard economics, MR reflects the demand curve. A possible interpretation of rising MR is that big tech firms face either an upward sloping or upward shifting demand curve in the short term, denoting higher user willingness to pay as output rises.[30] This property, which one may refer to as a special case of increasing returns to adoption,[31] could be a fundamental difference with the textbook monopoly model where demand is downward sloping and fixed.

All this suggests that big tech firms' short-term goal should be to expand output—no more, no less.[32] This is consistent with anecdotal observations of early loss-making by tech giants like Amazon, who prioritized growth over (net) profits in early years forecasting a long-term divergence between rising MR and MC. Moreover, this is consistent with theoretical arguments whereby MC is zero in digital markets (though our data shows that the latter is clearly not the case for Amazon and Netflix). When variables—like MC—have a constant zero value, they are not a constraint on decision-makers and may be ignored.

True, output also grows in the textbook monopoly model. First, output grows up to the profit maximizing level. And output may also grow strategically, when the monopolist attempts to keep potential rivals out of the market. But a difference with big tech firms is that when output increases in a traditional monopoly setting, it is always bounded: intersecting MR and MC prevents the monopolist from serving all quantities demanded. And when the threat of entry disappears, expansion ceases. This is not what we see here. Instead big tech appear to be a special case of increasing returns to adoption. Output growth seems unconstrained, and this at already high quantity levels.

The above analysis cautions against comparing tech giants to textbook monopolies. Big tech firms might be nominally called monopolies by virtue of their large share of output, or because the upward-sloping or shifting

---

30. Indeed, big tech firms may face a falling demand curve that is shifting upwards year after year. We discuss this eventuality in the following sections.
31. In the standard case of increasing returns to scale, the returns are increasing on the supply side because average total costs decrease over an infinite quantity of output. Here, this is a special case in the sense that the returns are increasing because marginal benefits to users increase over a substantial quantity of adoption by other users.
32. Up to the point where the whole demand is exhausted, and unless costs are increasing more rapidly.

demand curve they face may make it harder to dislodge them. But in effect, both their predicted and observed rational response to the specificities of the demand curve suggests absence of the classic monopoly harm (represented as the triangle ABC on Figure 3.1). In plain words, big tech firms do not appear to do the bad things that we normally expect monopolists to do. But this also leaves open a critical question: if big tech firms do not act like monopolies in the short term, what, if any, are the constraints on their competitive behavior?

C. Increasing Returns to Adoption, Network Effects, and Uncertainty

How do firms compete in the special case of increasing returns to adoption where the demand curve is upward sloping or shifting? We are not in darkness here. Since the 1970s, economics study firm behavior in markets with "network effects" where users' willingness to pay initially increases with quantity demanded.[33] A much underappreciated tenet of that literature emphasizes the uncertainty typical of network effects markets (1).[34] That finding is key. The theory corroborates the representations made by big tech firms and business analysts when they discuss the industry environment, as seen in the previous chapter (2).

1. Competition in Network Effects Markets

In this section, we sequentially introduce three related ideas, namely how the theory of network effects leads to an upward demand curve (a), how the upward demand curve leads to uncertainty (b), and how this uncertainty is compounded, not mitigated, by tipping effects (c).

---

33. This literature is discussed below. Other strands in the economics literature have considered upward sloping demand curves in markets with bandwagon effects. See Harvey Leibenstein, "Bandwagon, Snob, and Veblen Effects in the Theory of Consumers' Demand" (1950) 64(2) *The Quarterly Journal of Economics* 183 (hereafter Leibenstein, "Bandwagon"); Gary S Becker, "A Note on Restaurant Pricing and Other Examples of Social Influence on Price" (1991) 99 *Journal of Political Economy* 1109.

34. Note that most of the scholarly work does not concentrate on uncertainty, but on topics like lock in, winner take all, switching costs, price discrimination, and bundling.

a) Network Effects and the Upward Demand Curve

Let us start with a simplified presentation of the canonical model of net-work effects. In a market with network effects, users' willingness to pay ("WTP") depends on the number of other users consuming the service. Economists use a variety of concepts to denote this: "demand side econ-omies of scale,"[35] "positive consumption externalities,"[36] "network exter-nalities,"[37] and many others.[38] In some cases, the network effects are direct, when an individual user's utility increases as other users adopt the service. The typical example is a telephone network. In other cases, the network effects are indirect, where an individual user's utility grows as other suppliers of complementary products adopt the service. The typical example is a con-sole and video games. In both cases, the common idea is that an individual user's marginal benefit is based not only on the value (v) of the service's functional attributes—but also, and more remarkably, on the number (n) of (expected) users to join the network. This leads to a function $p(x)=v(x)n(z)$, where (p) is the reservation price, x is an individual user, and z is the popu-lation that can use the network.

Two diagrammatical representations of networks effects populate the lit-erature. The first gives an unordinary inverted U curve shape to the demand curve.[39] At low levels of (other) users' adoption of a network service, the network's value is null (see Figure 3.3, segment 0 to 2 on horizontal axis). The demand curve is flat. No one is willing to join. As more users join, the marginal WTP for the service increases. The demand curve slopes upward (see Figure 3.3, segment 2 to 6 on horizontal axis). At some point, adding users to the network brings positive, yet lower marginal value. The WTP

35. Hal R Varian and Carl Shapiro, *Economics of Information Technology* (Cambridge University Press 2004) 33.

36. Nicholas Economides, "The Economics of Networks" (1996) 14 *International Journal of Industrial Organization* 678 (hereafter Economides, "Economics of Networks").

37. Michael L Katz and Carl Shapiro "Network Externalities, Competition, and Compatibility" (1985) 75(3) *American Economic Review* 424 (hereafter Katz and Shapiro, "Network Externalities").

38. For example, Richard Langlois talks of "synchronization value." This denotes the fact that the number of platform users expands value up to a level that is higher than the platform's "autarky value," that is its value when the product is used in isolation by a user. See Richard N Langlois, "Written Evidence (OPL0073)" (2015) <http://data.parliament.uk/writtenev-idence/committeeevidence.svc/evidencedocument/eu-internal-market-subcommittee/online-platforms-and-the-eu-digital-single-market/written/25676.html>   accessed December 17, 2019.

39. We discuss below both the individual demand curve and the market demand curve.

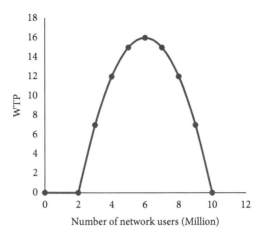

Figure 3.3 Demand Curve with Network Externalities

remains positive, but it decreases (see Figure 3.3, segment 6 to 10 on horizontal axis). The demand curve slopes downward.

The intuition behind this phenomenon is easy to understand: a marginal increase in one's consumption of a network good produces positive externalities on third parties who adopt it, triggering an increase in one's own consumption and WTP. This positive feedback loop stops at some point, when the marginal benefits that one derives from the network stem more from its own functionality than from other users' adoption. Moreover, some marginal disutility might kick in, due to congestion and other negative externalities resulting from mass adoption.

The second diagrammatical representation of network effects is one in which the demand curve is downward sloping, but shifts upwards with increases in users that join the network.[40] In this variant, each individual user derives positive yet decreasing marginal benefits from network service consumption. The demand curve slopes downward. Yet, because increases in individual consumption produce externalities on third parties, additional

---

40. Economides, "Economics of Networks" (n 36) 678. Network externalities "signifies the fact that the value of a unit of the good increases with the number of units sold. To economists, this fact seems quite counterintuitive, since they all know that, except for potatoes in Irish famines, market demand slopes downwards. Thus, the earlier statement, 'the value of a unit of a good increases with the number of units sold,' should be interpreted as 'the value of a unit of the good increases with the expected number of units to be sold.' Thus, the demand slopes downward but shifts upward with increases in the number of units expected to be sold."

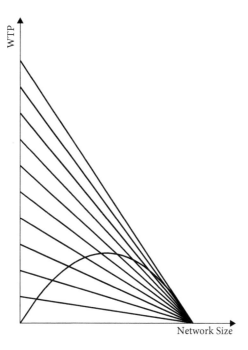

Figure 3.4 Alternative Demand Curve with Network Externalities

users join the network, increasing marginal benefits, and with it WTP, for the individual user. The demand curve shifts upward.

With an eye on Figure 3.4, we can see that each individual marginal user's WTP increases for some time, until it decreases.[41] Again, if we trace out the locus of (virtual) equilibrium for a network of size X (ie, we experience X-1 shifts in the downard sloping demand curve), we find that a typical user's demand curve slopes upward and then downward.[42]

The demand curve slopes upward as long as each individual user experiences increased benefits from others' consumption. And then it slopes

---

41. Economists technically refer to Figure 3.4 as a "fulfilled expectations demand curve" (Nicholas Economides, "Competition Policy in Network Industries" in Dennis W Jansen (ed), *The New Economy and Beyond: Past, Present and Future* (Edward Elgar Publishing 2006) 101–03). The quantity of users plays two roles. First, as in the conventional model of the demand curve, an increase in quantity makes the price decrease. Second, the actual quantity of users is also the expected quantity, which raises demand when it increases. On the diagram, we consider the number of users n to correspond to the initial expectations, so n plays the two roles at once.
42. The crossing points are virtual equilibrium points. On this, see the early work of Leibenstein, "Bandwagon" (n 33) 194.

downward when the value derived from increases in n(z) wears out. In that case, v(x) recovers a determinant role, yielding decreasing marginal benefits as under the standard demand curve.

The difference between both representations is a matter of exposition, not ideology. In the first case, the price effect and the consumption externality effects are accounted for together.[43] In the second representation, the price effect and the consumption externality are accounted for separately.[44]

Regardless of which diagrammatical representation best represents the real world (we could actually invent more of them, depending on how we formulate the problem), what matters is that the demand curve in network effects markets may contain an upward sloping segment.[45]

b) Upward Demand Curve and Uncertainty

The unordinary demand curve observed in network effects markets has a key implication. When firms operate in the demand curve's upward shifting or sloping region, there is much uncertainty. A perturbation in market conditions—including one due to the firm's own decisions—can precipitate the firm toward success or ruin. By contrast, when the demand curve slopes downward, a perturbation in market conditions—including one due to the firm's own decisions—will have trivial influence. Following a period of adjustment, the market will pursue its march toward the high participation equilibrium.[46]

43. Paul Belleflamme and Martin Peitz explain: "[T]he impact of the Law of Demand (according to which the quantity demanded decreases with the fee) is more than compensated by the network effect (which increases the consumers' willingness to pay as demand expands)." See Paul Belleflamme and Martin Peitz, *The Economics of Platforms* (Cambridge University Press, Forthcoming, 2020) Chapter 3 mimeo (hereafter Belleflamme and Peitz, *The Economics of Platforms*).

44. Traditional economists who consider that "an upward slopping demand curve is inconsistent with economic theory" tend to prefer the second representation. See Robert S Pyndick and Daniel Rubinfeld, *Microeconomics* (9th edn, Peason 2017) 737. We ought to note here that Gary Becker, hardly an untraditional economist, used the first method in his work on bandwagon effects. See Becker, "A Note on Restaurant Pricing and Other Examples of Social Influences on Price" (n 33).

45. Belleflamme and Peitz, *The Economics of Platforms* (n 43). In appendix 4, we show a diagrammatical representation of a discontinuous demand curve for a network market, where the network effects appear on the left hand side part of the diagram, and where the demand curve recovers its traditional slope on the right hand side.

46. Behind this complicated term lies a fairly simple idea: failure to add new users/keep existing users in the growth stage of the market decreases the realized utility of past adopters below their initial expectations. This leads to network churn. By contrast, failure to add new users/keep existing users in the mature stage of the market does not reduce utility below the expected level of quality that has been realized. This leads to network rigidity.

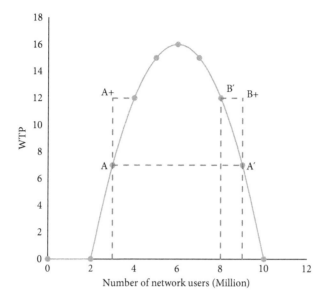

Figure 3.5 Demand Curve with Network Externalities and Ads

One should not blindly trust the model to understand this. A simple dia-grammatical illustration drives the point home. Consider the conventional representation of network users' WTP on Figure 3.5 above (eg, WTP might describe a subscription fee, tolerance to ads, or willingness to share personal data). A firm launches a social network service with a potential scale of 10 million users. The challenge for the firm is to recover a given level of production costs without undermining users' base growth. The firm knows that the demand curve is upward sloping/shifting but it cannot perfectly estimate users' WTP. How to best monetize the service?[47] Suppose now that the network has developed a small users' base of 3 million, and that demand is growing. The firm introduces ads at level A+. Ads can be thought of as a price paid by users.[48] As one can see on Figure 3.5 above, point A+ exceeds users' WTP. Marginal users leave the network. This triggers a negative

47. An example of the following approach showing how pricing decisions can place firms below or above equilibrium, and influence success or failure in reaching critical mass can be found in David Easley and Jon Klinberg, *Networks, Crowds, and Markets: Reasoning about a Highly Connected World* (Cambridge University Press 2010) 17.3.
48. See for a paper treating ads as prices, Rajiv M Dewan, Marshall L Freimer and Jie Zhang, "Management and Valuation of Advertisement-Supported Web Sites" (2002) 19(3) Journal of Management Information Systems, 87 at 89.

feedback loop of churn, that comes to an end with the collapse of the service at equilibrium point o. Had ads been set below WTP at level A, the
price would have been below the installed base reservation price, and the
network would have grown progressively until A', that is 9 million users.[49]

Now suppose that the firm has successfully built a user base of 9 million.
The firm raises ads to level B+ (which is equivalent now to what was previously A+). Again, this price level exceeds users' WTP. The firm's users base
will decrease to 8 million, and not below (point B'). What we see here is that
the cost of wrong business decisions is not qualitatively similar depending on
whether a firm operates in the upward or downward sloping region of the
market demand curve.

To describe the environment of firms that operate with an upward slopping or shifting demand curve, some economists use concepts like "disequilibrium,"[50] "out of equilibrium,"[51] or "unstable equilibria."[52] Many
economists however dislike the idea of non-equilibrium, and approach it
with disbelief if not scorn (economists generally assume that all markets
are in short-term equilibrium).[53] Letting the controversy aside, there is,

49. Or, to put it differently, a discrete decrease in price from A+ could result in a large increase in
    quantity, consistent with traditional demand curve effects.
50. Jeffrey Rohlfs, "Theory of Interdependent Demand for a Communications Service" (1974)
    5(1) *Bell Journal of Economics and Management Science* 16 (hereafter Rohlfs, "Theory of
    Interdependent Demand").
51. David S Evans and Richard Schmalensee, "Failure to Launch: Critical Mass in Platform
    Businesses" (2010) 9(4) *Review of Network Economics* Article 1 (hereafter Evans and Schmalensee,
    "Failure to Launch").
52. Rohlfs, "Theory of Interdependent Demand" (n 50).
53. A standard definition of equilibrium is that of a situation in which there is no room for
    voluntary improvement. Franklin Fisher, *Disequilibrium Foundations of Equilibrium Economics*
    (Cambridge University Press 1983) 3 (using the term non equilibrium: "As already stated,
    microeconomic theory is primarily about positions of equilibrium. The plans of agents (usu-
    ally derived from the solution of individual optimization problems) are taken together, and
    certain variables—usually prices are assumed to take on values that make those plans mutually
    consistent. Comparative static analysis then proceeds to compare equilibria corresponding to
    different values of underlying parameters. In all this, very little is said about the dynamics of
    the process that leads an equilibrium to be established in the first place or by which the system
    adjusts to a new equilibrium when the old one is displaced by a parameter shift. Attention
    is centered on the equilibria themselves (with some awkward problems when they are not
    unique), and points of nonequilibrium are discussed by showing that the system cannot remain
    at such points. But showing that disequilibrium points will not be maintained is necessary but
    very far from sufficient to justify analyzing only equilibria. The view that equilibria are the
    points of interest must logically rest on two underlying properties about the dynamics of what
    happens out of equilibrium. First, the system must be stable; that is, it must converge to some
    equilibrium. Second, such convergence must take place relatively quickly. If the predictions of
    comparative statics are to be interesting in a world in which conditions change, convergence
    to equilibrium must be sufficiently rapid that the system, reacting to a given parameter shift,

however, one interesting, and relatively consensual, insight in the main-stream economic literature. Both the firm, its competitors, and external observers face a "multiplicity of equilibria," and this creates uncertainty as to how the market will behave.[54] As Paul Belleflamme and Martin Peitz write, "a direct consequence of the existence of multiple equilibria is unpredict-ability."[55] Moreover, prices lose relevance. The market can sustain different network sizes for the same price.[56] And though static economic analysis can typically locate the multiple equilibria faced by firms in such markets (as we did on Figure 3.5), it usually "cannot tell us which one will be 'selected'."[57] In short, business seems more risky with increasing returns to adoption than in the standard case of the falling demand curve.[58] To capture this uncertainty in outcomes, Schumpeter figuratively talked of a "a ball that is perched on the top of an inverted bowl."[59]

c) Uncertainty and Tipping Effects
i) Brief Overview of Tipping Effects Theory

As much as they seem to generate uncertainty, network effects display another property that seems, at least facially, to work in reverse. The key concept here is "tipping."[60] In a network effects market, firms that reach a tipping point (or "critical mass") of users can expect a high participation equilibrium.[61] In accepted jargon, it is said that the market "tips." By con-trast, firms which do not reach that point can expect network collapse.

gets close to the predicted new equilibrium before parameters shift once more. If this is not the case, and, a fortiori, if the system is unstable so that convergence never takes place, then what will matter will be the 'transient' behavior of the system as it reacts to disequilibrium. Of course, it will then be a misnomer to call such behavior 'transient,' for it will never disappear").

54. Belleflamme and Peitz, *The Economics of Platforms* (n 43).
55. ibid.
56. Hung-Ken Chien and C Y Cyrus Chu, "Durable-Goods Monopoly with Network Effects" (2008) 27(6) *Marketing Science* 1012.
57. W Brian Arthur, "Competing Technologies, Increasing Returns, and Lock-In by Historical Events" (1989) 394 *The Economic Journal* 116 (hereafter Arthur, "Competing Technologies").
58. Of course, the model assumes reversibility of users' participation choices, but this is a reason-ably likely assumption especially when the demand is growing. By contrast, when demand is falling, reversibility is more constrained (for example, people have accumulated many friends on a social network), and this strengthens the movement toward the high participation equi-librium. Evans and Schmalensee, "Failure to Launch" (n 51).
59. Joseph A Schumpeter, *Historic Economy Analysis* (Allen & Unwin 1954).
60. Michael L Katz and Carl Shapiro, "Systems Competition and Network Effects" (1994) 8(2) *Journal of Economic Perspectives* 106 defining "'tipping' as "the tendency of one system to pull away from its rivals in popularity once it has gained an initial edge."
61. Another close concept is that of "critical mass." In economics, Thomas Schelling draws a parallel with nuclear engineering ("An example is 'critical mass'. An atomic pile 'goes critical'

There is a right and wrong way to think about tipping in network effects markets. To caricature, the wrong way considers the idea of tipping as an economic model able to predict a set and determinate threshold volume of users that, once crossed, will ignite an automatic domino effect of self-reinforcing technology diffusion that ends with near market monopoly.

The right way considers the principle of tipping not as a theory, but rather as a "mental model"[62] apt to characterize complex "recurrent behavior patterns" when "people's behavior depends on how many are behaving a particular way" in technology markets and but also other walks of life like sports or university seminars.[63] Historian Niall Ferguson recalls how the table turned during the French Revolution, when a hundred people lost their lives after soldiers defending the Bastille opened fire, triggering defection from some of the defenders who joined the crowd.[64]

Though economists are predominantly on the right side of the discussion, a number of hidden complexities of tipping effects leads non-economic savvy readers to cultivate misconceptions about it.[65] To paraphrase Hal Varian talking about network effects, tipping is one of these ideas "that you can explain to a regulator in five minutes and they can talk about it for five months."[66]

More specifically, the simplicity of the intuition obfuscates that markets vulnerable to tipping are actually a driver of complexity for firms. Let us discuss this in more detail.

---

when a chain reaction of nuclear fission becomes self-sustaining; for an atomic pile, or an atomic bomb, there is some minimum amount of fissionable material that has to be compacted together to keep the reaction from petering out"). See Thomas C Schelling, *Micromotives and Macrobehavior* (W.W. Norton & Company 2006) 89 (hereafter Schelling, *Micromotives*). Arthur, "Competing Technologies" (n 57).

62. Tren Griffin, "Two Powerful Mental Models: Network Effects and Critical Mass" (*Andreessen Horowitz*, March 7, 2016) <https://a16z.com/2016/03/07/network-effects_critical-mass/> accessed April 12, 2019 (hereafter Griffin, "Two Powerful Mental Models").

63. Schelling, *Micromotives* (n 61) 94.

64. Niall Ferguson, *The Square and the Tower* (Penguin Press 2018) 124.

65. Schelling observes that the concept of "mass" is technically inappropriate in physics, and that "number," which is its economic equivalent, is also unsatisfactory. He prefers to use it as a "shorthand." See Schelling, *Micromotives* (n 61) 95 ("whether the measure is the number of people engaged, or the number times the frequency or the length of time they engage in it, or the ratio of the number who do to the number who do not, or the amount of such activity per square foot or per day or per telephone extension, we can call it a 'critical-mass' activity").

66. Hal Varian, "Use and abuse of Network Effects" (*SSRN*, August 7, 2018) <https://papers.ssrn.com/sol3/papers.cfm?abstract_id=3215488> accessed April 12, 2019.

ii) The Tipping Point Is not a Set Measure

There is no tipping point corresponding to a set number of users against which firms can assess network adoption performance. Rather, there is a *range* of numbers that define a zone in which tipping is likely. In empirical works, this range is often expressed as a ratio of market users to market potential.[67]

Most economic works suggest that the tipping zone is difficult to estimate.[68] One difficulty owes to the fact that this range is an aggregate of individual users' vision of what constitutes critical mass,[69] and users' utility functions vary widely.[70] A lot of heterogeneity must therefore be accounted for.[71] This can be best understood with a real life example: a teenager's critical mass of connections on a social network is likely lower than Victoria Beckham's. And yet, to bring the teenager on board, the social network must convince Victoria Beckham to join (and use) the service. Like other marquee users, however, Victoria Beckham will not sponsor a low subscription service, raising the critical mass threshold challenge for the social network.

---

67. Michal Grajek and Tobias Kretchsmer, "Identifying Critical Mass in the Global Cellular Telephony Market" (2012) 30(6) *International Journal of Industrial Organization* 496 (hereafter Grajek and Kretchsmer, "Identifying Critical Mass"). ("Empirical work on critical mass focuses on identifying a percentage—typically varying between 10% (Mahler and Rogers 1999) and 25% (Cool et al. 1997)—of market potential as critical mass"); Evans and Schmalensee, "Failure to Launch" (n 51).
68. See Bob Briscoe, Andrew Odlyzko, and Benjamin Tilly, "Metcalfe's Law is Wrong" (*IEEE Spectrum*, July 1, 2006) <https://spectrum.ieee.org/computing/networks/metcalfes-law-is-wrong> accessed April 12, 2019 ("The fundamental flaw underlying both Metcalfe's and Reed's laws is in the assignment of equal value to all connections or all groups").
69. David Allen, "New Telecommunications Services: Network Externalities and Critical Mass" (1988) 12(3) *Telecommunications Policy* 257 (hereafter Allen, "New Telecommunications Services") ("each person has an individual vision of what constitutes critical mass").
70. Jose Luis Arroyo-Barrigüete, Ricardo Ernst, Jose Ignacio López-Sánchez, and Alejandro Orero-Giménez, "On the Identification of Critical Mass in Internet-based Services Subject to Network Effects" (2008) 30(5) *The Service Industries Journal* 643. The key problem with determining critical mass is defining the utility functions of the individuals who make up the market. For example, if one takes the user of a social network, then his utility function is conditional on at least two types of interaction with different people which are difficult to model (i) sphere of close influence; and (ii) rest of the population.
71. Schelling, *Micromotives* (n 61) ("Though perhaps not in physical and chemical reactions, in social reactions it is typically the case that the 'critical number' for one person differs from another's"; "When people differ with respect to their cross-over points, there may be a large range of numbers over which, if that number of people were doing it, for a few but only a few among them that number wouldn't be big enough, while the rest would be content. When those few for whom the number is not enough drop out, they lower the number, and some more drop out, and so on all the way. The fact that in the end nobody is doing it does not give us any measure of *how many* satisfied participants were lacking at any point along the way"); Allen, "New Telecommunications Services" (n 69).

Besides, another difficulty is that the tipping zone is not fixed. Market potential keeps changing as firms grow. The tipping zone is thus a moving target. Consider this: our estimate of Amazon's critical range is not the same depending on whether one looks at it as a firm seeking to become an online book retailer (in 1997), the world's "online" retailer (in 1999), or Earth's most consumer centric company (in 2003).[72] Or think about Netflix's entry into streaming content production in 2008. Streaming imposed on Netflix a new tipping challenge, for it subsequently had to build a library of titles of sufficient "mass" to convince viewers from other content networks to join its platform.[73] The upshot is simple. Markets that have tipped may re-tip.

One may still ask, however, whether the locus of the tipping point can be expected in the lower or the upper region of the upward sloping demand curve. But again, there is no clear response to this question. In the literature, tipping effects are one of those areas in the literature where the ratio of theory to evidence is quite large.[74]

What this means is simple. Firms are living organisms. And all growing firms, including large ones, face tipping effects challenges.[75]

iii) Tipping Effects and Business Strategy

Tipping effects do not arise in markets because of the laws of nature (or the nature of technology).[76] Already in 1985, economists Michael Katz and Carl Shapiro noticed this. Observing that one would like a theory that tells what leads to the zero adoption or to the high participation equilibrium, they asked "what can consumers and firms do to influence the market

---

72. See Amazon, Inc, Form 10-K, US SEC, 2003.
73. We could multiply examples. Facebook's critical mass threshold has evolved since the days when it launched as an undergrad college service at Harvard to become a worldwide unrestricted social network. Uber eats is another one. Though Uber's installed base of users in ridesharing services gives certain advantages, its critical mass of drivers is of no assistance when it comes to recruiting new restaurants.
74. In a thorough review from 2015, Ewa Lechman writes: "it is worth underlining that despite a relatively well-developed theoretical framework and conceptual background aiming to explain the 'critical mass'-like phenomenon, the number of empirical works seeking a quantitative assessment of it is very limited." See Ewa Lechman, *ICT Diffusion in Developing Countries: Towards a New Concept of Technological Takeoff* (Springer 2015) 54 (hereafter Lechman, *ICT Diffusion*).
75. One diagrammatical implication of this point is that network size cannot be normalized, and the demand curve should shift upward, without being tied to a fixed point on the horizontal axis.
76. Some authors have, however, come close to this assumption: see Lechman, *ICT Diffusion* (n 74) 50 for an overview of the literature.

outcome."[77] Katz and Shapiro captured early the intuition that because network effects vary in strength, other forces affect technology adoption.

Thirty-five years later, we still miss the theory, but we know a lot more. First, market institutions and firms' decisions influence technology adoption.[78] This influence is highest when firms are below the tipping zone, and lowest when firms are above it.

Second, below the tipping zone, price is only one of the numerous devices available to reach a high participation users' base.[79] By contrast, when the tipping zone is crossed, "installed base effects drive diffusion even in the absence of price decreases."[80] Crossing the tipping zone simplifies the set of firms' profit maximizing options, including by plausibly allowing exercise of power over price. This, as we shall see in Chapter V, has a straightforward policy consequence. Empirical data on firm-level performance allow to draw an inference that the market has tipped. For example, when we see a firm raising subscription or brokerage fees, increasing the intensity of advertisement, or phasing out freemiums, we may be observing a tipped market.

Third, when the demand grows in network effects markets, prices essentially serve as signals.[81] By contrast, prices recover their "mediating" role between supply and demand above the tipping zone.[82]

Fourth, externalities cause higher effects below the tipping zone. Ulrich Witt writes: "When critical point is high, innovation by third parties may lead to random fluctuations."[83] Put differently, there is higher uncertainty below the tipping point than above.

77. Katz and Shapiro, "Network Externalities" (n 37).
78. This, to some extent, is one of the key teachings of the economic literature on endogenous growth, which shows that technological change is not manna from heaven, but arises from the intentional actions taken by people who respond to market incentives. See Paul M Romer, "Endogenous Technological Change" (1990) 98(5) *Journal of Political Economy* S71.
79. Katz and Shapiro provide a list of firm strategies (pricing commitments on complementary software, "second sourcing," vertical integration, "penetration pricing," etc).
80. Grajek and Kretchmer, "Identifying Critical Mass" (n 67). The authors also note that the emergence of critical mass is conditioned on "strength of installed base effects, the size of the installed base, and the current market price." For this definition, see Grajek and Kretchmer, "Identifying Critical Mass."
81. Allen, "New Telecommunications Services" (n 69) at 269. This in turn, entails the equilibrium possibility of introductory pricing in network effects markets. See Luis M B Cabral, David J Salant, and Glenn A Woroch, "Monopoly Pricing with Network Externalities" (1999) 17 *International Journal of Industrial Organization* 199.
82. Allen, "New Telecommunications Services" (n 69).
83. Ulrich Witt, "'Lock-in' vs. 'Critical Masses'—Industrial Change under Network Externalities" (1997) 15 *International Journal of Industrial Organisation* 753.

With all this, the conclusion is unmistakable: unlike what terms like "snow-ball," "feedback loop," or "bandwagon effects" connote, there is no magic in markets with network effects. And claims about the self-sustaining nature and exponential rate of technology diffusion above the tipping zone must be taken with a grain of salt.[84]

iv) Tipping Effects and the Ghost Town Problem

There is no ratchet in markets subject to tipping effects. Firms can fail to maintain market relevance in spite of users' mass adoption of their product and services. In his seminal work on critical mass, Nobel prize winner Thomas Schelling uses the metaphor of the "dying seminar" to illustrate the situation of a university gathering that slowly peters out in spite of (sustained) academics' interest.[85]

One specific reason why firms in network markets might become "ghost towns" in spite of tipping effects is the following: as a network expands, users' growth yields a tyranny of connections, choice, and content, imposing irrelevance costs on users and control costs on the firm.[86] . Firms may therefore occupy what looks like an optimal above critical mass membership position, yet register user engagement decline and incremental network expenditures. Facebook's traditional way to deal with this problem has consisted in tweaking the algorithm of its newsfeed. To make things concrete, Facebook has decided to show top stories or family content, rather than relying on mere chronological order.

v) Tipping Effects Are Neither Firm nor Product-Related, but Market Specific

Often, the tipping effects story is not told carefully. Many works—including this one—discuss if, how, and when firms or products tip, when they should instead talk about markets. To put things differently, it is neither a firm that reaches critical mass nor its product that tips. It is the market.

To see what happens when the focus of analysis shifts, let us quote Tren Griffin: "What happens if a market does 'tip'... but it's the competitor that

---

84. For they are under-representative of the depth and sophistication of economics literature.
85. Schelling, *Micromotives* (n 61) 92.
86. For use of the expression "ghost town", see Alex Moazed and Nicholas L Johnson, *Modern Monopolies: What It Takes To Dominate the 21st Century Economy* (St Martin's Press 2016) (hereafter Moazed and Johnson, *Modern Monopolies*).

reaps those benefits?"[87] Griffin offers the following example: Myspace made the early investments in social networks, pushing the market toward tipping. But Myspace was impatient. Facebook was not. Facebook's slow monetization strategy eventually paid off.

The deeper point made by Griffin is that investments into critical mass are imperfectly appropriable.[88] Competitors can free ride on rivals' network specific investments. This property of network effects markets can work both to the benefit of late entrants (including, second, third, or fourth movers), as in the Facebook and Myspace story, and to the benefit of incumbents, as evidenced by Facebook's development of Instagram in a market initially developed by Snapchat.

2. Uncertainty

When network effects markets feature growing demand, firms operate under uncertainty. If we consider big tech firms' disclosures in 10-K reports (a) as well as industry fact patterns (b), there are sound reasons to believe that an economic model of competition with uncertainty better describes their environment than the standard monopoly model.

a) Anecdotes

One regularity observed in big tech firms' 10-Ks—and confirmed by our risk factor analysis in Chapter II—is a reported concern of disruption. Here is a short selection of the most commonplace big tech statements on disruption: "Our business is characterized by rapid change as well as new and disruptive technologies," "… many of the areas in which we compete evolve rapidly with changing and disruptive technologies, shifting user needs, and frequent introductions of new products and services"; "Our business is characterized by innovation, rapid change, and disruptive technologies."[89]

---

87. See Griffin, "Two Powerful Mental Models" (n 62).
88. The other point is that rival firms have distinct perceptions of the tipping zone levels.
89. Google CEO Eric Schmidt once declared "somewhere, someone in a garage is gunning for us." Eric Schmidt, "The New Gründergeist" (*Google Europe Blog,* October 13, 2014), <http://googlepolicyeurope.blogspot.com/2014/10/the-new-grundergeist.html>. See also Dominic Rushe, "Jeff Bezos Tells Employees 'One Day Amazon Will Fail'" *The Guardian* (November 16, 2018)("Amazon is not too big to fail … In fact, I predict one day Amazon will fail. Amazon will go bankrupt. If you look at large companies, their lifespans tend to be 30-plus years, not a hundred-plus years").

Outside of the Silicon Valley, big tech firms' litanies leave many cold. Critics deride tech giants' under-confidence as public relations talk serving to defuse attention from the public opinion, the press, and regulatory agencies. They rightly recall that Amazon, Netflix, and Google are twenty years old or so.[90] As years pass, the comparison with "murdered-by-disruption" giants like AOL, Blockbuster, Kodak, Myspace, Polaroid, and SUN Microsystems becomes untenable.

At the same time, the properties of network markets with increasing returns to adoption and the inherent estimation difficulties involved in identifying the tipping zone brings theoretical backing to big tech firms' alarmist declarations.

Moreover, it is not all certain that the risk of disruption which burdens big tech firms is one of terminal exit. If competitive extinction unlikely is a big tech concern, competitive irrelevance is perhaps a more credible one. To put the point clearly, big tech firms may not want to be relegated to the scrap heap of history like MapQuest, Nokia, or Yahoo!. Or they may simply not want to become also-rans like Oracle, a company that disrupted IBM and Cullinet, but that was later disrupted by Microsoft.[91]

Last, there is one more reason to give currency to big tech's reported under-confidence. Several tech firms today draw a share of their profits (and therefore of their ability to grow) from accidental discoveries: Amazon often recalls that it discovered the lucrative cloud services market by luck;[92] and Netflix did not initially believe in online streaming.[93] If this happened to them, why would not this happen to another firm?

---

90. At the same time, note that they are amongst the only new large firms that appeared in the economy in the past twenty years.

91. Clayton M Christensen, Mark W Johnson, and Darrell K Rigby, "Foundations for Growth: How to Identify and Build Disruptive New Businesses" (2002) 43(3) *MIT Sloan Management Review*, 22-31.

92. This is captured in Jeff Bezos' famous saying that there is a lot of uncertainty, and "no aha moment" when a company comes up with an idea. In a letter to shareholders, Jeff Bezos also wrote "Luck plays an outsized role in every endeavor, and I can assure you we've had a bountiful supply." See Brad Stone, *The Everything Store: Jeff Bezos and the Age of Amazon* (Little, Brown and Company 2013) and Jeffrey P Bezos, "2015 Letter to Shareholders" (Amazon. com 2015) <https://ir.aboutamazon.com/files/doc_financials/annual/2015-Letter-to-Shareholders.PDF> accessed April 21, 2020.

93. Netflix initially did not bet on online streaming, due to reservations about the ability of the Internet infrastructure and enabling technologies to deliver. See Netflix, Inc, Form 10-K, US SEC, 2004. The company perception will become more optimistic from 2007 onwards.

b) Industry Facts

When we look at sources of uncertainty in big tech markets, we observe a universe of risk factors all linked to the emerging properties of digital industries. To start, uncertainty stems from demand side factors. Estimating users' WTP is difficult. If this was not the case, the venture capital market would not exist.[94] Many factors enter a user's preference functions. Take privacy. If users of social networks value privacy in absolute terms, the relative weight of privacy is unclear when compared with other factors like convenience, personalization, or transaction costs economies.[95] In a 2019 experimental study, Eric Brynjolfsson, Avinash Collis, and Felix Eggers found that many unpriced goods produce significant consumer surplus, in spite of privacy loss.[96] This creates a challenge of setting the right monetization strategy, both level and time wise.

Besides, users' WTP in an upward sloping or shifting demand market is not fixed. WTP may decrease due to users' bad behavior. Common examples include Myspace users' exodus following reports of inappropriate content on the platform or Atari's demise due to failure to lock out unauthorized games.[97]

By contrast, when a network has overcome the tipping zone constraint, there is less uncertainty. AOL, once the dominant online Internet provider in the United States, provides a good example. In 1996, AOL moved from pricing by the hour to a monthly twenty hours' access subscription with incremental fees.[98] Intense customer backlash did not prevent AOL from

---

94. Since it is based on high risk bets with low probability of success. We could also all be as wealthy as Jeff Bezos or Marc Zuckerberg.

95. For an untechnical exposition, see Bowman Heiden and Nicolas Petit, "'Privacy Absolutism' masks how consumers actually value their data" (*The Hill*, December 12, 2019) <https://thehill.com/opinion/cybersecurity/474253-privacy-absolutism-masks-how-consumers-actually-value-their-data> accessed April 21, 2020.

96. Erik Brynjolfsson, Avinash Collis, and Felix Eggers, "Using Massive Online Choice Experiments to Measure Changes in Well-Being" (2019) 116(15) *Proceedings of the National Academy of Sciences* 7250. The study uses choice experiments to estimate the consumer surplus created by digital goods with zero price. It asks users how much compensation they would require to forego the digital good. Though the study does not compare monopolized digital goods to competitive ones, it estimates the consumer surplus generated by platforms like Facebook or digital services like search engines. The study finds that the monthly median consumer surplus for a Facebook user is USD 48. Emerging experimental work relativizes policy arguments that characterize users as unpaid data subjects.

97. Andrei Hagiu, "Strategic Decisions for Multisided Platforms" (2008) *Top 10 Lessons on Strategy, MIT Sloan Management Review* 4.

98. Kara Swisher, *AOL.com* (Three Rivers Press 1999) 160–62.

further growing its user base in the following years. Arguably, AOL's post-1996 growth took place in the downward sloping region of its demand curve. Closer to us, Netflix brings a possible example of a firm that may have reached critical mass, and knows it. In its 10-K for 2009, Netflix declared: "We have achieved a level of scale in our business that provides many operational and competitive advantages ... Such scale economies also have contributed over time to expanding operating margins which has made it possible for Netflix to aggressively price its service offering at levels difficult for competition to meet."[99]

This last example also suggests that uncertainty can arise from the supply side. Recall that in big tech markets, MP increase. The implication is clear: network markets with an upward demand and downward unit costs provide highest profit opportunities.[100]

The practical economic consequence is straightforward. One should witness relatively higher competitive entry in the portions of the demand curve that slopes upward. Again, anecdotal observations of bold big tech strategic moves seems to carry the point. Some illustrations are found in Microsoft's Bing attack against Google's Internet search service, Google's Android attack against Apple's closed smartphone ecosystem or Apple's entry into entertainment to challenge Netflix. Similarly, profit-making opportunities in markets with an upward demand may be the business rationale behind big tech firms' attempts to cream-skim specific market segments. Through that light, Microsoft's purchase of professional social network LinkedIn looks like specialist entry into social networks. The same can be conjectured about the launch of Facebook's ten minutes' video uploading IGTV service, which looks a lot like a pointed attack at Google's YouTube.

Complements are also a source of uncertainty. To think about this, consider the example of apps and operating systems ("OS"). On the one hand, apps bring added value to an OS, and increase users' WTP for the OS. On the other hand, apps capture value from the OS. The underlying economics

99. See Netflix, Inc, Form 10-K, US SEC, 2009.
100. Mario Rizzo goes as far as stating: "profits exist only in a world of uncertainty and disequilibrium." Mario J Rizzo, "Disequilibrium and all that" in Mario J Rizzo (ed), *Time, Uncertainty and Disequilibrium* (Lexington Books 1979) 10.

are straightforward: due to an "income constraint"—economic agents have finite resources—users faced with a new complementary application B or C, will devote relatively less to A.[101] Of course, A may still benefit from an anchoring effect if complement B or C makes the system more valuable. In this case, the loser might be unrelated pizza night, not A … unless B or C have figured out a way to capture all the increased value.[102] From this, one can instantly see that complements generate ambiguous effects. Add to this that complements sometime reconfigure the structure of an industry. In his famous Tidal Wave memo of 1995, Bill Gates speculated about the future of the Internet, a complement to Microsoft's OS and productivity software. Gates correctly conjectured the appearance of a whole host of competing products, like new file formats, browsers, and even less expensive devices for Web browsing. Competitive entry in adjacent, neighboring, or complement product spaces reinforces uncertainty, and therefore creates pressure on incumbents' products.

Last, firms in network effects markets may not only be victims, but also active agents of uncertainty. Because third party entry dissipates the likelihood of long-term profits, incumbents are incentivized to look for emerging or future network effects markets, adding even more uncertainty to the business environment. In the 1990s, AOL spent millions if not billions developing its own movie and media offering only to discontinue later.[103] In the 2000s, Microsoft invested successfully in games and less successfully in online press content. And today, we see the tech giants entering online banking and payments, entertainment, healthcare, or wearable devices like connected glasses or watches.

---

101. If you live in a neighborhood without a Starbucks, then you have a budget for detergent at Walmart that is x; now assume there is a Starbucks and you like it. You will spend y less at Walmart, where y<x.
102. We are grateful to Doug Melamed for bringing this to our attention. Note that firms' 10-K reports seem to suggest that complements may cannibalize revenue growth prospects for old products. See Microsoft 10-K for 2000 ("A market for handheld computing and communication devices has developed. While these devices are not as powerful or versatile as PCs, they threaten to erode sales growth in the market for PCs with pre-installed software").
103. The failed merger of AOL with TimeWarner—described as the "worst merger of all times" is anecdotal evidence of this. See Rita Gunther McGrath, "15 Years Later, Lessons from the Failed AOL-Time Warner Merger" (*Fortune*, January 10, 2015) <https://fortune.com/2015/01/10/15-years-later-lessons-from-the-failed-aol-time-warner-merger/> accessed April 21, 2020.

D. Conclusion

It is time to move on. Now that we have abstractly established the existence of a competitive constraint resulting from the uncertainty found in the special case of markets with increasing returns to adoption, network externalities, and tipping effects, we must address the next hard question: how do big tech firms concretely compete? This is what we do in the following chapter.

★

★   ★

IV

A Concrete Theory of Moligopoly

What do we know? To start, we saw that conventional methods of industry analysis identify levels of competition amongst big tech firms that are not discussed by competition and regulatory decision-makers. And we understand that simple economics do not support the idea of big tech monopolies.

Both findings bring about a novel hypothesis. If neither source of expert knowledge sees big tech firms as monopolies, one explanation might be that both antitrust and regulatory decision-makers discount facts of empirical significance. This chapter tries to identify these lost empirical facts.

Our ambition is dual. First, we hope to contribute to the ongoing policy conversation related to the behavior of firms in the digital economy.[1] Second, we are interested in elaborating a more concrete theory of big tech competition based on careful firm-level observation.

We start by introducing each tech giant (A). We then identify six critical properties common to many of them (B). On that basis, we can specify an original model of big tech "moligopoly" competition (C).

A. Meet Big Tech

1. Beyond Airport Books

Books on the tech giants have become a genre of their own. There is one for every taste, and in every airport. Some are biographies of big tech founders for the larger audience. Others discuss "how to win Wall Street,"

---

1. See Chapter I for a review of the literature.

Big Tech and the Digital Economy. Nicolas Petit, Oxford University Press (2020). © Nicolas Petit.
DOI: 10.1093/oso/9780198837701.001.0001

hoping to recruit readers among MBA students and young entrepreneurs. All are helpful learning resources. Yet, they carry judgment and interpretation. Moreover, they often focus on one specific firm, more than a group. For lack of a common methodology, they are thus of limited use to formulate empirical descriptions amenable to benchmarking.

To describe the economics, history, and strategy of big tech firms, we have turned (again) to 10-K reports. This is one of the few data sources common to all six firms that we focus on, namely Facebook, Apple, Amazon, Netflix, Google, and Microsoft.[2] 10-K information allows us to build comparable pictures. In particular, Item 7 "Management's Discussion and Analysis of Financial Condition and Results of Operations," and "Notes to financial statements" provide objective qualitative and quantitative insights.[3] Longitudinal treatment of 10-K reports avoids the shortcomings of static study of price, input, output, and accounting data, and gives a procedure to understand big tech firms' strategic moves. With that said, let us now meet the tech giants.

2. Facebook

Facebook is a social network. It develops a software platform and mobile application ("app") that enable users to freely share information with selected audiences in various form factors (ideas, opinions, photos, videos, etc). Facebook's stated mission is "to make the world more open and connected." Facebook was founded in 2004 by CEO Marc Zuckerberg, and held its Initial Public Offering ("IPO") in 2012.

Between 2011 and 2017, Facebook's monthly active users ("MAU") grew from 1.1 to 2.1 billion, its workforce from over 4.6 to 25.1 thousand, and shareholders' profits (net income) from USD 53 million to USD 15.9 billion. Facebook has expanded internationally, serving the United States, Europe, and Asia.[4] Facebook also diversified. In 2018, it described itself as a four "ecosystems" firm: the Facebook app and platform, Instagram, WhatsApp, and Messenger.[5] In 2018, Facebook spent 18 percent of its revenue on

---

2. The downside is that 10-Ks report less sensational stories than airport books on big tech.
3. We already discussed the objectiveness of 10-Ks in Chapter II.
4. In China, access to Facebook is restricted in whole or in part. According to Facebook, average revenue per user is more than five times higher in the United States and Canada than in Asia.
5. See 10-K for 2016, Facebook, Inc, Form 10-K, US SEC, 2016.

research and development ("R&D"). In relative terms, this makes it the biggest R&D spender of big tech.

Facebook's platform and mobile app are free to users. Facebook generates substantially all of its revenue by selling advertisement ("ad") products to marketers and/or advertising agencies.[6] Facebook's ad products are highly targeted, allowing marketers to reach specific and relevant audiences. Most of Facebook's ads are served to users of mobile devices. In recent years, the targeting of ads has nurtured intense privacy concerns in the public opinion and policy environments.

Careful study of Facebook's 10-Ks suggests that two sets of events served as catalysts for growth. First, in its early days, Facebook believed that fees collected on electronic payments from users (of games) to developers as well as purchases of its virtual currency would provide a significant revenue stream.[7] In 2011, Facebook even made its payment platform mandatory. This led payments and other fees to represent about 19 percent of Facebook's revenue.[8] A year later, however, Facebook introduced an important product change, deciding to display ads in the News Feed (previously, ads appeared in the right hand column of its webpage).[9] Ads displayed in News Feed were a turning point. By 2017, total advertisement amounted to 98 percent of Facebook's revenue. Moreover, about 90 percent of Facebook's revenue is generated by serving ads on mobile devices, and in particular News Feed ads.[10] For indeed, all of its daily and monthly active users access Facebook on mobile devices. This is significant, compared to 2012, when Facebook explained that mobile technology is not a boon because it "shows fewer ads on Mobile" (though this is "partially offset by higher price per ad for mobile").

---

6. See Facebook, Inc, Form 10-K, US SEC, 2018 ("Marketers pay for ad products either directly or through their relationships with advertising agencies, based on the number of clicks made by our users, the number of actions taken by our users or the number of impressions delivered").

7. See Facebook, Inc, Form 10-K, US SEC, 2012 ("Our users can make payments on the Facebook Platform by using credit cards or other payment methods available on our website. The primary process for these transactions is through the purchase of our virtual currency. Our users then use this virtual currency to purchase virtual and digital goods in games and apps from developers on the Facebook Platform. Upon the initial sale of the virtual currency, we record consideration received from a user as a deposit").

8. That is USD 810 million out of USD 4.2 billion.

9. Facebook forecasted that transaction fees would plateau, essentially nurtured by its exclusive relationship with the social game company Zynga.

10. In 2017, mobile ads represented 88 percent of Facebook's revenue.

What this means is simple: Facebook had not predicted the commercial potential of mobile technology.[11] At the same time, lack of adaptability could have meant stagnation. Facebook's mobile epiphany informed subsequent strategy. Seen through that light, later corporate events like the acquisition of WhatsApp—essentially a mobile messaging infrastructure—can be rationalized as investments intended to expand Facebook's foothold on mobile devices.

The second event is Facebook's acquisition of photo-sharing service Instagram in 2012. Seven years later, industry experts still speculate on the reason for the acquisition: acqui-hiring of thirteen employees, product buy of Instagram's superior photo technology, or strategic purchase of Instagram's 100 million active users' base? The 10-K numbers appear supportive of the strategic purchase story:[12] out of an accounted purchase price of USD 521 million, Facebook reported USD 74 million for the technology and USD 433 million as "goodwill."[13] In hindsight, 10-K reports show that Instagram software ownership increased users' "levels of mobile engagement and photo sharing," as compared to the more PC-centric Facebook service. We might also conjecture that the addition of Instagram buffered the year over year reduction in "younger" users' engagement on Facebook.[14]

11. Instead, it believed that ads on personal computers ("PCs") would remain king, plausibly discounting that users essentially use Facebook over leisure time, and not in the office.
12. Note however that in 2012, Facebook rationalized M&A generally on acqui-hiring grounds: "We have also made and intend to make acquisitions with the primary objective of adding software engineers, product designers, and other personnel with certain technology expertise." See Facebook, Inc, Form 10-K, US SEC, 2012.
13. The goodwill is an intangible asset for which the value corresponds to purchase price minus the value of all identifiable assets of a company. It consists on the value one can give to the customer base or the company's reputation. Despite its wide use, goodwill is still a vague concept. See Marco Giuliani and Daniel Brännström, "Defining Goodwill: A Practice Perspective" (2011) 9(2) *Journal of Financial Reporting and Accounting* 161.
14. In 2013, Facebook declared "some of our users have reduced their engagement with Facebook in favor of increased engagement with these other products and services. For example, in the third quarter of 2013, the best data available to us suggested that while usage by U.S. teens overall was stable, DAUs among younger teens in the United States had declined." And in yearly disclosure after the other, Facebook says that "user-provided data indicates a decline in usage among younger users" (adding "this age data is unreliable because a disproportionate number of our younger users register with an inaccurate age"). In 2017, Facebook repeated again: "We believe that some users, particularly younger users, are aware of and actively engaging with other products and services similar to, or as a substitute for, Facebook products and services, and we believe that some users have reduced their use of and engagement with our products and services in favor of these other products and services." See Facebook, Inc, Form 10-K, US SEC, 2013, 2014, and 2017.

Owing to this succession of more or less random events and strategic choices, Facebook has become a mobile advertisement business.[15] Looking ahead, delivering mobile ads on new form factors might also to be the logic behind Facebook's reported investments in long-term innovation projects like augmented reality devices, and improvements in global connectivity toward offline geographies.[16]

3. Amazon

Amazon is an electronic commerce company. Amazon sells a wide variety of retail goods to consumers through its online platform amazon.com. It also supplies web services to customers. Amazon's ambition is to be "earth's most customer-centric company." The company was started in 1995 by Jeff Bezos. Amazon became listed on the stock market in 1997.

Amazon's history is one of exponential growth. In 1997, a few hundred people worked at Amazon. Today it has 566 thousand employees. Amazon's 2017 revenue was about USD 177.9 billion, a factor 100 increase compared to 1997. Product offerings have also expanded. Initially started as an online bookstore, Amazon added products like music, cosmetics, consumer electronics, and food. Amazon has also vertically integrated into B2B web services (through its subsidiary Amazon Web Services, "AWS"),[17] devices (Kindle, Fire tablets, TV, and Echo), and content (streaming and online). Amazon operates in most countries in the world. It covers new geographies at rapid pace.

10-K reports give a good picture of the economics of Amazon. Amazon believes that there are cost efficiencies and productivity gains in many product and service areas. Long-term margins require a cost structure in which fixed costs are large relative to variable costs.[18] To improve "cost

---

15. In Facebook's disclosures, the sole company identified as a competitor is Google, also an advertisement business. See Facebook, Inc, Form 10-K, US SEC, 2013 and 2015.
16. See 10-K for 2015 talking of FB's "long-term innovation efforts, such as connectivity efforts, virtual reality, and artificial intelligence research." Facebook concedes that they do not (yet) provide "clear paths to monetization." See Facebook, Inc, Form 10-K, US SEC, 2015 and 2017.
17. In 1999, Amazon started reporting a new segment called "early stages businesses." In 2001, Amazon "began marketing three services for third-party sellers," namely Merchant@amazon.com, a merchant program and a syndicated stores program. In 2006 and 2007, Amazon noticed a take-up of web services for developers. In 2014, it started to report specifically on AWS. In 2015, AWS was the highest growth segment. See Amazon, Inc, Form 10-K, US SEC, 1999, 2001, 2006, 2007, 2014, and 2015.
18. In its 10-K for 1999, Amazon said that the platform business allows "economic incremental costs." See Amazon, Inc, Form 10-K, US SEC, 1999.

structure productivity," Amazon (i) "leverage[s] [its] fixed costs customer experience costs," ie the building and improvement of websites and fulfillment centers across a variety of products and services,[19] (ii) "minimize[s] growth in fixed costs [through] process efficiencies and lean culture,"[20] and (iii) "decrease[s] variable costs on a per unit basis" like "product costs, credit-card processing fees, picking, packaging, and preparing orders for shipment, transportation, customer service support, and certain aspects of our marketing costs."[21]

In turn, Amazon's strategies are designed to exploit economies of scale and scope. Low price programs—like Amazon Prime—[22] increase the scale of production.[23] Vertical integration in new product areas— like Amazon's entry in food products following the acquisition of Wholefoods—leverages infrastructure costs. Competition amongst sellers or between Amazon and sellers brings prices down and promotes users' adoption.[24]

Amazon's long-term focus leads to sustained short-term losses.[25] From 1997 to 2002, and in 2012 and 2014, Amazon recorded negative net income (but revenue grew). In 2001, Amazon even had to complete a restructuring plan, laying off 1.3 thousand employees. Arguably, Amazon sought to send a credible signal to investors that its business model was profitable. One open question, and a strategic challenge, for Amazon are whether a long-term commitment to "economical incremental costs" is compatible with rising labor costs.[26]

19. See Amazon.com, Inc, Form 10-K, US SEC, 2003 and 2015.
20. See Amazon.com, Inc, Form 10-K, US SEC, 2018.
21. See Amazon.com, Inc, Form 10-K, US SEC, 2003.
22. Amazon Prime was introduced in 2005. Prime offers free two-day shipping on retail purchases, on-demand video streaming, and free access to the Kindle library.
23. See Amazon.com, Inc, Form 10-K, US SEC, 2003 and 2004. In 2016, Amazon said that it is "operating at an ever increasing scale."
24. See Amazon.com, Inc, Form 10-K, US SEC, 2003 ("Our price reductions take several forms: we reduce the sales prices of products we sell we recruit third-party sellers to compete with us on product detail pages").
25. See Amazon.com, Inc, Form 10-K, US SEC, 2001 ("our financial focus is on long-term"). Thirteen years later, Amazon repeats that it is guided by "long term thinking." See Amazon.com, Inc, Form 10-K, US SEC, 2014.
26. This problem applies to many firms, and industries, with exception though of the performing arts, where labor cannot be substituted with capital and where economies of scale are not necessarily operative.

4. Apple

Apple is a computer manufacturer. It develops an ecosystem of proprietary hardware products and services (and related software). Its best known products are the Apple and Macintosh computer, the iPhone, and the iPad tablet. Apple was founded in 1976 by Steve Jobs and Steve Wozniak. Today, Apple's ambition is to bring "the best user experience to its customers through its innovative hardware, software and services."[27]

Since 1994, Apple's revenue has grown from USD 9 billion to USD 265 billion in 2018, though with a decrease between 1995 and 2003. In 2018, Apple generated a profit of USD 59 billion. Though Apple has diversified, about 60 percent of Apple's revenue is derived from iPhone sales. Since 2017, services like digital content (music), cloud storage, and payments are Apple's second revenue source (USD 29 billion), above Mac (USD 25 billion) and iPad (USD 19 billion) sales. Apple has a 132 thousand workforce.

In Apple's history, one industry event stands out. In 1994, Apple announced that it would develop a unified software platform for personal computers ("PC") in a bid to end several years of poor performance. Apple wanted to enter the PC market dominated by the Windows and Intel infrastructure ("Wintel") by licensing its proprietary Macintosh Operating System ("Mac OS") to PC original equipment manufacturers ("OEMs"). Apple entered into an alliance with IBM and Motorola.[28] However, Apple had few software applications to distribute with the Mac OS, and its main source of revenue remained hardware sales. The first effects of Apple's cross–platform licensing strategy did not take long to unfold. Apple's computers were commoditized by aggressive price competition from new Mac manufacturers. The firm PowerComputing sold a product known as a "clone." In 1996, Apple realized its blunder. It wrote: "The benefits to the Company from licensing the Mac OS to third parties may be more than offset by the disadvantages of being required to compete with them."

This episode had a durable influence on the economics of Apple. From this point, Apple migrated back to hardware (leaving software to Microsoft),[29]

27. See Apple, Inc, Form 10-K, US SEC, 2018.
28. Apple hopes to capture a share of the lucrative PC software market where Microsoft is leader with Windows and office applications.
29. In 1997, Apple signs a life-saving deal with Microsoft. In exchange for Apple abandoning its entry into the PC market, Microsoft accepts to write application software for Apple. Note also that the deal involves Apple accepting to bundle Internet Explorer as the default browser on its computers.

and developed a strategy focused on high-price devices, supply chain cost efficiencies, short product cycles, and a closed ecosystem. Let us examine more closely these four areas of strategic focus.

To start, Apple targets high margin markets[30] and avoids price competition.[31] Since 1997, this has been done through product differentiation.[32] When Jobs returned to Apple in 1998, escape from the PC commodity markets became the rallying cry. Apple foresaw profit maximization opportunities in new Internet devices, but was wary of risks of commoditization.[33] Jobs bet on "innovative industrial design" and "intuitive ease of use" to differentiate Apple's hardware products.[34] The strategy was introduced in 1998 with the release of the high end iMac, and was applied to subsequent product launches like the iPod, the iPhone, and the iPad. Apple's differentiation was also supported by aggressive branding, investments in distribution, and retailer selection.[35] Any reader of Apple's 10-Ks over the sample period will notice widespread association of ® or ™ symbols with product references. In 2002, Apple introduced a "retail initiative," building a high density network of shops where "knowledgeable salespersons" have a "direct interface with its targeted end customer" and can "effectively demonstrate the advantage of Apple over rivals."[36] In 2007, Apple concluded exclusive distribution agreements with selected carriers to sell iPhones to consumers.[37]

---

30. We can see in Apple's 10-Ks a careful targeting of low elasticity market segments. Around the 2000s, Apple devises a focused strategy for "education" and "creative customers," arguably on the anticipation that parents and artists constitute less price-sensitive segments. See Apple, Inc, Form 10-K, US SEC, 2002. Similarly, Apple's target of the watch market in 2015 is hardly a surprise. Watches are non-commodity goods, where above cost pricing is more the rule than the exception.

31. Apple is the sole firm of the big tech group to complain explicitly about price competition in its 10-Ks. See, eg, Apple, Inc, Form 10-Ks, US SEC, 2018.

32. In 2015, Apple talks of a "shift in mix to products with higher margins." See Apple, Inc, Form 10-K, US SEC, 2015.

33. See Apple, Inc, Form 10-K, US SEC, 2000 ("as the personal computer industry and its customers place more reliance on the Internet, an increasing number of Internet devices that are smaller, simpler, and less expensive than traditional personal computers may compete for market share").

34. See Apple, Inc, Form 10-K, US SEC, 1998.

35. Note that not all of Apple's products are subject to limited distribution. iPods are one exception. In 2005, Apple "significantly expanded the number of distribution points where iPods are sold. The iPod product line can be purchased in certain department stores, member-only warehouse stores, large retail chains, and specialty retail stores, …" See Apple, Inc, Form 10-K, US SEC, 2005.

36. See Apple, Inc, Form 10-K, US SEC, 2002.

37. In 2009, Apple will abandon exclusive distribution of iPhones.

Second, Apple's mid 1990s repositioning on hardware has had supply chain implications. To see this point, recall that hardware produces lower returns to scale than software. Apple's cost structure is now skewed toward variable costs.[38] Economies of scale contribute less to profit margins than savings on components, labor, and manufacturing costs.[39] This plausibly explains Apple's repeated supply chain changes, as can be seen from the 2005 switch from IBM to Intel for processor supply.[40]

Third, Apple launches new products at rapid pace.[41] Frequent product introduction, or new product versions, constitute a strategy to counter commoditization. Product upgrades also provide a value extraction tool. As reported in its 10-K for 1996 (in relation to software), Apple's upgrades reduce backward compatibility for users.[42] Apple is aware that product incompatibility causes churn.[43] But customer switching has been mitigated by selling to areas of demand that are relatively less elastic like "creative customers" or "education."[44]

Last, since the early 2000s, Apple employs an *ecosystem* strategy.[45] Apple views devices like computers or the iPhone as a "digital hub for advanced new digital devices such as digital music players, personal digital assistants, digital still and movie cameras, CD and DVD players, and other electronic devices."[46] The added value of the ecosystem business model can be seen

38. See Apple, Inc, Form 10-K, US SEC, 1995 ("The cost of goods sold is based primarily on the cost of components and, to a lesser extent, direct labor costs").
39. See Apple, Inc, Form 10-K, US SEC, 2014. Over the period 2012–14, Apple attributes increased profits essentially to "lower commodity and other products costs."
40. See Apple, Inc, Form 10-K, US SEC, 2005.
41. From 1998, Apple has been releasing new versions of its hardware products at more rapid pace, emulating what Microsoft had historically done with Windows. This strategy has been applied to all Apple hardware, and especially to the iPhone.
42. See Apple, Inc, Form 10-K, US SEC, 1996.
43. One could argue that Apple's focus on "education" was intended to build fidelity toward its products, and avoid the churn of consumers resulting from commoditization.
44. See n 30 above, referring to Apple, Inc, Form 10-K, US SEC, 2002.
45. See Apple, Inc, Form 10-K, US SEC, 2006. In its 10-Ks, Apple often takes pride in vertical integration: "the only participant in the personal computer industry that controls the design and development of the entire personal computer."
46. See Apple, Inc, Form 10-K, US SEC, 2001: "The company believes that personal computing is entering a new era in which the personal computer will function for both professionals and consumers as the digital hub for advanced new digital devices such as digital music players, personal digital assistants, digital still and movie cameras, CD and DVD players, and other electronic devices." In 2003, Apple says "The Company believes it maintains a competitive advantage by more effectively integrating the entire end-to-end music solution, including the hardware (iPod), software (iTunes) and music content (iTunes Music Store)." See Apple, Inc, Form 10-K, US SEC, 2003.

concretely in 2008. With substantial increase in iPhone sales, Apple recorded growth in all its revenue segments (ie Mac, iPods, iPhones, music, peripherals, and other hardware).[47] Moreover, combined with Apple's control over proprietary architectures, designs, and interfaces that prevent rivals from offering compatible equipment, Apple's ecosystem strategy limits churn by creating switching costs for customers.

In hindsight, Apple displayed adaptability and foresight. Apple's 1997 exit from the PC market was a lifesaving move.[48] And Apple correctly anticipated the success of Internet products[49] and in particular of form factors smaller than computers.[50]

5. Netflix

Netflix is an "internet television network." Incorporated in 1997, Netflix started operations as a DVD rental and sales service. Netflix changed the economics of DVD distribution by offering a large selection of titles on its website (www.netflix.com) and by getting them delivered to its clients' homes by postal mail.[51] Netflix completed its IPO in 2002. Today Netflix has developed a digital streaming service available to customers on any Internet-connected screen in exchange for a monthly subscription.[52] Netflix's corporate slogan is "see what's next."[53]

In 2018, Netflix achieved a revenue of USD 15.8 billion and a profit of USD 1.2 billion. Netflix has 5 thousand employees, 117 million users, and it

---

47. Note, however, that this is not a general trend. In 2009, not all segments will grow together.
48. Apple could have joined Amiga, Bull, Compaq, or Commodore, in the cemetery of dead computer hardware manufacturers.
49. They are discussed already in Apple's 10-K for 1996.
50. In 2000, Apple writes "as the personal computer industry and its customers place more reliance on the Internet, an increasing number of Internet devices that are smaller, simpler, and less expensive than traditional personal computers may compete for market share." See Apple, Inc, Form 10-K, US SEC, 2000.
51. Until then, customers rented DVDs by the title at the local store. Capacity constrained retailers focused primarily on new releases.
52. Subscribers have access to an unlimited number of titles per month. Note that Netflix was not the first to use a subscription model. In 2002, other online DVD subscription services, such as WalMart.com and FilmCaddy.com, a subsidiary of Blockbuster, Inc already existed.
53. David Ng, "Must Reads: As Netflix Surges, Original Content is the New Black. But Licensed Shows Still Take the Crown" *Los Angeles Times* (August 12, 2018) <https://www.latimes.com/business/hollywood/la-fi-ct-netflix-programming-surge-20180812-story.html>   accessed November 1, 2019.

streams more than 140 million of hours of content per day. Netflix operates in all countries in the world except China, Crimea, North Korea, and Syria.

Analysis of 10-Ks emphasizes the economic drivers of Netflix's strategy. First, Netflix is a highly specialized firm. Netflix has not pursued diversification opportunities in industries other than in-home film entertainment. And Netflix has only practiced vertical specialization to a limited degree. Hardware device and infrastructure supply has been contracted out to consumer electronic producers (like LG) and cloud computing providers (like Amazon).[54] Though Netflix has entered upstream content production (original movies and TV series), the logic has again been one of horizontal specialization. Investments in "exclusive and original programming," including TV series and movies are intended to "differentiate from competitors."[55]

A second characteristic of Netflix is its flexibility. Netflix's transition from DVD to streaming affords a good example. Netflix initially had reservations on the commercial viability of the Internet.[56] But in 2005, Netflix realized that Internet delivery of content to the home "will surpass DVD" in the future. In 2006, Netflix formulates a strategy to pivot away from its core DVD business.[57] But Netflix is not a pioneer in online download, and at that time several incumbent providers already offered movies downloading services like iTunes, Vongo, Movielink, and CinemaNow. Three business models compete: rental of online content; download to own; and ad-supported

54. When online streaming was developing in 2007, Netflix had to broaden the distribution of its instant viewing software across platforms (PCs, Macs, TVs, and video games devices). While others (like Apple, Amazon, Google, or Microsoft) had readily crossed the software/hardware boundary, Netflix pursued an outsourcing strategy through a partnership with LG and others consumer electronics suppliers to develop a set top box device or other devices. See Netflix, Inc, Form 10-K, US SEC, 2007.

55. See Netflix, Inc, Form 10-K, US SEC, 2012. In 2015, Netflix adds "we believe that original programming can help differentiate our service from other offerings, enhance our brand and otherwise attract and retain members." Netflix, Inc, Form 10-K, US SEC, 2015. It cannot be excluded that vertical integration may have also been a response to strategic supplier conduct, in line with textbook transaction economics and holdup theory. In previous 10-Ks, Netflix reported that entry was a response to episodes of business disruption with upstream content suppliers (eg, withdrawal of content from Starz Play Service in 2008 or exclusive deals between studios like Warner Bros and HBO).

56. See Netflix, Inc, Form 10-K, US SEC, 2004 ("The Internet may not become a viable commercial marketplace for many potential subscribers due to inadequate development of network infrastructure and enabling technologies").

57. See Netflix, Inc, Form 10-K, US SEC, 2006 ("the DVD format ... will continue to be the main vehicle for watching movies in the home for the foreseeable future and that by growing a large DVD subscription business, we will be well positioned to transition our subscribers and our business to Internet-based movie delivery as it becomes a mainstream method for movie distribution").

online viewing. In 2008, Netflix starts "bundling DVD and streaming as part of the Netflix subscription."[58] In the emerging online streaming market, this "creates a competitive advantage as compared to a streaming only subscription service." The transition is not frictionless. Netflix faces customer churn when it subsequently unbundles DVD and streaming subscriptions.[59] But Netflix eventually weathers the storm, raising the standard subscription fee for unlimited streaming from USD 7.99 in 2010 to USD 8.99 in 2014 and USD 9.99 in 2015.[60]

Third, non-price characteristics appear to be key drivers of competition. Netflix's 10-Ks stress the importance of a "broad and deep" selection of titles,[61] personalized recommendations based on users' ratings,[62] and convenience.[63] This is not boilerplate. The price war that broke out between 2004 and 2007 with Blockbuster Online brings anecdotal yet confirmative evidence that low fees are not enough to win viewers.[64] In 2007, Blockbuster registered 2 million subscribers in spite of lower prices than Netflix. In the same year, Netflix totaled 6.3 million subscribers, and had added 2.1 million subscribers to its service with a higher price.[65]

58. See Netflix, Inc, Form 10-K, US SEC, 2008.
59. In a second step, Netflix introduced "DVD only plans," and "separate[d] the combined plans," leading to a price increase for users of both services, and some consumer backlash. See Netflix, Inc, Form 10-K, US SEC, 2011 and 2012. Netflix reported that this led to "significant customer cancellations." Netflix had to take steps to retract plans to rebrand its DVD-by-mail service and separate the DVD-by-mail and streaming websites. Customer cancellation in the second half of 2011 "resulted in a 32.3% decrease in unique domestic net subscriber additions for the year ended December 31, 2011."
60. See Netflix, Inc, Form 10-K, US SEC, 2016 for a good overview of the fee evolution. Note also, that price increases often come with grandfathering protection for existing users. However, Netflix has systematically phased out grandfathering after some years.
61. See Netflix, Inc, Form 10-K, US SEC, 2007 ("broad and deep selection of DVD titles we offer subscribers").
62. See Netflix, Inc, Form 10-K, US SEC, 2007 (referring to Netflix's "ability to personalize" streaming library to each subscriber based on their selection history, "personal ratings" and "recommendation service").
63. See Netflix, Inc, Form 10-K, US SEC, 2007 ("the ease and speed with which subscribers are able to select, receive and return DVDs").
64. In 2003, Blockbuster acquired an online DVD subscription service called FilmCaddy.Com, planning to roll out an online subscription service. See Netflix, Inc, Form 10-K, US SEC, 2003. Blockbuster also tested a store-based subscription model for DVD in some of its locations. Its long-term plan was to integrate the online and store-based subscription programs sometime in 2005.
65. In August 2004, Blockbuster—incumbent video rental player since the mid-1980s—launched an online offering, setting prices 20 percent (or USD 3) lower than Netflix monthly subscription fee. Blockbuster also eliminated its traditional late fee policy (and offers a three-out formula). The timing was tricky. A couple of months before, Netflix had increased its subscription price from USD 19.95 to USD 21.99. Netflix will reverse course in November.

Fourth, the cost structure of Netflix involves high fixed costs and uncertain variable costs. Content acquisition from studios is Netflix's primary source of costs.[66] "Output deals" with studios specify a fee for a set of specific titles that stays fixed regardless of subscriber's base or viewing.[67] In 2017, output deals represented a cost of USD 3.3 billion.[68] Output deals also "include an unspecified or a maximum number of titles that we may or may not receive in the future and/or that include pricing contingent on certain variables, such as theatrical exhibition receipts for the title." Netflix estimates these unknown obligations to range between "approximately \$3 billion to \$5 billion over the next three years."[69]

6. Google

Google is an Internet search company. Founders Larry Page and Sergey Brin started Google in 1998 as a research project at Stanford University. Page and

---

It will lower the price of the most popular subscription plan to USD 17.99. Blockbuster will reply by slashing the price of its subscription to USD 14.99 in December 2004, and eliminate late fees for in-store rentals in January 2005. In late 2006, Blockbuster will launch "Total access," an integrated store-based and online program. Total Access was an attempt to leverage Blockbuster's massive offline capabilities to the online market. Under Total Access, subscribers could return DVDs delivered from Blockbuster Online to Blockbuster stores in exchange for an in-store rental. But Blockbuster will not keep up with operating losses, and will have to raise the price of total access. Netflix will give the coup de grace with a price reduction for its most popular subscription plans during the third quarter of 2007. In April 2006, Netflix also filed a complaint for patent infringement against Blockbuster. On June 13, 2006, Blockbuster filed a counterclaim alleging that the company had violated Section 2 of the Sherman Antitrust Act. The dispute was eventually settled. Netflix received a one-time payment of USD 7 million. In its 10-K for 2007, Netflix talks of an "apparent reduced competitive threat from Blockbuster Online." See Netflix, Inc, Form 10-K, US SEC, 2007.

66. They represent the "vast majority of cost of revenues." See Netflix, Inc, Form 10-K, US SEC, 2016.

67. Previously, Netflix had revenue-sharing agreements with studios, whereby it bought DVD copies at a lower upfront cost than traditional buying arrangements, and made more payments to the studios if subscribers rented DVD copies. Sometimes, the studios obtained equity in Netflix. This cost structure was highly predictable for a new entrant, and necessitated little capital advance. In 2002, Netflix explained that this improved its "ability to acquire larger quantities of newly released titles and satisfy a substantial portion of subscriber demand for such titles over a shorter period of time."

68. Netflix reported a USD 17.7 billion contingency in streaming content, which it amortized in a period of ten years as costs of revenue. In 2017, Netflix reported cost of revenue up to USD 7.7 billion. A back of the envelope calculus suggests that streaming content represents 23 percent of Netflix costs of revenue. See Netflix, Inc, Form 10-K, US SEC, 2017.

69. Netflix, Inc, Form 10-K, US SEC, 2017 ("with the payments for the vast majority of such amounts expected to occur after the next twelve months").

Brin developed a novel web indexing technology called PageRank,[70] which quickly became the most widely used automated search engine. Google had its IPO in 2004. Renamed Alphabet in 2015, it is today a "collection of businesses" centered around an offering of software services, hardware products, and advertisement. Alphabet's corporate slogan is "do the right thing."

In 2018, Alphabet generated a revenue of USD 136.8 billion to which Google contributed USD 136.2 billion. Alphabet's profits were USD 30.8 billion. Both Alphabet's revenue and profits have grown without interruption on a year over year basis. Alphabet has over 98 thousand full-time employees. Google search and advertisement services are supplied in most countries in the world.

The question of what defines the economic reality of Google can be answered by analysis of its 10-K reports. To start, Google is a firm specialized in advertising sales.[71] In 2017, Google generated a revenue of USD 95.4 billion on online advertising, and USD 14.2 billion on other activities (sales of apps, in-app purchases, digital content products, hardware, licensing, and service fees, including fees received for cloud offerings).[72] Google's advertising revenue stems from two distinct services. The first service is the AdWords platform. AdWords allow advertisers to bid for the display of ads on Google's websites (search engine, YouTube, Maps, Finance, etc) in reaction to specific search queries.[73] In 2017, AdWords made up 70.9 percent of Google's revenue. The second service is the AdSense platform. AdSense is a brokerage service that displays ads on behalf of advertisers on third-party websites, (ie not on Google's). Google distributes ads through search boxes or on spaces that partner websites—called Google's Network Members— set aside in exchange for a share of the fees collected from advertisers. In 2017, AdSense represented 16 percent of Google's revenue.

70. PageRank determines the importance of web pages by looking at the link structure of the web.
71. Initially, Google made money by licensing its search engine to other websites. In an Internet of portals filled with media content, taking money from websites in exchange for search capability was a good business concept. But Google foresaw a more distributed Internet, and a much larger market. In 2000, coincidentally with the dot.com crisis, Google experimented advertisement-based monetization. Since then, it has plowed the line in online ads.
72. See Alphabet, Inc, Form 10-K, US SEC, 2017.
73. Advertisers win the auction if they post the highest price adjusted for the ad quality score (as measured by the click-through rate and other factors). They only pay the second price for the auction. Advertisers pay a cost per click (with a minimal fee of USD 0.05), but may also be charged a cost per impression (or display).

Google's year over year revenue growth owes to the success of "targeted advertising"[74] technology (though Google stopped using this term in recent 10-Ks).[75] In 2013, Google declared that the "the main focus of our advertising programs is to help businesses reach people in the moments that matter across all devices with smarter ads that are relevant to their intent and context."[76] To match relevant advertisement to users, Google uses a variety of techniques including analysis of keywords, emails, group postings screening, and possibly of browser history, real time user activity, and geographic localization.[77]

Along with specialization comes diversification in advertisement services. Google is active in many "verticals." Google defines a vertical as a "particular industry" area, like finance or travel, which deploys "specialized sales teams" toward advertisers. In 2007, Google was present in eleven "advertising verticals."[78] Since 2008, Google no longer discloses a number, but reports activity in a "multitude" of advertising verticals. There are several likely reasons why Google adds verticals to its "general purpose" search engine. The reason most explicitly stated in its 10-Ks is a desire to avoid missing advertising revenue when users "navigate directly" and initiate search on specialist "websites," "content" platforms, or "apps" like Amazon, eBay, Kayak, or LinkedIn, even if Google supplies them with the search technology.[79] Revenue from searches on verticals that do not belong to Google—for instance through AdSense—[80] are shared with

---

74. See Google, Inc, Form 10-K, US SEC, 2006. For quite some time, Google's main technological challenge has been to reduce the number of ads on non commercial search queries, and to increase the number of ads on commercial search queries.

75. Compare 10-K for 2012, Item 7 ("We generate revenue primarily by delivering relevant, cost-effective online advertising. Businesses use our AdWords program to promote their products and services with targeted advertising") with 10-K for 2013, Item 7 ("Our Google segment generates revenues primarily by delivering relevant, cost-effective online advertising. Businesses use our AdWords program and AdSense program to promote their products and services with advertising on both Google-owned properties and publishers' sites across the web"). See Google, Inc, Form 10-K, US SEC, 2012 and 2013.

76. See Google, Inc, Form 10-K, US SEC, 2013.

77. Since 2015, Google sells "programmatic" and "reservation based advertising" which operates as an exchange market where advertisers enjoy "access to top-tier inventory across screens and formats, as well as the real-time insights," and thus can deliver hyper-targeted advertisement. See Google, Inc, Form 10-K, US SEC, 2013 or Alphabet, Inc, Form 10-K, US SEC, 2015.

78. In 2004, Google reported thirteen vertical markets. See Google, Inc, Form 10-K, US SEC, 2004.

79. See Alphabet, Inc, Form 10-K, US SEC, 2018.

80. Note though that traffic acquisition costs may also be incurred on Google properties. For example, mobile searches may take place on Google properties (like Google search for mobile), but represent traffic acquisition costs when Google pays handset manufacturers to preinstall its properties.

partners.[81] In 2011, these "traffic acquisition costs" ("TACs") represented 51 percent of AdSense advertising fees.[82] Understandably, Google views as "favorable" an evolution that consists in "a shift of mix from Google Network Members' websites revenue to Google websites revenue."[83] This, arguably, gives Google powerful incentives to try to decrease the payment of revenue share, end AdSense relationships, and integrate verticals served by Google Network Members.[84] Google may however rely on "revenue share" to enter new geographic markets, educate advertisers to technology (like programmatic advertising), or develop search on new platforms like mobile devices.

Google's diversification also extends to a range of other business that are "far afield" of its "core" of "Internet products," including communications devices, life science, or self-driving systems.[85] Consistent with Google's focus on advertisement, these investments are the consequence of technological change. Google's acquisition of Motorola in 2011 illustrates that well.[86] Google did not want to convert into a hardware mobile phone maker. But the Motorola acquisition was critical to advance Google's ongoing development of its homegrown mobile OS Android at a time where users increasingly accessed the Internet from mobile devices (Google had previously acquired mobile ads company AdMob in 2009).[87] By staying a PC-centric

81. Google fees to vertical partners are commonly referred to as "revenue share." In some cases, Google has committed to minimum revenue share and guaranteed payments with certain partners.
82. Traffic acquisition costs are defined as "amounts ultimately paid to our Google Network members under AdSense arrangements and to certain other partners (our 'distribution partners') who distribute our toolbar and other products (collectively referred to as 'access points') or otherwise direct search queries to our web site (collectively referred to as 'distribution arrangements')." See Google, Inc, Form 10-K, US SEC, 2005.
83. As it did in both 2016 and 2017. Granted, Google needs to rely on third party Google Network Members when it seeks to penetrate new geographies, educate advertisers to new advertisement technology (like programmatic advertising), or develop search on new platforms like mobile devices. For instance, in 2014, Google reported an "increase in the number of Google Network Members." See Google, Inc, Form 10-K, US SEC, 2014.
84. See Google, Inc, Form 10-K, US SEC, 2009 and 2011, where Google reports a "decrease in traffic acquisition costs as a percentage of advertising revenues" that is "primarily due to more revenues realized from Google Network members to whom we pay less revenue share."
85. See Alphabet, Inc, Form 10-K, US SEC, 2015 (discussing the "Other Bets" segment as a collection of "businesses that are generally pretty far afield of our main Internet products").
86. Google has previously sought to develop its own mobile phone Nexus in 2010.
87. See Google, Inc, Form 10-K, US SEC, 2012 ("The acquisition is expected to protect and advance our Android ecosystem and enhance competition in mobile computing"). Note that another reason explaining the acquisition might have been that Google wanted to buy patents to use as litigation weapons amidst a growing number of patent disputes between industry players in cellular technologies.

search engine, Google risked leaving substantial advertising revenue to third parties.[88] Moreover, mobile devices collect lots of contextual information useful for non-keyword advertisement.

Through this lens, one can also make sense of Google's diversification in new form factors like virtual reality, digital assistants, or self-driving vehicles.[89] Superficially, Google's investments look like vertical integration in traditional industries like optical devices, audio speakers, or car manufacturing. But the reality is that they are attempts to distribute ads on the "multiple screens" that people use online.[90] To put the point graphically, Google will unlikely build cars, speakers, or sunglasses. Rather, it invests in the technology that will show ads on visual headsets and on the windshields of self-driving vehicles.[91] Google's strategy seems to be present, in the future, on all devices—regardless of what they are (screens, display boards, speakers, car windshields, glasses, etc)—[92] where ads can be served to users.[93] As Google said in 2013, it wants to "reach people in the moments that matter across all devices."[94]

Third, Google displays a commitment to long-term, uncertain, and serendipitous research. Google's restructuring into Alphabet illustrates this point. In 2015, Alphabet became the holding structure of a collection of "individual business run separately." Alphabet reports a separate "Google" segment, which covers revenue-making activities like Internet products, hardware, and newer items like virtual reality. "Other bets" is the other

88. See Google, Inc, Form 10-K, US SEC, 2012 ("consumers are using multiple devices to access information. Over time these trends have resulted in changes in our product mix, including a significant increase in mobile search queries and a deceleration in the growth of desktop queries").

89. See Alphabet, Inc, Form 10-K, US SEC, 2016 and 2017 where these new products are mentioned.

90. See Alphabet, Inc, Form 10-K, US SEC, 2015 ("Mobile computing power continues to grow and users want to feel connected no matter where they are or what they are doing. We seek to expand our products and services to stay in front of this shift in").

91. This does not preclude the possibility that Google will seek to make revenue by licensing the software to car manufacturers and opticians.

92. Google often says it invests using the "toothbrush test," which means asking whether the "product will be used by hundreds of millions of people everyday, hopefully twice a day." See Google, Inc, Form 10-K, US SEC, 2014. Latest efforts today include the "knowledge graph," "Google Now," and Google's digital assistant Duplex. See Google, Inc, Form 10-K, US SEC, 2013. The point is basically to build a predictive and conversational Wikipedia.

93. Including offline ones. Recall that Google tried to offer offline ads in 2007 and 2008, by adding Google Print Ads, Google Audio Ads, and Google TV Ads, to schedules and places advertising into newspapers and audio and TV programs. Today, 10-Ks say little of these programs, and most have seemed discontinued.

94. Google, Inc, Form 10-K, US SEC, 2013.

reportable segment which comprises non-revenue-making research activities in areas like smart homes, self-driving systems, or life science research.[95] Google has explained that the "Alphabet reorganization was implemented to better allow us to structure teams in ways that we believe will produce the fastest, most focused innovation possible for moonshot projects."[96] The logic goes beyond a simple division of labor. The corporate reorganization promotes transparency toward investors. Alphabet can invest in high-risk projects, knowing that investors will less readily penalize the entire business of Google if "moonshots" fail to meet expectations.

7. Microsoft

Microsoft is a computer software firm. Microsoft was founded in 1975 by Bill Gates and Paul Allen. Microsoft developed the MS/DOS operating system for PCs which ended IBM's computer software dominance. Microsoft's iconic products include Windows (a graphical extension of MS/DOS), Office (a suite of productivity applications including word processing and spreadsheets), and the Xbox (a video game console). Microsoft's current focus is on "platforms and productivity services for an intelligent cloud and an intelligent edge infused with artificial intelligence."[97] Its stated mission is "to empower every person and every organization on the planet to achieve more."[98]

In 2019, Microsoft generated a total revenue of USD 125.8 billion and a profit of USD 39.2 billion. Since 1994, Microsoft's revenue has steadily grown (with an exception in 2016). Microsoft's profits have recorded more variance on a year over year basis, though the company never incurred losses. Today, Microsoft employs 124 thousand workers, 40 thousand of whom are involved in R&D work. Microsoft operates in over 190 countries worldwide.

Five features emerge from the analysis of Microsoft's 10-Ks. First, Microsoft has undergone diversification. Microsoft is no longer the Windows-centric firm that pundits from the 1990s were talking about. Compared to the 1990s where Windows and Office brought in 99 percent of Microsoft's

---

95. The collection of business comprises "Access/Google Fiber, Calico, Nest, Verily, GV, Google Capital, X, and other initiatives." See Alphabet, Inc, Form 10-K, US SEC, 2015.
96. Alphabet, Inc, Form 10-K, US SEC, 2015.
97. See Microsoft Corporation, Form 10-K, US SEC, 2019.
98. See Microsoft Corporation, Form 10-K, US SEC, 2019.

revenue, both products account today for 37 percent of Microsoft's revenue.[99] Since 2016, Windows is no longer a standalone reporting segment in Microsoft's 10-Ks.

More concretely, the breadth of Microsoft's entry has been substantial: consumer devices (Zune and Lumia phones); interactive content (portals like MSN); television (MSNBC, a news partnership with NBCUniversal News Group, and ActiMate's Interactive Barney product for kids); Internet dial-up access; search engine (Bing), browsers, and other Internet related software; online payment systems (Trans Point E-Bills); online advertisement; portable computers and tablets (Surface); entertainment hardware and software (Xbox and Mojang); productivity software (MySQL); cloud computing (Azure); and open source software (GitHub).[100]

Second, we notice path dependence to a business model known as "Commercial Software Development" ("CSD"). Under CSD, developers bear the fixed costs of R&D, which are subsequently offset by revenue made from software sales to users.[101] In hindsight, path dependence to CSD give us an alternative explanation for Microsoft's moderate success in the Internet compared to the OS era. There is little doubt that Microsoft correctly forecasted the economic potential of the Internet. Microsoft developed a free email service and a free Internet browser in the mid-1990s. And Microsoft spent the late 1990s and early 2000s developing widely used websites and applications like Expedia.com, CarPoint, MoneyCentral, MapPoint. But Microsoft's monetization strategy has invariably been one in which users pay at some point or the other, through subscriptions for narrowband Internet or access to premium services. Multisided business models in which users do not pay for software (development costs are offset by others groups of users) have by contrast been the exception rather than the rule in Microsoft's business strategy.[102]

<hr/>

99. In 2017, Windows accounted only for 9.59 percent of Microsoft revenue. See Microsoft Corporation, Form 10-K, US SEC, 2017.
100. This is consistent with our observations whereby Microsoft changed reporting segments six times over the period 1994 to 2017. This, in turn, reflects a history of rapid and more or less successful movements in Microsoft's product portfolio and strategy.
101. See Microsoft Corporation, Form 10-K, US SEC, 1995 noting the "fixed nature of a significant portion of expenses."
102. This is clear in Microsoft 10-K for 1996. Microsoft alludes to a free policy in relation to browsers ("policy of offering customers the latest Internet technology at no additional cost"). But then it adds that this is offset by Windows sales ("because Internet browsers are a fundamental and integral part of Windows-based operating system"). See Microsoft Corporation, Form 10-K, US SEC, 1996.

The story of Microsoft's lukewarm entry in online advertisement is suggestive of a similar logic. Initially, Microsoft had correctly identified online advertising as a means to support product development,[103] and betted on the development of "portals" and "channels" (and emails) where publishers could display ads to Microsoft's subscribers.[104] However, in 2001 and 2002, Microsoft reports a "decline" in the online advertising market. In 2005, it declares "richer user experience means fewer advertisements and links."[105] The endgame is a known story. Combined with a decline of dialup access subscriptions (outcompeted by broadband offerings), Microsoft's portals and channels no longer offer attractive advertisement channels. Advertisers' interest in Microsoft's display ads platform collapsed.

Of course, one may ask, why has Microsoft been so path dependent to CSD, and more generally to charging users? This is where a third economic feature of Microsoft's business model is relevant. Over the full period covered by our 10-K sample (ie, 1996–2017), Microsoft has been subject to intense antitrust scrutiny.[106] Continuous exposure to antitrust proceedings may have imparted caution in the choice of business models. Instead of experimenting with innovative multisided monetization strategies, Microsoft may have plausibly preferred to follow industry norms like subscription, versioning, and licensing models. An alternative explanation may be related to Microsoft's market power. Confident in its ability to leverage its OS near monopoly, Microsoft kept directly or indirectly charging users for new products. If the latter hypothesis is true, then hindsight tells us that

103. In 1995 and 1996 Microsoft says that its MSN network "may be supported by advertising and commerce." In 1998 and 1999 it explains that it provides systems to clients for "targeted online advertising and marketing" but does not seem to make much use of it for itself. And in 1999, while revenue of online ads increases, it talks of a decline of the Internet advertising market in 2001 and 2002. See Microsoft Corporation, Form 10-K, US SEC, 1995, 1996, 1998, and 1999.
104. See Microsoft Corporation, Form 10-K, US SEC, 2004.
105. See Microsoft Corporation, Form 10-K, US SEC, 2006, where Microsoft reports on its focus on "display advertising for portals, channels, emails and messaging services." Profits are thus contingent on selling access to the Internet. For years, Microsoft will lose money on access revenue, when dialups subscriptions go down. See Microsoft Corporation, Form 10-K, US SEC, 2007. As a result, Microsoft portals and channels cease to be a critical user interface. Advertisers' interests in the purchase of display ads on Microsoft properties will recede.
106. In 1996, Microsoft's 10-K reports on the US Department of Justice 1996 nascent investigation in web browsers. In 2017, Microsoft's 10-K still discusses the process of mandatory internal antitrust compliance imposed under the settlement in *Barovic v Ballmer et al.* See Microsoft Corporation, Form 10-K, US SEC, 1996 and 2017.

market power played here as a disadvantage for Microsoft, who failed to notice or anticipate disruptive business models.[107]

The fourth defining economic feature of Microsoft is imitation of competition in products and services.[108] Microsoft's 10-Ks show a pattern of catch-up entry and horizontal segmentation. Consider the following facts: Microsoft did not invent its OS for PC. It purchased a system called QDOS, enhanced it for the IBM PC, and then derived MS/DOS from its IBM-enhanced version of QDOS; Microsoft's Internet portal MSN copied AOL and CompuServe's access services, with emphasis on online content; Microsoft followed Yahoo!, Google, and others in search but focused on display ads; Microsoft entered social networks by targeting professionals with the purchase of Yammer in 2012 and LinkedIn in 2016.

A noticeable feature of Microsoft's imitation competition strategy is to involve established firms through mergers and acquisitions ("M&A") or strategic alliances. In 1999, Microsoft invested USD 5 billion in an alliance with AT&T and other broadband companies in order to ramp up its online efforts. In 2009, Microsoft entered into a ten-year agreement with Yahoo! to become the exclusive algorithmic and paid search platform for Yahoo! websites. In 2014, Microsoft established a strategic alliance with Nokia to jointly create new mobile products and services.[109] And in 2015, Microsoft concluded agreements with AOL to outsource its display sales efforts.

This short list will strike anyone's eye. Microsoft appears to have consistently cooperated with the industry leader of a previous technology paradigm.[110] And yet, Microsoft is still alive today. This, in turn, raises a hard question: why has Microsoft not lost out to other firms, like many forgotten computer firms from the 1980s and 1990s (eg, Atari, Novell, Sun, Digital Equipment Corporation, Lotus, Claris, CompuServe, Prodigy, AOL, Sega, etc)? Key to this might be Microsoft's adaptability. Over the period 1994 to 2017, Microsoft announced multiple strategic changes and an almost equal number of "internal reorganisations," "functional realignments," and

---

107. Note, however, that the declining sales of Windows and Office over the reporting period do not support the market power hypothesis.
108. This is not to suggest that Microsoft does not differentiate. Microsoft won the OS battle because it chose to license its software to PC manufacturers, while rivals like IBM and Apple were vertically integrated.
109. This paved the way to the subsequent purchase of Nokia by Microsoft for USD 9.5 billion.
110. In spite of its stated ambition to "establish leadership in new businesses." See Microsoft Corporation, Form 10-K, US SEC, 2000.

"restructurings." Reserving the case of monopoly rents under the CSD model, Microsoft displays a clear turnaround culture.

B. Common Properties of Big Tech

As George Stigler wrote, any scientist seeking to construct or improve a theory faces the question: "what common trait in the phenomena should be incorporated in the theory?"[111] Social sciences give no model to discriminate between relevant and irrelevant regularities or between the peculiar and the general. We address this problem specifically in relation to big tech firms by making our method explicit. We then discuss six common properties of the tech giants.

1. Method

This section assumes that big tech are an ontology. We try to see if we can find some regularities amongst the tech giants within an acceptable interval of firm-level heterogeneity. We ask: beyond "bigness," what are the tech giants' common properties?[112]

In our research, we focus on pattern identification. But how to separate pattern from noise? We cannot dispense with the formulation of a test for the selection of the facts that can be found of general validity for the analysis of big tech's competitive environment. As we just said, firm-level heterogeneity invites suspicion toward the very idea of a big tech ontology. Moreover, many deeper attributes of firms, like their sets of capabilities, are not directly observable or measurable.[113]

At an abstract level, we can start by disqualifying observed properties that are not regular amongst the tech giants.[114] At a more concrete level, we can

---

111. Georges J Stigler, *Theory of Price* (4th edn, Macmillan USA 1987) 6.
112. An open examination should be ready to find out that there are none. We found in Chapter II a degree of heterogeneity in the group. But the press, the public opinion, and to some extent policy-makers seem to see an ontology in the group, so we are forced to examine the issue.
113. John Sutton, *Competing in Capabilities* (Oxford University Press 2012) 11 (hereafter Sutton, *Competing in Capabilities*).
114. We leave aside irrelevant features for competitive analysis like high market capitalization or US origins, which are either formulated as investment thesis or for political economy purposes.

select properties that meet two tests. First, the property must be relevant to at least three out of the six current tech giants. Second and cumulatively, the property must be relevant to at least one of the old tech giants, that is either Apple, Microsoft, or Amazon. In applying these tests, we allow for a degree of generalization, considering that getting a perfect fit to reality is impractical.

On that basis, we identify six common properties of tech giants-like businesses: diversification, discontinuity, long termism, growth, exploration and discovery, and flexibility.[115] This list is the result of our own deliberations and domain expertise, informed by careful study of the economics, organizational theory, entrepreneurship, and strategic management literature,[116] and augmented with casual readings as well as insights gathered from informal conversations with academics, industry representatives, and officials.

2. Diversification

a) The Single Product Illusion

In his essay *The Square and the Tower*, historian Niall Ferguson describes several big tech firms as follows: "Google is essentially a vast global library … Amazon is a vast global bazaar … and Facebook is a vast global club."[117] Understandably, both theorists—who search for abstraction—or pundits—who look for simplification—describe firms through the prism of the main product that they supply.[118] In all cases, the nature of the product is irrelevant. The trope intends to constraint the observers' analytical focus on the

---

115. We have avoided buzzwords like "disruption" or abstract concepts like "innovation." And we have tried to stay as close as possible to terms of art used in the economics literature.
116. We reviewed seminal studies on the subject that have been published in leading journals such as Academy of Management Journal, Academy of Management Review, Administrative Science Quarterly, Journal of Management, Journal of Management Studies, Organization Science, and Strategic Management Journal. Note, however, that we are aware of some limitations of management literature. In particular, management studies are often perceived as qualitative ex post rationalization. Moreover, management scholars are often criticized on the ground that they derive theory from arbitrarily selected industry/firm examples, a form of cherry picking.
117. Niall Fergusson, *The Square and The Tower: Networks and Power, from the Freemasons to Facebook* (Penguin Press 2018).
118. This tradition is actually quite old. Since the early nineteenth century neoclassical price theory, monopolists, and oligopolists have been described as suppliers of single commodities (like coal, rice, wood, steel) or utilities (like water or railways). A significant exception, of course, is the vast amount of economic research devoted to strategic complements. But even in cases of complementary, the relevance of diversification only goes as far as functional price and/or output relationships can be established between distinct non-substitute products.

firms' essential outputs, and leave aside the noise generated by other productive activities.[119]

But are Ferguson and others' single product tech giants' descriptions an
accurate, or even just reasonable, account of the empirical reality? Consider
what big tech firms do. Google has developed an email service, a browser,
a mobile OS, and a social network. Amazon has grown from a specialist
online bookseller to a generalist online retailer as well as a cloud computing services provider, and it now owns a brick and mortar grocery chain.
And Facebook is a firm structured along two market segments, that is social
networks and messaging.

10-K reports convey the same picture. Revenue recognition choices,
representations of operating segments, and product offering descriptions
suggest diversified tech giants, not single product ones.[120] Apple recognizes
revenue under five segments, that is "sale of hardware, software, digital content and applications, accessories, and service and support contracts."[121]
Microsoft has three revenue-reporting segments—productivity and business processes, intelligent cloud, and more personal computing—each of
them consisting in a "portfolio" of products and services (eg, more personal
computing includes Windows, devices like Surface, gaming including Xbox
hardware, and software and search advertising).[122] Alphabet's two reporting
segments cover "*a combination of multiple operating segments*" in areas as diverse
as autonomous vehicles, biotechnologies, and venture capital funding, as well
as a variety of products "such as Ads, Android, Chrome, Commerce, Google
Cloud, Google Maps, Google Play, Hardware, Search, and YouTube."[123] In
one Note to Consolidated Financial Statements, Amazon lists its product

---

119. Some economists have long criticized this tendency, and tried to work under the assumption of multiproduct firms, since this is "the only case encountered in reality." See William
J Baumol, Elizabeth E Bailey, and Robert D Willig, "Weak Indivisible Hand Theorems on
the Sustainability of Multiproduct Natural Monopoly" (1977) 67(3) *The American Economic
Review* 350.

120. All firms must identify "reporting segments" which correspond to sources or revenue that
are materially significant. Though reporting segments may be suggestive of product diversification, they do not cover operating segments that do not meet the quantitative thresh-
olds to qualify as reportable segments. Interestingly, reporting firms often disclose operating
segments that are not material and thus do not qualify as reportable segments. Even when
reporting firms do not provide information on operating segments, other sections of 10-Ks
may provide information. This is, in particular, the case of 10-K sections on business overview,
revenue recognition, or notes to consolidated financial statements.

121. See Apple, Inc, Form 10-K, US SEC, 2017.

122. See Microsoft Corporation, Form 10-K, US SEC, 2017.

123. See Alphabet, Inc, Form 10-K, US SEC, 2017.

offerings as "retail websites and physical stores," "electronic devices," "programs" for "merchants," "authors, musicians, filmmakers, app developers"; "compute, storage, database" services through AWS; "fulfillment, publishing, certain digital content subscriptions, advertising, and co-branded credit cards."[124] Though it has "a single reportable segment and operating segment structure," Facebook describes five product categories in the overview section of its 10-K, namely Facebook, Instagram, WhatsApp, Messenger, and Oculus.[125] Netflix is the outlier with two business segments in streaming and DVDs, though 10-Ks point to increased investments in "content production activities."[126]

b) Conglomeralism Renewed

Based on the above, some scholars were quick to note a "resurgence of conglomeralism."[127] Conglomerates were a popular form of corporate organization in the 1960s through the 1970s, before they fell into disgrace with investors.[128] General Electric or the UK firm Hanson are commonly cited examples.

In economic literature, there are two main efficiency theories to the formation of multiproduct firms. Their relevance to big tech is obvious. One predicts that conglomerates occur in the presence of economies of scope in production.[129] This applies correspondingly well to big tech. Economies of scope arise due to the low marginal cost of leveraging intangible inputs

---

124. See Amazon, Inc, Form 10-K, US SEC, 2017.
125. See Facebook, Inc, Form 10-K, US SEC, 2017.
126. Netflix has three reportable segments, but only two of them are product segments. See Netflix, Inc, Form 10-K, US SEC, 2017.
127. See Marc Bourreau and Alexandre De Streel, "Digital Conglomerates and EU Competition Policy" [2019] *ETNO—European Telecommunications Network Operators' Association* 1. See also our earlier work, Nicolas Petit, "Technology Giants: The 'Moligopoly Hypothesis' and Holistic Competition: A Primer" (*SSRN*, October 22, 2016) <https://papers.ssrn.com/sol3/papers.cfm?abstract_id=2856502> accessed November 1, 2019.
128. In the past, conglomerates were seen as internal capital markets, providing an alternative to inefficient (external) capital markets. However, the theory of finance later found that conglomerates had been subject to a 13 to 15 percent discount in stock market valuation as compared to single segment firms, due to the fact that corporate diversification creates agency problems. See Larry H P Lang and Rene M Stulz "Tobin's q, Corporate Diversification and Firm Performance" (1994) 102 *Journal of Political Economy* 1248. Philip G Berger and Eli Ofek, "Diversification's Effect on Firm Value" (1995) 37(1) *Journal of Financial Economics* 39. Evgeny Lyandres, 'Strategic Cost of Diversification" (2007) 20(6) *Review of Financial Studies* 1901. In the 1980s and 1990s, many firms spun off product segments, and refocused on core activities.
129. And the related absence of market exchange mechanisms for a diversified set of inputs. See David J Teece, "Economies of Scope and the Scope of the Enterprise" (1980) 1(3) *Journal of Economic Behavior & Organization, 223-247* (hereafter Teece, "Economies of Scope").

like digital information or the technical know-how residing in personnel.[130] The other theory views conglomerates as a substitute to external capital markets, in particular when the funding of R&D is risky.[131] This also fits well tech giants' diversification. Big tech firms operate in markets where existing appropriability institutions like intellectual property rights ("IPR") only imperfectly apply.[132] Diversification entitles big tech firms to cross-monetize fixed R&D investments and increase total returns to innovation (which, as we previously saw, reaches high intensity levels).[133] This is particularly the case when firms diversify in complements, that is when due to a decrease in the quality adjusted price of good A, consumers demand for complementary good B increases. In non-technical terms, complements lift all boats. For example, Apple recorded a huge growth of iPhone sales in 2008. This led to a corresponding revenue increase in all other segments for Apple, as if there was a feedback loop.

c) Diversification Direction

In considering the direction of big tech firms' diversification, we face a harder inquiry. Though they differ from pure financial conglomerates like Warren Buffet's Berkshire Hathaway, the tech giants have entered markets weakly related to their origins market: Microsoft pursued diversification in

130. A variant of this theory insists on the fact that digital information and know how are imperfectly contractible inputs. In this context, diversification might provide new labor opportunities for engineers with tacit knowledge, and avoid the transfer of non-excludable information to other firms. This might be tied to the policy debate on the non-enforceability of non-compete clauses in labor contracts. See Teece, "Economies of Scope" (n 129).

131. Kenneth J Arrow, "Economic Welfare and the Allocation of Resources for Invention" in National Bureau of Economic Research (ed), *The Rate and Direction of Inventive Activity: Economic and Social Factors* (Princeton University Press 1962) 616 (hereafter Arrow, "Economic Welfare") (observing low incentives for investment in research and inventive activities, Arrow notes: "The only way, within the private enterprise system, to minimize this problem is the conduct of research by large corporations with many projects going on, each small in scale compared with the net revenue of the corporation. Then the corporation acts as its own insurance company. But clearly this is only an imperfect solution").

132. As evidenced by the fact that young tech giants have often been involved in IPR disputes (on both sides).

133. David J Teece, "Profiting from Technological Innovation: Implication for Integration, Collaboration, Licensing and Public Policy" (1986) 15 *Research Policy* 301 (hereafter Teece, "Profiting from Technological Innovation") provides a good formulation of the argument ("The innovator can improve its total return to R&D, however, by adjusting its R&D investment portfolio to maximize the probability that technological discoveries will emerge that are either easy to protect with existing intellectual property law, or which require for commercialization cospecialized assets already within the firm's repertoire of capabilities").

games, Google in self-driving systems, Facebook in payment systems, and Amazon in video content production.

We cannot accept the simple idea that big tech firms go wherever they may roam. A more reasonable assumption is that big tech firms are sophisticated organizations where business decisions are subject to deliberation. This is all the more so since the tech giants are publicly listed companies, subject to investors' and regulatory scrutiny. Though appealing, the commonplace "move fast and break things" story whereby big tech firms enter new markets on a founder's whim is implausible.[134]

Now, suppose the existence of a rational justification to tech giants' choice to diversify in apparently unrelated markets. What is it? In a 2013 article, business and management scientists Barhadwaj and his co-authors give us an intuition:

> Amazon's corporate scope of e-retailing and web services may be considered an unrelated portfolio under traditional strategy conceptualization because of the distance between these two business lines within Amazon. Recognizing and mapping the underlying connections among e-retailing, the role of hardware (Kindle) and web services (AWS) requires a more nuanced understanding of the effect of digital technologies than simply computing distances based on SIC-codes and industry classifications. Therefore, Amazon's corporate portfolio may be wrongly characterized as unrelated while we can easily see the related linkages between the constituent parts …
> The same logic can be extended to firms such as Google, Netflix, Microsoft, and others as they continue to adjust and fine-tune their corporate scope to take advantage of the developments in hardware, software, and Internet connectivity.[135]

The insight here is that the tech giants diversify in industries where computation and digital information can be leveraged to offer "greater opportunities for competitive advantage."[136] But a theory of diversification whereby tech giants enter product markets where information in digital form increases marginal output is too crude.[137] It is implausible that big tech firms

134. And discredited by anecdotal evidence. Most big tech "moonshots" have been pursued as outside projects, like Amazon's CEO ventures in space transportation.
135. Anandhi Bharadwaj, Omar A El Sawy, Paul A Pavlou, and N Venkat Venkatraman, "Digital Business Strategy: Towards a Next Generation of Insights" (2013) 37(2) *MIS Quarterly* 474 (hereafter Bharadwaj et al, "Digital Business Strategy").
136. See Andrew McAfee and Erik Brynjolfsson, "Big Data: The Management Revolution" [2012] *Harvard Business Review* 10.
137. By raising the productivity of capital and labor.

will integrate into coffee shops, simply because they can e-manage baristas more efficiently. Moreover, it is hardly new that information is a source of substantial economic surplus.[138] Digital information firms have known this since the emergence of relational databases about forty years ago.[139]

We may return to Niall Fergusson's work to refine the intuition. In the age of discovery, Portuguese sailors developed nautical instruments, ships like the caravel and the galleon, and breakthroughs in cartography in a "bid to establish a new and superior trade network viable."[140] Like Portuguese sailors, the tech giants develop technology to overcome real world constraints. Today, the constraint is that information is distributed while computation requires centralization.[141] In the modern division of labor, big tech firms specialize in building (i) *sensors* that collect, convert, disseminate, label, and restructure distributed information (both digital and analog); and (ii) *servers* that centralize analysis, computation, correlation, reproduction, search, storage, retrieval, and filtering of sensed information.

Concrete examples of sensors are apps, application programming interfaces ("APIs"), smartphones, search engines, social networks, home assistants, smart watches, augmented reality glasses, payments systems, video conferencing apps, etc.

Concrete examples of servers are cloud computing platforms, software as a service, data centers, super computers, artificial intelligence systems, etc. In the future, we should observe big tech firms' further diversification in digital information servers and sensors like self-driving cars or quantum

---

138. For decades, it is known that information has significant economic value. In 1994, Peter Drucker discussed "… the epoch that began early in this century, and an analysis of its latest manifestations: an economic order in which knowledge, not labor or raw material or capital, is the key resource." See Peter F Drucker, "The Age of Social Transformation" (1994) 274(5) *The Atlantic Monthly* 53. And in 1945, Friedrich Hayek stressed the importance to economic life of "a body of very important but unorganized knowledge" that is "the knowledge of the particular circumstances of time and place" possessed by "practically every individual." See Friedrich A Hayek, "The Use of Knowledge in Society" (1945) 35(4) *The American Economic Review*, 519-530.

139. See Michael L Brodie, "Data Integration: From Relational Data Integration to Information Ecosystems" (2010) *24th IEEE International Conference on Advanced Information Networking and Applications*.

140. Fergusson, *The Square and The Tower* (n 117) 74.

141. Hsinchun Chen, Roger H L Chiang, and Veda C Storey, "Business Intelligence and Analytics: From Big Data to Big Impact" (2012) 36(4) *MIS Quarterly* 1174, citing Surajit Chaudhuri, Umeshwar Dayal, and Vivek Narasayya, "An Overview of Business Intelligence Technology" (2011) 54(8) *Communications of the ACM* 88 ("unlike traditional transaction records collected from various legacy systems of the 1980s," big data "from the web are less structured and often contain rich consumer opinion and behavioral information").

computers—subject to possible regulatory restrictions informed by privacy, cybersecurity, and free speech concerns.

Observe that we do not discuss here the tech giants' diversification through the prism of "data." The reason is that big tech firms do not specifically discuss "data" in 10-Ks.[142] But why would they? Due to imperfect appropriability, data hardly constitutes an "asset" for disclosure purposes. Moreover, in our current state of knowledge, we lack a theory of value or of externalities that considers "data" as an explanatory variable for economic profits amenable to estimation.

d) Summation

We now appreciate that diversification is a feature common to several tech giants, not a bug. We also know that there are firm-level variations. On one end of the spectrum are the less diversified Netflix and perhaps Facebook. On the other end of the spectrum are the more diversified Microsoft, Amazon, and Google, with Apple in the middle.

3. Discontinuity

The tech giants operate in an environment characterized by discontinuity. By this, we mean changes, events, or shifts which alter the competitive environment by reallocating strategic advantages and disadvantages among firms. Former Intel CEO Andy Grove has talked of "strategic inflection points."[143] Three categories of discontinuities can be distinguished.

a) Technology

Economists say that digital information technologies display modularity. They can be combined (and recombined) at little cost adding new products

---

142. A rare exception is Facebook. In its 10-K for 2013, Facebook discussed how it forecasted the market by usage of data: "In the third quarter of 2013, we worked with third parties to develop models to more accurately analyze user data by age in the United States. These models suggested that usage by U.S. teens overall was stable, but that DAUs among younger U.S. teens had declined. The data and models we are using are not precise and our understanding of usage by age group may not be complete." See Facebook, Inc, Form 10-K, US SEC, 2013. Observe incidentally that it can be conjectured that the Instagram acquisition in 2012 led to an interruption in that trend.

143. Andrew Grove, "Navigating Strategic Inflection Points" (1997) 8(3) *Business Strategy Review*, 12 ("During a Strategic Inflection Point, the way a business operates, the very structure and concept of the business, undergoes a change").

and services to markets.[144] Matt Ridley once talked of "ideas having sex."[145] The smartphone is the best illustration. In 2007, Apple described the iPhone as a "handheld device that combines in a single product a mobile phone, a widescreen iPod with touch controls, and an Internet communications device".[146]

Modular technologies are characterized by pervasiveness. They create market opportunities for new products and services. Smartphones are a good example. Widespread user adoption led to the creation of entirely new areas of supply and demand like the selfie stick industry or—perhaps more contributive to social welfare—proximity mobile payments.[147]

The modularity of digital information technologies causes competition to result in random arrival of innovation outputs. Nambisan and his co-authors write: "Most digital designs remain somewhat incomplete or in a state of flux."[148] Accordingly, "there is an unprecedented level of unpredict-ability and dynamism with regard to assumed structural or organizational boundaries of a digital innovation, be it a product, platform or service."[149] Table 4.1 hereafter provides a historical overview of random innovation arrivals in the digital economy.

The correlate of technological modularity is that the competitive envi-ronment displays uncertainty.[150] This can be contrasted with other industries

144. See Ming Dong, David A Hirshleifer, and Siew Hong Teoh, "Stock Market Overvaluation, Moonshots and Corporate Innovation" (*SSRN*, December 3, 2016), <https://papers.ssrn.com/sol3/papers.cfm?abstract_id=2878418> (accessed October 31, 2019) (hereafter Dong et al, "Stock Market Overvaluation") (suggesting that the idea that innovation is a process of recombinant search is not new, dating as far back as Schumpeter in 1934, and giving the example of the discovery of the double helix structure of DNA by James Watson and Francis Crick).
145. Matt Ridley, "When Ideas Have Sex" (2010) *TEDGlobal* <https://www.ted.com/talks/matt_ridley_when_ideas_have_sex/up-next>.
146. See Apple, Inc, Form 10-K, US SEC, 2007.
147. Bharadwaj et al, "Digital Business Strategy" (n 135) 471, "[D]igital technologies are funda-mentally reshaping traditional business strategy as modular, distributed, cross- functional, and global business processes that enable work to be carried out across boundaries of time, dis-tance, and function."
148. Satish Nambisan, Kalle Lyytinen, Ann Majchrzak, and Michael Song, "Digital Innovation Management: Reinventing Innovation Management Research in a Digital World" (2017) 41(1) *Mis Quarterly, 223-238.*
149. ibid.
150. For instance, Matt Marx, Joshua S Gans, and David H Hsu, "Dynamic Commercialization Strategies for Disruptive Technologies: Evidence from the Speech Recognition Industry" (2014) 60(12) *Management Science* 3103 write that "automatic speech recognition technology is an industry where considerable "uncertainty" surrounds the value of new innovations."

Table 4.1 Sequence of Historical Discontinuities in Digital Technology

---

Graphical User Interfaces ⟶ Operating Systems ⟶ Portals ⟶ Search (incl search engines and online commerce) ⟶ Smartphones (incl devices, OS and Apps) ⟶ Social Networks ⟶ Cloud Computing, SaaS and ML ⟶ Home Assistants? ⟶ Augmented Reality? ⟶ Self-Driving Systems?

---

like defense, pharmaceuticals, or semi-conductors in which innovation processes are more linear, predictable, and structured.[151]

Our 10-K evidence anecdotally supports the uncertainty argument. Many big tech firms did not correctly anticipate the trends of the next generation of digital information technology. In the early 2000s, Microsoft adopted an approach to the Internet focused on control of content and networks, not search engines. Until 2004, Netflix had reservations about the potential of streaming over DVD. In 2012, Facebook expressed reservations about mobile ads monetization, arguably given screen and user attention constraints. We now know that none of these blunders were fatal. Yet, they required significant adaptability from Microsoft, Netflix, and Facebook.

b) Entry

One suggestion that has been made previously is that big tech firms are paranoid. 10-Ks are filled with claims of significant risks of competitive entry. In 1996, Microsoft—at the supposed height of its monopoly reign—declared that the "extremely rapid pace of technological change constantly creates new opportunities for existing competitors and start-ups and can quickly render existing technologies less valuable."[152] More particularly, the tech giants report to be under threat from a particular class of new, smaller, and faster entrant firms. In 2009, Google wrote: "Emerging start-ups may be able to innovate and provide products and services faster than we can."[153]

---

151. In these industries, technology frontiers are known and pipelines of research are delineated years ahead. This structuring may come from (i) a coordinated approach to innovation within industry groups like standard development organization (eg, in semi-conductors) or (ii) regulatory constraints (eg, clinical trials in pharmaceutical research).

152. Microsoft Corporation, Form 10-K, US SEC, 1996.

153. See Google, Inc, Form 10-K, US SEC, 2009. See also Google, Inc, Form 10-K, US SEC, 2004 (referring to a "trend toward industry consolidation among our competitors, and so smaller competitors today may become larger competitors in the future.") See Google, Inc, Form 10-K, US SEC, 2011 (suggesting competition "with new and established companies" in relation to online products and services).

Often, big tech firms liken themselves to failed incumbents like AOL, Lycos, Altavista, Yahoo!, or Myspace.[154]

Taken together, big tech firms' declarations are suggestive of a high degree of subjective vulnerability to new firm entry, competition, and expansion. In fact, tech giants' own experience is one of market success through a process of competition with established incumbents.

Many, however, consider such declarations to be cheap talk. Economists who, *ex visu*, observe persistently high big tech market shares instead support a theory of incumbency advantage, not of incumbency vulnerability. In short, the argument goes, established tech giants would be different from digital incumbents of the past. The reason, although seldom explained let alone expressed, would lie in big tech's qualitatively superior network effects. [155]

The loose ends of this reasoning are clear. As Frank Knight has shown, there is no intellectual basis to discount the relevance of the subjective feeling of probability for firm behavior as compared to objective probability.[156] To fix the idea more clearly, let us recall that one of the most popular topics discussed in business and management science relates to creative destruction of incumbents by new firms.[157] Theories of incumbent failure in their

---

154. See, for instance, Eric Schmidt, "The New Gründergeist" (*Google Europe Blog*, October 13, 2014) <https://europe.googleblog.com/2014/10/the-new-grundergeist.html>. Jason Furman et al, "Unlocking Digital Competition: Report of the Digital Competition Expert Panel" (*HM Treasury* 2019) §1.98 <https://www.gov.uk/government/publications/unlocking-digital-competition-report-of-the-digital-competition-expert-panel>.

155. See Chapter I. As well as extreme returns to scale, and the role of big data.

156. See Frank H Knight, *Risk and Uncertainty* (The Riverside Press 1921) 229.

157. Anna Bergek, Christian Berggren, Thomas Magnusson, and Michael Hobday, "Technological Discontinuities and the Challenge for Incumbent Firms: Destruction, Disruption or Creative Accumulation?" (2013) 42(6–7) *Research Policy* 1210 (hereafter Bergek et al, "Technological Discontinuities") (noting an abundance of papers related to the creative destruction of incumbents by new firms). Amongst these works, Clayton Christensen's theory of technological disruption stands out as the norm in diverse disciplines and topic areas. Clayton M Christensen *The Innovator's Dilemma: When New Technologies Cause Great Firms to Fail* (Harvard Business School Press 1997) (hereafter Christensen, *The Innovator's Dilemma*). Clayton M Christensen, Michael E Raynor, and Rory McDonald, "What Is Disruptive Innovation?" [2015] *Harvard Business Review 44*. Christensen's theory is known as the "innovator dilemma" (though it is more a theory of manager's dilemma). The theory states that managers from large firms all too often follow two erroneous precepts: listen to the needs of their best customers and focus investments on projects that promise the best returns. Those principles are in fact paradoxically the wrong thing to do, because established firms fail to notice disruptive innovation that arises either in the low ends of their core or in new market footholds. Business scholar Constantinos Markides has proposed an alternative theory of "business model innovation," namely the discovery of a fundamentally different business model in an existing business. Markides gives the following formulation: "The end result of this is that the early pioneers that create these new-to-the-world markets are very rarely the

many variants and nuances—organizational inertia, disruptive innovation, incumbent myopia, competence destruction, business model innovation — [158] are taught at virtually all business schools in the world, and we should thus proceed on the assumption that they form part of the educational background of many executives including at big tech companies.[159] Neglect of this empirical fact in the discussion of the economics of digital technologies is a mistake that can be best understood with a metaphor: if subjective perceptions do not matter, we should let doctors perform surgery without anesthesia because pain is caused by the brain.

Second, that new entry is a low objective probability event in big tech markets ignores that not all risks are equal. Nassim Nicholas Taleb has popularized the lost wisdom that it is rational for individuals and societies to worry (in their actual decisions, not beliefs) about certain classes of low probability and high cost risks like climate events, pandemics or a third world war.[160]

ones that scale them up from little niches to big, mass markets. The companies that eventually scale up new markets jump into the market right before the dominant design emerges." See Constantinos Markides, "Disruptive Innovation: In Need of Better Theory" (2006) 23(1) *The Journal of Product Innovation Management*, 19, 23 (hereafter Markides, "Disruptive Innovation"). Though scholars are today divided on the mechanics of business discontinuity, many join Christensen in relativizing the importance of first mover advantages.

158. Since then, the literature has nuanced theories of incumbent failure. In a scathing review of Christensen's work, management scholar Erwin Danneels suggests that we overstate incumbents' inertia. Erwin Danneels, "Disruptive Technology Reconsidered: A Critique and Research Agenda" (2004) 21(4) *The Journal of Product Innovation Management* 246, 252 (hereafter Danneels, "Disruptive Technology Reconsidered"). A more appropriate description of the reality is that "not all, but some incumbents fail." The relationship between the order of market entry and survival is more ambiguous, affected by a whole array of other variables, like strategy, innovation, or organization type. See Sungwook Min, Manohar U Kalwani, and William T Robinson "Market Pioneer and Early Follower Survival Risks: A Contingency Analysis of Really New versus Incrementally New Product-Markets" (2006) 70(1) *Journal of Marketing* 15 (hereafter Min et al, "Market Pioneer and Early Follower Survival Risks"); Stefan Tongur and Mats Engwall, "The Business Model Dilemma of Technology Shifts" (2014) 34(9) *Technovation* 525 (hereafter Tongur and Engwall, "The Business Model Dilemma Of Technology Shifts"); Bergek et al, "Technological Discontinuities" (n 157).

159. Observe that survival probability may be even lower in digital. See Min et al, "Market Pioneer and Early Follower Survival Risks" (n 158) 30; See also Bharadwaj et al, "Digital Business Strategy" (n 135) 474 suggesting that uncertainty is even higher in digital ("This opens up a whole new portfolio of digital business strategy approaches around the digitization of information for products and services"). Note that Christensen said in later work that the Internet is disruptive to some but sustaining to other firms. See Danneels, "Disruptive Technology Reconsidered" (n 158) 247 for references.

160. Nassim N Taleb, *The Black Swan: The Impact of the Highly Improbable* (Random House 2007).

Third, the fact that no big tech firm went under to date is no basis to draw an inference of lack of vulnerability. Firms rarely fall from a cliff. Rather the relevant question to ask is whether the tech giants face a credible risk of decline, irrelevance, or stagnation as experienced by firms like eBay[161] or Groupon.[162] This, then, brings to mind industry episodes like Apple's near death experience when Mac OS clones entered the market or Netflix's 2004–07 price war following Blockbuster streaming entry. Both firms stayed afloat, yet it is hard to refute that new entry created significant business discontinuity.

Fourth, economist have shown that established firms that are diversified face diseconomies of scope, and that this phenomenon might be a substantial source of failure in a context of discontinuity. Contrary to conventional wisdom—which assumes that *"anything an entrant can do an incumbent can do better"*—established firms might struggle to deploy inherited strengths in new markets, while entrants do not.[163] A careful study of IBM and Microsoft's history by Bresnahan, Greenstein and Henderson shows that failure in new markets is more likely if the costs of organizational conflict are considerable and if the marketplace does not value the benefits of increased coordination.

Last, and we cannot stress this point strongly enough, the business and management literature predicts that incumbent replacement by disruptive entry should be taken more seriously in the case of old rather than young firms. An empirical study even found that survival risk is greater for incumbents in new product markets after six years.[164]

---

161. Around 2015, eBay started to report declining revenue. It reported again a decline in 2017. Overall, the trend is one of stasis, and the company is no longer the first game in town.

162. Since 2014, Groupon has experienced no growth in revenue, and even a decline in 2015, 2016, and 2018. Net revenue for Groupon from 2014 to 2018 were USD 2.8 billion in 2014, USD 2.9 billion in 2015, USD 3 billion in 2016, USD 2.8 billion in 2017, and USD 2.6 billion in 2018. See Groupon, Inc, Form 10-K, US SEC, 2014–18.

163. Timothy F Bresnahan, Shane Greenstein, Rebecca M Henderson, "Schumpeterian Competition and Diseconomies of Scope: Illustrations from the Histories of Microsoft and IBM", in Josh Lerner and Scott Stern (eds), *The Rate and Direction of Inventive Activity Revisited* (University of Chicago Press 2012) 203.

164. Min et al, "Market Pioneer and Early Follower Survival Risks" (n 158) 29. The authors note that pioneers have consistently lower survival risks in incrementally new product markets, yet as said above, big tech firms seem to operate in markets with many new product introductions.

c) Regulation

Discontinuity also occurs when the law changes. Business and management science indicates that "regulatory events" are sources of "discontinuous environmental change" and of firm "survival" or "selection."[165] Michael Tushman and Charles O' Reilly discuss the example of US airline deregulation in the 1970s, which "led to waves of mergers and failures as firms scrambled to reorient themselves to the new competitive environment." And economic historian Zorina Khan has empirically shown that there is a substantial increase in litigation when new, transformative technologies are introduced.[166]

In their 10-Ks, big tech firms express significant concern about regulatory events. This is hardly surprising. The tech giants are exposed to a relatively high probability of regulatory events because of the emergent properties of digital information technologies. To see this, recall that modularity leads to new form factors, product designs, and business models. Technological novelties thus produce novel externalities, both positive and negative. Social networks' repertoire of emergent concerns affords a good example (eg, echo chambers, political polarization, privacy losses, or hate speech). In turn, the inherent uncertainty surrounding the possibility of free market exchange to bargain away externalities under existing legal arrangements fuels demand for ad hoc rules and institutions.[167] Judge Frank Easterbrook once talked of a "law of the horse" syndrome to deride the tendency of lawyers to build new and specialist areas of the law around new technology.[168]

It would be a herculean task, and a fastidious read, to document in detail big tech's exposure to regulatory events. However incomplete, a simple sketch of the new legal rights and duties adopted in the European Union ("EU") around the tech giants' activities carries the point: "right to be forgotten," the "meme ban," the General Data Protection Regulation

---

165. Michael L Tushman and Charles A O'Reilly, "The Ambidextrous Organizations" (2004) 4 *Harvard Business Review* 11 (hereafter Tushman and O'Reilly, "The Ambidextrous Organizations").

166. See B Zorina Khan, "Trolls and Other Patent Inventions: Economic History and the Patent Controversy in the Twenty-First Century" (2014) 21 *Georges Mason Law Review* 825, 838 ("new innovations like the telegraph, telephone and automobile were inevitably accompanied by an upswing in total civil litigation"). See also B Zorina Khan, "Innovations in Law and Technology, 1790–1920" in Michael Grossberg and Christopher Tomlins (eds), *Cambridge History of Law in America*, Vol II (Cambridge University Press 2008) 483–530.

167. Digital information technology and regulatory institutions co-evolve.

168. Frank H Easterbrook, "Cyberspace and the Law of the Horse" [1996] *University of Chicago Legal Forum* 207.

("GDPR"), the "GAFA tax," or the "copyright link tax." Of significance is also the fact that regulatory events often coincide with big tech firms' product launches. In 2007, Apple faced a barrage of antitrust complaints as soon as it introduced its iPhone under exclusive distribution arrangements. Last, but not least, regulatory events may pressure firm strategy in unrelated fields. In 2001, Microsoft had to cancel the launch of a personal online repository project called Hailstorm amidst rising industry and privacy concerns.[169] Though we cannot tell for sure whether this was dispositive, the press established connections with ongoing antitrust scrutiny, and in particular statements from the Attorney General for Connecticut, Richard Blumenthal, who had declared that "some of the same kinds of antitrust issues seem to be raised."[170]

Upshot? The law is in flux. As Bruce Sewell, a former General Counsel of Apple said "every so often, you're going to get it wrong."[171] Unfortunately, 10-Ks do not give direct evidence of the costs expended by tech giants on legal budgets (and lobbying ones). A reasonable assumption, nevertheless, is that they may be significant relative to firms in industries with a stable legal environment.[172] More important, perhaps, is the fact that regulatory events produce indirect effects on firms, including disrupting key officials and executives from what they are supposed to do, ie manage the company.

d) Summation

Recall that we encountered uncertainty in the previous chapter. The treatment was essentially theoretical: big tech firms operate under a competitive

169. See John Markoff, "Technology; Microsoft Has Quietly Shelved Its Internet "Persona" Service" *The New York Times* (April 11, 2002) <https://www.nytimes.com/2002/04/11/business/technology-microsoft-has-quietly-shelved-its-internet-persona-service.html?login=facebook&auth=login-facebook>.
170. See Andrew Orlowski, "Sun, AOL take MS Hailstorm to the Feds" (*The Register*, March 20, 2001) <https://www.theregister.co.uk/2001/03/20/sun_aol_take_ms_hailstorm/>. This illustrates the point of management scholars Ming-Jer Chen and Danny Miller who suggested that "confrontational competitive aggressiveness" can get large companies into trouble. See Ming-Jer Chen and Danny Miller, "Reconceptualizing Competitive Dynamics: A Multidimensional Framework" (2015) 36(5) *Strategic Management Journal* 769.
171. See Jeremy Horwitz, "Apple's Former Top Lawyer: $1 Billion Budget Enabled High-Risk Strategies" (*Venture Beat*, June 10, 2019) <https://venturebeat.com/2019/06/10/apples-former-top-lawyer-1-billion-budget-enabled-high-risk-strategies/>.
172. The political economy literature has recently argued that the size of these expenses did not really matter, and that the large market shares of firms as well as indirect threats were more effective channels of firm influence on public policy. See Luigi Zingales, "Towards a Political Economy of the Firm" (2017) 31(3) *The Journal of Economic Perspectives* 113.

constraint because of the uncertainty typical of network effects markets with increasing returns to adoption. At this stage, we understand more concretely the economic forces that work to create uncertainty. Technology, entry, and regulation reallocate competitive advantages and disadvantages amongst firms.[173] In its 10-K report for 2000, Microsoft described a process of "Rapid change, uncertainty due to new and emerging technologies, and fierce competition" as "challenging because the pace of change continues to accelerate, creating new opportunities for competitors and subjecting business planning to substantial uncertainty."[174] Discontinuities, in particular technological ones, appear to be a key source of competitive pressure on big tech firms.

4. Long Termism

One of the notable features of the tech giants is their commitment to a long-term horizon. Big tech behavior displays significant deviations from the short-term baseline of both established business wisdom and received economic theory.[175] For example, where economics predict that below cost pricing leads to recoupment or exit in the short term, Amazon successfully maintained a low price business model in spite of consistent losses in the first six years of its listing on the stock market.

This feature is disturbing. Can we supply more than anecdotal evidence of big tech's long termism? To confront this task, we must first address a methodological issue: how do we differentiate firms with short-term and long-term horizon?[176] One way of straightening out the arbitrary separation between the short term and the long term is to draw a clear line. Economists understand the short term as the period over which capacity is fixed, and in which all investments (purchases) are exhausted. This allows us to formulate

173. Dean A Shepherd, "Venture Capitalists' Assessment of New Venture Survival" (1999) 45(5) *Management Science* 622 ("When the key success factors in an industry are unstable, there is uncertainty").
174. See Microsoft Corporation, Form 10-K, US SEC, 2000.
175. For a review, see David Marginson and Laurie McAulay, "Exploring the Debate on Short-Termism: A Theoretical and Empirical Analysis" (2008) 29(3) *Strategic Management Journal* 273. There is copious literature on the controversial subject of short termism. That discussion focuses on three sets of questions: are business organizations short termist, why are they short termist, and is short termism individually and socially harmful?
176. Keynes famously joked that "in the long run, we are all dead." John M Keynes, *A Tract on Monetary Reform* (London Macmillan and Co 1923) (scorning advocates of laissez faire suggesting that in the long run, money markets would reach equilibrium).

a good enough definition of the long-termist firm. A firm has a long-term horizon if a significant number of its decisions aims at modifying capacity.

In turn, study of two types of business decisions allows to draw qualitative inference of long termism.[177] The first is the R&D decision.[178] The literature correlates R&D with investments in the future.[179] Figure 4.1 below records firm-level R&D expenditures and intensity figures in 2018 for the tech giants (dark grey dots) based on EU official data.[180] Google, Microsoft, and Apple outspend pharmaceutical firms' (light grey dots) R&D budget, though they are generally less R&D intensive.[181] The results hold if we include Amazon—whose reporting does not disaggregate technology and content investments—using the conservative assumption that only half of its reported technology and content budget of USD 22.6 billion is R&D.[182]

177. Other tests have been proposed. See, eg, François Brochet, Maria Loumioti, and George Serafeim, "Short-termism, Investor Clientele, and Firm Risk" (2012) *Harvard Business School Working Paper 12-072* who offer to use language used by senior managers in quarterly earnings calls. They find significant firm-level heterogeneity.

178. This way, we avoid the reductionism that consists in equating R&D to innovation.

179. See Brian J Bushee "The Influence of Institutional Investors on Myopic R&D Investment Behavior" (1998) 73(3) *Accounting Review* 305. Some rely on Laverty's work to suggest that R&D indicators are bad proxies of the long term. See Kevin J Laverty, "Economic 'Short-Termism': The Debate, The Unresolved Issues, and the Implications for Management Practice and Research" (1996) 21(3) *Academy of Management Review* 825 (hereafter Laverty, "Economic Short-Termism"). This is not an entirely accurate reading of Laverty's views. Laverty has questioned the representativeness of R&D data as a proxy for "desirable" long-run investments, as part of the discussion on alleged excessive short termism of managers who would prioritize undesirable short-term investments over better, long-term ones. In reality, Laverty consistently categorizes R&D as "investments in the future" or "long-run investments." See Laverty, "Economic Short-Termism" 838. Granted, in a 1993 paper, Laverty questions the reliability of R&D as a good indicator of long termism. However, he concedes that his empirical work is based on a limited sample of two industries. And he notes that long-term R&D choices may be consistent with declining long-term prospects, undermining his initial hypothesis. At the end, Laverty essentially criticizes R&D as an imperfect indicator because it is not fully comprehensive. Kevin J Laverty, "How Valid are R&D Measures in Empirical Tests of 'Short-Termism'?" (1993) 1 *Academy of Management Annual Meetings Proceedings* 27.

180. See The 2018 EU Industrial R&D Investment Scoreboard, European Commission—Joint Research Centre <https://iri.jrc.ec.europa.eu/scoreboard18.html> (hereafter "The 2018 EU Industrial R&D Investments Scoreboard"). The data includes capitalized R&D. We do not record results for Netflix because it does not appear in the EU Industrial R&D investment scoreboard.

181. The firms in the pharmaceutical industry are (by decreasing ranking in the EU scoreboard) Roche, Johnson & Johnson, Merck, Novartis, Pfizer, and Sanofi.

182. See The 2018 EU Industrial R&D Investments Scoreboard (n 180) Box 4.1, 55. We convert Amazon's turnover from USD 177.9 billion to EUR 148.2 billion at the Euro exchange rate of USD 1.20 = EUR 1 as followed in the scoreboard. We assume half of Amazon's technology and content (USD 22.6 billion) is R&D, ie USD 11.3 billion. We convert Amazon's estimate

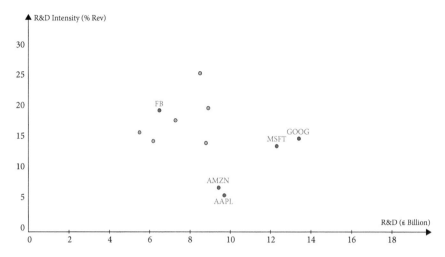

Figure 4.1 Big Tech (dark grey) v Pharma (light grey) R&D (2017–18) (2018 EU Industrial R&D Investment Scoreboard)

Only two pharmaceutical firms record higher R&D intensity than Facebook.[183]

The second is "earnings" decisions. To set the ground for this, a definition of earnings is in order. Earnings are firm's accounting profits. In turn, firms make two types of earnings decisions. Either they pay out earnings to shareholders as dividends (or in the form of share buybacks). Or they retain earnings for subsequent use such as investment, M&A, or research. In the latter case, we talk of "retained earnings" (equal to net income minus dividends).[184]

Decisions to payout "dividends" are a good proxy of short termism. The underlying intuition is as follows: when a firm distributes dividends, it might display less concern for the future than when it retains earnings; in

R&D from USD 11.3 billion to EUR 9.4 billion (using the same exchange rate). This gives us a 6.36 percent R&D intensity figure.

183. Respectively Merck and Roche. Net sales of Merck is EUR 14.5 billion in 2017 (Merck Annual Report 2018 <https://www.merckgroup.com/investors/reports-and-financials/earnings-materials/2018-q4/en/2018-Q4-Report-EN.pdf> accessed December 18, 2019) and net sales of Roche is CHF 50.6 billion (Roche Finance Report 2018, p 48 <https://www.roche.com/investors/annualreport17.htm> accessed December 18, 2019). We convert Roche's turnover from CHF 50.6 billion to EUR 43.2 billion at the Euro exchange rate of CHF 1.17 = EUR 1 as followed in the 2017 Roche Finance Report (p 28).

184. Jonathan Berk and Peter DeMarzo, *Corporate Finance* (4th edn, Pearson 2017) 66 (hereafter Berk and DeMarzo, *Corporate Finance*).

the case of retention, the firm expects that there is some future capacity to finance that is not covered by existing investments (not so much the long term as such, but close). Though cash retention may have tax implications and creates its own set of agency problems (which are arguably lower in the case of founder firms like many tech giants), retaining cash can reduce the costs of raising capital in the future.[185] Moreover, cash retained is not fluid capital that can be moved in the near term by third parties. It stays at the disposal of the firm, providing more long-term certainty.[186]

Of course, long-termist firms may distribute dividend, and rely on debt or equity to finance the future. But real world observations show that firms typically finance long-term investments like R&D first on retained earnings, followed by debt, and ultimately by equity.[187] Moreover, it is conventional in the field of industrial organization theory to correlate retained earnings conduct with survival, entry deterrence, or delayed exit motivations, again denoting concern for the long term (and competition).[188]

With this in mind, we may now ask: do the tech giants retain or pay out earnings? The data show that big tech firms retain significant earnings. With the exception of Microsoft and Apple (since 2012), none of the other big tech firms paid cash dividends.[189] And even with dividend payouts, Microsoft

185. ibid fig 17.5, 647.
186. Laverty, "Economic Short-Termism" (n 179) 833–34.
187. This is confirmed by a financial economics theory known as the "pecking order hypothesis." Berk and DeMarzo, *Corporate Finance* (n 184) 615–16 and fig 16.4. In addition, and more specifically, empirical studies show that there is "solid evidence that debt is a disfavored source of finance for R&D investment." See generally, Berk and DeMarzo, *Corporate Finance* 608 and specifically, Bronwyn H Hall, "The Financing of Innovation" in Scott Shane (ed), *Handbook of Technology and Innovation Management* (Wiley-Blackwell 2009) 409–21. A 1987 empirical study of 140 firms by John Guerard, Alden Bean, and Steven Andrews found that research activities are normally negatively associated with dividends. John B Guerard Jr., Alden S Bean, and Steven Andrews, "R&D Management and Corporate Financial Policy" (1987) 33(1) *Management Science* 1 1419.
188. See Martha A Schary, "The Probability of Exit" (1991) 22(3) *The RAND Journal of Economics* 339; Daron Acemoglu, Philippe Aghion, and Fabrizio Zilibotti, "Distance to Frontier, Selection and Economic Growth" (2006) 4(1) *Journal of the European Economic Association* 37 (talking of the use "retained earnings of old entrepreneurs (or, equivalently, the cash in the hands of existing businesses) to shield them against the threat of entry by new entrepreneurs"); Drew Fudenberg and Jean Tirole, "A 'Signal-Jamming' Theory of Predation" (1986) 17(3) *The RAND Journal of Economics* 366 (noting, in relation to predatory pricing conduct, that "A firm with higher retained earnings has a higher probability of staying in the market, independently of the source of earnings").
189. Microsoft started in 2003 and Apple restarted paying dividends in 2012 after a pause of fifteen years (previously, 1996 had been the last year with a dividend). This might also be consistent with the theory whereby more mature firms pay dividends (because they have fewer investments opportunities than younger ones), a hypothesis known as the life cycle theory

and Apple have retained significant earnings. Since 2012, Microsoft has kept USD 24.1 billion. And Apple has retained USD 70.4 billion in 2018.[190]

Skeptical readers should at this point object that cash dividends are not a very deep measure of a firm's pay-out policy. Firms may pay out money to shareholders through a share repurchase or buyback. And corporate finance theory considers that dividends and buybacks are perfect substitutes (the so-called Modigliani-Miller irrelevance hypothesis).[191] To their credit, it is true that there is substantial heterogeneity amongst big tech firms. Amazon and Netflix have not used buybacks since 2012. Google and Facebook have respectively introduced buybacks in 2015 and 2017. Microsoft repurchases shares since 1994. And Apple has restarted buybacks in 2012 after years of retention. But does this invalidate our previous suggestion that tech giants are long termist?

The Modigliani-Miller irrelevance hypothesis only suggests that dividends and buybacks have a similar effect on *firm value*. It does not say that the decision to dividend or buyback is neutral in all respects. To the contrary, signaling theory suggests that buyback programs carry less commitment value than dividends.[192] This is because, "unlike with dividends, firms do not smooth their repurchase activity from year to year. As a result, announcing a share repurchase today does not necessarily represent a long-term commitment to repurchase shares. In this regard, share repurchases may be less of a signal than dividends about future earnings of a firm."[193]

Plausible (though not definitive) implication? Big tech buybacks may signal a short-term constraint to return cash to shareholders, while retaining long-term ability to invest in capacity growth.

Let us wrap up. A majority of big tech firms invests in R&D and keeps large cash reserves. This evidence leads us to infer a long-term competitive

in financial economics. However, our conjecture need not be inconsistent with the life cycle theory, and can in fact perfectly work together with it. See Harry DeAngelo, Linda DeAngelo, and René M Stulz, "Dividend Policy and the Earned/Contributed Capital Mix: A Test of the Life-Cycle Theory" (2006) 81(2) *Journal of Financial Economics* 227. Moreover, if there is discontinuity in tech markets, investment opportunities should be the same for younger and older firms.

190. Netflix, here, is the outlier. Netflix has used debt a lot, relative to retained earnings. But Netflix also displays low R&D figures, which is not incompatible with your hypothesis. In short, Netflix does not seem to be very long termist.
191. See Franco Modigliani and Merton Miller, "Dividend Policy, Growth, and the Valuation of Shares" (1961) 34(4) *Journal of Business* 411.
192. Berk and DeMarzo, *Corporate Finance* (n 182) fig 17.6, 656.
193. ibid.

horizon.[194] Taken together with the uncertainty previously discussed, the tech giants' R&D and earnings decisions might be rational adaptations to risks of discontinuous phenomena that are unobservable in the short term.[195] Through this lens, R&D intensity maximizes big tech firms' chances to become active agents of discontinuity. And big tech firms' earnings policy reduces the risk of being a victim of discontinuity.

5. Growth

a) What Tech Giants Attempt to Maximize

Any casual reader who spends time observing the operations of big tech will come away impressed with the extent of management's occupation with growth.[196] Expansion is a theme which (with some variations) is dinned into the ears of stockholders. Indeed, in going through big tech firms' disclosures, one may easily come to believe that growth of the firm is the main preoccupation of top management.

The above paragraph is not from us. We adapted to big tech the opening lines of William Baumol's 1962 article "On the Theory of Expansion of the Firm."[197] Through repeated interaction with entrepreneurs—in the context of his consultancy work—Baumol observed that managers prioritize growth over other *motivations*, and especially profit maximization. Hoping to improve the empirical relevance of mainstream economics (in which the entrepreneur is assumed to be a profit maximizing automaton), Baumol elaborated a model of firm maximizing sales revenue subject to a profit constraint.[198]

---

194. Our point is not that tech giants want to stay in market, as forever companies. Recall that both Google and Netflix tried to sell to third parties (Google to Excite and Netflix to Blockbuster). Incentives to stay or exit markets may change over the life of a firm.

195. Much research insists on "importance of the subjective perspective of time in understanding competitive phenomena." Sucheta Nadkarni, Tianxu Chen, and Jianhong Chen, "The Clock Is Ticking! Executive Temporal Depth, Industry Velocity, and Competitive Aggressiveness" (2016) 37(6) *Strategic Management Journal* 1132 (hereafter Nadkarni et al, "The Clock Is Ticking!").

196. See Microsoft Corporation, Form 10-K, US SEC, 2000, saying that handheld devices erode Microsoft's revenue growth in traditional markets.

197. William J Baumol, "On the Theory of Expansion of the Firm" (1962) 52(5) *American Economic Review* 1078 (hereafter Baumol, "On the Theory of Expansion of the Firm").

198. William J Baumol, *Business Behavior, Value and Growth* (Macmillan 1959) (see, in particular, for oligopoly firms: "Specifically, I have suggested that management's goal may well be to maximize 'sales' (total revenue) subject to a profit constraint"). Baumol's point was that firms attempt to maximize a *rate of growth* of sales revenue, and *profits* is a means to that end (retained earnings and payment of dividends to induce outside investors).

Baumol's work seems prescient. At a high level, his observation rings true for many tech giants. 10-K disclosures insist more on the "extent" to which the firm has "progressed" rather than on the size or profitability of their current operations.[199]

And yet one's first thought here might be skeptical: this may just be an artefact of the disclosure exercise. For indeed, reporting firms are required to discuss material changes from prior periods (though nothing requires them to discuss "growth" as a factor of change).[200] Moreover, when Baumol wrote his theory, neither his "highly impressionistic" evidence,[201] nor his "elegant"[202] model convinced his peers.[203] So what should give us more confidence today that growth is a plausible motivation for big tech firms (one that belongs to the lost empirical facts that we ambition to document)?

To start, Baumol wrote before the Internet. Since then, economists have witnessed the rise of information goods industries with a zero marginal cost.[204] And industries subject to zero marginal cost enjoy increasing returns to production.[205] But this is not all. Recall the simple empirical economics of Chapter III. Coupled with zero (or low) marginal costs, network effects create increasing marginal benefits and remove the stationary short-term equilibrium constraint that defines optimal firm size. This means even more

---

199. Again, see Baumol, "On the Theory of Expansion of the Firm" (n 197) 1085 ("First, maximization of rate of growth of sales revenue seems a somewhat better approximation to the goals of many management groups in large firms than is maximization of the current level of sales. For example, most company publicity materials seem to emphasize the extent to which the firm has 'progressed' rather than the sheer magnitude of its current operations").

200. Moreover, there is no question that investors' strategies are heterogeneous in terms of holding portfolio of value and growth stock, so signaling is not a plausible reason.

201. Marshall Hall, "Sales Revenue Maximization: An Empirical Examination" (967) 15(2) *The Journal of Industrial Economics* 143.

202. John Williamson, "Profit, Growth and Sales Maximization" in Charles K. Rowley (ed) *Readings in Industrial Economics, Vol. I* (The Macmillan Press 1972) 46.

203. Though Baumol has presumably been more aligned with academics from outside of his field who had already talked of the plurality of motivation of business organizations. See Richard M Cyert and James G March, *A Behavioral Theory of the Firm* (Prentice Hall 1963) 3.3 (listing five goals).

204. See Hal R Varian and Carl Shapiro, *Information Rules: A Strategic Guide to the Network Economy* (Harvard Business Review Press 1998) 91 (hereafter Varian and Shapiro, *Information Rules*).

205. Varian and Shapiro actually wrote that the "the marginal cost of producing information goods is close to zero." ibid., 287. Note that this is more an approximation than an observation. Not all information goods have a zero marginal cost of production, simply because variable costs are not always constant. For example, electricity may cost more at some periods than others. Moreover, not all digital economy goods are information products. Think, for example, of an iPhone.

increasing returns. And this gives further theoretical backing to the idea that tech giants' short-term motivation is to grow output.

There is, perhaps, a testable way to see whether growth is a motivation of big tech firms. At a high level, the main implication of Baumol's model is that a growth-minded firm will prefer a mix of input costs with relatively higher fixed costs than variable costs. With this background, do 10-K reports tell us anything about tech giants' costs preferences? If readers recall well, we saw in Chapter III that in spite of a growing scale, both Facebook and Google maintain low and constant (or slowly ascending) incremental costs, suggesting a large share of fixed costs. Similarly, and even though the quantitative evidence was less compelling for Amazon and Netflix (whose incremental costs rise with scale), both firms' costs preferences could be inferred from anecdotal evidence. Netflix, for one, converted variable content acquisition costs due under revenue-sharing contracts with studios into fixed costs pursuant to output deals.[206] And Amazon has been explicit on its strategy to rebalance its labor intensive cost base, in particular by increasing reliance on automation. Recall that Amazon is the sole tech giant in the six firms studied here that has undertaken layoffs.

Last, observations of tech giants' M&A activity accord with our previous findings. Mergent Industrial Manual reports data on the tech giants' acquisitions.[207] We record the following numbers of transactions: Facebook 35, Amazon 43, Apple 66, Microsoft 212, and Google 246.[208] No data is provided for Netflix.

M&A data alone is insufficient to draw inference of a firm-level growth *motivation* in digital industries. But it coincides with a substantial amount of business management, strategy, and entrepreneurship literature that discusses M&A as a growth strategy. In the standard narrative, M&A constitutes the last stage of a division of labor between large and small firms. The larger

---

206. In 2013, Netflix describes its "increasingly long-term and fixed-cost nature of our content acquisition licenses." Netflix, Inc, Form 10-K, US SEC, 2013.
207. Mergent Industrial Manual provides historical data on companies listed in the United States, including corporate events like M&A. Mergent relies upon information obtained directly from the corporations or from stockholders' reports and Securities and Exchange Commission reports and registration. The database sometimes includes the target's line of business and the terms of the transaction.
208. With the exception of Netflix, all tech giants have been quite active on the M&A market. These might be conservative estimates. Several studies provide indirect evidence of higher numbers. See Axel Gautier and Joe Lamesch, "Mergers in the Digital Economy" (2019) *Working Paper* <https://orbi.uliege.be/bitstream/2268/241664/1/Gafam_19_07_19_revAG.pdf> accessed December 18, 2019.

firm delegates to smaller organizations the task of exploring technological discontinuities in exchange for a future opportunity to scale through
a cooperative acquisition.[209] A variant of this theory consists in the larger
firms letting smaller firms compete in the race for a dominant design, and
later entering the industry through M&A or vertical integration, scaling the
selected technology and removing fragmentation.[210]

b) Discussion

Before we draw implications from the above analysis, one clarification is
in order. We are not making the argument that tech giants grow. They do.
What we are suggesting is that regardless of realized output, one of big tech
firms' key motivations might be to maximize growth.[211] Or put differently,
both profit and growth maximization may compete with, and/or complement, each other in tech giants' preference function.[212]

Against this backdrop, if big tech firms operate under a growth maximization motivation, zero sum game rivalry might not be a first best goal.
Business and management scholars stress that in markets characterized by
"ample resources and growth opportunities firms face little competitive
pressure" to denote that growth-minded firms have low incentives to enter

---

209. See Markides, "Disruptive Innovation" (n 157) 24 ("Established companies should not even
attempt to create such innovations but should leave the task of creating these kinds of markets to small, start-up firms that have the requisite skills and attitudes to succeed at this
game. Established firms should, instead, concentrate on what they are good at—consolidating
young markets into big, mass markets … it is in fact a widely accepted business model in
industries where companies live and die on their ability to continuously bring creative new
products to the market—industries such as music and book publishing, Hollywood movies, theater plays, and art galleries"); Ming-Jer Chen and Danny Miller, "Reconceptualizing
Competitive Dynamics: A Multidimensional Framework" (2015) 36(5) *Strategic Management
Journal* 758, 760 (growth by joint ventures and mergers and acquisitions is also at the heart
of competition-cooperation strategies in big tech or in the "lift all boats," relational idea of
platform as ecosystems theory); Matt Marx, Joshua S Gans, and David H Hsu, "Dynamic
Commercialization Strategies for Disruptive Technologies: Evidence from the Speech
Recognition Industry" (2014) 60(12) *Management Science* 3103 (treating M&A with smaller
innovative competitor as a "cooperate strategy").
210. C. Jay Lambe and Robert E. Spekman, "Alliances, external technology acquisition, and discontinuous technological change" (1997) 14(2) Journal of Product Innovation Management, 102.
211. This does not exclude that they have a profit maximizing motivation. After all profits feed
retained earnings and dividends which are instrumental to growth.
212. Profits allow retention and payouts that fund the future, but beyond some point they compete with growth. See Baumol, "On the Theory of Expansion of the Firm" (n 197) 1085
("From the point of view of a long-run growth (or sales) maximizer, profit no longer acts
as a constraint. Rather, it is an instrumental variable-a means whereby management works
towards its goals. Specifically, profits are a means for obtaining capital needed to finance
expansion plans").

into competitive market share (or profit) stealing behavior.[213] Upshot? We should not expect to see growth-minded tech giants *intentionally* adopt pro or anticompetitive conduct.

Second, firms with a growth mindset are essentially worried about stagnation. A product segment making significant profits yet with low growth potential is arguably irrelevant. This might explain the paradox of firms with entrenched market positions and profit-making operations that do not sit still, like Microsoft's investments in various product areas in spite of a reported monopoly position in OS for PC and Office.[214]

Third, while growth might relax competitive pressure as seen above, it creates a new type of pressure on firms. Tushman and O'Reilly write:

> Older, larger firms develop structural and cultural inertia—the organizational equivalent of high cholesterol ... as companies grow, they develop structures and systems to handle the increased complexity of the work. These structures and systems are interlinked so that proposed changes become more difficult, more costly, and require more time to implement ... this results in structural inertia—a resistance to change rooted in the size, complexity and interdependence in the organization's structures, systems, procedures and processes.[215]

One relevant question for us is whether this pressure that is common to many firms is mitigated by network effects as far as big tech is concerned.

6. Exploration and Discovery

Management theory exhorts firm to be "ambidextrous."[216] The underlying wisdom is that firm performance requires both exploration and exploitation in innovation strategies. In real life, limited resources often impose on firms a choice between exploration and exploitation.[217] Big tech firms,

---

213. See Augustine A Lado, Nancy G Boyd, and Susan C Hanlon, "Competition, Cooperation, and the Search for Economic Rents: a Syncretic Model" (1997) 22(1) *The Academy of Management Review* 130 (hereafter Lado et al, "Competition, Cooperation, and the Search for Economic Rents").

214. These are not pure financial investments.

215. See Tushman and O'Reilly, "The Ambidextrous Organizations" (n 165) 18.

216. For a good literature review, see Sebastian Raisch and Julian Birkinshaw, "Organizational Ambidexterity: Antecedents, Outcomes, and Moderators" (2008) 34(3) *Journal of Management* 375-409.

217. Dovev Lavie, Uriel Stettner, and Michael L Tushman, "Exploration and Exploitation Within and Across Organizations" (2010) 4(1) *The Academy of Management Annals* 116 (hereafter Lavie et al, "Exploration and Exploitation Within and Across Organizations") ("Although both exploration and exploitation are essential for survival and prosperity, limited resource

however, appear to practice exploration and exploitation as complements not substitutes. Before we discuss some evidence of the extent of the phenomenon (b) and big tech firms' possible motivations (c), let us say a word on both concepts (a).

a) Concepts

Organization theorist James March gives a good definition of exploration: "Exploration includes things captured by terms such as search, variation, risk taking, experimentation, play, flexibility, discovery, innovation."[218] March contrasts exploration with exploitation that "includes such things as refinement, choice, production, efficiency, selection, implementation, execution." Often, the difference between exploration and exploitation is "a matter of degree rather than kind."[219]

When exploration is applied to innovation choices, it denotes innovation that is not goal-directed.[220] The firm puts research money in a black box. It commits to an open ended innovation *process*, rather than to a set technological *outcome*.[221]

Why, one may ask, would a firm make such risky bets? A plausible reason is the scientific consensus that great discoveries can be achieved unpredictably.[222] Columbus' or Pasteur's breakthroughs changed the course of history.

---

availability compels organizations to favor one type of activity over the other. The trade-offs between exploration and exploitation underscore these inherent differences").

218. James G. March, "Exploration and exploitation in organizational learning" (1991) 2(1) *Organization science*, 71.

219. Lavie et al, "Exploration and Exploitation Within and Across Organizations" (n 217). Note also that exploration and exploitation cut across organizational structure, strategy, and innovation. Justin J P Jansen, Frans A J Van den Bosch, and Henk W Volberda, "Exploratory Innovation, Exploitative Innovation, and Performance: Effects of Organizational Antecedents and Environmental Moderators" (2006) 52(11) *Management Science* 1661 (hereafter Jansen et al, "Exploratory Innovation, Exploitative Innovation, and Performance").

220. Susan Stipp "Strategic or Blue Sky Research?" (2010) 6(3) *Elements* 139. Scientists talk of "blue sky" research (as opposed to "strategic" research).

221. Exploration differs from widespread notions of radical, disruptive, or generative innovation, which are all based on ex post rationalizations of observed outcomes. Similarly, Dong et al talk of moonshots, and also take an outcome driven perspective (defining "a moon shot as a risky project involving radical solutions to problems, breakthrough technology, and major scope for improving the welfare of customers") (see Dong et al, "Stock Market Overvaluation" (n 144)).

222. Vannevar Bush, "Science—The Endless Frontier, Report to the President by Vannevar Bush, Director of the Office of Scientific Research and Development" July 1945 ("We must remove the rigid controls which we have had to impose, and recover freedom of inquiry and that healthy competitive scientific spirit so necessary for expansion of the frontiers of scientific knowledge").

And yet, neither of them found what they were after. Now make no mistake: our point is not that great scientific discoveries owe to luck or accident. Both Columbus and Pasteur enjoyed support from significant research organizations, resources, and structures. Instead, as Paula Stephan writes, the point is simply that the realized research outcomes were "unexpected."[223]

In the empirical business and management literature, scholars assess firms' exploration and exploitation choices through a variety of lenses, like cultural (risk taking/fail well spirit), relational (cooperation and competition at individual/divisional levels), and organizational choices (spin offs like AT&T's Bell Labs).[224]

b) Patterns of Exploration and Discovery?

Judging by anecdotes of discontinued product development processes, the tech giants seem adept of exploration. 10-Ks are rife with examples of failed product experiments, like Microsoft's ActiMate dolls, Amazon's Fire phone, Facebook's virtual currency, or Google TV. But can we move beyond anecdotes to give more rigorous evidence of a big tech exploration preference? Though they are imperfect, four data points are worth considering.

First, we may try to disaggregate the firm-level allocation of resources for invention between exploration and exploitation.[225] One way to do this consists in looking at R&D, patent, and research workforce data, and breaking it down under both categories. This procedure can be applied to Google. Since 2015, Alphabet reports on its exploratory ventures under a separate segment named "Other Bets." We can thus reconstruct an approximate R&D budget for Google's exploration choices (see Table 4.2 below).[226] Since 2014, Other Bets reports net losses. Though not all losses are R&D expenses, a plausible great deal of these costs are research expenses. When we relate these losses

223. Paula E Stephan, "The Economics of Science" (1996) 34(3) *Journal of Economic Literature* 1199-1235.

224. Nicholas Negroponte, "Creating a Culture of Ideas" *MIT Technology Review* (February 1, 2003). Lavie et al, "Exploration and Exploitation Within and Across Organizations" (n 217).

225. Note that there is no legal obligation on publicly listed companies to report on non-revenue generating segments. And firms might have few incentives to do this. Disclosure may lead to loss of a competitive advantage to rivals. Also, over-disclosure of exploratory innovation may alarm investors (arguably seeking to maintain investors' trust, Facebook's first 10-K even declared that its "product development philosophy is centered on continuous innovation in creating products that are social by design"). See Facebook, Inc, Form 10-K, US SEC, 2012.

226. We use here the method employed by JackDaw Research. See Jan Dawnson, "Breaking Down Alphabet's Other Bets" (*Beyond Devices*, February 1, 2016) <http://www.beyonddevic. es/2016/02/01/breaking-down-alphabets-other-bets/>.

Table 4.2 Alphabet's Exploration R&D (as % of total R&D)

	2014	2015	2016	2017	2018
Other Bets Losses	1.556 bn	3.011 bn	2.949 bn	2.152 bn	2.763 bn
Alphabet R&D	9.832 bn	12.282 bn	13.948 bn	16.625 bn	21.419 bn
Other Bets R&D	15.8%	24.5%	21%	12%	12.8%

to Alphabet, we can see that Other Bets absorbs between 12 and 25 percent of total R&D spend (see last line in Table 4.2 below).[227]

Second, we can use the benefit of hindsight to look for qualitative 10-K evidence of tech giants' non Net Present Value ("NPV") projects. Rita Gunther McGrath argues that experimental firms follow "real options" investments models, placing small bets—read investments—on many projects without NPV.[228] In less technical terms, the idea is that exploration involves uncertain, distant, and diversified payoffs.[229]

Against this backdrop, several big tech facts point out an exploration—or non-NPV—mindset. Facebook's apps like Stories or WhatsApp, Google's Maps or Street View, and Microsoft's HoloLens were all developed at low levels of monetization and/or without a clear business model proposition.[230] In Facebook's 10-K for 2018, the exploratory approach to monetization is in clear display: "the Stories format is becoming increasingly popular for sharing content across our products, and we do not currently monetize Stories at the same rate as News Feed."[231] Similarly, in relation to WhatsApp and Messenger, Facebook declared: "We have also invested, and expect

227. Note that in 2018, Alphabet started to report Nest revenue together with Google other revenue, due to Nest transfer to Google's hardware team. Prior period segment information was recast to conform to the current period segment presentation. We have however used here the non-recast information found in 10-Ks.
228. Rita Gunther McGrath, "Business Models: A Discovery Driven Approach" (2010) 43(2-3) *Long Range Planning* 255 (hereafter McGrath, "Business Models: A Discovery Driven Approach") ("business model experimentation can often be designed to honor such real-options concepts as keeping initial investments small until concepts are proven and only investing more substantially when there is greater evidence that an idea will work—but then being prepared to scale up with vigor").
229. Without a computable Net Present Value. See Lavie et al, "Exploration and Exploitation Within and Across Organizations" (n 217) 112–14 ("Compared to returns from exploitation, returns from exploration are systematically less certain, more remote in time, and organizationally more distant from the locus of action and adaption"). ("In turn, exploration entails a shift away from an organization's current knowledge base and skills.")
230. See Tongur and Engwall, "The Business Model Dilemma of Technology Shifts" (n 158).
231. See Facebook, Inc, Form 10-K, US SEC, 2017.

to continue to invest, significant resources in growing our WhatsApp and Messenger products. We have historically monetized messaging in only a very limited fashion, and we may not be successful in our efforts to generate meaningful revenue from messaging over the long term."[232]

Third, we may get a hint of big tech firms' commitment to exploration by looking at organizational arrangements.[233] Business and management science suggests that the returns to exploration are greater with goal and supervision autonomy.[234] When this idea is introduced, we can make sense of some tech giants' practice of internal competition: Google lets Maps and Waze compete for users' navigation demand; Facebook's Messenger and WhatsApp compete for users' text communication demand; and Microsoft offers rival videoconferencing services through Skype for Business and Teams.[235] One way to think about big tech firms' practice of internal competition is as a strategy to *explore* consumer preferences.

Last, we can find a good example of a realized exploration strategy by studying the history of Amazon's Alexa. In 2004, Amazon started to develop Alexa.com as a search engine software and an Internet browser. In the following years, Alexa took an *unexpected* turn. It morphed into a *voice* enabled platform, a hardware form factor known as "Echo" and is now sold as a standard off the shelf good.[236] Study of older 10-Ks shows that this evolution was largely unplanned.

What has been said so far has excepted Apple and Netflix. This should not be taken as a suggestion that Apple and Netflix do not follow exploration

---

232. ibid.
233. Lubatkin et al (2006) suggest that structural exploration (ambidexterity) may be more appropriate for large and diversified firms. See Michael H Lubatkin, Zeki Simsek, Yan Ling, and John F Veiga, "Ambidexterity and Performance in Small- to Medium-sized Firms: The Pivotal Role of Top Management Team Behavioral Integration" (2006) 32(5) *Journal of Management* 646.
234. See Rita Gunther McGrath, "Exploratory Learning, Innovative Capacity and Managerial Oversight" (2001) 44(1) *The Academy of Management Journal* 118 (hereafter McGrath, "Exploratory Learning").
235. Note that we cannot tell from the outside whether these competing apps are operated independently, or whether there is full divisional and technological integration between them.
236. In his letter for Shareholders for 2018, Jeff Bezos writes "The vision for Echo and Alexa was inspired by the Star Trek computer. The idea also had origins in two other arenas where we'd been building and wandering for years: machine learning and the cloud. From Amazon's early days, machine learning was an essential part of our product recommendations, and AWS gave us a front row seat to the capabilities of the cloud. After many years of development, Echo debuted in 2014, powered by Alexa, who lives in the AWS cloud." Jeffrey P Bezos, "Letter to Shareholders" (2018) <https://ir.aboutamazon.com/static-files/4f64d0cd-12f2-4d6c-952e-bbed15ab1082> (hereafter Jeff Bezos, "2018 Letter to Shareholders").

strategies. Apple is well known for its secretive culture, both internally and externally. But let us recall, for what it is worth, that Apple pioneered the smartphone revolution in 2007 by recombining a touchscreen mobile phone, the iPod, and a set of Internet communications services.[237] Similarly, we know that Apple did not have a specific and well-thought monetization strategy for the AppStore until it introduced a 30 percent fee drawing inspiration from industry practice in software licensing. Netflix, by contrast, presents a profile perhaps more aligned on exploitation.[238]

c) Motivations?

Why do the tech giants explore?[239] Three big tech-specific factors appear relevant. The first are technological idiosyncrasies. Digital information is a "slack resource" that can be combined (and recombined) at low incremental cost, resulting in infinite input permutations and indeterminate innovation arrivals.[240] This feature produces powerful incentives to exploration for firms in digital information industries.[241] All the more so given increasing economic evidence that innovation breakthroughs are combinatorial.[242] Moreover, data removes some uncertainty, defined as an "*absence of information*", and thus the risk cost of innovation.[243] Big tech's data capabilities might allow them to pursue bolder exploration strategies than firms in other industries, for which uncertainty deters investment and innovation.

Second, industry or firm-level events play a role in building a path dependent culture of exploration. In his own words, Jeff Bezos recounts as follows the history of Amazon Web Services ("AWS"):

---

237. Note, however, that the evidence is mixed. In contrast to pure experimentalism, Apple "makes choices about which technologies to ride based on keen market insight." See Loizos Heracleous, "Quantum Strategy at Apple Inc." (2013) 42(2) *Organizational Dynamics* 92.
238. Its most significant experiments are adaptive streaming, offline viewing, and a social networking feature called Friend.
239. See Lavie et al, "Exploration and Exploitation Within and Across Organizations" (n 217) 118 (noting "Empirical research has produced limited or mixed evidence on the causes of exploration and exploitation").
240. ibid 122.
241. Including in relation to hardware. See Marcel Bogers, Henry Chesbrough, and Carlos Moedas, "Open Innovation: Research, Practices, and Policies" (2018) 60(2) *California Management Review* 5 ("Bringing the technological and scientific component together implies a creative combination of hardware and software").
242. Martin Weitzman, "Recombinant Growth" (1998) 113(2) *Quarterly Journal of Economics* 331.
243. Arrow, "Economic Welfare" (n 131).

Wandering is an essential counter-balance to efficiency. You need to employ both. The outsized discoveries—the "non-linear" ones— are highly likely to require wandering. AWS itself—as a whole—is an example. No one asked for AWS. No one. Turns out the world was in fact ready and hungry for an offering like AWS but didn't know it. We had a hunch, followed our curiosity, took the necessary financial risks, and began building—reworking, experimenting, and iterating countless times as we proceeded.[244]

The rest is well known. AWS became Amazon's money-making segment. Given the historical role of serendipity at Amazon, it is of little wonder why it plays a role in the firm's contemporary innovation strategy. The same argument applies to other tech giants' products or service areas in which exploration has been the industry norm. Management specialist Rita Gunther McGrath explains that Google's success with advertising-supported Internet searches "builds upon the many previous experimental efforts made by preceding companies," and in particular Infoseek and Yahoo!.[245]

Finally, there is what we may call environmental factors. Broadly speaking, business and management scientists consider that two forces may influence firms to explore.[246] Competition, understood as interfirm rivalry, is the first.[247] Economic dynamism, understood as technological discontinuity, is the second.

Let us look at both factors in turn. Business and management scholarship points out almost unambiguously to a functional relationship between competitive intensity and exploration.[248] When there is intense competitive

---

244. Jeff Bezos, "2018 Letter to Shareholders" (n 234). A story commonly heard, and hard to document, is that Amazon realized the potential of AWS at Christmas, when servers got suddenly busy due to a spike in online orders. Walmart had a cap set a some million of orders, including at Christmas, which diverted huge traffic to Amazon.

245. McGrath, "Business Models: A Discovery Driven Approach" (n 228).

246. See Lavie et al., "Exploration and Exploitation Within and Across Organizations" (n 217) 118 and following. The authors survey four environmental "antecedents," namely, environmental dynamism, exogenous shocks, competitive intensity, and appropriability regime. In the literature, environmental dynamisms and exogenous shocks are often accounted for together, and we follow this approach here. Moreover, we do not study appropriability because as seen before, institutions and regulations are in a state of flux in big tech industries.

247. That is the "number of competitors" and "number of areas in which there is competition." See Jansen et al, "Exploratory Innovation, Exploitative Innovation, and Performance" (n 219). See also William P Barnett, "The Dynamics of Competitive Intensity" (1997) 42(1) *Administrative Science Quarterly* 128.

248. In a literature review of 2010, Lavie, Stettner, and Tushman (n 217) write "Intensifying competitive pressures call for exploration that can drive change and nurture new sources of competitive advantage" (citing Daniel A Levinthal and James G March, "The Myopia of Learning" (1993) 14 *Strategic Management Journal* 95 (hereafter Levinthal and March, "The

pressure in an industry, firms have incentives to develop exploration strate-gies.[249] In an influential 2005 book, W Chan Kim and Renée Mauborgne argue that successful companies are those that break out of "red oceans," that is known market places where rivalry brings prices down, and create "blue oceans," that is new market spaces that make the competition irrele-vant.[250] Kim and Mauborgne write: "The only way to beat the competition is to stop trying to beat the competition."[251] Common examples are Uber, Airbnb, Marvel, or Zappos.[252]

This is a startling proposition. As we previously saw, many consider that big tech firms are monopolies subject to limited competition. How can it be therefore that we see tech giants exploring to such a degree? Two hypotheses arise here. Either we have overstated the extent of big tech firms' exploration. Or the monopoly finders have understated competition.

Myopia of Learning"). They also note that "some evidence suggests that exploration is pre-ferred to exploitation as a means for strengthening an organization's foothold in existing markets and establishing presence in new markets during periods of competitive rivalry. In contrast, the incentives to exploit dominate when the competitive tension is dampened and organizations generate reasonable return on investment by leveraging existing products, ser-vices, and technologies without incurring exploration risks."

249. One empirical study makes a somewhat similar, yet more nuanced finding: in a context of competition, exploitation is a performance maximizing choice, while exploration is *not* a per-formance reducing one. See Jansen et al, "Exploratory Innovation, Exploitative Innovation, and Performance" (n 219).

250. W Chan Kim and Renée Mauborgne, *Blue Ocean Strategy* (Harvard Business School Publishing Corporation 2005) 4. Often a blue ocean strategy requires an intermediate step, that consists in moving to a "droplets," ie, product extensions in existing markets so as to mit-igate downside risk aversion by shareholders and management. See Ioannis Christodoulou and Paul Langley, "A Gaming Simulation Approach to understanding Blue Ocean Strategy Development as a Transition from Traditional Competitive Strategy" [2019] *Journal of Strategic Marketing* 1 (hereafter Christodoulou and Langley, "A Gaming Simulation Approach to Understanding Blue Ocean Strategy Development").

251. ibid, p. 4. Note that Kim and Mauborgne build on previous research by Gary Hamel, at note 17, p 218 ("Gary Hamel (1998) argues that success for both newcomers and industry incum-bents hinges upon the capacity to avoid the competition and to reconceive the existing indus-try model. He further argues (2000) that the formula for success is not to position against the competition but rather to go around it"). We also refer readers to the famous research on Judo Economics, whose first principle is "Move rapidly to uncontested ground to avoid head-to-head conflict." See David B Yoffie and Michael A Cusumano, "Judo Strategy—The Competitive Dynamics of Internet Time" (1999) 77(1) *Harvard Business Review 70*. ("Skilled judo players use rapid movement to avoid head-to-head confrontations with potentially superior opponents—moving the battle to terrain where they have an advantage or, at least, where their opponents do not.")

252. See Christodoulou and Langley, "A Gaming Simulation Approach to Understanding Blue Ocean Strategy Development" (n 250).

Because we cannot refute the first hypothesis, let us concede the monopoly point. This leaves explanatory room for the second factor, namely environmental dynamism. The idea here is that "industry growth, dynamism, an abundance of technological opportunities and the environment's demand for new products" may be determinant in incentivizing exploration choices.[253] Theoretical and empirical studies in organization theory, strategy, management science, and industrial economics point to the fact that exploration strategies maximize survival and prosperity.[254] Conservatively assuming that the tech giants are aware of this literature, environmental dynamism plausibly explains firm-level observations of exploration strategy.

Both competitive intensity and environmental dynamisms are tied. In a 1993 seminal paper, Daniel Levinthal and James March observed: "Power allows an organization to change its environments rather than adapt to them. Thus, firms with strong market positions impose their policies, products, and strategies on others, rather than learn to adapt to an exogenous environment."[255] But "in the long run, however, the use of power to impose environments is likely to result in atrophy of capabilities to respond to change."[256] Perhaps big tech firms just put theory to practice,

253. Sebastian Raisch and Florian Holtz, "Shaping the Context for Learning: Corporate Alignment Initiatives, Environmental Munificence and Firm Performance" in Stuart Wall, Carsten Zimmermann, Ronald Klingebiel, and Dieter Lange (eds), *Strategic Reconfigurations: Building Dynamic Capabilities in Rapid Innovation-Based Industries* (Edward Elgar 2010) 68.

254. ibid, confirming empirically that firms with a bias toward exploration outperform their peers (in return on equity terms) in environments of high environmental munificence ("Our findings demonstrate that exploration-oriented alignment behavior is linked to superior performance" at p 77; observing also that "the data also show that firms are moving towards a more balanced orientation in times of low environmental munificence" and that they "did not find evidence of such a balanced alignment having a superior performance effect" at p 78); Jansen et al, "Exploratory Innovation, Exploitative Innovation, and Performance" (n 219) ("Specifically, results suggest that organizational units operating in more dynamic environments increase their financial performance by pursuing exploratory innovations"); McGrath, "Exploratory Learning" " (n 234) 119 (the consensus cuts across adaptative systems theory, empirical research and real options reasoning. McGrath notes that it is a "quite well accepted idea that it is useful to generate internal variety for organisations facing change." She adds that "Organizations that prove to have superior abilities to manage exploration will be better able to adapt to changing circumstances"); Nadkarni et al, "The Clock is Ticking!" (n 195) ("in unpredictable industries, firms and particularly incumbent try out large numbers of ventures in the hope that at least some of them generate competitive advantage").

255. Levinthal and March, "The Myopia of Learning" (n 248) 102.

256. ibid 97.

Table 4.3 Big Tech Origin v Current Market

	Origins market	Current market
FB	Online transactions	Online advertisement
AMZN	Online bookselling	Online retail
AAPL	Desktop computer	Smartphones
NFLX	Online DVD	Online streaming
GOOG	Search licensing	Search advertising
MSFT	Licensable operating systems	Productivity software

understanding that exploration is key to avoiding the long run "traps of power."[257]

7. Flexibility

In a book on globalization, economist John Sutton has discussed how firms adapt to competition from low wage countries.[258] One of Sutton's key findings is that a "primary survival mechanism lies in switching the balance of a firm's activities towards new product lines."[259] Sutton tells the story of Aquafresh, a Ghanaian firm that started operations in textile and "reinvented itself as a maker of soft drinks."[260]

What, one may ask, is the relevance of Sutton's work to big tech? Leaving aside diversification, Table 4.3 above shows that most tech giants' core operations are today localized in a product or service area distinct from the "origin" market in which they historically entered.

Business and management scholars Tushman and O'Reilly provide an interesting framework to think more granularly about big tech change. They suggest looking at shifts in strategy, structure, skills, and culture.[261] When we apply this framework to the tech giants, a much richer picture emerges. Let us look at them in turn.

---

257. ibid 102.
258. Sutton, *Competing in Capabilities* (n 113). Sutton's book talks of industries, but his examples are firm specific.
259. ibid 12.
260. ibid.
261. Tushman and O'Reilly, "The Ambidextrous Organizations" (n 165) 15 ("To succeed over the long haul, firms have to periodically reorient themselves by adopting new strategies and structures that are necessary to accommodate changing environmental conditions. These shifts often occur through discontinuous changes—simultaneous shifts in strategy, structures, skills, and culture").

Strategy shifts include monetization,[262] differentiation,[263] technology,[264] or product changes.[265] Possible big tech instantiations are Facebook's turn-around from a brokerage business model (payments on games and virtual currency) to an ad-based one; Netflix's cost base conversion from revenue sharing to output deals; Google's transition from search engine licensing to search advertising; or Apple's exit from the open PC market toward a closed ecosystem.

Structural change occurs through corporate reorganizations, M&A trans-actions, or divestitures.[266] Some big tech examples stand out, like Google's 2015 corporate reshuffling into Alphabet, Amazon's 2017 acquisition of Whole Foods, and Microsoft's 2018 operational reorganization that led to spread Windows capabilities across divisional lines.[267]

Skills change is noticeable in leadership, compensation, or workforce management movements: Steve Jobs' spectacular return to Apple or the hiring of Satya Nadella at Microsoft in replacement of Steve Ballmer spring to mind. Less obvious, though not less relevant, is Google's liberal manage-ment of workers' time.[268] Google has historically encouraged its engineers

262. See McGrath, "Business Models: A Discovery Driven Approach" (n 228) 248. McGrath uses the example of Hewlett Packard moving from a hardware to a services business model in corporate following arrival of CEO Mark Hurd ("On the corporate side, he shifted HP toward more of an integrated solutions and services model than it had previously adopted, culminating most recently in its decision to acquire the consulting and outsourcing firm EDS to fill out its capabilities to support client corporations' needs more comprehensively").

263. Tushman and O'Reilly take the example of Apple, who moved from a single product strategy (selling the Apple I PC) to sell a "broader range of products," with a "market wide emphasis." See Tushman and O'Reilly, "The Ambidextrous Organizations" (n 165) 14.

264. Michael A Cusumano, *Staying Power: Six Enduring Principles for Managing Strategy & Innovation in an Uncertain World* (Oxford University Press 2012) 62 (hereafter Cusumano, *Staying Power*) (showing how Nintendo, early loser of the "consoles war" later won by changing, and embracing "a clever system-level innovation combining hardware and software that changed the player's experience: a wireless remote control for its Wii console").

265. More generally, a strategy shift means that a firm moves from a business goal to another, for instance, from being a technological leader toward being the low cost player, or from being a corporate partner, toward building a consumer centric relationship.

266. Richard R Nelson, *The Sources of Economic Growth* (Harvard University Press 2000) 111 (hereafter Nelson, *The Sources of Economic Growth*) gives the following definition: "Structure involves how a firm is organized and governed, and how decisions actually are made and carried out."

267. Satya Nadella "Embracing our future: Intelligent Cloud and Intelligent Edge" (*Microsoft*, March 29, 2018) <https://news.microsoft.com/2018/03/29/satya-nadella-email-to-employees-embracing-our-future-intelligent-cloud-and-intelligent-edge/> accessed April 21, 2020.

268. For a parallel, see Cusumano, *Staying Power* (n 264) 250 (taking Toyota as example of flexibil-ity, and mentioning its "liberal use of worker overtime").

to devote as much as 30 percent of their time to work on side projects, hoping for them to discover new products or services.[269]

Cultural change is less easy to measure. Microsoft's 2018 acquisition of GitHub, an open source software provider, offers a good example. Until then, Microsoft had spent years criticizing open source.[270] Netflix's vertical integration into video content is also a possible illustration.

Having identified anecdotal evidence of tech giants' flexibility, we can now consider further refinements. Business and management literature distinguishes two qualitative forms of firm change. On the one hand, "tactical" change relates to short-term adjustments to price, costs, inventory and product features.[271] On the other hand, "strategic" change is about long-term shifts in strategy, structure, culture, and people.[272] This new distinction allows us to separate two polar types of big tech firms. A first group alternates periods of strategic and tactical change:

- From 1997 to 2007, Apple has undergone strategic change. Besides calling back Steve Jobs as interim CEO and cutting product areas like peripherals, Apple abandons its strategy to openly license the Macintosh OS, and incrementally focuses on "Internet devices that are smaller, simpler, and less expensive than traditional personal computers."[273] This shift culminates with the introduction of the iPhone in 2007. By contrast, over the period 2007 to 2017, Apple has invested mostly

269. See Google, Inc, Form 10-K, US SEC, 2006 ("we encourage our engineers to devote as much as 30% of their time to work on independent projects. Many of our significant new products have come from these independent projects, including Google News, AdSense for content and Orkut").

270. This was a constant feature of Microsoft 10-Ks. For example, in 2003 Microsoft declared that one problem of open source software is "that no single entity is responsible for the Open Source software, and thus users have no recourse if a product does not work properly or at all." See Microsoft Corporation, Form 10-K, US SEC, 2003.

271. See for good definitions of tactical and strategic change, Brian L Connelly, Laszlo Tihanyi, S Trevis Certo, and Michael A Hitt, "Marching to the Beat of Different Drummers: The Influence of Institutional Owners on Competitive Actions" (2009) 53(4) *Academy of Management Journal 723–742*. For an example of tactical change, "Gillette executes about 20 product transitions per year." See Kathleen Eisenhardt and Shona L Brown, "Time Pacing: Competing in Markets that Won't Stand Still" (1998) 76(2) *Harvard Business Review 59–69*.

272. Connelly et al., "Marching to the Beat of Different Drummers" (n 271).

273. In 1998, Apple refocuses on the iMac, and drops peripheral products like Messagepad and Emate. In 1999, Apple talks of an effort to simplify and focus. See Apple, Inc, Form 10-K, US SEC, 1999 ("the discontinuance of these peripheral products and portable computing

in tactical change. We do not witness many significant product introductions—the iWatch is an exception—and the firm practices product upgrades and planned obsolescence;[274]

- 2005–10 is a period of strategic change that sees Netflix moving away from DVD toward online streaming. Though it expresses technical reservations about the potential of the Internet in 2004,[275] Netflix forecasts that online streaming will overtake DVD.[276] And Netflix correctly sees that studios keep prioritizing the DVD segment. In 2007, Netflix launches the "Instant Viewing" feature, starts a cooperation with set-top boxes suppliers like LG, and bundles DVD and streaming subscriptions to boost customer acquisition. The rest is well known. In 2010, Netflix has more subscribers to its online streaming service than to its DVD service. From this point, Netflix will embrace tactical change. Its innovation investments are mostly "incremental in nature,"[277] though one may wonder whether Netflix's increased focus on content production investments since 2015 augurs a new shift to "strategic" change.

In business and management science, this is often referred to as the "punctuated equilibrium model" where long periods of incremental choice are interrupted by brief periods of discontinuous change.[278]

products was part of the overall strategy by the Company to simplify and focus its efforts on those products perceived as critical to the Company's future success").

274. Already in 1996, Apple described product upgrades and planned obsolescence as follows: "*To extend the life of its current operating system*, the Company intends to issue periodic releases consisting of discrete operating system components. The Company expects that this will enable it to introduce some new functionality for the current operating system sooner than it would be able to introduce a completely new operating system. Concurrently, the Company will continue development of its next-generation operating system, focusing on increased functionality at the possible expense of some backward compatibility. Diminished backward compatibility in its new operating system could result in a loss of existing customers."

275. See Netflix, Inc, Form 10-K, US SEC, 2004.

276. See Netflix, Inc, Form 10-K, US SEC, 2005 ("At some point in the future digital delivery directly to the home will surpass DVD").

277. See Netflix, Inc, Form 10-K, US SEC, 2011 talking of "making improvements to our service offering, including testing, maintaining and modifying our user interfaces, our recommendation and merchandising technology, as well as, telecommunications systems and infrastructure and other internal-use software systems."

278. Elaine Romanelli and Michael L Tushman, "Organizational Transformation as Punctuated Equilibrium: An Empirical Test" (1994) 37(5) *Academy of Management Journal* 1141.

The other type of big tech firms appears to practice strategic change more continuously.[279] Microsoft is the archetypical example. Besides daily tactical adaptations, Microsoft has been breathlessly changing strategies since 1997. We can track Microsoft's strategic evolution as follows: OS and client software ➔ interactive content (TV) ➔ portals ➔ payments ➔ mobile phones ➔ online advertising ➔ search engines ➔ mobile phones (again) ➔ tablets and other computing hardware ➔ wearables ➔ cloud computing.

Since it is in no part our present purpose to go into an exhaustive discussion of big tech change, we may just observe that diversified firms like Google and Amazon probably sit somewhere between both groups, while Facebook likely belongs to the second group.

What matters more is that our qualitative observations counterbalance the applicability to digital information industries of the received narrative whereby large firms that become fraught with "organizational inertia,"[280] managerial "myopia,"[281] "value network" immobility,[282] and "core rigidities."[283]

279. Shona L Brown and Kathleen M Eisenhardt, "The Art of Continuous Change: Linking Complexity Theory and Time-Paced Evolution in Relentlessly Shifting Organizations" (1997) 42(1) *Administrative Science Quarterly* 1. For a plausible reason, see Bharadwaj et al, "Digital Business Strategy" (n 135) 476 ("Although time has been recognized as an important driver of competitive advantage for firms in the strategic management literature for quite some time (eg, Stalk and Hout 1990), it takes on a more central role in digital business settings").

280. Dean A Sheperd, "Venture Capitalists' Assessment of New Venture Survival" (1999) 45(5) Management Science 621. See also Richard N Langlois and Paul L Robertson, *Firms, Market and Economic Change: A Dynamic Theory of Business Institutions* (Routledge 1995) 104 ("Inertia is often a product of successful adaptation to earlier innovations, as a firm develops ways of operating that appear to be so well suited to its internal and external environment that it sees no reason to change").

281. Myopia is often illustrated by quoting Ken Olsen, President of Digital Equipment who once said "There is no reason for any individual to have a computer in their home" (Quote Investigator, "There is No Reason for Any Individual To Have a Computer in Their Home: Ken Olsen? Savid H. Ahl? Gordon Bell? Apocryphal?" (*Quote Investigator*, September 14, 2017) <https://quoteinvestigator.com/2017/09/14/home-computer/> accessed November 1, 2019). Similarly, RIM founder reportedly told employees "that no one would buy the iPhone because people didn't want to have a personal computer on their phone" (Eric Jackson, "The 6 Reasons Research in Motion Shot Itself In the Foot" (*Forbes*, July 18, 2011) <https://www.forbes.com/sites/ericjackson/2011/07/18/the-6-reasons-research-in-motion-shot-itself-in-the-foot/#6a6foaf15fd3> accessed November 1, 2019).

282. Christensen, *The Innovator's Dilemma* (n 157).

283. Dorothy Leonard-Barton (1992), cited by Lado et al, "Competition, Cooperation, and the Search for Economic Rents" (n 213).

To avoid confusion, let us recall that flexibility is not deterministically linked to market performance.[284] Flexibility may limit the costs of missed market opportunities or of late entry in a context of technological discontinuity.[285] Google and Amazon's respective success in mobile phone OS and online advertising in spite of a late entry are corroborating observations. On the other hand, flexible firms may be too unfocused to achieve critical mass.[286] Microsoft's dispersion may be part of the explanation of its moderate success in mobile phone OS or search advertisement.

8. Summation

What can we cull from this? Beyond bigness, some tech giants share other regularities that are not generally accounted for in the literature. Though no systematic empirical evidence is available, what gives us confidence in our findings is the consistency between all or most six features. While writing this section, we realized that they often work together. Take diversification. It draws on exploration. It reflects a growth oriented mindset. And it requires flexibility.[287]

284. Ronald Klingebiel, "Deploying Strategic Initiatives: Further Consideration of the Flexibility-Stability Balance" in Stuart Wall, Carsten Zimmermann, Ronald Klingebiel, and Dieter Lange (ed), *Strategic Reconfigurations: Building Dynamic Capabilities in Rapid Innovation-Based Industries* (Edward Elgar 2010) 198 (hereafter Klingebiel, "Deploying Strategic Initiatives") ("Few studies, however, have empirically observed a direct link between flexibility and performance").

285. Jay B Barney, "Types of Competition and the Theory of Strategy: Toward an Integrative Framework" (1986) 11(4) *The Academy Journal of Management Review* 796 ("Other firms may have the unique ability to rapidly adapt to whatever revolutionary changes might occur … Firms that possess either of these organizational capabilities may have a greater likelihood of survival in industries threatened by revolutionary Schumpeterian changes than firms without these capabilities"). Nelson, *The Sources of Economic Growth* (n 266) 69 ("To be successful in a world that requires that firms innovate and change, a firm must have a coherent strategy that enables it to decide what new ventures to go into and what to stay out of"). Tushman and O'Reilly explain that changes are necessary for an incumbent to survive when it faces competence destroying innovation. See Tushman and O'Reilly, "The Ambidextrous Organizations" (n 165). Varian and Shapiro, *Information Rules* (n 204) 278 ("Rigidity is death, unless you build a really big installed base, and even this will fade eventually without improvements").

286. Klingebiel, "Deploying Strategic Initiatives" (n 284) ("In addition, excessive flexibility in the deployment of strategic initiatives can, for example as a consequence of modularisation, mean a lack of strategic focus and critical mass").

287. The literature often links flexibility with diversification and exploration. See McGrath, "Exploratory Learning" (n 234) 118 (suggesting that effective adaptation to disruptive change requires "internal variety" and that this is associated with exploration, meaning "search for new organizational routines, and the discovery of new approaches to technologies, businesses, processes, or product").

Against this background, we can now move to a more concrete question: if some firms—including possibly some outside of the group studied here (Twitter, Oracle, or Tencent come to mind)—develop most or all of the six properties, how does this influence the process of competition? This is what we look at next.

C. Moligopoly Competition

We can now return to the drawing board. Conceive of a world in which hypothetical tech giants were to develop most of the above properties at orders of magnitude. And then ask yourself what competitive equilibrium would result? This is the question that we now explore, because the real world of big tech may be closer to it than the monopoly world seen by neo-structuralists.

Before we proceed with theorizing (2) and discuss implications (3), let us restate in a stylized way the few key facts that we know (1).

1. Oligopoly Competition with Monopoly Positions

Our six tech giants started in a distinct product segment, service area, or industry. In all cases, the tech giants entered an environment subject to significant network effects and increasing returns to adoption. Today, big tech firms hold structural positions akin to monopoly in their origin market. At the same time, observed big tech firms' behavior is inconsistent with the conduct of a monopolist, and if it is not consistent the implication has to be that some oligopoly competition exists.[288] One alternative concept to characterize the state of big tech competition as one of "moligopoly" in which tech giants compete against each other or against non-big tech firms, either known or unknown to them.[289]

---

288. See Chapter III above.

289. The concept is close to business and management literature works on "cognitive oligopoly" or on subjective perception of competitive dynamics. Joseph F Porac, Howard Thomas, and Charles Baden-Fuller, "Competitive Groups as Cognitive Communities: The Case of Scottish Knitwear Manufacturers" (1989) 26(4) *Journal of Management Studies* 397. Joseph F Porac and Howard Thomas, "Taxonomic Mental Models in Competitor Definition" (1990) 15(2) *Academy of Management Review* 224.

Now, let us go back to the initial question. If the tech giants are oligopolists with near monopoly positions in distinct product segments, markets, or industries, what kind of equilibrium outcome should we expect? Relatedly, is this equilibrium a competitive or an anticompetitive one? We discuss hereafter the two main scenarios underlined in economics literature, excluding from the outset static models of oligopoly because their basic assumptions are violated in the case of big tech.[290]

2. Big Tech Cooperation or Competition?

a) Multimarket Competition and Mutual Forbearance?

Economists talk of "multimarket competition" to describe the situation in which firms compete against each other simultaneously in several markets.[291] The term was first coined by economist Corwin Edwards in the 1950s in relation to large conglomerates competing with one another in several product areas.[292] Today, multimarket competition is often studied in relation to firms that operate in many distinct geographic markets, like airlines, supermarkets, or banks.

Edwards' work suspected multimarket competition to lead to anticompetitive outcomes. Edwards developed a concept of "mutual forbearance" in which diversified firms "may acquire a sphere of influence within which its primacy is respected by the others, and in turn may accord primacy elsewhere to others,"[293] in turn leading to "structural developments that are

---

290. In particular the tech giants explore, grow, and diversify in multiple markets.
291. Satish Jayachandran, Javier Gimeno, and P Rajan Varadarajan, "The Theory of Multimarket Competition: A Synthesis and Implications for Marketing Strategy" (1999) 63(3) *Journal of Marketing*, 49–66 (hereafter Jayachandran et al, "The Theory of Multimarket Competition").
292. Corwin D Edwards, "Conglomerate Bigness as a Source of Power" in Universities-National Bureau, *Business Concentration and Price Policy* (Princeton University Press 1955) (hereafter Edwards, "Conglomerate Bigness").
293. In 1955, Edwards is reported to have written: "When one large conglomerate enterprise competes with another, the two are likely to encounter each other in a considerable number of markets. The multiplicity of their contacts may blunt the edge of their competition … Each may informally recognize the other's primacy of interest in markets important to the other, in the expectation that its own important interests will be similarly." This quote, however, is apocryphal. It does not appear in the above mentioned paper. Frederic Scherer cites it in his 1980 book, and many works have relied on it since then. Bernheim and Whinston are no exception. They refer to Edwards as quoted in Scherer's book. See Frederic M Scherer, *Industrial Market Structure and Economic Performance* (Houghton Mifflin Company 1980). B Douglas Bernheim and Michael D Whinston, "Multimarket Contact and

anticompetitive in tendency."[294] Mutual forbearance is more than a theory of market sharing. Edwards had in mind a setting in which diversified firms A and B shared monopolies in markets 1 and 2. But he also conjectured that A and B would wield low competition at each other in *most* or *all* other markets 3, 4, 5, and *n* in which they are active, not just the monopoly ones.

Since Edwards, formal and empirical works have studied the possibility that multimarket contacts allow firms in oligopoly to develop "spheres of influence."[295] In the standard model, mutual forbearance involves a sort of "tacit collusion" equilibrium.[296] Each firm compares the benefits of cheating in a market with the cost of punishment (eg, a price war) in other markets.[297] The seminal paper of Douglas Bernheim and Michael Whinston shows that firms (including differing ones) specialize in the market in which they are more efficient, and forbear from cheating in the other markets where they are less efficient than the other firms.[298] For each firm, the profits derived from this tacitly colluding equilibrium increase, while the possible gains from deviations in markets where it is less efficient fall. The endgame is a "live and let live" outcome in which firms do not attack each

Collusive Behavior" (1990) 21(1) *The RAND Journal of Economics* 1 (hereafter Bernheim and Whinston, "Multimarket Contact and Collusive Behavior"). See also Allyn D Stryckland, "Conglomerate Mergers, Mutual Forbearance Behavior and Price Competition" (1985) 6(3) *Managerial and Decision Economics* 153.

294. Corwin D Edwards, "The Future of Competition Policy: A World View" (1974) 16(4) *California Management Review* 112.

295. The seminal paper is Bernheim and Whinston, "Multimarket Contact and Collusive Behavior" (n 293). Later works on airlines or mobile communications have confirmed the empirical possibility of multimarket (tacit) collusion.

296. Note that Edwards talked of "similar reciprocal recognitions of primacy." See Corwin Edwards, "Economic Concepts and Antitrust Litigation: Evolving Complexities" (1974) 19(2) *The Antitrust Bulletin* 317. For a good review of empirical studies, see Jayachandran, Gimero, and Varadajaran noting in 1999 that the available evidence "by and large, lends support to the mutual forbearance hypothesis." See Jayachandran et al, "The Theory of Multimarket Competition" (n 291) 52.

297. See Edwards, "Conglomerate Bigness" (n 292) 355 ("The anticipated gain to such a concern from unmitigated competitive attack upon another large enterprise at one point of contact is likely to be slight as compared with the possible loss from retaliatory action by that enterprise at many other points of contact"); see also Bernheim and Winston reworking his hypothesis and criticizing its underlying logic ("the problem with this argument is that once a firm knows that it will be punished in every market, if it decides to cheat, it will do so in every market." See Bernheim and Whinston, "Multimarket Contact and Collusive Behavior" (n 293) 3.

298. Bernheim and Whinston, "Multimarket Contact and Collusive Behavior" (n 293) 12–13.

other's sphere of influence.[299] Moreover, multimarket contacts enable firms to construct more severe punishments.[300]

Is mutual forbearance a convincing explanatory theory of big tech behavior?[301] At first blush, there is anecdotal and formal evidence supporting the hypothesis. A well-known fact is indeed that each tech giant holds a strong position in its origin market. Besides, recent economic research shows that oligopoly markets in which coordination is unlikely because cheating is imperfectly observable—for example zero price markets which are common in digital information industries—are prone to mutual forbearance.[302]

And yet, much evidence discredits a mutual forbearance equilibrium. Two big tech features are relevant. First, observed patterns of big tech behavior deviate from the mutual forbearance hypothesis. In the standard economic model that has just been described, oligopolists appear to pursue nominal diversification strategies. This situation contrasts with big tech firms' practice of effective diversification. Online advertisement (Google and Facebook), cloud computing services (Amazon, Google, and Microsoft), and payment services (Facebook, Apple, and Google) are examples of tech giants' competition in multiple markets with close to symmetrical positions.

Second, it is useful to remember the discussion on big tech firms' long-term horizon. Under the mutual forbearance hypothesis, multimarket contacts should constrain tech giants' behavior in most or all output markets (including the specialized market), and by reverse reasoning, in input decisions. But the investment patterns discussed previously are not consistent with tacit collusion theory. The facts are that we find industries with persistently high, and increasing, R&D expenses.[303] This point is of considerable

---

299. Joel A C Baum and Helaine J Korn, "Dynamics of Dyadic Competitive Interaction" (1999) 20(3) *Strategic Management Journal* 251, 256 (hereafter Baum and Korn, "Dynamics of Dyadic Competitive Interaction").

300. Bernheim and Whinston, "Multimarket Contact and Collusive Behavior" (n 293) 21.

301. To date, the claim of mutual forbearance has not (yet) been made with tech giants, yet, it is sometimes heard that the Chinese firms equivalent to US big tech companies (known as BATX for Baidu, Alibaba, Tencent and Xiaomi) follow a coordinated approach, orchestrated by the central government.

302. Bingyong Zheng, "Multimarket Contacts under Imperfect Monitoring" (*SSRN*, March 28, 2019) <https://papers.ssrn.com/sol3/papers.cfm?abstract_id=3361592> accessed October 31, 2019.

303. Under accepted theory, firm-level asymmetries, industry growth, and innovation all make collusion difficult to sustain. On growth, see John Sutton who observes that "as the market gets bigger, the extra profit available to the firm with the best design, or the top performance product, rises and this induces all firms to invest more in capability building." Sutton,

relevance. Unless we assume that big tech firms' R&D investments are pure social waste, we should accept that they will translate in measurable output at some point, be it more output in one or more of the multiple markets subject to mutual forbearance or in entirely new markets. The upshot is that R&D makes mutual forbearance a finite equilibrium though one with an uncertain end. If they reason back, firms realize that they will not suffer punishment if they cheat in the short term, because R&D outputs will reconfigure markets in the long term.[304] Mutual forbearance is not impossible.[305] It is just not rational.

Moreover, a word can be said on the fact that mutual forbearance models have not been updated to assess the influence of big tech's key industry properties such as direct and indirect network externalities, increasing returns to adoption, tipping effects, switching costs, personalization, and stochastic uncertainty. Do these properties soften or strengthen tech giants' incentives to cheat, and with the sustainability of a collusive division of labor? Do they tilt the risk-reward calculus towards cheating, given the low costs and outsized payoffs of cheating?[306] And if big tech firms compete *for* the markets rather than *in* the markets, should we not logically conclude that tech giants' oligopolistic interaction is a succession of "finite" games for which the theory predicts a competitive equilibrium?

Mutual forbearance thus gives at best a superficial theory of big tech competitive behavior. Let us explore an alternative scenario.

Competing in Capabilities (n 113) 26. On asymmetries and innovation, see Marc Ivaldi, Bruno Jullien, Patrick Rey, Paul Seabright, and Jean Tirole, "The Economics of Tacit Collusion" Final Report for DG Competition, European Commission, March 2003, 66 ("collusion is easier to sustain in mature markets where innovation plays little role than in innovation-driven markets").

304. This is consistent with findings of competition in the "preparadigmatic" stages of an industry, for new designs, form factors, products, and services. See Teece, "Profiting from Technological Innovation" (n 133) 288 ("in the early stages of industry development, product designs are fluid, manufacturing processes are loosely and adaptively organized, and generalized capital is used in production. Competition amongst firms manifests itself in competition amongst designs, which are markedly different from each other. This might be called the preparadigmatic stage of an industry … Once a dominant design emerges, competition shifts to price and away from design").

305. Previous scholarly observations have established that mutual forbearance may constrain short-term competitive moves, like pricing or advertisement, but not "more fundamental research and development driven innovations." See Jayachandran et al, "The Theory of Multimarket Competition" (n 291).

306. McGrath talks of "huge premium." See McGrath, "Business Model: A Discovery Driven Approach" (n 228) 53.

b) Direct v Indirect Entry

The question before us now is: what alternative theory of oligopoly behavior in dynamic markets can give us a realistic model of big tech competition? We lay out such a theory, devise specifications, and then draw several competitive equilibrium hypotheses.

i) Framework: A Game of Entry

How do the tech giants compete if not as monopolists or tacitly colluding oligopolists? There are two non-exclusive possibilities to look at. One: big tech firms compete by late entry in known markets or existing industries. Scholars have produced many concepts to refer to this: "rivalry," "imitation," "commoditization," "catch-up," "me too," "copycat innovation," "fast follower," or "red ocean" competition. Common examples are Apple's decision to license the Mac OS in order to compete with Windows in PC markets; Microsoft's launch of Bing.com to challenge Google's dominance in search; or Amazon's attempt to build a smartphone OS to compete with Google's Android and Apple's iPhone.

Two: big tech firms compete by initial entry into new segments, markets, or industries. That is, tech giants pursue "new areas of demand,"[307] following strategies known as "competition fleeing," "competition avoidance," "differentiation," "disruption," "disintermediation," "segment founding," "competition against the non-consumption,"[308] or "blue ocean" competition. In the late 1990s, Amazon and Netflix both followed this path against Blockbuster. Amazon specialized in online DVD sales. Netflix developed online DVD rental. Closer to us is Google's decision to build the semi open-source OS Android for smartphones, distinct from Apple's proprietary ecosystem.

The many confusing labels produced by economic and management theorists to refer to both strategies does not support an inference of disagreement. In reality, most works converge on a model of firm strategic entry decision with two branches: one of "direct entry" and one of "indirect

307. Timothy F Bresnahan and Shane Greenstein, "Technological Competition and the Structure of the Computer Industry" (1999) 47(1) *The Journal of Industrial Economics* 1 (hereafter Bresnahan and Greenstein, "Technological Competition").
308. Clayton M Christensen, Mark W Johnson, and Darrell K Rigby, "Foundations for Growth: How to Identify and Build Disruptive New Businesses" (2002) 43(2) *MIT Sloan Management Review* 7 (hereafter Christensen, "Foundation for Growth") ("Companies seeking to create disruptive growth should first search for ways to compete against non-consumption").

entry". Often, however, it is hard to classify tech giants' choices as one or the other. Consider the following examples:

- The Apple II computer was a direct entry in the PC market, yet it was indirect to the extent that it was designed as a toy for children, unlike other machines designed to automate the office;[309]
- Google search was a direct entry in a market occupied by incumbents like Yahoo!, Lycos, Excite, Infoseek, and AltaVista. Yet Google's entry was indirect in that it entered with a new technology not exclusively based on analysis of keywords found on webpages, but on hyperlinks pointing to a given website;
- When Facebook launched in 2003, the product was conceived as an attack on incumbent social networks like Myspace or Friendster, yet it was indirect because it was not focused on music, and reserved to students;[310]
- Amazon entered the book retail business in 1996; it did so by attracting new customers on the basis of a new business model competing in fundamentally different ways from Barnes and Nobles.[311]

This problem of categorization, we believe, owes to a lack of standardized definitions in the literature. To waive confusion quickly, we will use here a narrow concept of direct entry that refers to the supply of perfect substitutes in existing product markets. And we will use the terminology indirect entry to refer to the supply of imperfect substitutes or of perfect complements in existing product markets.

Besides these controversies, we can draw from the above examples two regularities. First, no big tech firm launched by attacking another firm. Or put distinctly, nascent tech giants did not follow a direct entry strategy.[312] Second, tech giants' entry strategy has seemed to change once they became established. Subsequent big tech diversification choices display both direct and indirect entry strategies. Amazon tried direct entry in the search market

---

309. ibid 25 (also noting that Apple entered into handheld devices by positioning Newton as a computer, while Palm's pilot was a simple organizer).
310. David S Evans and Richard Schmalensee, "Failure to Launch: Critical Mass in Platform Businesses" (2010) 9(4) *Review of Network Economics* 1.
311. Markides, "Disruptive Innovation" (n 157) 20.
312. This is even true for Microsoft. Coordinated by IBM, Microsoft focused on operating system, peripherals, software applications, and computer languages. See Bresnahan and Greenstein, "Technological Competition" (n 307).

in 2003 with its subsidiary A9.com.[313] Google's current efforts in automotive focus on indirect entry into self-driving systems.

These observations raise two essential questions: what is big tech best entry strategy at launch? And what is big tech best entry strategy once established? Given that this book is an attempt to discuss the competitive behavior of existing large digital firms like the tech giants, we are essentially interested in the second question. We will however also consider the first question since hypothetical entry by a new tech firm (eg, US videoconferencing Zoom or Chinese firm TikTok) may discipline established big tech firms' behavior.

As a result, the question may be reformulated as follows: what is big tech firms' allocation criterion between direct and indirect entry, and is there a first and a second best strategy?

To answer this question, we must make additional specifications. At a high level, the direct versus indirect entry decision can be conceived of as a game in which tech giants and other firms are players seeking to maximize their best interest, that is growth. The payoffs from direct versus indirect entry differ in the following dimensions. When entry is indirect, segments, markets, or industries are new, and therefore "smaller."[314] Growth is limited. At the same time, indirect entry gives a relatively higher likelihood of critical mass than direct entry.[315] Growth is fast. Indirect entry creates relatively less exposure to incumbent counter-attack than direct entry.[316]

Besides, an established big tech firm will generally commit to indirect entry with less uncertainty (typically, it will concentrate on scaling young markets),[317] while a startup will tolerate a higher degree of uncertainty.[318]

---

313. See Amazon, Inc, Form 10-K, US SEC, 2003 referring to ("'A9.com', our wholly-owned subsidiary focused on search technology on www.A9.com"; "www.a9.com and www.alexa.com that enable search and navigation"; and "entry into search advertising: marketing and promotional services, such as sponsored search").

314. Christensen et al, "Foundations for Growth" (n 308) 24 ("every major, attractive market that exists today was at its inception small and poorly defined—just as the major growth markets of tomorrow are small and poorly defined today").

315. Bresnahan and Greenstein, "Technological Competition" (n 307) 21 ("Thus, a new platform will have the highest likelihood of attracting enough customers to get over the 'acceptance' hump if it serves a completely new, uncontested, segment of demand").

316. Baum and Korn, "Dynamics of Dyadic Competitive Interaction" (n 299) 254. "This *counter-competition* strategy anticipates further entry moves and attempts to keep potential entrants in check by signaling the ability to respond immediately to their aggressive actions in their home markets (Caves, 1984; Karnani and Wernerfelt, 1985; van Witteloostuijn and van Wegberg, 1992)." See also Tongur and Engwall, "The Business Model Dilemma of Technology Shifts" (n 158) 526.

317. Markides, "Disruptive Innovation" (n 156) 24.

318. In concrete terms, the more established the tech giant, the higher it will rely on NPV assessments. By contrast, the younger the tech giant, the least it will compute risk return payoffs.

Last, because of fragmented technological leadership amongst the tech giants, direct versus indirect entry choices are presumed neutral from both resources and capabilities perspectives.[319]

These parameters allow us to build relatively simple payoffs hypotheses in the form of a matrix reflecting tech giants' entry decisions. We also overcome the common uncertainty objection whereby risk-return payoffs are difficult to calculate in dynamic markets, and firm behavior cannot be conjectured. We simply follow Sutton's observation, trying to understand firms' "intangible judgment as to the pluses and minuses of going in a given direction."[320]

In pursuit of the task of identifying the equilibrium outcome of big tech competition, we look at the three following entry games: big tech v big tech, big tech v non big tech, and startup v big tech.[321]

ii) Big Tech v Big Tech

In our first game, an established big tech firm ("F1") competes with another big tech firm ("F2"). F1's choice of entry is primarily based on what will generate the highest growth, dependent on what the other firm chooses to do. The payoffs are illustrated in Table 4.4 below. Direct entry gives F1 a small fraction (25 percent) of F2's monopolized market (100 percent). Indirect entry gives F1 a monopoly fraction (100 percent) of a smaller market. To be conservative, and reflect the cost of uncertainty as compared to direct entry, we

---

319. See Bresnahan and Greenstein, "Technological Competition" (n 307). Anecdotal proof that big tech industries are under fragmented technological leadership can be found in the *US v Adobe* antitrust case, where several of the tech giants had concluded a horizontal collusive agreement to stop poaching each others' engineers.

320. A standard way to look at investments in dynamic markets would suppose the firms have access to a payoff function which is either deterministic or that introduces a stochastic element. The assumption is that the firm can (i) identify alternative states of the world and (ii) attach to them (at least) subjective probabilities. But as Sutton noted, investment decisions often are not following this idea: "the decision to build capability is one that is taken not on the basis of some explicit estimation of likely costs and benefits, but rather on the basis of a much more intangible judgment as to the pluses and minuses of going in a given direction." Instead, firms operate in a world of "Knightian uncertainty" (Sutton, *Competing in Capabilities* (n 113) 104). They do not calculate payoffs. They just try to head in the right direction.

321. We draw here inspiration from the simple game modeling found in John Kay, *Foundations of Corporate Success: How Business Strategies Add Value* (Oxford University Press 1993) and Avinash K Dixit and Barry J Nalebuff, *Thinking Strategically: The Competitive Edge in Business, Politics, and Everyday Life* (W.W. Norton & Company 1993).

Table 4.4 Payoffs (growth) Big Tech (F1) v Big Tech (F2)

		F2	
		Counter attack	Accommodate
F1	Direct entry	5 -5	25 -25
	Indirect entry	10 10	20 0

suppose that this market represents 20 percent of the market monopolized by F2.[322] In both instances of F1 entry, F2 has two choices: counter-attack or accommodate. Because of network effects, switching costs, and users' expectations, if F2 counter-attacks in response to direct entry, F1 only gets 5 percent of the market. If F2 counter-attacks in response to indirect entry, F1 and F2 split the new market in half, so they both grow by 10 percent.

We can see on Table 4.4 that F1 has no dominant strategy. By contrast, F2 has a dominant strategy, which is to counter-attack. The game tree on Figure 4.2 below shows the possible outcomes of the big tech v big tech game. Knowing F2's dominant strategy, F1 will choose its best strategy, namely indirect entry, even though it is not the decision that yields the

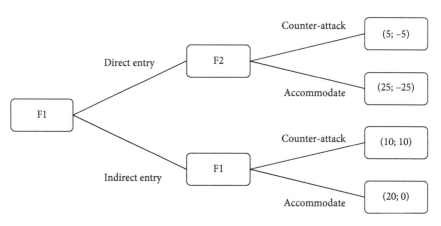

Figure 4.2 Game Tree: Big Tech (F1) v Big Tech (F2)

322. We are conservative in this estimation, because an unknown market represents more uncertainty than a known monopoly market.

highest possible growth in the game. In fact, it would be better for F1 to have F2 always accommodate.

This simplified representation of big tech v big tech competition has explanatory power. The low payoffs to direct entry might be illustrated by Apple's entry into the PC market, by Microsoft's entry in search against Google, or by Google+ entry into social networks against Facebook. By contrast, the high payoffs to indirect entry are illustrated by many tech giants' indirect entry into new markets like smartphone OS, payments, or cloud computing.

At an even finer level, the big tech's indirect entry equilibrium might be particularly relevant for specific firms like Amazon or Google. As seen in Chapter II, Amazon is perceived as a competitor to all tech giants and Google is reported to take on competition from most other tech giants. In sum, Amazon and Google might be the archetypal F1 and F2 firms in our game.

iii) Big Tech v non-Big Tech

Our second game features a big tech firm ("F") competing with a non-big tech firm ("NF"). We bring here one significant variation to the previous game by introducing an efficiency bias in favor of F.[323] This efficiency bias is the result of tech giants' control of digital information resources and capabilities.

In our new game, direct entry gets F a larger share of the NF market if the latter accommodates, namely 75 percent. If NF counter-attacks, however, it is again true that F gets a large share though it peaks at 50 percent. The efficiency bias also affects indirect entry. If NF counterattacks, F still gets 75 percent of the smaller market, that is 15 percent. NF gets the rest, that is 5 percent. The payoffs are illustrated on Table 4.5 below.

Table 4.5 Payoffs (growth) Big Tech (F) v non-Big Tech (NF)

		NF	
		Counter attack	Accommodate
F	Direct entry	50 / -50	75 / -75
	Indirect entry	15 / 5	20 / 0

---

323. Here, there is probably less fragmented technological leadership between F and NF. Put differently, F have superior technological capabilities and resources.

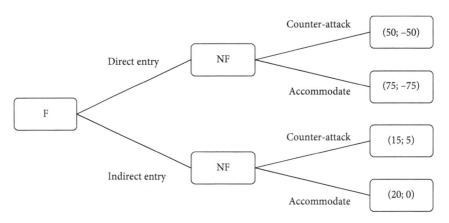

Figure 4.3 Game Tree: Big Tech (F) v non-Big Tech (NF)

What is the outcome of this second game? The game tree in Figure 4.3 above shows the possible outcomes of the big tech v non-big tech game. F's dominant strategy is direct entry. NF dominant strategy is to counter attack.

The direct entry equilibrium is supported by anecdotal evidence of non-big tech disruption like Apple's introduction of the iPhone or Microsoft's launch of Xbox. Also, our findings in Chapter II allow us to conjecture that a direct entry route is probably more realistic for firms like Apple, Amazon, and Microsoft, who count non-big tech firms as their closest competitors.[324] By contrast, Netflix or Facebook represent a lesser direct attack potential for non-big tech firms. To illustrate the point, recall for example, that Netflix and Facebook are the only tech giants that have not tried to build mobile devices, OS, or tablets.

iv) Startup (New Big Tech) v Big Tech

In a hypothetical game of startup ("S") entry, the modeling must be slightly amended because the growth payoffs are more difficult to estimate, even under extreme simplifications like the ones above. Moreover, the moves by the big tech firm ("F") are distinct. F can either compete with the startup or buy it.[325]

---

324. We also saw in Chapter II that Apple, Amazon, and Microsoft enjoy relatively stronger offensive positions than others (suggesting possible entry).
325. In line with Coasian theory, buying might be seen as an implicit admission that competing is too costly or risky.

The payoffs for this game is as follows. Each side has two possible moves, so there are four possible outcomes. Suppose S chooses direct entry. F can decide to compete, leading to a *poor* outcome for S (little growth) and a *good* outcome for F (large growth). These payoffs follow from the "kill-zone" idea whereby F can copy S's services easily (Facebook's copycat expropriation of Snapchat's features is the best example) and that established tech giants have committed sunk resources to their origin market (Amazon's Prime investments is the best example).[326] Alternatively, F decides to buy S. This leads to a *good* outcome for S, and a *poor* outcome for F which has to line up significant money for the purchase. Suppose now that S chooses indirect entry. F can respond with compete, which leads to the *best* outcome for both. F can also respond with buy, and the outcome for both is *acceptable* (reasonable growth). Note that the value that S gets from a F buy is lower here than under direct entry because the new market is smaller. Table 4.6 below gives the payoffs of the game.

We can see in Figure 4.4 that S has no dominant strategy. And F's best strategy is to compete. Knowing this, the strategic move that maximizes S's payoffs is an indirect entry.

Again, this game has explanatory power for the entry path followed by tech firms when they were startups. Amazon did not attack Walmart or Barnes & Nobles in physical retail. Instead, it built an e-commerce platform. And it may have predictive power for startups attacking big tech firms. Slack attacked Microsoft's moat in office software applications with a distinct approach to workplace collaboration centered on rich chat

Table 4.6 Payoffs (growth) Startups (S) v Big Tech (F)

		F			
		Compete		**Buy**	
	Direct entry	Poor		Good	
			Good		Poor
S		Best		Acceptable	
	Indirect entry				
			Best		Acceptable

326. See Business, "Into the Danger Zone: American Tech Giants are Making Life Tough for Startups" *The Economist* (San Francisco, June 2, 2018).

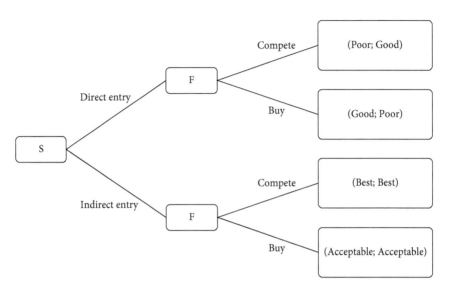

Figure 4.4 Game Tree: Startup (S) v Big Tech (F)

and communication services. Similarly, Zoom's Covid-19 attack against Microsoft and Cisco is not targeted at their origin market, but rather at peripheral videoconferencing services. And like Slack, Zoom opted for a different approach to gain critical mass: there is no need for an account, the service is free to use for up to forty minutes, and meetings can be accessed with a simple hyperlink or code.[327]

More generally, the game's results are broadly in line with received entrepreneurship theory. Steven Blank emphasizes that the "majority of startups are not going after known markets."[328] And, metaphorically, we may expect in the future to see startups use tech giants' markets more as "lighthouses" signaling market risk, than as kill zones.

327. Tom Warren, "Microsoft's Skype Struggles Have Created a Zoom Moment" (*The Verge* March 31, 2020) <https://www.theverge.com/2020/3/31/21200844/microsoft-skype-zoom-houseparty-coronavirus-pandemic-usage-growth-competition> accessed April 21, 2020.
328. Steven G Blank, *The Four Steps to the Epiphany—Successful Strategies for Products that Win* (K&S Ranch Consulting 2005) 12. Steven Blank argues that startups predominantly use three other entry options namely "Bringing a new product into a new market," "Bringing a new product into an existing market and trying to resegment that market as a low-cost entrant," or "Bringing a new product into an existing market and trying to resegment that market as a niche entrant."

v) Limitations

As all model-building exercises, our hypothetical games have shortcomings.[329] First, the big tech v big tech game does not explain observed patterns of direct entry like Microsoft's series of catchup acquisitions (eg, Jammer, Nokia, aQuantive, or Skype). That said, we cannot rule out that Microsoft did not fully display big tech properties when it executed catchup moves. The press is replete with stories on the Gates-Ballmer culture of zero sum game rivalry. This is distinct from the growth, exploration, and discontinuity-spirited model of big tech competition.

Second, our games say nothing of markets in which big tech firms make no entry. For example, Facebook never tried to build a mobile OS, a smartphone, or tablet hardware. This, we concede, is the single most important limitation of our model.

3. Implications

Big tech firms are moligopolies. Each of them enjoys a monopoly in its origin market. And direct entry in their market is more the exception than the rule, owing to tipping effects. Tech giants however practice exploration competition. Indirect entry is their favored strategy, especially in untipped markets. Direct entry remains however an option in non-big tech markets. In the long term, this process leads tech giants to compete as oligopoly.

The dynamic of indirect entry is a feature of moligopoly markets, not a bug. The pursuit of new areas of untipped market demand by indirect entry is a rational choice, compared to the hazards of zero sum game competition in tipped markets. In 1997, direct rivalry between Microsoft and Apple left the former with near monopoly and the latter in agony. The end result was a truce. Apple and Microsoft concluded an agreement whereby Apple would

---

329. Douglas A Melamed and Guido Calabresi, "Property Rules, Liability Rules, and Inalienability: One View of the Cathedral" (1972) 85(6) *Harvard Law Review* 1128 (observing two shortcomings of model building, namely "The first is that models can be mistaken for the total view of phenomena, like legal relationships, which are too complex to be painted in any one picture. The second is that models generate boxes into which one then feels compelled to force situations which do not truly fit"). Along these lines, skeptical readers might object that our hypotheses are not robust, because many real life firms do not neatly belong to the S, F, or NF groups (think of Adobe, IBM, Oracle, or SAP). But as we said previously, we use big tech as a mental model for any firm that displays most of the six features identified above at levels of significance.

abandon productivity software in exchange for cross-licensing and a USD 150 million investment that allowed it to reposition on hardware products. The rest is history.

Big tech firms have drawn the lessons. They do not need an oligopoly agreement to achieve superior payoffs through indirect entry, vertical competition, and differentiation. Unilateral decision-making alone leads to this realization. Consider Amazon and Netflix. The two firms were initially positioned on very close market segments, that is online video selling and rental.[330] In hindsight, we can now rationalize Amazon and Netflix's choices as deliberate differentiation strategies. Today, Amazon is essentially a gigantic online supermarket offering "earth biggest selection." By contrast, Netflix is an "Internet Television Network." Many more industry anecdotes carry the point.[331]

Of course, one may observe that the moligopoly equilibrium means less competition, not more. But this is only superficially true. The sequence of tech giants' indirect entry moves reconfigures and creates new channels of competition amongst them and other firms. While Amazon and Netflix were initially close competitors, today's main competitor to Netflix is Apple, which has made an indirect entry into original movies and TV by sinking large resources into the development of its own content. In turn, Disney and other non-big tech firms have joined the streaming war.

Moreover, the logic of exploration attracts indirect entry by tech giants in untipped product and service applications like cloud computing, payments, home assistants, TV, banking, podcasting, healthcare, self-driving cars, augmented and virtual reality. To stay with our Netflix and Apple example, it is not an unattractive conjecture to think that the augmented and virtual reality devices developed by firms like Microsoft and Facebook will at some point divert users' revenue from Netflix and Apple's content services. Such likely future competition is again evidence of moligopoly.

---

330. In its 10-K for 1998, Amazon describes itself as "the number one online video seller." And when Netflix enters around 2002, it describes itself in its 10K as "an online movie rental subscription service." We see here Netflix making indirect entry against Amazon and direct entry against Blockbuster and Walmart. Amazon, Inc, Form 10-K, US SEC, 1998. Netflix, Inc, Form 10-K, US SEC, 2003.

331. For example, in the cloud market, Microsoft is focused on business clients, while Amazon serves all stakeholders. Microsoft also uses proprietary solutions, while Amazon uses an open source Linux backend.

D. Conclusion: Voodoo Economics or Neoclassical Redux?

During a sabbatical in the United States, a neoclassical economist incredulous about the moligopoly hypothesis asked: how does the market competition in cloud remove monopoly power in online commerce? At the time, this prompted the idea that his question was typical of all that was wrong with existing economic models of industry structure and firm behavior: their inability to consider competition across markets holistically. On further inquiry, our intuition was wrong. The six properties model is inherently classical. Many established economists have previously built models of industry structure and firm behavior including growth,[332] flexibility,[333] or long termism.[334]

And yet, the wisdom of these economists has not carried the day, eclipsed by other works like the famous theory of multisided markets.[335] As a result, we remain today close to the situation that Michael Porter was describing in the early 1980s:

> another intriguing frontier for [industrial organization] research is the development of a model of the competitive interaction among multibusiness firms with business units in partly overlapping markets. Such overlapping complicates coordination among firms, but offers possibilities for threats, deterrence, and side payments that go beyond those possible when competition is on a market-by-market basis. In view of the prevalence of large, diversified firms in many markets, this avenue of research seems to hold great interest.[336]

---

332. See above, our reference to Baumol's work.
333. The idea of flexibility can be tied to Harvey Lebenstein's work on X inefficiency, see Chapter III above. Note also that some writers have claimed that Alfred Marshall, who is the father of price theory, was in reality an evolutionary economist. See J Stanley Metcalfe, "Alfred Marshall and the General Theory of Evolutionary Economics" (2007) 15(1) *History of Economic Ideas* 81.
334. See John R Hicks, "The Process of Imperfect Competition" (1954) 6(1) *Oxford Economic Papers*, 45 and in particular his reference to snatchers and stickers ("The entrepreneur who is mainly interested in seizing a quick profit (I shall call him the Snatcher) will have a high [weight for short period profit] relatively to his [weight for long period profit]; the one who is mainly interested in building up a steady business (I shall call him the Sticker) will have a high [weight for long period profit] relatively to his [weight for short period profit]. Such types of psychology are, I think, readily recognizable in the pages of business history").
335. This theory is reviewed in Chapter V.
336. Michael Porter, "The Contributions of Industrial Organization to Strategic Management" (1981) 6(4) *The Academy of Management Review* 617.

Moligopoly theory fills this gap. Big tech firms are players in a dynamic oligopoly game. Network externalities, increasing returns to adoption, tipping effects, and other properties of digital information industries give big tech firms a monopoly subject to a discontinuity constraint. The constraint renders the game *finite*. It is also stochastic, resulting in distinct and indeterminate payoffs, players, and rules in the next repetition of the game.[337] Like in a standard prisoner dilemma, the upshot is to create incentives for big tech firms to *cheat*—read compete—at each repetition.[338] But again because of network externalities, increasing returns to adoption, and tipping effects, the short-term dominant strategy for each big tech firm is to compete by indirect entry in untipped markets. They pursue exploration, flexibility, and growth strategies. When successful, the observed outcome is one of big tech diversification, and the reconfiguration of existing channels of competition.

The previous discussion makes it clear that all six properties work together toward a competitive equilibrium. Moligopoly may well be an economically efficient industry structure, in line with our findings in Chapter III—recall that we observed big tech output growth, suggesting allocative efficiency. Next, emerging work suggests that industry concentration in information technologies might just reflect the superior productivity of "superstar firms," suggesting productive efficiency.[339]

Moreover, moligopoly appears to lead to a substantial allocation of resources to invention. To that extent, our theory is consistent with the works of economists Joseph Schumpeter and Kenneth Arrow who, contrary to common belief, both concurred on the dynamic efficiency effects of large firms. Indeed, while readers certainly recall that Schumpeter stressed that monopoly is a driver of "creative destruction,"[340] they may not realize

---

337. Both in their origin market, segment, or industry and in the new market, segment, or industry.
338. And reduces the cost of punishments in future repetitions.
339. David Autor, David Dorn, Lawrence F Katz, Christina Patterson, and John Van Reenen, "The Fall of the Labour Share and the Rise of Superstar Firms" (2020) 135(2) Quarterly Journal of Economics 645.
340. Joseph A Schumpeter, *Capitalism, Socialism and Democracy* (Harper & Brothers 1942) 106: "What we have got to accept is that [the large-scale establishment or unit of control] has come to be the most powerful engine of that progress and in particular of the long-run expansion of total output not only in spite of, but to a considerable extent through, this strategy which looks so restrictive when viewed in the individual case and from the individual point of time. In this respect, perfect competition is not only impossible but inferior, and has no title to being set up as a model of ideal efficiency. It is hence a mistake to base the theory of government regulation of industry on the principle that big business should be made to work as the respective industry would work in perfect competition."

as clearly that Arrow considered diversification (in small projects) by "large corporations" to be the "only way" to minimize private disincentives to invest in the risky process of invention.[341]

At the same time, our moligopoly model is an emendation of Schumpeter and Arrow's appropriability theories. In our view, the rate and direction of tech giants' innovation investment is determined by the vulnerability of their monopoly positions and the inefficiency of large corporate organizations.[342] At its core, our theory of incentives to innovation is thus more one of inappropriability than of appropriability.[343] If this is right, then we may have reached a better understanding of the firm-level properties needed for the competitive system to achieve dynamic efficiency.

The antitrust and regulatory policy implications of this new theory are unclear. This is what we examine in the next chapters.

341. An often overlooked statement of Kenneth Arrow is the following: "The only way, within the private enterprise system, to minimize this problem is the conduct of research by large corporations with many projects going on, each small in scale compared with the net revenue of the corporation. Then the corporation acts as its own insurance company. But clearly this is only an imperfect solution." See Arrow, "Economic Welfare" (n 131) 616. In reality, contemporary economic literature may have overplayed the opposition between Schumpeter and Arrow, and downplayed that both converged on the appropriability or hedging of private firms' investments into innovation. In both Schumpeter and Arrow's views, a monopoly position or a large corporate organization could increase tolerance to risk bearing. By contrast, the contemporary literature stresses that Arrow had emphasized the ambiguous effects of appropriability, which on the one hand creates investments incentives, but also counter incentives due to the monopolist reluctance to cannibalize its preinvention monopoly. See Carl Shapiro, "Did Arrow Hit the Bull's Eye" in Josh Lerner and Scott Stern (eds), *The Rate and Direction of Inventive Activity Revisited* (University of Chicago Press 2012) 361–404. To our knowledge, Arrow never explained why conglomerates are an "imperfect solution."
342. In digital information industries, monopolies are not stable entitlements for the various reasons that have already been discussed.
343. This can be seen in our discussion of retained earnings in section B.4. When firms do not return profits to shareholders, which is what Schumpeterian appropriability is, they are *retaining* and *reinvesting* them in R&D and/or conglomerate activities. This is a subtle difference, but one of major significance.

V

Antitrust in Moligopoly Markets

The previous chapter has key implications for antitrust law and policy (hereafter, antitrust). And it is probably not those the reader would expect. Let us start from the triviality that the function of antitrust is to maintain competition in the digital economy. As we saw, in industries with increasing returns to adoption, economic forces discounted in received theory produce incentives on structural monopoly firms to compete by indirect entry in untipped markets, and avoid privately and socially inefficient rivalry in tipped markets.[1] A sound antitrust regime should thus preserve competitive pressure on monopoly firms in markets that have tipped and in which incentives to indirect entry have therefore disappeared. The concrete implications of this idea are both substantive and methodological. First, antitrust should focus on cases of harm to competition in markets that have tipped, and be more forgiving toward the leveraging of market power in untipped markets. Second, antitrust should adopt tools that allow fact finders to draw a finer line between tipped and untipped markets, complementing inferences of monopoly power drawn from structural methods of market definition and evaluation of market power.

A. Limits and Possibilities under Existing Antitrust Doctrine

This section discusses the flexibility of existing antitrust doctrine to cope with the distinctive features of digital industries, firms and markets seen in

---

1. Rivalry in tipped markets is privately inefficient because it is very costly for the direct entrant, and it is socially inefficient when there are increasing returns to scale due to rising marginal benefits.

Big Tech and the Digital Economy. Nicolas Petit, Oxford University Press (2020). © Nicolas Petit.
DOI: 10.1093/oso/9780198837701.001.0001

Chapter IV (2). To set the scene, we first recall what the function of anti-trust is (1).

1. Antitrust's Function: Rivalry

Antitrust seeks to deter or remove bad conduct that limits rivalry. It does so by a series of behavioral and structural proscriptions. In the United States, Sections 1 and 2 of the 1890 Sherman Act prohibit anticompetitive business coordination as well as monopolization and attempts to monopolize.[2] And in a preventive spirit, the Clayton Act of 1914, the Celler Kefauver Act of 1950, and the Hart–Scott–Rodino Antitrust Improvements Act of 1976 subject significant corporate mergers to preliminary review by the Federal Trade Commission ("FTC") or the Antitrust Division of the Department of Justice ("DoJ").[3] The European Union ("EU") competition law is a "modem restatement" of the Sherman Act, with variations and additions.[4]

---

2. See Sherman Act 1890, ss 1 and 2 (hereafter "The Sherman Act"). Section 1 provides "Every contract, combination in the form of trust or otherwise, or conspiracy, in restraint of trade or commerce among the several States, or with foreign nations, is declared to be illegal. Every person who shall make any contract or engage in any combination or conspiracy hereby declared to be illegal shall be deemed guilty of a felony, and, on conviction thereof, shall be punished by fine not exceeding $10,000,000 if a corporation, or, if any other person, $350,000, or by imprisonment not exceeding three years, or by both said punishments, in the discretion of the court." Section 2 provides "Every person who shall monopolize, or attempt to monopolize, or combine or conspire with any other person or persons, to monopolize any part of the trade or commerce among the several States, or with foreign nations, shall be deemed guilty of a felony, and, on conviction thereof, shall be punished by fine not exceeding $10,000,000 if a corporation, or, if any other person, $350,000, or by imprisonment not exceeding three years, or by both said punishments, in the discretion of the court."

3. The Clayton Antitrust Act 1914, s 7(1) and 7(2). Section 7(1) provides "No person engaged in commerce or in any activity affecting commerce shall acquire, directly or indirectly, the whole or any part of the stock or other share capital and no person subject to the jurisdiction of the Federal Trade Commission shall acquire the whole or any part of the assets of another person engaged also in commerce or in any activity affecting commerce, where in any line of commerce or in any activity affecting commerce in any section of the country, the effect of such acquisition may be substantially to lessen competition, or to tend to create a monopoly." Section 7(2) provides "No person shall acquire, directly or indirectly, the whole or any part of the stock or other share capital and no person subject to the jurisdiction of the Federal Trade Commission shall acquire the whole or any part of the assets of one or more persons engaged in commerce or in any activity affecting commerce, where in any line of commerce or in any activity affecting commerce in any section of the country, the effect of such acquisition, of such stocks or assets, or of the use of such stock by the voting or granting of proxies or otherwise, may be substantially to lessen competition, or to tend to create a monopoly." See also The Celler-Kefauver Anti-Merger Act 1950 and The Hart-Scott-Rodino Antitrust Improvements Act 1976.

4. James A Rahl, "International Antitrust" (1981) 79(4) *Michigan Law Review* 982.

Articles 101 and 102 of the Treaty on the Functioning of the EU ("TFEU") prohibit, on the one hand, anticompetitive agreements, concerted practices, and decisions by associations of undertakings, and on the other hand, abuses of a dominant position.[5] Council Regulation (EC) No 139/2004 requires firms to notify corporate concentrations of European dimension to the European Commission ("EC") for prior approval.[6] Both antitrust regimes have in common the use of legal tests of purpose or effect to establish liability. Since the 1970s in the United States and the 2000s in Europe, antitrust liability has increasingly been established in terms of effects. Similarly, presumptive rules of inference of purpose and effect—called "*per se*" rules in the United States or "by object" restrictions in Europe—have receded across most areas, with a culmination in merger law, and an exception in cartel law. In all other areas, antitrust doctrine has elaborated sophisticated

5. See Consolidated Version of the Treaty on the Functioning of the European Union [2012] OJ C/326/01 (hereafter "TFEU"). Article 101(1) TFEU provides "The following shall be prohibited as incompatible with the internal market: all agreements between undertakings, decisions by associations of undertakings and concerted practices which may affect trade between Member States and which have as their object or effect the prevention, restriction or distortion of competition within the internal market, and in particular those which:

(a) directly or indirectly fix purchase or selling prices or any other trading conditions;
(b) limit or control production, markets, technical development, or investment;
(c) share markets or sources of supply;
(d) apply dissimilar conditions to equivalent transactions with other trading parties, thereby placing them at a competitive disadvantage;
(e) make the conclusion of contracts subject to acceptance by the other parties of supplementary obligations which, by their nature or according to commercial usage, have no connection with the subject of such contracts".

Article 102 TFEU provides "Any abuse by one or more undertakings of a dominant position within the internal market or in a substantial part of it shall be prohibited as incompatible with the internal market in so far as it may affect trade between Member States. Such abuse may, in particular, consist in:

(a) directly or indirectly imposing unfair purchase or selling prices or other unfair trading conditions;
(b) limiting production, markets or technical development to the prejudice of consumers;
(c) applying dissimilar conditions to equivalent transactions with other trading parties, thereby placing them at a competitive disadvantage;
(d) making the conclusion of contracts subject to acceptance by the other parties of supplementary obligations which, by their nature or according to commercial usage, have no connection with the subject of such contracts."

6. Council Regulation (EC) 139/2004 on the control of concentrations between undertakings (EC Merger Regulation) [2004] OJ L24/1 (hereafter "EC Merger Regulation 2004"). Article 4 provides "Concentrations with a Community dimension defined in this Regulation shall be notified to the Commission prior to their implementation and following the conclusion of the agreement, the announcement of the public bid, or the acquisition of a controlling interest."

burden-shifting rules, which have attracted considerable commentary from legal scholars and practitioners.

But let us return to our initial topic. Antitrust's rivalry function operates more as an admonition than as an injunction. Losses in rivalry are neither a necessary nor sufficient condition of antitrust liability. Antitrust, in particular in the United States, tolerates conduct or transactions that limit rivalry upon proof or presumption of consumer welfare benefits. In past decades US agencies have cleared horizontal mergers in heavily concentrated industries like home appliances, agrochemical products, or airlines. Similarly US and EU antitrust implicate specific categories of firm conduct without a need to show adverse effect on rivalry. Conventional examples are horizontal price fixing[7] or, in the European Union, minimum resale price maintenance ("RPM") in vertical contracts between sellers and buyers.[8]

And yet, antitrust's main function remains the protection of rivalry.[9] Courts in the United States and the European Union have historically

---

7. *United States v Socony-Vacuum Oil Co* [1940] 310 US 150.

8. RPM is not prohibited *per se* in the United States, but presumptively unlawful in the EU. See Article 4 of Commission Regulation (EU) No 330/2010 on the application of Article 101(3) of the Treaty on the Functioning of the European Union to categories of vertical agreements and concerted practices [2010] OJ L102/1 (excluding from exemption "the restriction of the buyer's ability to determine its sale price, without prejudice to the possibility of the supplier to impose a maximum sale price or recommend a sale price, provided that they do not amount to a fixed or minimum sale price as a result of pressure from, or incentives offered by, any of the parties").

9. In *United States v Philadelphia National Bank* [1963] 374 US 321, the Supreme Court read Congressional intent as follows: "it seems to the Court that the Congress, by the use of the word 'competition', intended to preserve free and open markets wherein the rivalry of the commercial firms, in the same line of endeavor, for the patronage of the common customer, would be demonstrated by a business atmosphere where free purchasers and free sellers, under no obligation to buy, and under no obligation to sell, would enter into contracts of purchase and sales (or service contracts) because of the actual inducements offered, such as quality of product, terms, delivery and the many other factors which make for good business relations, having in mind the peculiar situations, facts and circumstances which govern the particular transactions between individuals or organizations." In *Citizen Publishing Co v United States* [1969] 394 US 131, the Supreme Court applied the *per se* prohibition rule to a joint operating agreement between two newspapers noting that "All commercial rivalry between the papers ceased." In *United States v E I du Pont de Nemours & Co* [1956] 351 US 377, the majority quoted a report of the Attorney General's National Committee to Study the Antitrust Laws stating "In the interest of rivalry that extends to all buyers and all uses, competition among rivals within the industry is always important." In his dissent in *Associated Press v United States* [1945] 326 US 1, Justice Murphy refused to consider that the conduct in discussion "necessarily" restrained trade, because a "brisk rivalry" had erupted between the defendant and a major competitor. In *Meritor*, the Third Circuit supported a treatment of exclusive dealing under the rule of reason, on the ground, amongst others "that competition to be an exclusive supplier may constitute 'a vital form of rivalry' which the antitrust laws should encourage." See *ZF Meritor LLC v Eaton Corp* [2012] 3d Cir No 11-3301. See also, *Fabrication Enterprises, Inc v*

insisted on the maintenance of "pluralistic competition."[10] In *Alcoa*, Learned Hand powerfully captured the key role of rivalry: "immunity from competition is a narcotic, and rivalry is a stimulant, to industrial progress."[11] In Europe, the case law has made rote reference to the protection of the "structure of competition."[12]

The problem with this is that there is not only one, but several "ecologies of competition."[13] Rivalry is only one of them. And it need not be the dominant one. The point can be made with a metaphor. Most marathon runners endure demanding training and lifestyle habits to be competitive.[14] And yet, competition is just one motivation amongst a universe of others, including self-esteem, life meaning, fitness, longevity, and personal goal achievement. In short, marathon runners are competitive regardless of rivalry.

Hygenic Corp [1994] SDNY 848 F Supp 1156 ("'industrial' rivalry which is encouraged under antitrust principles") and *Menasha Corporation, Plaintiff-appellant, v News America Marketing In-store, Inc, and News America Marketing In-store Services, Inc, Defendants-appellees* [2004] 7th Cir 354 F3d 661 ("competition for the contract is a vital form of rivalry, and often the most powerful one, which the antitrust laws encourage rather than suppress").

10. See Kenneth S Carlston and James M Treece "Antitrust and the Consumer Interest" (1966) 64(5) *Michigan Law Review* 777.

11. *United States v Aluminum Co of America* [1945] 2d Cir 148 F2d 416.

12. *Europemballage Corporation and Continental Can Company Inc v Commission* [1973] ECLI:EU:C:1973:22, § 26 ("[t]he provision is not only aimed at practices which may cause damage to consumers directly, but also at those which are detrimental to them through their impact on an effective competition structure, such as is mentioned in article 3 (f) of the treaty"); *British Airways plc v Commission* [2003] ECLI:EU:T:2003:343, § 311 ("Since Article 82 EC is aimed at penalising even an objective detriment to the structure of competition itself … BA's argument that there is no proof of damage caused to consumers by its reward schemes cannot be accepted"); *Post Danmark A/S v Konkurrencerådet* [2015] ECLI:EU:C:2015:651, §§ 70–72 ("As regards, in the second place, the serious or appreciable nature of an anticompetitive effect, although it is true that a finding that an undertaking has a dominant position is not in itself a ground of criticism of the undertaking concerned … the conduct of such an undertaking may give rise to an abuse of its dominant position because the structure of competition on the market has already been weakened … In addition, since the structure of competition on the market has already been weakened by the presence of the dominant undertaking, any further weakening of the structure of competition may constitute an abuse of a dominant position"); *Gencor Ltd v Commission* [1999] ECLI:EU:T:1999:65, § 314 ("In the light of the seventh recital in its preamble, which states that 'a new legal instrument should therefore be created … to permit effective monitoring of all concentrations from the point of view of their effect on the structure of competition in the Community', the principal objective of the Regulation is to monitor market structures, and not the behaviour of undertakings which is essentially to be controlled only under Articles 85 and 86 of the Treaty.)"

13. James G March, "Exploration and Exploitation in Organizational Learning" (1991) 2(1) *Organizational Science* 71.

14. Sima Zach, Yan Xia, Aviva Zeev, Michal Arnon, Noa Choresh, Gershon Tenenbaum, "Motivation Dimensions For Running a Marathon: A New Model Emerging from the Motivation Marathon Scale (MOMS)" (2017) 6(3) *Journal of Sport and Health Science* 302.

So the real question is this: should we abandon, or at least radically alter, traditional antitrust principles modeled on rivalry in digital markets?[15] The answer is yes. Protecting rivalry is not perforce socially beneficial in industries with increasing returns to adoption.[16] Let us contemplate this idea for a minute. Markets with increasing returns to adoption exhibit tipping effects (some also talk of *winner take all* or *winner take most* effects). Even apart from the fact that most inputs to production at some point exhibit decreasing returns,[17] industries with increasing returns to adoption on the demand side lead to what Theodore Levitt disapprovingly called "a technological inevitability of monopoly and oligopoly" in 1952 in relation to electronics and atomic energy.[18]

Besides, enforcing rivalry is costly. An example drives the point home. Consider a breakup of Facebook in four social networks. Each social network receives an initial allocation of 25 percent of Facebook's user base, and is free to technologically and commercially diversify. The logic of network effects means that as soon as one social network lures a marginal user from one of its competitors, it should benefit again from a winner take all effect. Economic theory suggests that these effects might not take much time to materialize.

Moreover, governmental actions expended to move from a monopolized to a rival market structure are not trivially uncostly. Compatibility remedies in digital industries are likely to impose significant enforcement costs. This is because enforcement of rivalry in network effects markets is akin to forcing a square peg into a round hole. Once the square is in the hole, it must be kept under pressure to remain in it. Rivalry-spirited remedies like breakups, interoperability, or data-sharing measures thus entail recurring

---

15. This is a reformulation of the question phrased by FTC Commissioner Christine Wilson in a speech titled "Promoting Sound Policies for the Next Decade." See Christine Wilson, "Promoting Sound Policies for the Next Decade" (Federal Trade Commission, March 26, 2019) <https://www.ftc.gov/news-events/audio-video/audio/promoting-sound-policies-next-decade-ftc-commissioner-christine-wilson> accessed January 10, 2020.

16. Nicholas Economides, "Competition Policy in Network Industries: An Introduction" (2004) *NET Institute Working Paper No 04-24*, Center for Law and Business Research Paper No 03-10 (hereafter Economides, "Competition Policy") ("in industries with significant network externalities, under conditions of incompatibility between competing platforms, monopoly may maximize social surplus").

17. Hal R Varian, "Use and Abuse of Network Effects" (2017) SSRN Working Paper <https://papers.ssrn.com/sol3/papers.cfm?abstract_id=3215488> accessed December 4, 2019.

18. Theodore Levitt, "The Dilemma of Antitrust Aims: Comment" (1952) 42(5) *American Economic Review* 895.

costs, owing to the ongoing necessity to repress nascent feedback loops.[19] Placing industries under permanent government supervision is alien to the "discrete" nature of antitrust enforcement.[20]

More importantly, in digital industries, monopolies might be self-depleting. As the preceding analysis in Chapter IV suggests, untipped areas of demand where rivalry is low attract indirect entry, in turn shifting economic value to new markets. Owing to network externalities, tipping effects and increasing returns to adopters (manifest in user lock-in and switching costs), firms seldom compete by direct entry against an incumbent platform. Instead, firms try to bypass, leapfrog, envelop, or re-segment established markets. One story commonly heard in the Silicon Valley is that Microsoft's "take-no-prisoner approach" to OS and productivity software in the 1990s forced innovators to focus efforts on disruptive Internet applications like search engines and social networks.

Of course, one might object that antitrust is empirical, so reform is not needed for new technologies with increasing returns to adoption. Study of antitrust history appears to bring confirmatory evidence. In the twentieth century, industries like transportation, finance, food and drugs, and communications have gone through massive waves of technological progress without need to reform our antitrust laws. This logic is, however, only superficially attractive. Antitrust has undergone indirect reform. Sector-specific regulation has been adopted to inject competition in airlines, banking, pharmaceutical products, or telecommunications. In all four cases, regulatory reform accompanied business model innovation—low cost carriers and "hub and spoke" networks in airlines—or technological progress— automated teller machines in banking, biotechnology in food and drug, and cellular connectivity and networks limiting natural monopolies in telecommunications.[21] Both in the United States and the European Union, adoption of sector-specific regulation led to a revisitation of the role of antitrust, and doctrinal adjustments. In the United States, the Supreme Court mostly limited admission of antitrust claims in regulated industries.[22]

---

19. Economides, "Competition Policy" (n 16) 14 ("it is possible to have situations where a breakup of monopoly into two competing firms of incompatible standards reduces rather than increases social surplus").
20. See Justice Scalia Dissent, in *Eastman Kodak Co v Image Technical Servs., Inc* [1992] 504 US 451.
21. See OECD, "Regulatory Reform and Innovation" <https://www.oecd.org/sti/inno/2102514.pdf> accessed December 4, 2019.
22. *Verizon Communications, Inc v Law Offices of Curtis V Trinko, LLP* [2004] 540 US 398 ("But just as the 1996 Act preserves claims that satisfy existing antitrust standards, it does not create new

In the European Union, the courts have envisioned a bigger, complementary role for antitrust, giving confidence to antitrust decision-makers that they could act in regulated industries as a matter of priority.[23]

The conclusion is that industries with increasing returns to adoption where potentially beneficial monopolies compete by indirect entry in untipped areas of demand ought to receive special treatment under antitrust law. The question is: what margin of flexibility is there in our antitrust regimes to accommodate these specificities?

2. Antitrust Flexibility?

This subsection discusses whether antitrust law in the United States (a) and European Union (b) provide flexibility by asking under what circumstances its doctrine has tolerated deviation from rivalry. Given the uncertainty around the antitrust lawmakers' intent, it seems appropriate to focus on statutory language and substantive court precedents.

a) US Antitrust Law

With exceptions, US antitrust doctrine has recognized that rivalry is not to be pursued at all costs. This evolution is more the byproduct of a general economic conception of the law, than a deliberate recognition of the social welfare properties of increasing returns to adoption in digital markets.

Since the 1970s, a desire to avoid "efficiency" losses in a broad sense has guided the application of US antitrust law, resulting in a degree of doctrinal agnosticism toward industry structure. Though inferences of specific allocative (price) efficiency losses might be drawn from market power situations in which rivalry is limited, this might not necessarily be the case. Moreover, concentrated market structures might also produce productive (cost) and dynamic (innovation) efficiency benefits. Accordingly, US courts have laid to rest the 1960s judicial attitude that sought to ensure "the maintenance of

---

claims that go beyond existing antitrust standards; that would be equally inconsistent with the saving clause's mandate that nothing in the Act 'modify, impair, or supersede the applicability' of the antitrust laws"). *Credit Suisse Securities (USA) LLC v Billing* [2007] 551 U.S. 264 ("there is a serious risk that anti-trust courts, with different non expert judges and different nonexpert juries, will produce inconsistent results ... Allowing an antitrust lawsuit would threaten serious harm to the efficient functioning of the securities market").

23. See eg, Nicolas Petit "Circumscribing the Scope of EC Competition Law in Network Industries? A Comparative Approach to the US Supreme Court Ruling in the Trinko Case" (2004) 3(4) *Journal of Network Industries* 347.

markets with a large number of small players," and that treated with inhospitality any conduct or transaction that reduced rivalry.[24]

Section 2 cases show this neatly. Established doctrine holds that successful monopolization is not sufficient to find a violation of antitrust law. Under *United States v Grinnell Corp*, the basic standard for monopolization requires proof of "the willful acquisition or maintenance of that power as distinguished from growth or development as a consequence of a superior product, business acumen, or historic accident."[25] And predatory pricing law requires not only an elimination of rivalry, but also proof of allocative efficiency-reducing recoupment by means of supra-competitive prices (or output restriction) to establish unlawful monopolization.[26] In *Olympia*, Judge Posner noted in relation to Section 2 that in the late 1970s "the emphasis of antitrust policy shifted from the protection of competition as a process of rivalry to the protection of competition as a means of promoting economic efficiency."[27]

In merger law too, rivalry is no longer a first order concern. Federal courts and government agencies ignore the 1963 *Philadelphia National Bank* presumption whereby mergers between rivals in concentrated industries are presumptively unlawful without proof of anticompetitive effects.[28] Only a subset of rivalry-reducing mergers to monopoly, or near monopoly, are deemed categorically problematic. When they are, the rationale is not the protection of rivalry. The rationale seems to be an absence of productive efficiency gains due to the general property of decreasing returns.[29]

It is also important to stress that US doctrine manifests a concern for dynamic efficiency, and that this has legitimized deviation from market rivalry. In its 2003 Opinion in *Trinko* the Supreme Court held that "to

---

24. Herbert Hovenkamp, *The Antitrust Enterprise—Principle and Execution* (Harvard University Press 2008) 208 (hereafter Hovenkamp, *Antitrust Enterprise*).
25. *United States v Grinnell Corp* (1966) 384 US 563.
26. *Brooke Group Ltd v Brown & Williamson Tobacco Corp* [1993] 509 US 209 ("whether the claim alleges predatory pricing under § 2 of the Sherman Act or primary-line price discrimination under the Robinson-Patman Act, two prerequisites to recovery remain the same. First, a plaintiff seeking to establish competitive injury resulting from a rival's low prices must prove that the prices complained of are below an appropriate measure of its rival's costs").
27. *Olympia Equipment Leasing Company, Alfco Telecommunications Company, and Paula Jeanne Feldman v Western Union Telegraph Company* [1986] 7th Cir 797 F2d 370.
28. *United States v Philadelphia National Bank* [1963] 374 US 321.
29. William J Kolasky and Andrew R Dick, "The Merger Guidelines and the Integration of Efficiencies into Antitrust Review of Horizontal Mergers" (2010). See Hovenkamp, *Antitrust Enterprise* (n 24) 211.

safeguard the incentive to innovate, the possession of monopoly power will not be found unlawful unless it is accompanied by an element of anti-competitive conduct."[30] Similarly, US coordinated conduct law treats most vertical restraints under the rule of reason, on the ground that contractual reductions in intrabrand price rivalry "encourag[e] retailers to invest in tangible or intangible services."[31]

The broader point is that influenced by the common law process, US courts have reassessed antitrust doctrine in light of progress in economic theory. There is no reason to believe it cannot adapt to the specific non-rival economics of digital markets. In its 1992 Opinion in *Eastman Kodak v Image Technical Services, Inc, et al*, the Supreme Court relied on the new economics of customer lock-in to reject the neoclassical price theory assumption that firms cannot charge supra-competitive prices in secondary good markets absent market power in the primary good market.[32] The Supreme Court "instructed lower courts to judge parties' economic theories by how well they described 'actual market behavior'."[33] The District Court followed the invitation in the 1999 *US v Microsoft* case. One can discern there an application of Brian Arthur's theory—whereby the "small events of history" can "tip" markets outcomes in the presence of "positive feedback" loops[34]—to fight against Microsoft on the ground that it had "retarded, and perhaps altogether extinguished, the process by which [two] middleware technologies could have facilitated the introduction of competition into an important market."[35] And in 2019, the Supreme Court in *Ohio, et al v American Express Company* relied on the economic theory of multisided markets to raise the burden of proof on plaintiffs in vertical restraints cases involving transactions platforms like credit cards or online commerce markets.[36]

---

30. *Verizon Communications, Inc v Law Offices of Curtis V Trinko, LLP* [2004] 540 US 398.
31. *Leegin Creative Leather Products, Inc v PSKS, Inc* [2007] 551 US 877. See also *Continental TV, Inc v GTE Sylvania, Inc* [1977] 433 US 36.
32. *Eastman Kodak Co v Image Technical Services, Inc et al* [1992] 504 US 451. Note that Kodak actually promotes a radical rivalry-based vision of antitrust policy.
33. See Rudolph R Peritz, *Competition Policy in America* (Oxford University Press 2001) 318.
34. See W. Brian Arthur, "Competing Technologies, Increasing Returns, and Lock-In by Historical Events" (1989) 99(394) *The Economic Journal* 394, 127.
35. *United States v Microsoft Corp* [1999] CA 98-1232, Court's Findings of Fact, 206. Microsoft was held guilty of unlawful exclusion of non-rival firms by "impeding another form of innovation that bore the potential to diminish the applications barrier to entry," capable to bring rivalry in the monopoly "market for Intel-compatible PC operating systems."
36. *Ohio v American Express Co* [2018] 585 US. Commentators remain divided on whether the Supreme Court drew the correct normative implications of the theory of multisided markets.

Though US courts' permeability to economics makes doctrine adaptive, it might at the same time lead to indeterminate antitrust policies in digital markets. This is due to two reasons. The first is that economic study of digital markets has not (yet) produced unequivocal normative prescriptions. In short, learning takes time. The second is more general, and has to do with the fact that use of economics in antitrust renders enforcement facts-driven. This is a challenge in new industries which exhibit emergent patterns of behavior that cannot be rationalized by recourse to prior knowledge or experience. This uncertainty might plausibly explain the moderate levels of antitrust intervention by US government agencies in digital markets. To date, US agencies have not brought any Section 1 or 2 charges against big tech firms, and only a few merger enforcement proceedings have been started against them.[37]

And yet, the US doctrinal paradigm has two key features that are particularly accommodating for a non–rivalry-based special antitrust regime. First, there is no categorical inhospitality toward monopoly positions, leaving aside the particular case of merger to monopoly. Second, incentives matter. As much as new entrants, successful firms with a dominant share must entertain an opportunity to appropriate the profits of innovation.

b) EU Competition Law

Contrary to US law, the trend of EU competition doctrine has been to give greater weight to rivalry, at least until recent years. This trend is arresting if one considers US and EU antitrust's initial positions. Unlike US antitrust's historical focus on small firm protection, European competition law initially did not object to industry concentration.[38] This is apparent from the language of the competition rules found in the 1957 Treaties—still in force today. The 1957 Treaties do not prohibit dominance in itself, just its abuse.[39]

---

37. Department of Justice, "Justice Department Requires Google Inc. to Develop and License Travel Software in Order to Proceed with Its Acquisition of ITA Software Inc." (2011) *Press Release Number 11-455* <https://www.justice.gov/opa/pr/justice-department-requires-google-inc-develop-and-license-travel-software-order-proceed-its> accessed December 4, 2019.

38. See Pinar Akman and Hussein Kassim, "Myths and Myth-Making in the European Union: The Institutionalization and Interpretation of EU Competition Policy," (2010) 48(1) *Journal of Common Market Studies* 111 (hereafter Akman and Kassim, "Myths and Myth-Making in the European Union").

39. For about a decade, the rules on anticompetitive unilateral conduct were not enforced. See David J Gerber, *Law and Competition in Twentieth Century Europe: Protecting Prometheus* (Oxford University Press 2001) 356.

And the 1957 Treaties did not establish a merger control system, in spite of the fact that merger rules had just been strengthened in the United States. Pinar Akman has rightly noted that post-war European economic policy was essentially about growing domestic firms and promoting business efficiency through consolidation, not protecting rivalry.[40]

But EU doctrine soon departed from this position, incrementally making rivalry the public policy of competition rules. In unilateral conduct cases, the EU courts have subjected dominant firms to strict behavioral constraints, including duties of assistance to rivals.[41] The courts have repeatedly established liability on the ground that rivals' "access to the market" is abusively made "more difficult" by the dominant firm.[42] Doctrine has allowed agencies to establish dominant firm liability at minimal levels of rival foreclosure, insisting that "competitors should be able to compete on the merits for the entire market and not just for a part of it."[43] And judicial dicta have held that there is no need to show "serious or appreciable" effects to establish abuse.[44]

Merger law has undergone a similar evolution. The policy of the EU Commission is here more relevant than courts' decisions which are inherently rare in this area of the law.[45] The Commission has shown heightened concern for the protection of rivalry in contemporary cases. In *Dow/DuPont*, the Commission prohibited a merger amongst large biochemical producers on the ground that the industry would feature one less firm that was vertically integrated into most or all significant aspects of research and development.[46] The Commission's assessment of a post-merger loss to innovation competition paid no heed to the possibility of new divisions

---

40. Akman and Kassim, "Myths and Myth-Making in the European Union" (n 38).
41. EU courts consider that a dominant firm is under a "special responsibility" not to impede competition. The rationale for this is an inference that in a market with a dominant position, the "degree of competition is already weakened". See *NV Nederlandsche Banden-Industrie Michelin v Commission* [1983] ECLI:EU:C:1983:313 (*Michelin I*), § 70; *British Airways plc v Commission* [2007] ECLI:EU:C:2007:166, § 66; *Post Danmark II v Konkurrencerådet* [2015] ECLI:EU:C:2015-651, § 26.
42. *Post Danmark II v Konkurrencerådet* [2015] ECLI:EU:C:2015-651, § 42.
43. *Tomra Systems ASA and others v Commission Case* [2012] ECLI:EU:C:2012:221, § 42.
44. *Post Danmark II v Konkurrencerådet* [2015] ECLI:EU:C:2015-651, §§ 72–73. See also the statement "fixing an appreciability (de minimis) threshold for the purposes of determining whether there is an abuse of a dominant position is not justified" (§§ 73–74).
45. Firms seldom challenge prohibition decisions because the slow timing of annulment proceedings makes it unlikely to revitalize a forbidden transaction.
46. Commission Decision of 27.3.2017 declaring a concentration to be compatible with the internal market and the EEA Agreement [2017] C(2017) 1946 final (Case M.7932—Dow/DuPont).

of labor toward innovation within the merged firm. By contrast, the EU Commission is yet to clear a merger on grounds of procompetitive efficiencies, even though the possibility has been theoretically envisioned in policy documents.

Last, an examination of EU law toward the dynamic efficiency effects of market power shows a preference for rivalry. The statutory language of Article 102 TFEU empowers agencies and courts to correct monopoly power in action by regulating dominant firms' prices, in violation of the Schumpeterian wisdom whereby it is the perspective of profits that drives investments in innovation.[47] Similarly, in coordinated conduct law, EU regulations enunciate a *quasi per se* prohibition rule against resale price maintenance, that denies the defendant an opportunity to invoke the free rider problem that deters dealer investment as justifications for their conduct.

In doctrine, reverse *Trinko* is law in the EU.[48] In 2007, the General Court dismissed as implausible Microsoft's defense that a duty to license interoperability protocols to rivals would reduce incentives to innovate. And in its 2018 decision in *Google Android*, the Commission rejected Google's alleged objective justification to its tying of the Search app and Chrome with Play Store, on the ground that "Google would still have benefitted from a significant stream of revenue from search advertising, given its market shares on PCs."[49]

Overall, it is easy to see that, in EU antitrust law, rivalry trumps efficiency. Granted, several recent cases in unilateral and coordinated conduct law might change the orientation of contemporary doctrine. In 2017, the

47. Admittedly, cases have been rare, and circumscribed to exceptional circumstances in which prices show a "persistent" and "significant" difference from other industries. See *Autortiesību un komunicēšanās konsultāciju aģentūra/Latvijas Autoru apvienība (AKKA/LAA) v Konkurences padome* [2017] ECLI:EU:C:2017:689, § 55.
48. We borrow this expression from Michael Kades who used it in relation to the *Amex* case. See Michael Kades, Hal Singer, Randy Picker, and Chris Sagers, "Will the Supreme Court's Amex Decision Shield Dominant Tech Platforms From Antitrust Scrutiny?" (*Forbes*, July 18, 2018) <https://www.forbes.com/sites/washingtonbytes/2018/07/18/antitrust-enforcement-of-dominant-tech-platforms-in-the-post-american-express-world/> accessed December 4, 2019.
49. European Commission Press Release, "Antitrust: Commission Fines Google €3.34 Billion for Illegal Practices Regarding Android Mobile Devices to Strengthen Dominance of Google's Search Engine" (July 18, 2018) <https://ec.europa.eu/commission/presscorner/detail/en/IP_18_4581> accessed December 4, 2019. See also Commission Decision of 18 July 2018 relating to a proceeding under Article 102 of the Treaty of the Functioning of the European Union (the Treaty) and Article 54 of the EEA Agreement (2018) C(2018)4761 final (Google Android Case AT.40099).

Intel judgment placed a lesser focus on the protection of rivalry.[50] In a case about discount schemes, the upper EU court endorsed the idea that dominant firms can lawfully exclude less efficient rivals.[51] In coordinated conduct cases, judicial dicta have also occasionally recognized that competition might efficiently lead to reduced rivalry through concentration.[52] And in other cases, the court has upheld theories of liability that affirmed violations of the law when firms jointly reduced market uncertainty, not strictly rivalry.[53]

The full implications of these decisions for the future of EU competition policy remain debated. To focus on *Intel*,[54] it is unclear whether the EU court's greater acceptance of efficiency cuts beyond the special case of dominant firm pricing conduct.[55] In other areas of unilateral conduct law, precedents are still closer to what could be described as the intellectual equivalent of the anti-concentration spirit of the 1960s doctrine of the Supreme Court in the United States.[56]

Wherever the case law goes, the single most important difference between US and EU law is this: the European approach to competition enforcement signals less faith in the tendency of monopoly markets to self-correct short term deviations from rivalry, and more trust in the ability of government to restore it.

---

50. *Intel Corp v European Commission* [2017] ECLI:EU:C:2017:362.

51. This policy had been previously promoted by the EU Commission in a 2009 policy paper. However, the Court did not act upon Advocate General Nils Wahl's invitation to declare that efficiency is the aim of competition law. See Opinion of Advocate General Wahl in *Intel v Commission* [2016] ECLI:EU:C:2016788 "given its economic character, competition law aims, in the final analysis, to enhance efficiency."

52. *Competition Authority v Barry Brothers* [2008] ECLI:EU:C:2008:643, § 35. To declare an agreement anticompetitive, the court considered that absent the coordination, the firms "would have ... no means of improving their profitability other than by intensifying their commercial rivalry or resorting to concentrations."

53. Though the loss in rivalry resulting from uniform oligopoly pricing seemed the underlying concern. See *John Deere Limited v Commission* [1998] ECLI:EU:C:1998:256, § 90.

54. See Nicolas Petit, "Intel and the Rule of Reason in Abuse of Dominance Cases" (2018) 43(5) *European Law Review* 728.

55. The court explicitly mentioned at § 136 of its judgment that "Article 102 TFEU prohibits a dominant undertaking from, among other things, *adopting pricing practices* that have an exclusionary effect on competitors considered to be as efficient as it is itself."

56. See *Utah Pie Co v Continental Baking Co* [1967] 386 US 685. The Supreme Court held that any adverse effect on a competitor, including on a quasi-monopolist, could support a finding of liability under US antitrust law. See Ward S Bowman, "Restraint of Trade by the Supreme Court: The Utah Pie Case" (1967) 77 *Yale Law Journal* 70.

c) Summation

Neither US nor EU antitrust laws refer to rivalry as their explicit function. At the same time, the common feature of the "conduct" component found in the US and EU statutory proscriptions is to address rivalry suppressing conduct, that is "conspiracy," "agreement," "abuse," and "monopolization."

Close examination of US and EU doctrine however highlights differences that reflect distinct conceptions of the role of rivalry in antitrust. The European Union appears to take a more uncompromising view of rivalry as the main function of competition rules. By contrast, US antitrust more readily tolerates deviation from rivalry toward monopoly, on the ground of conjectured efficiency gains.[57] As we shall see, US antitrust might thus be more adaptable to our normative theory of antitrust for digital markets than EU law.

This issue is not unimportant. Together with other factors, the stance of antitrust doctrine toward rivalry might plausibly explain observable outcomes in the economy in general, and in the digital economy in particular. In the United States, an antitrust policy environment historically accommodating to deviations from rivalry might have contributed to the rise of "superstar firms" and higher economic dynamism. At the same time increased concentration has lent credence to suspicion of capture of regulatory agencies by corporate interests, in particular in the digital industry.[58]

Bottom line? In the European Union, firms—especially large ones—must be more vigilant than they are in the United States. With other factors like national market divisions and high regulatory intensity, this might have played a contributory role to weakened entrepreneurialism and investments in the European Union, absence of large firm creation in digital markets, and complaints from politicians of weak EU industrial policy in a globalized world. At the same time, industry concentration has been contained, and prices of goods and services have decreased in a broad number of markets.[59] Also, there has been less critique of regulatory capture in the EU. But this ought not to mean that EU competition policy is less corporatist. The EU's plaintiff-friendly competition rules have drawn to Brussels gigantic

57. This tendency has long been diagnosed, and criticized. See Harry S Gerla, "Restoring Rivalry as a Central Concept in Antitrust Law" (1996) 75(2) Nebraska Law Review 209.
58. See Luigi Zingales, "Towards a Political Economy of the Firm" (2017) 31(3) *Journal of Economic Perspectives* 113.
59. Thomas Philippon, *The Great Reversal: How America Gave up on Free Markets* (Harvard University Press 2019).

regulatory wars amongst US firms. To fix the idea, recall that Microsoft, once a defendant before the European Union, was the initial complainant in the first European abuse of dominance case against Google.[60]

B. Defining Antitrust Doctrine
for Digital Markets

To date, antitrust doctrine does not offer a substantive framework apt to capture the harms and efficiencies, both static and dynamic, which are idiosyncratic to digital markets. We believe the research set out in previous chapters sketches a path forward. The main function of antitrust in digital markets should not be to promote rivalry—it cannot be presumed to be socially efficient—but a *pressure* equivalent to it. In particular, by maintaining pressure on monopoly rents, antitrust creates an uncertainty equivalent to rivalry that produces powerful incentives on established big tech firms to invent new products and introduce market-shifting innovations. Antitrust remedies should be introduced to promote uncertainty in big tech firms' monopoly markets when it has disappeared as a result of bad conduct and structural market failures or features like network effects, increasing returns to adoption, and market tipping.

Our proposed theory of antitrust in digital markets has two clear implications. First, antitrust should focus on cases of harm to competition in digital markets that have *tipped.* One way to create pressure on incumbent big tech firms without losing the efficiency of large market shares consists in limiting the monopoly rents in the tipped market, so as to incentivize them to pursue indirect entry and competition in untipped markets.

Second, antitrust should be agnostic toward conduct or transaction by both incumbent and new firms in *untipped* markets, unless there is a suspicion that the incumbent firm will "turn off" the pressure created by the new market.[61] Antitrust neutrality toward incumbent and new firms

---

60. Kelly Fiveash, "Microsoft Pulls out of Google Antitrust Actions" (*ArsTechnica,* April 22, 2016) <https://arstechnica.com/tech-policy/2016/04/microsoft-drops-antitrust-complaint-against-google-in-brussels/> accessed December 18, 2019.

61. See Nicholas Economides, "Public Policy in Network Industries" (2006) *New York University Law and Economics Working Papers 78,* 21 ("there should be no presumption that anti-competitive actions are responsible for the creation of market share inequality"; the "but for world against which actions in network industries are to be judged should not be perfect competition but an environment of significant inequality and profits"; "firms do not reach their high output

is based on several reasons that will be later elaborated on: there are docu-
mented efficiencies to lateral integration; errors might be less costly for the
large firm; and integration of innovation by large firms and exit of small
firms is a common mode of operation in many industries (creative content,
movies, etc).

Why is our theory superior? After all, we are not the first observer to call
for a special antitrust doctrine for digital markets. Mark Lemley and David
McGowan have argued that "[a]rguments based on network effects may
suggest that the law must rethink the rationality of behavior considered
unlikely under neoclassical theory, such as predation in antitrust jurisprudence, and address new risks not considered under models based on declining returns."[62] With more limited ambitions, Howard Shelanski has argued
in favor of a differentiated approach to competition on the Internet, that
"might sometimes take the form of less aggressive antitrust intervention"
but that "might also take the form of new emphases, approaches, and remedies."[63] At the other end of the spectrum, Geoffrey Manne and Joshua
Wright rely on the error-cost framework to caution against inefficient
intervention, and stress that concerns of substantial risk of false positives are
not lesser in the digital economy, much to the contrary.[64]

The limitations of most of these works is that they do not confront three
hard problems that are either created, or exacerbated, by digital markets.
The first is: how to distinguish competitive and anticompetitive strategy
when there is evidence of monopoly market shares? The second is that
the monopoly market share might be socially efficient in the presence of
increasing returns to adoption on the demand side.[65] And the third is that
the monopoly market share often arises in a *new* market as a result of indirect entry, including by incumbent firms. Put differently, monopoly firms
change.

In supporting a stricter antitrust regime toward tipped markets and more
moderate antitrust toward untipped markets our framework avoids the risk

and market domination by exclusion, coercion, tying, erecting barriers to entry or any other
anti-competitive behavior"; "no anticompetitive activity has led firms to this equilibrium").

62. Mark A Lemley and David McGowan, "Legal Implications of Network Economic Effects"
(1998) 86 *California Law Review* 479.
63. Howard A Shelanski, "Information, Innovation and Competition Policy for the Internet"
(2013) 161(6) *University of Pennsylvania Law Review* 1963.
64. Geoffrey A Manne and Joshua D Wright, "Google and the Limits of Antitrust: The Case
Against the Antitrust Case Against Google" (2011) 34 *Harvard Journal of Law and Public Policy* 1.
65. And costly compatibility/interoperability remedies in rapidly moving markets.

of decisional mistakes in unknown environments, that is "causing harm from interfering in complex businesses that are both rapidly moving and not fully understood."[66] Moreover, controlling market outcomes over structures safeguards the efficiencies linked to increasing returns to adoption on the demand side, and opens up opportunities for entrants in tipped markets from which established tech firms attempt to pivot away. Last, our theory also meets the traditional concern of over-deterrence of error cost theory against antitrust enforcement.[67] In particular, by allowing the monopoly firm to compete in untipped markets, it avoids antitrust being turned into a rent-seeking device amongst competitors. And at any rate, over-deterrence concerns should not excessively clutter enforcement activity, because the evidence suggests that firms disregard antitrust risk as a cost of doing business, possibly due to tipping effects. As a friend once put it: the existence of monopoly billionaires suggests that antitrust is not a limit. More seriously, neither Microsoft, nor Netflix, has been discouraged to bundle new products to dominant offerings, even when they were in the middle of antitrust proceedings.

To date, antitrust doctrine has tangentially referred to the specificities of digital markets. In its 2004 decision against Microsoft, the EC stressed "the externalities ... which tend to insulate network markets once they have tipped."[68] In *Microsoft/Skype*, the EU General Court relativized the relevance of market shares in the assessment of mergers in markets "characterised by short innovation cycles" like the fast-growing "consumer communications sector."[69] And in *Heinz/Beechnut*, the US Court of Appeals for the District of Columbia suggested that product innovation claims were implausible in the baby food industry "given the old-economy nature of the industry."[70] However, these have remained isolated pronouncements.

With the following subsections, we hope to give confidence to courts, agencies, and antitrust practitioners in their ability to fashion tractable antitrust doctrine for digital markets. To assist them, we illustrate the implications

---

66. David S Evans, "Antitrust Issues Raised by the Emerging Global Internet Economy" (2008) 102(4) *Northwestern University Law Review* 285.
67. Frank H Easterbrook, "Limits of Antitrust" (1984) 63 *Texas Law Review* 1.
68. Commission Decision relating to a proceeding under Article 82 of the EC Treaty (Case COMP/C-3/37.792 Microsoft) [2004] C(2004)900 Final, § 946.
69. See *Cisco System Inc and Messagenet SpA v European Commission* [2013] ECLI:EU:T:2013:635.
70. *FTC v HJ Heinz C, et al* [2001] DC Cir No 00-5362.

of the theory with a series of retrospective case studies, taken from US and EU interventions against large tech firms.

C. Essential Role of Antitrust in Tipped Markets

Antitrust can play an essential role by dissipating monopoly rents in tipped markets. There are two alternative ways to do this. One involves direct antitrust control of the exercise of monopoly power (1). The other involves indirect antitrust limitation of monopoly rents (2). In addition to this, antitrust might adopt a presumption against horizontal mergers in tipped markets (3).

1. Direct Antitrust Control on Exercise of Monopoly Power?

Antitrust law might prohibit the exercise of monopoly power in digital markets that have tipped. Concretely, antitrust law might declare unlawful levels of profitability that reflect monopoly rents. There are, however, doctrinal limitations to this. US law leaves firms free to enjoy the "fruits" of monopoly power. A firm with market power does not violate the antitrust laws by increasing price or otherwise extracting supra-competitive rents from trading partners. To the contrary, as the Supreme Court put it in *Trinko*, "the mere possession of monopoly power, and the concomitant charging of monopoly prices, is not only not unlawful; it is an important element of the free-market system."[71] The focus of US antitrust is on tactics, not outcomes.[72]

By contrast, EU law allows more direct control of dominant firms' unfair prices or trading conditions. However, while the prohibition of exploitative behavior by dominant firms remains on the books, the EU courts have struggled to define administrable standards of application. In *United Brands*, the

---

71. *Verizon Communications Inc v Law Offices of Curtis V Trinko, LLP* [2003] 540 US 398. Long before *Trinko*, it was understood that one that gains a monopoly by "skill foresight and industry" is permitted to reap the fruits of the monopoly. See *United States v Aluminum Co of America* [1945] 2d Cir 148 F2d 416.
72. David S Evans and Keith N Hylton, "The Lawful Acquisition and Exercise of Monopoly Power and Its Implications for the Objectives of Antitrust" (2008) 4(2) *Competition Policy International* 203.

court defined as abusive a price that "has no reasonable relation to the economic value of the product supplied,"[73] increasing rather than reducing legal
uncertainty.[74] The result is that the prohibition has been *de facto* abandoned
by non-enforcement (or confined to exceptional circumstances). Exploitative
monopoly conduct has been mostly addressed under sector specific regulation.

Compelling normative reasons counsel against a relaxation of current
doctrinal limits to the direct control of exercise of monopoly power in
digital markets. The first is definitional. Economic theory has not devised
a method that separates monopoly profits from increased profits attribut-
able to superior bargaining power, and that difficulty does not disappear
in network effects markets.[75] When the antitrust fact finder looks at profit
levels, obstinate problems prevent distinguishing monopoly rents—revenues
that exceed the long-term cost of capital—from quasi rents—revenues in
excess of short-term total costs.[76] The 1992 Supreme Court Opinion in
Kodak provides an obvious example. The court inferred from the evidence
before it that a producer of photocopiers and micrographic equipment both
enjoyed and had "exerted" monopoly power in the aftermarkets for parts
and services "where locked in customers, high information costs, and discriminatory pricing limited and perhaps eliminated any long term loss"
for the producer due to lack of substitution in the primary market.[77] In his
dissent, Justice Scalia reduced the issue to a "brief perturbation in competitive conditions," outside of the core business of the antitrust laws.[78] This

73. See *United Brands v Commission* [1978] ECLI:EU:C: 1978:22, § 250. See also § 251 ("This
    excess could, *inter alia*, be determined objectively if it were possible for it to be calculated
    by making a comparison between the selling price of the product in question and its cost of
    production which would disclose the amount of the profit margin").
74. See *Scandlines Sverige AB v Port of Helsingborg* [2004] Case COMP/A568/D3, § 226 where the
    Commission struggled with the *United Brands* test, and had to elaborate on it. The Commission
    considered that the "determination of the economic value of the product/service should also
    take account of other non-cost related factors, especially as regards the demand-side aspects of
    the product/service concerned."
75. Academics have thus often employed monopoly power for both situations, recognizing a "non
    usual" deviation from the term of art. See Benjamin Klein, Robert G Crawford, and Armen A
    Alchian, "Vertical Integration, Appropriable Rents, and the Competitive Contracting" (1978)
    21(2) *The Journal of Law & Economics* 299.
76. See Roger G Noll, "'Buyer Power' and Economic Policy" (2005) 72(2) *Antitrust Law
    Journal* 589.
77. *Eastman Kodak Co v Image Technical Services, Inc et al* [1992] 504 US 451.
78. In his dissent, Justice Scalia—citing himself a dissent from judge Posner—did not disagree on
    the possible existence of consumer harm in the aftermarkets ("Though that power can plainly
    work to the injury of certain consumers, it produces only 'a brief perturbation in competitive
    conditions—not the sort of thing the antitrust laws do or should worry about'").

disagreement over what constitutes short-term versus long-term profits, and the indeterminacy assumed by both the majority and the dissent in *Kodak* leaves antitrust enforcement subject to "I know it when I see it" guesses as to what are monopoly rents, and conditions outcomes in antitrust enforcement to decision-makers' unstated preferences as to the time value of economic surplus.[79] The risk is to transform antitrust into a "vehicle for fixing contracts that might be unfair."[80] One example of use of antitrust to redress unfair contracts in digital markets is the German antitrust agency 2017 *Facebook* decision, which deemed abusive the dominant social network "take it or leave it" privacy policies toward users, in disregard of evidence showing that firms without market power apply similar policies to their users.[81]

Of course, the law could incorporate a presumption whereby tipped markets suggest (long-term) monopoly rather than (short-term) quasi rents. But then a fatal impracticality arises: a presumption of monopoly rent does not tell antitrust agencies and courts the alternative price, output, or privacy level that would dissipate the monopoly rent, and incentivize exit toward untipped markets by the dominant defendant. This difficulty is compounded in digital markets, where outputs supplied to users are often unpriced.

The second reason is ideological. A policy of direct control of monopoly profits tends to signal antipathy toward dynamic efficiency. Both conservative and progressive antitrust thinkers (including enforcers) agree that monopoly profits reward innovative investments. They (only) disagree on their estimation of the probability that short-term entry will bring about market share and rent erosion that limits consumer harm. This explains the weak support toward direct control of monopoly rents amongst US and EU antitrust experts. It is quite telling that in the United States—where the law does not prohibit exploitative abuses—neo-structuralist advocates of legislative reform have not suggested importing the EU model.

---

79. Understandably, many US courts have subsequently declined to apply *Kodak*.
80. Hovenkamp, *The Antitrust Enterprise* (n 24) 101.
81. The German antitrust agency held that: "Due to market power users cannot avoid the processing of their data" (§ 385). It disposed of the argument that Facebook did not enjoy market power by considering that users' demand is less elastic in relation to data extraction than to price increases in general (§ 382). Note, however, that this counter-argument says nothing of whether demand for social networks is inelastic due to a market power situation of the kind apprehended by antitrust law. See Administrative Decision under Section 32(1) German Competition Act (GWB) [2019] 6th Decision Division, B6-22/16.

2. Indirect Antitrust Control on Exercise of Monopoly Power?

In light of the problems involved in directly controlling profit levels, an alternative approach to dissipate monopoly rents might consist in reducing the size of tipped markets or, to be precise, the share of output going to the dominant firm in a tipped market. An often overlooked normative application of the economic theory of multisided markets is indeed that adjustments to a firm's price structure (not levels) can lead to *reduced* output. Though most cases like *Amex* in the United States and *Cartes Bancaires* in the European Union respectively stress how vertical and horizontal restraints might pro-competitively increase output in multisided markets,[82] antitrust law could equally use the theory to work toward the promotion of pro-competitive decreases of dominant firms' output in tipped markets. After all, antitrust doctrine ordinarily sets constraints on the way firms structure, rather than set, their prices. Together, these observations might invite consideration of effective, legitimate, and practical remedies that limit monopoly rents in digital markets that have tipped. Let us look closer.

a) Multisided Markets Theory

The theory of multisided markets was developed in papers by Bernard Caillaud and Bruno Jullien,[83] Jean-Charles Rochet and Jean Tirole,[84] Mark Armstrong,[85] and others published in the early 2000s. The best presentation of the theory begins with the idea that in some markets, profit-seeking manufacturers who wish to remain competitive attempt to get two (or more) separate groups of users "on board." The case of console and video games producers is often used as illustration. In this market, no developer would produce games for a console that has no gamers. Likewise, no gamer would buy a console if there were no compatible games (and thus developers).

---

82. See *Ohio v American Express Company (AMEX)* [2018] 585 US __, 16 ("There is no such evidence in this case. The output of credit-card transactions grew dramatically from 2008 to 2013, increasing 30%"). *Groupement des cartes bancaires v European Commission* [2014] ECLI:EU:C:2014:2204.

83. Bernard Caillaud and Bruno Jullien, "Chicken & Egg: Competition among Intermediation Service Providers" (2003) 34(2) *The RAND Journal of Economics* 309.

84. Jean-Charles Rochet and Jean Tirole, "Platform Competition in Two-Sided Markets" (2003) 1(4) *Journal of the European Economic Association*, 990.

85. Mark Armstrong, "Competition in Two-Sided Markets" (2006) 37(3) *The RAND Journal of Economics* 668 (hereafter Armstrong, "Competition in Two-Sided Markets").

According to multisided markets theory, a solution to this "chicken and egg" problem is for the console manufacturers to "choose a price structure and not only a price level."[86] This decision is not benign in terms of output. In their 2006 paper, Rochet and Tirole find that for a given (total) price level, output can increase "by charging more to one side and less to the other relative to what the market delivers."[87] One side (gamers) also known as the "money side"[88] will be called to cross-subsidize the participation of the other side (developers), also referred to as the "subsidy side."[89] In such settings, the price structure is "non neutral." As Michael Katz puts it, the volume of transactions realized on a platform varies with the individual pricing values charged on both sides (p1 and p2) though the total platform price, (p1+p2) remains constant.[90] In addition—and of equal importance— Rochet and Tirole argue that users must be prevented from negotiating away the platform's price structure through Coasian bargaining or thanks to monopoly power.[91] Unfortunately, this last limb of the definition has been somewhat neglected in subsequent scholarship.[92]

The logical implication of the theory of multisided markets is that the share of output from which a firm extracts a monopoly rent on a tipped market can be reduced by adjustments to its price structure.

A simple fictional example carries the point. Let us start with a basic situation. Suppose there is only one nightclub in town.[93] The owner wishes

86. Jean-Charles Rochet and Jean Tirole, "Two-Sided Markets: A Progress Report" (2006) 37(3) The RAND Journal of Economics 645, 648 (hereafter Rochet and Tirole, "Two-Sided-Market"). See also Daniel F Spulber, "Solving the Circular Conundrum: Communication and Coordination in Internet Markets" (2010) 104(2) Northwestern University Law Review 537, (Spulber talks of a "circular conundrum").
87. Rochet and Tirole, "Two-Sided-Market" (n 86) 648.
88. Console manufacturers typically earn royalties from each game that is sold. These royalties, ultimately paid by gamers, appear to make up the bulk of console manufacturers' earnings. See notably Julia Wood, "Teardown of Xbox, PS4 Reveal Tight Margins" (CNBC, November 27, 2013) <http://www.cnbc.com/id/101230904> accessed December 4, 2019.
89. A developer kit for Sony's new PS4 console usually costs $2,500 and is sometimes given to developers free of charge. See Colin Campbell, So How Much Does it Cost to Develop for Playstation 4? (Polygon, July 24, 2013) <http://www.polygon.com/2013/7/24/4553842/so-how-much-does-it-cost-to-develop-for-playstation-4> accessed December 4, 2019.
90. Michael L Katz, "Platform Economics and Antitrust Enforcement: A Little Knowledge is a Dangerous Thing" (2019) 28(1) Journal of Economics & Management Strategy 138.
91. Rochet and Tirole, "Two-Sided-Market" (n 86) 649. In other words, there must be transaction costs preventing "the bilateral setting of prices between buyer and seller."
92. See Dirk Auer and Nicolas Petit, "Two-Sided Markets and the Challenge of Turning Economic Theory into Antitrust Policy" (2015) 60 The Antitrust Bulletin 4.
93. See Armstrong, "Competition in Two-Sided Markets" (n 85) (supporting our choice of night-clubs as a good example noting that nightclubs are "sometimes far enough away from others that the monopoly paradigm might be appropriate").

to maximize total participation. She knows that men gain more from inter-
acting with women than vice versa.[94] If she sets an equal fee of USD 10 for
both groups, the nightclub will attract fifty participants of each group. But if
she cuts the fee for female patrons to USD 5, she will attract eighty of them.
Given this new situation, the platform owner can raise the fee for males to
USD 15, minimizing participation loss in this group to only forty-five. We
observe here that demand by females is quite elastic (-1.2), while demand by
males is quite inelastic (-0.2).[95] But more importantly, we see that when the
nightclub changes the price structure, participation moves from 100 to 125.
Moreover, though the change does not modify the total price level (USD
10 + USD 10 = USD 15 + USD 5), total revenue grows from USD 1,000
to 1,075. Under certain cost conditions, the change in the price structure
might be both privately and socially efficient.

Now, assume a benevolent social planner perceives that the nightclub is
serving too many users, and wants to reduce output. One way to do this
consists in changing the nightclub's price structure. There are many other
methods available, rather than simply regulating the admission price of the
nightclub. Assume the female patrons' reduction took the form of a free
drinks ticket worth USD 5. The social planner might issue an executive
order barring free drinks coupons beyond USD 2. Assuming the parameters stay the same, the effective fee for female patrons is now USD 8. Given
the elasticity of demand by females (-1.2), this leads to a reduction of female
participation of 22.5. For simplicity, we say twenty-two which leads to fifty-
eight females attending, and a corresponding decrease in male participation
below forty-five.

b) Normative Applications

The normative applications of the theory of multisided markets are pretty
clear. First, antitrust might specify doctrines that *directly* regulate the relative
price levels set by the platform itself in tipped markets. Second, antitrust
might *indirectly* influence the relative price levels charged on the various
sides of the platform by allowing third party users to wield market power
through horizontal merger or coordination. Third, antitrust law might also
indirectly undermine the price structure by restricting vertical restraints

---

94. ibid.
95. We use standard metrics for the price elasticity of demand. When the value is between -1 and
    0, the demand is inelastic. When the value is below -1, the demand is elastic. When the value
    is 0, the demand is perfectly inelastic.

adopted by the platform that limits user bypass. Let us review these three options in turn.

i) Direct Regulation of Price Levels

Direct regulation of price levels is alien to the free market.[96] And it would be indeed antithetic to antitrust's consumer welfare DNA to use it to *increase* prices directly. Given this, the best approach is to develop indirect antitrust rules that lower the output of a tipped market on which a dominant firm extracts a monopoly rent. So what type of indirect rules can antitrust develop to reduce output on tipped markets?

ii) Market Power Conduct by Users on the Money (and Subsidy) Side

Under our second option, antitrust might select the rule of reason to assess market power conduct by users on the inelastic (money) side of a tipped market. Conversely, antitrust might select a stricter *per se* or *quasi per se* prohibition rule to treat market power conduct by users on the elastic (subsidy) side. Let us review both alternatives.

To reduce the dominant firm's output, US and EU antitrust doctrine might allow users on the inelastic side to adopt market power enhancing conduct like horizontal agreements, joint ventures, or trade associations. To illustrate, consider the Supreme Court Opinion in *Broadcast Music, Inc v Columbia Broadcasting System* (hereafter, "*BMI*")[97]—a case that predates multisided market theory. In *BMI*, 20 thousand artists had granted to collecting societies ASCAP and BMI the right to negotiate blanket licenses to copyrighted musical materials with television network CBS and two hundred affiliated stations. CBS challenged the arrangement under Section 1 of the Sherman Act as illegal price fixing.[98] In a multisided market perspective, CBS might be analogized to a platform with three different sides, that is content producers, affiliated stations, and viewers. Though the case does not give an estimate of CBS's market power—CBS was described as a "giant of the world in the use of music rights"—the Opinion correctly refused to

---

96. The arguments here are similar to the points made previously in relation to antitrust control of exploitative conduct by monopolists, but different in that they do look at reducing prices, but also at increasing them.
97. *Broadcast Music, Inc v Columbia Broadcasting System, Inc* [1979] 441 US 1.
98. CBS would have apparently preferred that all music be made available at standard per use rates within negotiated categories of use.

treat copyright owners' concerted action as price fixing, and dealt with it under the rule of reason.[99] Had *BMI* been decided in 2019, the Opinion would have provided a useful illustration of our theory.

An alternative approach consists in using strict legal rules against users' coordination on the subsidy side. The aggressive logic developed in the European case *Expedia Inc* provides an illustration.[100] Here, two firms had formed a joint venture to create an online travel agency. On that market, platform intermediaries called Global Distribution Systems ("GDS") charge fees to airlines, bus, and rail suppliers on the money side, and pass through benefits to online travel agents on the subsidy side (and sometimes retail travel agents). Had the joint venture been allowed to proceed, this might have resulted in growing platform output, in a market already very concentrated. Though not adopted in a GDS multisided market context, the EU court's judgment held that no *de minimis* defenses can be raised against a price fixing arrangement covering 2 percent of a market. Price fixing, said the court, is by "nature and independently of any concrete effect" an "appreciable restriction of competition" prohibited under Article 101(1) TFEU.[101] Obviously, *Expedia Inc* makes no sense in a standard economic context. But it does in a multisided market context. For indeed, market power enhancing conduct on the subsidy side of a tipped market may result in excessive adoption of platform services.

US and EU doctrine seem more hospitable to the first alternative than the second. In the United States, the Supreme Court has considerably reduced the scope of its Opinion in *United States v Socony-Vacuum Oil Co*[102] in which it held necessary to treat under the *per se* rule any combination which tampers with the price system.[103] In EU case law, horizontal

---

99. *Broadcast Music, Inc v Columbia Broadcasting System, Inc* [1979] 441 US 1, 5.

100. *Expedia, Inc v Autorité de la concurrence and Others* [2012] ECLI:EU:C:2012:795.

101. ibid § 37.

102. *United States v Socony-Vacuum Oil Co* [1940] 310 US 150.

103. Most commentators underline that *Socony* remains good law, yet they stress that the Supreme Court has practically brought derogations by permitting defendants to raise rule of reason type arguments. See for instance, Ernest Gellhorn and William Kovacic, *Antitrust Law and Economics in a Nutshell* (4th edn, West Academic Publishing 1994) 195 who note: "Since the late 1970s, with the notable exception of Maricopa, the Court's horizontal pricing jurisprudence has demonstrated a willingness to modify the traditional *per se*/rule of reason dichotomy. At a minimum, BMI and NCAA authorize courts to expand the characterization component of the traditional *per se* standard and explicitly entertain a fuller assessment of defendants' claims that the price-setting behavior has nontrivial procompetitive merit". See also *In re Sulfuric Acid Antitrust Litig* [2012] 703 F3d 1004, 1012 (7th Cir 2012) ("The plaintiffs retreat to the general language in the Socony–Vacuum Opinion, an Opinion 72 years old

coordination is no longer treated under a quasi *per se* prohibition standard. In *Groupement des cartes bancaires v European Commission*, the court adopted a restricted scope requirement by holding that the notion of a restriction of competition by object "can be applied only to certain types of coordination between undertakings which reveal a sufficient degree of harm to competition."[104] The court made express reference to multisided markets theory in its Opinion.

Perhaps most important, however, is that doctrine should accept to modulate the standard of antitrust liability depending on whether defendants are active on the subsidy or the money side. To date, the case law does not allow for such an approach.

iii) Anticompetitive Restraints that Limit Users' Power to Set Prices
A third constraint on monopoly rents in tipped markets consists in using antitrust *indirectly* to limit restraints of users' power to set prices. To see this, consider the example of payment card systems. Payment card platforms adopt various rules to enforce their preferred price structure.[105] One such rule is the no surcharge rule. Payment card platforms like Visa, MasterCard, or American Express prohibit merchants to pass through to cardholders the transaction fees that they owe to the payment card platform as a result of a payment card being used. This no surcharge rule allows payment cards platforms to keep control of the price structure, and raise their own output against that of rival platforms or payment instruments (eg, cash). By contrast, if the merchant is free to shift part or all of the costs to the other party, it overturns the price allocation decided by the platform which may be procompetitive. This simple logic explains why "pro competition" antitrust and regulatory instruments have restricted use of no surcharge rules.[106] Note, however, that the point that we want to make here is slightly different.

---

and showing its age"). In this case, Judge Posner proceeded to examine the many relaxations brought to *Socony* by the Supreme Court's case law.

104. *Groupement des cartes bancaires v European Commission* [2014] ECLI:EU:C:2014:2204, § 58.
105. See Benjamin Edelman and Julian Wright, "Price Restrictions in Multi-sided Platforms: Practices and Responses" (2014) 10 *Competition Policy International* 2.
106. See Regulation (EU) 2015/751 of the European Parliament and of the Council of 29 April 2015 on interchange fees for card-based payment transactions [2015] OJ L123, Article 11. For analysis, see Cyril Ritter, "Antitrust in Two-Sided Markets: Looking at the U.S. Supreme Court's Amex Case from an EU Perspective" (2019) 10(3) *Journal of European Competition Law & Practice* 172.

Our proposed introduction of constraints on the price structure primarily ambitions to reduce the output of a tipped market on which a firm extracts a monopoly rent, regardless of whether this leads to more rivalry by competitors or new entrants.

The European Union has more relevant experience here than the United States. To date, EU antitrust law has been applied to restrict platform rules that seek to avoid losing transactions to other firms. A growing body of decisions in coordinated and unilateral conduct cases has developed to limit use of "most-favored-nation clauses," whereby platforms like Airbnb, eBay, or App Stores require "parity" between the products/services sold through their platforms and the supplier's (eg, hotel's) own website and or other sales channels.[107] But the primary focus of EU antitrust is on promoting non-platform transactions and outside competition. This is more tangential than the clear, yet indirect, price limit to monopoly rents that we envision. To move the law one step further, one possibility would be to relax the strict *per se* rule against resale price maintenance ("RPM") and allow users to set prices on the other side in the specific context of tipped markets.[108] Another option might be to make antitrust doctrine more biting toward "agency" relations between platform and suppliers like app stores and developers.[109] Currently, agency relations escape—at least in theory—application of Article 101 TFEU, depriving agencies and courts from antitrust remedies on one side of the price structure. Last, merger assessment could also be strengthened, to limit platform's opportunities to vertically integrate into products sold by competing suppliers, and subsequently bid prices down in order to raise output. Put differently, price leadership by a platform in an already tipped market might not be in the social interest.

In the United States, by contrast, antitrust's favorable bias toward practices that expand output appears to prevent application of our proposal. In

---

107. Pinar Akman, "A Competition Law Assessment of Platform Most-Favored-Customer Clauses" (2016) 12(4) *Journal of Competition Law and Economics* 781, at 804–14.

108. Commission Regulation (EU) 330/2010 of 20 April 2010 on the application of Article 101(3) of the Treaty on the Functioning of the European Union to categories of vertical agreements and concerted practices [2010] OJ L102/1. See Commission Decision of 17 December 2018 relating to proceedings under Article 101 of the Treaty on the Functioning of the European Union and Article 53 of the Agreement on the European Economic Area [2018] C(2018)8455 final (Case AT.40428 Guess).

109. See, arguing generally against that idea (though in ways unrelated to the arguments advanced in this book), Pinar Akman, "Online Platforms, Agency, and Competition Law: Mind the Gap" (2019) 43(2) Fordham International Law Journal 209.

spite of their commitment to evidence, this bias leads courts in the United States to occasionally rely on abstract factual evidence that comports with theoretical economic predictions, and disregards "actual market realities" as required under *Kodak*. This problem has been observed in *Ohio, et al v American Express Company*, where industry evidence that credit card trans-actions had increased by 30 percent sufficed to convince the majority that Amex's specific anti-steering clauses produced no competitive injury. In a scathing dissent, Justice Breyer observed that by such reasoning, the major-ity came close "to saying that the Sherman Act does not apply at all."[110]

And yet. The subsequent *Apple v Pepper* Opinion opens a possibility for US antitrust to play a role in constraining a platform price structure.[111] Here, the Supreme Court has accepted claims that iPhone users who download apps from the Apple Store are "direct purchasers" of Apple, entitled to sue the latter on grounds of unlawful monopolization. Though the court has said nothing of whether the lock-in of iPhone owners into buying apps only from the App Store and paying Apple's 30 percent fee constitutes an antitrust violation, the Opinion in effect discourages use of "per transac-tion" charging. Recall that to sell an app in the App Store, app developers pay a moderate annual membership fee, but retrocede 30 percent of the retail price to Apple.[112] This fee model may lead to excessive developer par-ticipation. This is because developers need not worry about how well the platform does at manufacturing transactions with users on the other side. By contrast, when the law raises the costs to platforms of "per transaction" charging—as the Supreme Court did in *Apple v Pepper*—it raises incen-tives to introduce (possibly higher) membership fees. Armstrong has indeed argued that "when there is a monopoly platform, it makes no difference if tariffs are levied on a lump-sum or per-transaction basis."[113] So in tipped markets, the law might affect the platform fee choice, by inducing monop-olists to replace per transaction charging on users with (possibly higher) membership fees on developers. In turn, a membership fee might bring developers to consider participation choices more carefully in the first place, and decrease platform output.

---

110. See Justice Breyer dissent in *Ohio v American Express Co* [2018] 585 US __.
111. *Apple v Pepper* [2019] 587 US __.
112. To sell an app in the App Store, app developers must pay Apple a USD 99 annual membership fee. Apple requires that the retail sales price end in USD 0.99, but otherwise allows the app developers to set the retail price.
113. Armstrong, "Competition in Two-Sided Markets" (n 85).

3. Presumption against Horizontal Mergers

Independent of the above proposals, antitrust might subject horizontal merg-ers on a tipped market to a non-rebuttable presumption of consumer harm. One may object that a presumption against horizontal mergers is super-fluous in markets that have already ripened into monopoly. Most mergers are unlikely to harm competition because fringe rivals do not represent a competitive constraint. Worse, a presumption against horizontal mergers in a tipped market might foreclose exit opportunities for unsuccessful firms and delay efficient industry reordering.[114] And yet, a limited economic case might be made that horizontal mergers in tipped markets harm compe-tition (a). As far as the law is concerned, the presumption formalizes pre-existing approaches tested in the United States and the European Union, yet with some practical limitations (b).

a) Economic Case

Let us return to our nightclub example. Suppose that some users of the nightclub also value country music. Until now, due to fixed costs and net-work effects, no country music club has ever entered. The market inef-ficiently undersupplies variety. Economist Joel Waldfogel has talked of a "tyranny of the majority."[115] Now, assume that surviving night clubs' fixed infrastructure can be acquired at salvage value by an indirect entrant. Entry by merger is now less costly, and in the social interest. The indirect entrant faces cheaper fixed costs and might be able to repurpose the infrastructure to serve portions of demands with distinct music preferences (unless the incumbent night club scoops up the assets first).

Granted, a presumption against horizontal mergers by the dominant plat-form of a tipped market will not restore rivalry. But it prohibits marginal increases of the output share on which the firm takes a monopoly rent, compared to the but-for world that would prevail without merger. And more importantly, allowing third party purchase of distressed assets might promote indirect entry. Recall from Chapter IV that indirect entry is the main channel of competition for both big tech firms and startups. Indirect

---

114. See Elad Gil's book, mentioning that "YouTube exited to Google in part due to the threat of lawsuits from the media industry," Elad Gil, *High Growth Handbook: Scaling Startups from 10 to 10,000 People* (Stripe Press 2018) Ch 6.
115. Joel Waldfogel, *The Tyranny of the Market* (Harvard University Press 2007).

entry will be stronger in tipped markets where diversification might matter. Social networks are a good example, because the preferences of younger and older users are different. Text messaging is a bad example, because there is little scope for product differentiation.

In doctrine, competition agencies are not allowed to prohibit welfare enhancing transactions on the ground that the merger would prevent another merger from taking place, which would increase social welfare even more.[116] A better legal standard would allow the imposition of such prohibition, through a presumption against horizontal mergers to monopoly in tipped markets.

On its face, the presumption is radical. Parties to a merger to monopoly are deprived of the right to raise an efficiency defense.[117] This is even stricter than the infamous rebuttable 1962 *Philadelphia National Bank* presumption.[118] At the same time, the presumption is narrower. It does not prevent any merger in a tipped market, just mergers that involve a firm in control of a tipped market.

Contemporary merger practice allows agencies to outlaw transactions that remove a "maverick" firm from the market.[119] Our proposal prescribes an adjustment to this theory of liability. The idea is to consider the target's operating assets as disruptive on the conjecture that they might be owned by a future entrant. The key issue is whether the target's assets can be repositioned. This (difficult) inquiry is a standard feature of horizontal merger assessment.[120] The modularity of digital markets should allow us to confidently presume that repositioning is available, hence the choice of a non-rebuttable presumption.

---

116. Svend Albaek, "Consumer Welfare in EU Competition Policy" in Caroline Heide-Jørgensen (ed), *Aims and Values in Competition Law* (DJØF Publishing 2013).
117. Note that many practitioners complain that the possibility of raising an efficiency defense is essentially a theoretical one.
118. *United States v Philadelphia National Bank* [1963] 374 US 321.
119. See US Merger Guidelines, § 2.1.5. See also Guidelines on the assessment of horizontal mergers under the Council Regulation on the control of concentrations between undertakings [2004] OJ C31, § 42 ("However, a merger may also increase the likelihood or significance of coordinated effects in other ways. For instance, a merger may involve a 'maverick' firm that has a history of preventing or disrupting coordination, for example by failing to follow price increases by its competitors, or has characteristics that gives it an incentive to favour different strategic choices than its coordinating competitors would prefer").
120. Amit Gandhi et al, "Post-Merger Product Repositioning" (2008) 56(1) *The Journal of Industrial Economics* 49.

b) Legal and Practical Feasibility

A fair amount of decisional activity suggests that our proposed approach is the common currency of antitrust practice, though not explicitly on the books. In 2008, the US Department of Justice ("DoJ") threatened to prosecute a horizontal agreement between Yahoo! and Google. The DoJ was concerned about the preservation of Yahoo!'s incentives to invest in its own search advertising business under the outsourcing agreement with Google.[121] The firms abandoned the transaction. Two years later, the US Department of Justice (DoJ) cleared the horizontal merger between Yahoo! and Microsoft,[122] observing that it would be likely to increase competition by creating a more viable competitive alternative to Google.[123] By contrast, other merger cases might have been decided differently under the presumption. The 2013 *Google/Waze* clearance by the UK Competition and Markets Authority ("CMA") is a case in point.[124] The presumption would have led to the merger being struck down, given Google Maps' clear market leadership at the time.[125] Last, the presumption would also work against mergers in which a number two competitor buys the leading firm of a tipped market. This scenario occurred in *Microsoft/Intuit*, where Microsoft sought to acquire its "most significant competitor."[126] The DoJ, correctly in our view, filed for injunctive relief on the ground that the combination of Intuit's Quicken dominant 69 percent share with Microsoft's Money 22 percent

---

121. US Department of Justice Press Release, "Yahoo!Inc. and Google Inc. Abandon their Advertising Agreement" (November 5, 2008) https://www.justice.gov/archive/atr/public/press_releases/2008/239167.htm accessed December 4, 2019.

122. ibid.

123. US Department of Justice Press Release, "Statement of the Department of Justice Antitrust Division on Its Decision to Close Its Investigation of the Internet Search and Paid Search Advertising Agreement Between Microsoft Corporation and Yahoo! Inc." February 18, 2010   <https://www.justice.gov/opa/pr/statement-department-justice-antitrust-division-its-decision-close-its-investigation-internet> accessed December 4, 2019.

124. Completed acquisition by Motorola Mobility Holding (Google, Inc) of Waze Mobile Limited [2013] Competition and Markets Authority, Office of Fair Trading ME/6167/13.

125. In line with Elena Argentesi, Paolo Buccirossi, Emilio Calvano, Tomaso Duso, Alessia Marrazzo, and Salvatore Nava, "Ex-post Assessment of Merger Control Decisions in Digital Markets: Final Report" (May 9, 2019) Document prepared by Lear for the Competition Markets Authority <https://assets.publishing.service.gov.uk/government/uploads/system/uploads/attachment_data/file/803576/CMA_past_digital_mergers_GOV.UK_version.pdf> accessed December 4, 2019 (hereafter Argentesi et al, "Ex-post Assessment of Merger Control Decisions") (observing that the CMA "discarded valuable pieces of evidence signaling that Waze may have become a relevant competitor to Google Maps").

126. See complaint for injunctive relief against combination in violation of section 7 of the Clayton Act, *United States of America v Microsoft Corporation* (1995), <https://www.justice.gov/sites/default/files/atr/legacy/2012/08/07/0184.pdf> accessed December 4, 2019.

share would eliminate competition in personal finance software market, and more generally, the emerging home banking marketplace.

The presumption's main limitation is practical. Like all line drawing exercises, it demands impossible determinacy in delineating horizontal relationships. Take Facebook's acquisition of Instagram. Under what category should we look at this merger: horizontal or non-horizontal merger? At a high level, Facebook and Instagram both offer social networks, and appear to belong to the horizontal category. At the same time, evidence of distinct user bases as well as multi-homing by common users is not suggestive of the high degree of substitutability necessary to classify the transaction as a horizontal merger.

In past practice, antitrust agencies have "fallen back on functional market definitions on the user side," discounting possible horizontal overlaps.[127] In *Facebook/Instagram*, the UK CMA considered horizontal overlaps, but did not find in favor of their existence, endorsing the view that photo apps like Instagram "are complementary to social networks."[128] This difficulty has nurtured reflection on a substitute concept of "attention markets" in which platforms compete to induce users to spend time on their service.[129] Attention markets facilitate findings of horizontal overlaps, thus reducing the burden of proof of harm to competition compared to theories of harm based on complementary goods and services.

But attention markets might also reduce merger enforcement. Restaurants, weekend TV shows, and bedtime compete in the nightclub attention market. An indeterminate, and perhaps infinite, range of substitutes compete in an attention market. Hence, the concept of attention markets decreases the chances that agencies intervene by raising the costs of enforcement. Put differently, the attention markets concept does not lower the practical difficulty of administering antitrust. The concept actually deepens difficulties, by increasing antitrust claims which are hard to believe—for example social media dancing platform TikTok competes with nightclubs—and hard to refute.

---

127. Andrea Prat and Tommaso Valletti, "Merger Policy in the Age of Facebook" (*VOX, CEPR Policy*, 26 July 2018) <https://voxeu.org/article/merger-policy-age-facebook> accessed December 4, 2019 (hereafter Valletti and Prat, "Merger Policy").

128. Anticipated acquisition by Facebook Inc of Instagram Inc [2012] Competition and Markets Authority, Office of Fair Trading ME/5525/12, 21.

129. David S Evans "Attention rivalry among online platforms" (2013) 9(2) *Journal of Competition Law & Economics* 313.

More reasonable is the objection that our presumption lacks teeth, because "most M&A transactions involving tech platforms do not have a clear horizontal element."[130] This objection, however, can be relativized on the ground that as platforms diversify into conglomerates, the probability of horizontal overlaps with a target firm increases.

4. Beyond Antitrust?

A straightforward alternative to an indirect weakening of monopoly rents by antitrust consists in promoting revenue sharing through entitlements (a), tax (b), or open standards (c). Let us review these three alternatives in turn.

a) Entitlements

The point is easy enough to state: by granting property rights to the various sides of a platform, a social planner might affect the distribution of value to the benefit of users. Property rights provide opportunities for payments through excludability. This is relevant in digital markets "where institutions have not arisen to manage negative prices."[131] Property rights might facilitate opportunities for platform bypass through direct bilateral market transactions between users on distinct sides. And property rights allow same-side individual parties to form collective rights organizations that bargain with the platform from a more efficient position.

The European Union has been a faster adopter of revenue sharing policies than the United States. A real life example of a revenue sharing device with the subsidy side is the attribution of property rights on personal data to individual users of platforms under the General Data Protection Regulation ("GDPR").[132] And a real life example of a revenue sharing device with the

---

130. Argentesi et al, "Ex-post Assessment of Merger Control Decisions" (n 125).

131. "Final Report of the Stigler Committee on Digital Platforms" (2019) *Center for the Study of the Economy and the State*, 33 (hereafter the Stigler Center Report).

132. Though its stated objective is sociopolitical, not economic. See Regulation (EU) 2016/679 of the European Parliament and of the Council of 27 April 2016 on the protection of natural persons with regard to the processing of personal data and on the free movement of such data, and repealing Directive 95/46/EC (General Data Protection Regulation) [2016] OJ L119 (Article 1(2) and 1(3) ("This Regulation protects fundamental rights and freedoms of natural persons and in particular their right to the protection of personal data. The free movement of personal data within the Union shall be neither restricted nor prohibited for reasons connected with the protection of natural persons with regard to the processing of personal data").

money side is the EU copyright directive that creates an intellectual property right ("IPR") over press content like extracts and images.[133]

A possible outcome of introducing revenue sharing devices in tipped
markets is not less, but more monopoly. Again, multisided market theory provides the general framework of analysis. Take property rights on
data. When users are compensated for their personal data, property rights
increase the subsidy to users.[134] The social planner raises the benefits of user
participation in the platform. Non-users have increased incentives to join.
And the subsidy might compensate a possible decline in quality (eg, congestion) for existing users.

Similar effects might arise when property rights are introduced on the
money side. Take copyright for content creators. At first glance, the entitlement might seem to limit the size of the platform monopoly rent—the
platform now pays copyright licensing fees. Closer analysis however suggests
that this will not be the case under all circumstances, in particular when
property rights are simultaneously introduced on the subsidy side. Payments
of copyright licensing fees to users on the money side limit incentives to
bypass the platform, and to negotiate directly with more elastic users—by
necessary assumption—on the subsidy side. The platform shields property
rights owners on the money side from direct indemnification of property
rights owners on the subsidy side. To be fair, the platform might pass through
payments to property right owners on the subsidy side to the money side,
in which case incentives to bypass remain plausible. But even then, unless
one assumes absence of transactions costs, the choice of the platform as a
contractual partner for property right owners on the money side dominates,
because of the efficiencies arising from the centralization of payments with

---

133. Except very short extracts. See Directive (EU) 2019/790 of the European Parliament and of
the Council of 17 April 2019 on copyright and related rights in the Digital Single Market and
amending Directives 96/9/EC and 2001/29/EC [2019] OJ L130.

134. An often mentioned analogy to support the attribution of property rights on personal data
is number portability in telecommunications. Number portability clearly increased competition between telecommunications services. The analogy works well at the intuitive level,
because it is hard to deny that users of telecommunications service deserve to be the owners
of their number. But on closer analysis, the analogy founders. To start, data is the money side
of a subsidized product, like internet search or social networking. In telecommunications,
the money side is the subscription service. Then, and more important, investments from
a telecommunications supplier into a phone number are infinitesimal, relative to the large
investments that go into data collection, curation and analysis.

the dominant platform, and its superior bargaining power.[135] Put differently, the allocation of entitlements on various sides might convert platforms into collecting societies, with legally enforceable monopoly power.

b) Tax

Tax, and in particular sales tax, might be employed to limit monopoly rents in tipped markets.[136] But tax is not obviously more efficient than antitrust. The reason is not conceptual, it is practical. Let us fully set out the consequences of a sales tax. Undoubtedly, a sales tax reduces revenue made on the money side, and affects the price structure. Conceive of a sales tax on targeted ads revenue. Due to the non-neutrality of the price structure in a multisided market, the sales tax limits targeted ads' output and achieves the goal of monopoly rent limitation. But fiscal design is such that sales taxes are rarely firm or market specific. In practice, the lowest unit of implementation of a sales tax appears to be an industry sector. Under this assumption, a sales tax will not only hit the monopoly firm. It will also affect firms in neighboring markets, including these best placed to make indirect entry. In the example, the sales tax hits Google, Facebook, and Verizon as well as ad technology providers. Moreover, even if one could restrict implementation of the sales tax to a properly delineated relevant market, the modification of the price structure in this market reduces the expected payoffs of indirect entry for new firms, especially if they are smaller and face relatively higher liquidity constraints. Again, use of antitrust limited rules to reduce the rent of monopoly firms in tipped markets appears advantageous.

c) Open Standards, Compatibility, and Interoperability

A case might be made that the monopoly share is socially inefficient if compatibility can be ensured with horizontal competitors.[137] For example, the Stigler Center would like to impose interoperability among digital platforms, similar to the way governments mandated interoperability

---

135. See Guido Calabresi and A Douglas Melamed, "Property Rules, Liability Rules, and Inalienability: One View of the Cathedral" (1972) 85(6) *Harvard Law Review*, 1096 ("no one makes an assumption of no transaction costs in practice").

136. A tax is a government charge that increases costs. Here, we consider the case of a sales tax, and not of an income tax. For indeed, an income tax would indiscriminately cover all of the firm's activities, not only the tipped market.

137. Economides, "Competition Policy" (n 16) 107 noted that consumers and total surplus might be higher under compatibility.

among phone companies, as a way of weakening network effects.[138] To put things graphically, under an interoperability regime, LinkedIn users might be able to interoperate with Facebook users, by viewing pictures posted on Facebook's Newsfeed through the LinkedIn graphical user interface.

Interoperability might decrease the monopoly rent in a tipped market. Particularly when the platform itself has chosen to restrict interoperability, excluding the rest of the industry from the benefit of network effects.

But the cost of achieving interoperability, and in particular the specification of open standards, might consume a lot of resources over a long period of time. This is not ideal in markets hit by discontinuities. Moreover, it is legitimate to ask why big tech firms do not already practice compatibility. This might be because institutions and rules have not emerged to allow tech companies to appropriate their investments. As long as this remains the case, big tech firms will remain reluctant to develop open interoperability protocols in the context of standard-setting organizations.[139]

But there is an even more fatal problem with open standards and interoperability. A duty of interoperability adds one side to the platform, leading to possible modifications to the price structure. To see this, assume that the platform had only one money and one subsidy side. The duty of interoperability brings a new side on board, that is other platforms seeking access (eg, to application programming interfaces ("API")). If access under the open standard is free, then agents on the money side will enjoy increased utility from their interaction with the platform because they now cater to a larger number of third parties. This might entice the platform to charge higher prices on the money side, meaning more, not less, monopoly rent. Moreover, with interoperability, users on both the money and subsidy sides have lower incentives to leave the platform for competing ones, because they now enjoy access to an even richer set of products and services. Interoperability requirements might thus limit multi-homing, and create incremental entrenchment.

To date, antitrust efforts to impose interoperability have a spotty record. In 2004, the EC tried forcing Microsoft to provide interoperability for work

---

138. See The Stigler Center Report (n 131) 118.
139. On this aspect, the Stigler Center Report (n 131) notes the necessity of ongoing monitoring due to "the likelihood of technical change, and the incentive for non-cooperation by the incumbent firm."

group servers operating systems.[140] Fifteen years later, not one significant competitor to Microsoft has emerged on this government-created market.

D. Residual Role of Antitrust in Untipped Markets

1. Elaboration

A firm charging monopoly rents in a tipped market will attract indirect entry from other firms in untipped markets. And an antitrust regime that reduces the rents charged in a tipped market should produce incentives to indirect entry in untipped markets by the monopoly firm. As a result, one should observe increased efforts by *all* firms to make indirect entry in untipped markets.

In general terms, the social gains from indirect entry might be substantial. Indirect entry increases output. When firms re-segment tipped markets with low cost or differentiated products, indirect entry eliminates deadweight losses. For example, there is no question that smartphone output increased when open source operating systems for mobile phones like Android were introduced.[141]

Indirect entry also reduces monopoly rents. When firms create new products in new markets, indirect entry changes the relative preferences of users, raises the opportunity cost of purchases in the tipped market, and shifts inwards the demand curve on which the incumbent charges a monopoly rent.[142] For example, there is no question that users derived less relative utility from desktop computers when mobile phones were introduced. Admittedly, the opposite might also be true, *sometimes*.[143] Indirect

---

140. Commission Decision relating to a proceeding under Article 82 of the EC Treaty (Case COMP/C-3/37.792 Microsoft) [2004] C(2004)900 final.

141. Statista, "Global smartphone sales by operating system 2009-2018, by quarter" (February 27, 2020) <https://www.statista.com/statistics/266219/global-smartphone-sales-since-1st-quarter-2009-by-operating-system/> accessed April 22, 2020.

142. It is well known that complements are not priced independently, and yield pressure on each other. At the same time, the disrupted platform still benefits from anchoring effects if it earns relatively lower yet supra-competitive profits.

143. We say sometimes because complementarity sometimes does not work to the benefit of the monopoly good. The example here is the eBay/PayPal merger/demerger, in which it was clearly seen that eBay little benefitted from integration with an online payment service.

entry of a complement may render the monopoly product more valuable. For example, the combination of an online store with an online payment service increases marginal benefit to users of the monopoly product. But in this case again, indirect entry increases social welfare. Even if positive externalities toward the monopolized product increase the monopoly rent, this is due to a shift upward of the demand curve, not to market power.

What do we draw from this? A guideline under which a consumer welfare spirited antitrust regime should protect indirect entry by *all firms* in untipped markets. Put differently, it is unwarranted to treat firms with monopoly positions in tipped markets more strictly than others when they make indirect entry in untipped markets. To paraphrase a famous antitrust dictum, the incumbent firm, having been urged to exit from the tipped market, must not be turned upon when it does.[144] Unless the law is willing to ignore the possibility that monopolists adjust market conduct to policy incentives—in which case antitrust should just condemn monopoly *per se*—incumbent firms should be afforded equal opportunities to indirect entry. More important, there is no economic basis to prefer indirect entry by an incumbent firm from a tipped market over entry from (i) a new firm or (ii) an established firm from an untipped market. Firm type is not determinative of the weight of social welfare brought by a unit of innovation.[145] Controversially, one might even advance that the cost of errors is lower for incumbent firms that benefit from a monopoly in a tipped market. In consequence, it might be socially beneficial to promote indirect entry by incumbents over entry of other firms.

But a rule of *per se* legality that would totally exonerate indirect entry from antitrust liability is unwarranted. One can conceive of circumstances where a monopoly firm entry in untipped markets might be anticompetitive. There are two scenarios, one unproblematic, the other not. First, the untipped market cannibalizes the monopoly rent, but the network effects position of the incumbent firm in the tipped market produces no externalities in the new market. Consider a nightclub facing indirect entry from a movie theater, keeping in mind the men and women cross group externalities discussed previously. The movie theater attracts 30 percent of the

144. *United States v Aluminum Co Of America (ALCOA)* [1945] 2nd Cir 148 F2d 416, 430.
145. Entrepreneurship literature discusses the division of innovative labor between a large firm and a small firm, and stresses the complementarity between both organizations. The small firm invents and exits, the large one scales it and expands. In both cases, there is indirect entry by the two types of firms.

demand that went to the nightclub. At the same time, the demand that deflects to the theater finds irrelevant whether all female patrons or just a few of them go to the movies. Upshot? Entry into movies by a nightclub monopolist is unproblematic, because the network effects advantage held in the tipped market are not portable in the untipped market.

Second, the untipped market cannibalizes the monopoly rent, and the network effects position of the incumbent firm in the tipped market produces externalities in the new market. Suppose that a nightclub faces indirect entry from a restaurant. Indirect entry again limits the monopoly rent, because nightclub goers spend some of their evening time, and money, at the restaurant. Yet, because the nightclub monopolist knows that some of the restaurant clients will join the nightclub, it can exploit relevant network effects advantages. A quick numerical example drives the point home: assume the nightclub has 100 clients. Each client spends USD 100 per night there. The nightclub total revenue per night is USD 10,000. The total cost of servicing client in the nightclub is USD 4,000. When indirect restaurant entry occurs, each client spends USD 30 at the restaurant. The nightclub total revenue per night now falls to USD 7,000. The nightclub can launch its own onsite restaurant for trivial cost, offer free dining—a USD 30 voucher to each client in the nightclub—and attract all 100 users (as long as incremental costs do not exceed USD 3,000). In such circumstances, the indirect entrant has no incentives to entry: matching the nightclub offer is a zero profit making strategy.

The hard question for antitrust is this: on what conditions should antitrust restrict indirect entry of a monopoly firm in an untipped market? A preliminary consideration is that the conditions imposed on indirect entry have to be exceptional. Recall that the main implication from our theory is that antitrust should try to encourage monopoly firms to exit from tipped markets. At the same time, the position of the monopoly firm in the tipped market should not be prohibited in and of itself. There is no antitrust principle that requires entry to take place from zero positions. Antitrust does not require that a monopoly firm in country A should not enter in country B by using advantages developed in country A. Of course, antitrust agencies and courts occasionally try to impose a "level playing field" between the incumbent and the new entrant.[146] But in industries with networks

---

146. See Ian Ayres and Barry Nalebuff, "Going Soft on Microsoft? The EU's Antitrust Case and Remedy" (2005) 2 *The Economists' Voice 2, 1–12*.

externalities and increasing returns to adoption, this idea is less compelling than in traditional industries because this means penalizing the incumbent firm for advantages essentially due to users' preferences. Moreover, the test should require a showing of adverse anticompetitive effects in the tipped market—that is monopoly power in the tipped market compared to the "but for" world without entry in the untipped market—otherwise antitrust might indiscriminately penalize incumbent pro-competitive exit from tipped markets (for instance, a declining one).

The answer is to try to construct an antitrust rule or standard that allows to capture indirect entry conduct that by purpose or effect maintains, enlarges, or prolongs the monopoly rent in the tipped market. In our view, the test should call for *four* basic inquiries. The first asks whether there is a leveraging of network effects from the tipped to the untipped market. The point is to insulate from liability entry into markets where network effects from the tipped market afford no competitive advantage in the untipped market, like in our example of the nightclub and the movie theater. The second asks whether the firm's conduct deters or forecloses indirect entry. The anticompetitive effect will be easier to show when the incumbent penetrates a market in which there is already one or more indirect entrants or when the strategy is targeted. The third asks whether indirect entry pressures the monopoly rent. It requires evaluating whether indirect entrants offer products or services that directly or indirectly constrain the rent extracted in the tipped market. The fourth asks whether the monopoly firm has ability and incentives to withhold participation, discontinue investments, or delay innovation in the indirect entry market.[147] The condition seeks to determine if the incumbent firm's indirect entry is a cheap entry deterrence commitment—[148] in which case it is deemed to be anticompetitive—or

---

147. The economic logic is close to that related to a monopolist investing R&D resources in "sleeping patents" that are then withheld from use. See Richard Gilbert and David M Newberry, "Preemptive Patenting and the Persistence of Monopoly" (1982) 72(3) *The American Economic Review* 514 (hereafter Gilbert and Newberry, "Preemptive Patenting"). Our scenario slightly differs from the patent literature because here, the investment into the complementary market is not necessarily a preemptive strategy, as in the patent case of Newberry and Gilbert.
148. See, for an economic model showing this, Dennis W Carlton and Michael Waldman, "The Strategic Use of Tying to Preserve and Create Market Power in Evolving Industries" (2002) 33(2) The RAND Journal of Economics (hereafter Carlton and Waldman, "The Strategic Use of Tying").

whether it is a long-term commitment that manifests strategic change—in which event it is deemed lawful.[149]

The test contemplated here can be generalized to all areas of antitrust law where firms adopt indirect entry strategies through coordinated or unilateral conduct or by merger. It should be construed as a mental model, not as a strict legal norm with cumulative conditions. Depending on one's preferences in terms of legal certainty and decisional flexibility, the test might be accommodated either as a rule or standard.

The boundary between lawful and unlawful conduct under our proposed test is, conceivably, a blurry line. Two antitrust cases decided on both sides of the Atlantic provide a possible example and counter-example of our antitrust test. The first is the US *Microsoft* case. The second is the EU *Google Android* case.

2. Example: *Microsoft* (US)

Microsoft is one of the most high-profile cases of contemporary US antitrust policy. The case is important for two reasons: one, advocates of higher activity levels under the consumer welfare standard often mention *Microsoft* as an example of sound antitrust policy (at least in relation to the theory of liability); two, the US courts' approach in *Microsoft* is close in spirit to our proposed antitrust rule.[150]

In *Microsoft*, the US government case focused on Microsoft's maintenance of its Windows operating system ("OS") monopoly through the

---

149. There are many examples of tech giants' discontinuation of new homegrown or acquired products, services, and applications. See for example, Google's phasing out of restaurant recommendation service Zagat. Kate Krader, "How Google Almost Destroyed Zagat" (*Bloomberg*, March 7, 2018) <https://www.bloomberg.com/news/articles/2018-03-07/here-s-how-google-almost-destroyed-zagat> accessed January 10, 2020. See also, Facebook's abandonment of face filter app MSQRD. Rob Price, "Facebook Abandoned a Red-Hot App after Promising to Keep it Shows how Far the Social Network Goes to Stay Dominant" (*Business Insider*, January 2, 2020) <https://www.businessinsider.com/facebook-msqrd-acquisition-tech-competition-2019-12?international=true&r=US&IR=T≥ accessed January 10, 2020. For a review of acquisitions and subsequent shutdowns by Google and Facebook, see Tim Wu and Stuart A Thompson, Opinion, "The Roots of Big Tech Run Disturbingly Deep" *The New York Times* (June 7, 2019) <https://www.nytimes.com/interactive/2019/06/07/opinion/google-facebook-mergers-acquisitions-antitrust.html> accessed January 10, 2020.

150. *United States v Microsoft Corp* [1999] DDC 84 FSupp2d 9 (findings of fact); *United States v Microsoft Corp* [2000] DDC 87 FSupp2d 30, aff'd in part, rev'd in part, *United States v Microsoft Corp* [2001] DCCir 253 F3d 34; and *Microsoft Corp v United States* [2001] 534 US 952 *cert denied*.

exclusion of middleware developers such as Netscape and Sun. The District and Appellate Courts found that Microsoft had sought to protect its OS monopoly from the platform threat posed by middleware providers. This was achieved through several tactics, such as indirect entry into middleware products, contractual restrictions on original equipment manufacturers ("OEMs") from preinstalling rival browsers, integration of Internet Explorer and Windows (notably by removing Internet Explorer's Add/Remove utility), attempts to exclude Java, and so forth. Ultimately, the Court of Appeals upheld large parts of the District Court's ruling, which found that Microsoft had unlawfully drawn developers away from rival platforms that might otherwise have challenged Microsoft's OS monopoly.[151] Both courts affirmed liability under Section 1 and 2 of the Sherman Act.

Of overwhelming importance to the case was Microsoft's obsession to maintain the "applications barrier to entry."[152] Users only chose PC OS for which a large and varied set of software applications are written. Software developers thus tended to write applications first, and often exclusively, for the OS that was already used by a majority of PC users. This made it "prohibitively expensive" for a new OS to attract enough developers and consumers to become a viable alternative to Windows.[153] With the development of the Internet, however, Microsoft conjectured that developers might write applications that relied solely on middleware or servers, and no longer on the OS and its Application Programming Interface ("APIs") thus weakening the applications barrier to entry, and making it easier for firms "already in the market" to present a "viable alternative to Windows."[154] As the District Court made clear in its findings of fact and conclusions of law, Microsoft recognized middleware as the "Trojan horse that, once having … infiltrated the applications barrier" could open the way for non-Microsoft OS to "emerge as acceptable substitutes to Windows."[155]

---

151. See *United States v Microsoft Corp* [2001] DCCir 253 F3d 34 (though most of the District Court monopoly maintenance case stood, the Appellate Court dismissed liability for exclusivity deals with ICPs, on lack of evidence of a specific share of foreclosure; dismissed liability for Microsoft general "course of conduct," apart from Microsoft's specific acts; dismissed the claim of attempted monopolization of the browser market short of evidence of barriers to entry; vacated the District Court's finding of a *per se* tying violation, and remanded the case for analysis under the rule of reason in so far as platform software products were concerned; and vacated the District Court decree remedy).
152. *United States v Microsoft Corp* [1999] DDC 84 FSupp2d 9 (Findings of Fact) § 407.
153. ibid, Findings of Fact, § 40.
154. ibid, Findings of Fact, § 56.
155. ibid, Findings of Fact, § 77.

Broadly, the theory of liability used in *Microsoft* articulates most, not all, branches of our antitrust rule. The first and second prongs are the easy parts. Leveraging was undisputable. Microsoft withheld technical information on Windows, bartered pre-installation icons on Windows desktop with internet access providers in exchange for Internet explorer usage, provided financial incentives to OEMs paid by Windows OS revenues, and pursued aggressive "Windows integration" of Internet Explorer.[156] Prima facie foreclosure was equally clear. There were pre-existing competitors, and Microsoft made indirect entry into middleware as a late entrant. The judicial record contains evidence of *actual* adverse market share effects on Netscape and Sun's middleware distributions.[157]

The third prong of the test is more interesting. It requires showing a link between foreclosure in the untipped market and monopoly maintenance in the tipped market. Though the US courts never attempted to show that Netscape Navigator or Sun's Java would backward integrate into the PC OS market, their theory was that Netscape Navigator would develop into a substantial platform for applications development, in turn allowing "other firms" to develop competing OS that would end Windows' reign on the market. The District Court, however, recognized "insufficient evidence" that the middleware layer would have ignited genuine competition in the OS market. And yet two facts convinced the District Court to accept a lower burden of production with respect to incipient OS competition. First, the District Court abstractly singled out the OS computer platform as an "important market."[158] Second, the District Court insisted that "firms already in the market" like IBM or Be Inc. had sought to develop a viable alternative to Windows, thereby backing its entry conjecture with empirically observed industry facts. On appeal, the court stressed the "added uncertainty" of this theory. The Appellate Court however also supported a lower burden of production, although by somewhat distinct reasoning. The court relied on theoretically plausible propositions about the purpose of the Sherman Act to protect "nascent competitors" in "industries marked by

---

156. ibid, Findings of Fact, § 379 ("Microsoft could still defray the massive costs it was undertaking to maximize usage share with the vast profits earned licensing Windows").

157. Navigator's share fell from above 80 percent in January 1996 to 55 percent in November 1997, and Internet Explorer rose from 5 percent to 36 percent over the same period. ibid, Findings of Fact, 179.

158. ibid, Findings of Fact, § 411.

rapid technological advance and frequent paradigm shifts," and the specific economics of industries with zero marginal costs and network effects, where nascent competitors allegedly represent more "lethal" threats to incumbents than in more traditional industries. Though there was certainly a kernel of truth to both courts' justifications for a lowered burden of production, the lack of an explicit criterion, in particular in relation to the tipped market "importance," leaves an impression of subjectivism in the determination of antitrust liability.

The fourth prong of our test is not discussed in *Microsoft*. But the District court involuntarily considered whether Microsoft's entry in the browser market was a cheap commitment. Nuancing its finding of anticompetitive exclusion, the court remarked that "though the suspicion lingers, the evidence is insufficient to find that Microsoft's ambition is a future in which most or all the content available on the Web would be accessible through its own browsing software."[159] Requiring antitrust agencies and courts to establish that the dominant firm will be a slacker allows to dispense with a delicate weighing of gains and losses to consumers in both markets. In particular, proof of product withholding or discontinuation, deferral, or reduction of investments in the indirect entry market, avoids weighing the consumer harm inflicted by monopoly maintenance in the tipped market against the consumer benefits of the dominant firm's investments in the untipped market.[160] And we know in insight that while Internet Explorer 6.0 was released in 2001, Internet Explorer 7.0 was only released in 2006, and Internet Explorer 8.0 in 2009.[161] Having framed Microsoft's conduct as "predatory," the court should have logically been examined whether following exclusion, Microsoft had ability and incentives to live the quiet life (in line with US law requirements on anticompetitive price predation).

159. ibid, Findings of Fact, § 384.
160. Note that the firm should be allowed the benefit of demonstrating a valid business justification, eg, that the market turned out to be less promising than it thought or that the product required high initial investments and lower subsequent investments.
161. See Commission Decision of 6.3.2013 addressed to Microsoft Corporation relating to a proceeding on the imposition of a fine pursuant to Article 23(2)(c) of Council Regulation (EC) No 1/2003 for failure to comply with a commitment made binding by a Commission decision pursuant to Article 9 of Council Regulation (EC) No 1/2003 [2013] C(2013) 1210 final (Case AT.39530—Microsoft (tying)), § 54.

3. Counter-Example: *Google Android* (EU)

The EU *Google Android* case is a counter-example in that our test produces a distinct outcome from that reached by the European Commission ("EC"). In *Google Android*, the EC found unlawful the complex contractual provisions that Google applied to OEMs and mobile network operators ("MNOs") in exchange for the free licensing of its smart mobile OS Android and App Store. There, Google had tied the licensing of the Android App Store to the pre-installation of its search app and Chrome browser, restricted the ability of licensed OEMs to develop forked versions of Android that did not use Google search as the default search provider for all web searches, and paid financial incentives to OEMS and MNOs in exchange for exclusive pre-installation of Google's general search services. In concluding that Google was guilty of abuse of dominance, the EC endorsed the view that Google had used Android as a "carrot and stick [to] protect and strengthen a dominant position in general search services and thus its revenues via search advertisements."[162]

At a superficial level, clear analogies exist between the US *Microsoft* and EU *Google Android* decisions. Both are shining examples of indirect entry cases in which monopolists eliminate nascent threats to their rents in tipped markets. And yet, unlike *Microsoft*, the facts of *Google Android* appear to fail all four prongs of our proposed antitrust test. Blinded by Google's dominating market share in each national market for general search services, the EC failed to see that the threat to Google's rents in search did not so much come from future rivalry as in *Microsoft* (or search advertising, though this was not considered a relevant market by the EC), but from the widening of revenue streams resulting from the new market for smart mobile advertisement. To see the point by analogy, consider globalization. With the widening of national markets, local monopolists that used trucks to transport goods had every incentive to lease or own ships and airlines to capture a fraction of the larger market, and this regardless of zero sum game rivalry in local markets.[163]

---

162. See Commission Decision of 18.7.2018 relating to a proceeding under Article 102 of the Treaty on the Functioning of the European Union (the Treaty) and Article 54 of the EEA Agreement [2018] C(2018) 4761 final (AT.40099—Google Android), § 739.

163. When sunk costs are present or specialized assets are needed, ownership is a better alternative than a lease contract. See Benjamin Klein, Robert G Crawford, and Armen A Alchian, "Vertical Integration, Appropriable Rents, and the Competitive Contracting" (1978) 21(2) *The Journal of Law & Economics* 297.

All of this is so commonsensical that one would have expected caution in the EC's approach to antitrust intervention against Google's indirect entry. And yet, the EC affirmed liability unhindered, discounting claims of immaterial anticompetitive effects and substantial pro-competitive efficiencies arising from Google's conduct. Most disconcerting of all is the message that the decision conveys to dominant firms, who are advised to act with caution when they devise indirect entry strategies to adapt to growing markets.

Of course, one might object that the EC did not prevent Google from competing in untipped markets through indirect entry, simply from engaging in exclusionary contracts to tilt the scale. But a standard economic rule is that when firms cannot use the market contracting process to appropriate quasi rents, an alternative is vertical integration. The relevant question—wholly ignored by the EC—is then: is antitrust working toward social welfare improvements when it creates inducements on firms to substitute contracts with vertical ownership (here, in handset devices and OS)?[164] Moreover, an argument might be made that Google relied on contracts in the anticipation of limited opportunistic OEM behavior. Recall that OEMs enjoyed a free OS, and sometimes payments—the EC actually blamed Google for its "carrot and stick" strategy.[165] This anticipation falls if OEMs must, at some point, economically contribute to the distribution of Android. Incentives to opportunistic expropriation by OEMs, and to vertical integration by OS manufacturers, rise.

But let us return to our four-pronged test. The first condition is manifestly satisfied. It is perfectly undisputable that Google leveraged its market position in App Stores toward the general search engine markets.[166] But an inordinate feature that invites skepticism is that leverage occurred by use of monopoly power held in the *entry* market for smartphone OS.[167] Logic should invite deduction that Google had no, or at best had contestable, market power in search services—or that the market had de-tipped. By

---

164. Carlton and Waldman, "The Strategic Use of Tying" (n 148) advise that efficiencies achieved through product integration are higher than efficiencies achieved through contracts.
165. As an aside, no OEM officially complained to the EC.
166. Note that in EU law, leveraging can be prohibited as long as there is an effect in the non-monopolized market, regardless of whether the conduct produces anticompetitive effects in the monopolized market.
167. Google's origins market is search, and it only entered the smartphones OS and app stores markets subsequently. To be fair, note that the part of decision that focuses on exclusivity payments considers how Google used its search engine advantage in the tipped market. Yet, the gravitational center of the decision is mostly on the use of Play store as a leveraging device.

extension, Google's conduct might have been equally regarded as competition on the merits to keep or regain market share, not monopoly maintenance.[168] This would have been clear, had the EC used a market definition including the money side of the search market, where personal data intensive technologies and form factors other than search compete for the attention of advertisers. With eyes focused on the market for the provision of general search services, and Google's commanding share of it, the EC did not only ignore multisided market theory. It obfuscated levels of competition potentially relevant to antitrust analysis, and denied the defendant the opportunity to assert a cognizable pro-competitive justification for its conduct.

Google Android fails the second prong more clearly. Recall that in *Microsoft*, the courts carefully established the channels of rivalry—for example "middleware threats"—which credibly threatened Windows' dominance, and which Microsoft sought to exclude by maximizing Internet Explorer's usage share. In other words, *Microsoft* was a case of targeted exclusion.[169] The EC decision by contrast is lighter on evidence that Google's maximization of Android OS or App Store share came "at the expense" of specific rivals, as Internet Explorer did toward Netscape Navigator. Empirical data on global smartphones sales by operating system over 2009–2018 are inconsistent with the idea that Android did introduced a zero sum game phase, and show that Android expansion is consistent with the steady growth of the global market for smartphones.[170]

That evidence calls to mind a teaching from the business and management literature. In the presence of network externalities, firm with a solid reputation for high quality products "may adopt a strategy that encourages other firms to clone its innovations,"[171] not exclude them. And the various exclusivity conditions imposed for the free licensing of Android to OEMs might have just been a strategy to promote *perfect* cloning.

---

168. The inference is true under both an offensive or defensive leveraging scenario.
169. Bill Gates' "Tidal Wave memorandum" clearly mentioned Netscape.
170. Statista, "Global smartphone sales by operating system 2009-2018, by quarter" (27 February, 2020) <https://www.statista.com/statistics/266219/global-smartphone-sales-since-1st-quarter-2009-by-operating-system/> accessed April 22, 2020.
171. See Augustine A Lado, Nancy G Boyd, and Susan C Hanlon, "Competition, Cooperation, and the Search for Economic Rents: A Syncretic Model" (1997) 22(1) *The Academy of Management Review* 129.

Of course, these are just possibility theorems. But *Google Android* is additionally devoid of the concealed boycott threats formulated by Microsoft toward firms like Intel, Apple, or IBM to name just a few.[172] The EC merely found that that OEMs subject to Google licenses were generally prevented from licensing Android Forks (like Amazon's Fire OS) or of internally developing Android Forks even though they would have been "well-placed" to do so.[173] And by contrast to a case of "naked exclusion" without efficiency justifications like *Microsoft*,[174] the EC never seriously addressed whether OEMs had—with or without the contractual restrictions—rational incentives to choose the Android OS and myriad applications over a costly course of vertical integration. This point is not just theoretical. When OEMs have no other choice, they can launch smartphone OS, including non-Android Forks. Chinese OEM Huawei is a case in point. Banned from Google licenses in 2019 as part of the Trump administration's trade war with China, Huawei developed its own smartphone OS Harmony.[175] Huawei has announced that it would only launch Harmony commercially if the ban was not suspended. The Huawei Harmony story shows two things: one, provided exit from Android licenses is free, Google's contractual practices cannot be a cause of competitive exclusion if OEMs who leave Android can develop competing mobile OS; two, Huawei's decision to keep using Android in countries other than the United States suggests that Google's Android OS licensing has benefits over vertical integration.[176]

---

172. True, the EC discussed motivational exclusionary evidence, as the District Court did in *Microsoft*. And it might be legitimate to use evidence of motivation in "exceptional" cases. See Carlton and Waldmann, "The Strategic Use of Tying" (n 148). But in fairness, the documentary evidence adduced is both different in tone, extent, and nature from that in *Microsoft*. Consider the following example. When a Google executive says "Every time I see an Android device shipping with Bing I die a little," he complains about competition as in standard business chit-chat. This seems different from Bill Gates' targeted bellicosity in an internal memo about discussions with AOL ("We have to be sure that we don't allow them to promote Netscape as well").

173. See Commission Decision of 18.7.2018 relating to a proceeding under Article 102 of the Treaty on the Functioning of the European Union (the Treaty) and Article 54 of the EEA Agreement [2018] C(2018) 4761 final (AT.40099—Google Android), § 1106.

174. By naked exclusion, we mean "conduct unabashedly meant to exclude rivals, for which no one offers any efficiency justification." See Eric B Rasmusen, J Mark Ramseyer, and John S Wiley, Jr, "Naked Exclusion" (1991) 81(5) *The American Economic Review* 1137.

175. Angela Moon "Exclusive: Google Suspends some Business with Huawei after Trump Blacklist-Source (*Reuters*, May 19, 2019) <https://www.reuters.com/article/us-huawei-tech-alphabet-exclusive/exclusive-google-suspends-some-business-with-huawei-after-trump-blacklist-source-idUSKCN1SP0NB> accessed December 4, 2019.

176. Jon Porter, "Huawei's New Operating System Is Called HarmonyOS" (*The Verge*, Augusts 9, 2019) <https://www.theverge.com/2019/8/9/20798251/huawei-harmonyos-hongmengos-smartphones-internet-of-things-operating-system-android> accessed December 4, 2019.

Failure to consider this allows us to conjecture that the EC might have fallen prey to what economist Harold Demsetz called the Nirvana fallacy.[177] Of course, one may ask, why did Google then contractually limit OEMs' right to develop Android Forks? The answer, again, lies in the fine print of the US *Microsoft* case: contractual restrictions to Android Forks on the OEM side give assurances to applications developers on the other side that their investment in writing applications is portable across OEMs and generations of the OS.[178] In turn, OEMs choose OS based on the number of apps in an App Store. Put differently, while OEM fragmentation played as an "applications barrier to entry," contractual restrictions with OEMs weakened it.[179]

The third prong of the test requires a link between exclusionary conduct and monopoly maintenance in the tipped market. We discussed this under the first condition. We can now go deeper. A year ago, a lawyer supportive of the case told us: "Android is Google's Trojan Horse for search over mobile!" We begged to remind him that it was not all clear that the Greeks were the bad actors of the Trojan war. The Trojans had committed the biggest crime by abducting the wife of their hosts. And the Greeks were the clever side of it. They built a machine able to transport their skills within Troy. Unlike the Greeks' strategy, however, Google's Android strategy was not a hidden trick.[180] The metaphor calls attention to context. The *Google Android* decision offers a static evaluation of market power positions and contractual restraints, and lumps them together in support of a narrative of abusive

---

177. See Harold Demsetz, "Information and Efficiency: Another Viewpoint" (1969) 12(1) *The Journal of Law & Economics* 1 and Chapter I, Section C(1). See also Geoffrey Manne, "The EU's Google Android Antitrust Decision Falls Prey to the Nirvana Fallacy" (*Truth on the Market*, July 18, 2018) <https://truthonthemarket.com/2018/07/18/the-eus-google-android-antitrust-decision-falls-prey-to-the-nirvana-fallacy/> accessed December 4, 2019.

178. Note also that the maintenance of contractual restrictions toward forks after Android had become a popular OS might be justified on the ground that users do benefit from a stable OS across generations, in terms of the investment they have made in applications, training, and certain hardware.

179. Google might not plausibly have entered into exclusive dealing requirements with app developers, because this might have fallen foul of antitrust liability. See Economides, "Competition Policy" (n 16) 113 referring to Nintendo's exclusive dealing requirement with game developers, abandoned thanks to antitrust challenge. See full set of FTC documents available at <https://cdn.muckrock.com/foia_files/2017/01/18/FOIA-2017-00161_Production.pdf> accessed December 4, 2019.

180. Which to some extent relativizes the weight of my former research assistant Norman Neyrinck's remark that "cutting throats when Trojans are asleep hardly qualifies as a fair fight."

monopoly maintenance in the tipped market.[181] To be fair, the EC decision discusses the "PC to mobile shift" of the "mid/late 2000s" in the preliminary section that precedes its antitrust evaluation. But the following legal and factual analysis turns into a formal inquiry of post-2011 conduct that disregards the history and economic complexity of the matter at hand. Our reading is that the EC did not confront whether Google's indirect entry with Android was anticompetitive or pro-competitive monopoly maintenance. But a serious case might be made on the basis of positive economics literature that monopolists too have incentives to innovate, be it to replace a monopoly with another.[182] Unless this set of alternatives is considered, antitrust agencies and courts might negate the principle of equal opportunity of indirect entry.

The fourth prong of the test asks whether the dominant firm will exit the indirect entry market following exclusion. Under existing doctrine, the EC was not required to prove this to establish an unlawful abuse. However, the decision alludes to some direct and indirect evidence in the decision that Google's indirect entry might be a serious commitment. To start, the development of Android substitutes variable costs known as traffic acquisition costs (paid to OEMs, MNOs, and websites) for sunk ones (R&D, marketing, etc.), creating exit barriers in the untipped market. Besides, study of anecdotal information found in the decision and elsewhere is suggestive. Over the course of the period of infringement, Google has vertically integrated into devices like Nexus and Pixel, and ramped up investments into parallel mobile and Internet of Things ("IoT") OS like Fuschia or Android Things.

4. Applications to Contemporary Concerns in Digital Markets

This interpolated discussion of *Microsoft* and *Google Android* shows that our antitrust test works both to establish liability and immunity in cases of

---

181. Daniel A Crane, "Does Monopoly Broth Make Bad Soup" (2009) 76(3) *The Antitrust Law Journal* 663. *Cont'l Ore Co v Union Carbide & Carbon Corp* [1962] 370 US 690, 699 (plaintiffs "should be given the full benefit of their proof without tightly compartmentalizing the various factual components and wiping the slate clean after scrutiny of each"); *City of Mishawaka v Am Elec Power Co* [1980] 7th Cir 616 F2d 976, 986 ("It is the mix of various ingredients ... in a monopoly broth that produces the unsavory flavor").

182. See Gilbert and Newberry, "Preemptive Patenting" (n 147). See also Jennifer F Reinganum, "Uncertain Innovation and the persistence of Monopoly: Reply" (1984) 74(1) *The American Economic Review* 243.

indirect entry by a monopoly firm. It satisfies the requirement of neutrality toward monopoly and other firms' indirect entry.

Our antitrust test is not contingent on categorical or formalistic distinctions. We can draw from the above discussion that it broadly covers monopoly firms' strategies, including product design and technological integration (Microsoft's "commin[gling]" of OS and browsers' routines),[183] contractual restraints (Google's anti-fragmentation agreements), organic growth strategies (development of Internet Explorer), and M&A transactions (Google's acquisition of Android).

In this light, let us now examine how our antitrust test dovetails with the ongoing policy conversation on anticompetitive conduct and consumer harms in digital economy.[184]

a) Self-Preferencing

Self-preferencing might breach our antitrust test. Self preferencing is a form of discrimination. The monopoly firm uses its position in the tipped market to favor its own products in the untipped market. This might either exclude rivals or reduce the surplus transfers they receive from users (even if the monopoly firm products are not used).[185] Self-preferencing has a clear leveraging component. At the same time, no antitrust liability should attach unless rivals in the untipped market are a threat to monopoly rents in the tipped market.[186] To illustrate, consider the facts of the EC 2017 decision in *Google Shopping*.[187] The EC found abusive Google's prominent display of its own comparison shopping service ("CSS") on general search pages combined with demotion of rival CSS websites. Our antitrust test might have condemned Google's self-preferencing vis-à-vis rival CSS because

---

183. *United States v Microsoft Corp* (1999) DDC 84 FSupp2d 9 (Findings of Fact) § 174.
184. For a reminder, see Chapter I. To organize the discussion clearly, we rely on the categories of conduct discussed in Keith Hylton, "Digital Platforms and Antitrust Law" (2019) 98(2) Nebraska Law Review (hereafter Hylton, "Digital Platform and Antitrust Law").
185. See Dennis W Carlton, Joshua S Gans, and Michael Waldman, "Why Tie a Product Consumers Do Not Use?" (2010) 2(3) *American Economic Journal: Microeconomics* 85.
186. We leave aside the question of whether self-preferencing increases the monopoly rent, in violation of our first antitrust principle whereby we should limit monopoly rent extension. As seen previously, however, this increase in the size of the rent is not a direct consequence of monopoly power, but of the externality created by complementary goods, that drives marginal benefits up, and moves the demand curve upward.
187. Commission Decision of 27.6.2017 relating to proceedings under Article 102 of the Treaty on the Functioning of the European Union and Article 54 of the Agreement on the European Economic Area [2017] C(2017) 4444 final (AT.39740—Google Search (Shopping)).

the latter competed with the former for a fraction of the untipped market for merchant commissions or specialist search advertising revenue, meeting condition one and two.[188] At the same time, our test might have immunized self-preferencing toward comparison shopping services, because conditions three and four were not satisfied. There was no suggestion in the case the CSS would directly or indirectly threaten Google's dominance over general search. And Google's shopping service has not been discontinued.[189]

b) Copycat Expropriation

Copycat expropriation might only exceptionally fall foul of our antitrust test. Copycat expropriation occurs in digital markets when a monopoly firm copies, imitates, or replicates a third party product, service, application or functionality. Copycat expropriation is generally procompetitive, unless it infringes upon IPRs—the law then embodies a social preference against unauthorized copying. Firms compete for lead time, and imitation dissipates economic rents. Users might enjoy higher benefits from using functionality within rather than outside the platform.[190] And in industries with little *ex ante* cooperation over product development, standards emerge by trial and error imitation. The last entrant eliminates the bad design and sets the dominant one.[191]

Copycat expropriation is the common currency in food products. Much of the burger wars between Mc Donald's and Burger King involve cloning. Or consider Pepsi's enlisting of Michael Jackson. The whole industry moved to celebrity advertising, imitating Pepsi's strategy.

Unfortunately, the paucity of legal cases on copycat expropriation in digital markets imposes reliance on real life illustrations. A commonly used

---

188. Note, however, that under this market definition, one does not clearly see the two markets situation required to establish leverage under the first condition. The EC nonetheless affirmed liability. It established two relevant markets for "general search services" and "comparison shopping services." It then moved on to establish exclusionary effects on the ground that Google had diverted "user traffic" away from CSS, leaving unanswered why this direct rivalry for merchant or advertiser revenue needed not be characterized as the sole and proper relevant market for antitrust evaluation.

189. See § 446 of EC Decision, where the Commission indirectly recognizes this rivalry, but does not connect it to a relevant market (AT.39470—Google Search (Shopping)).

190. Keith Hylton, "Digital Platforms and Antitrust Law" (n 184).

191. Peter Thiel and Blake Masters, *Zero to One: Notes on Startups, or How to Build the Future* (Crown Business 2014). Some examples of that strategy are IBM patiently waiting that UNIVAC became dominant on mainframe to penetrate the market; Apple copying the Xerox UI; Google emulating thirty-five search engines before it, and perfecting the technology; and Android closely drawing inspiration from the iPhone UI.

example in the antitrust conversation is Facebook's copy of Snapchat's features like stories. Here, we see that the fourth condition of our test is not satisfied, because Facebook entry in Snapchat's market is a durable strategy.

Amazon's private labels strategy gives another example. In Amazon's case, however, condition four might be satisfied. Often, Amazon's entry into specific product categories appears to be temporary. At the same time, the second condition might not be fulfilled. As seen previously, Amazon's recourse to vertical integration might be a way to induce merchants to sell at a low enough prices, not exclude them.[192] To be sure, under some circumstances, Amazon might have excluded merchants from highly profitable product segments like diapers, batteries, or beauty products, then satisfying the second condition of our test. Even so, imitation of a specialist product category might unlikely represent a threat for Amazon in the tipped market, so that the third condition is not fulfilled.

c) Killer Acquisitions

"Killer acquisitions" might fall within a merger version of our antitrust test if, and only if, the target is shut down. The theory of killer acquisitions is very simple. Consider a monopoly firm acquiring a growing startup. The startup is active outside of the monopoly firm market. It is, however, a horizontal threat because it operates within a same technological or user "space."[193]

Where, one might ask, is the kill? In a best-selling book on information communications industries, Tim Wu claimed that history supported the existence of an industry specific "Kronos effect," namely "efforts undertaken by a dominant company to consume its potential successors in their infancy."[194] In a subsequent empirical study that popularized the term "killer" merger, pharmaceutical firms were found to discontinue targets' innovative projects with potential to create future rivalry in 6.4 percent of

---

192. Short of being able to use controversial contractual practices like resale price maintenance, especially in Europe.
193. To date, these mergers are looked at as "conglomeral" transactions. In the absence of clear horizontal overlaps or risks of input foreclosure, they are presumptively innocuous.
194. See Tim Wu, *The Master Switch: The Rise and Fall of Information Empires* (Vintage 2011). Reference to Kronos is not very apposite, because in most merger cases the acquired successor is not home grown. Kronos, by contrast, ate its own progeny.

the sample cases.[195] Voices in the antitrust community have remarked that 6.4 percent is not a small number.[196]

Subject to a relaxation of the moot condition of leverage in a setting of entry by merger, killer acquisitions appear to breach the second and third conditions of our antitrust test.[197] But killer acquisitions do not obviously breach the fourth condition if the monopoly firm has ability and incentives to grow the target. Some, in the policy discussion, would nonetheless like to outlaw such acquisitions because the target could "grow as a self-standing competitive force if not acquired by the incumbent, or if other companies may be realistically interested."[198] Our test is superior to this proposal. No formal or empirical works to date allow an assumption that a startup brings a higher contribution to social welfare—read industry output—under standalone growth or M&A with a third party competitor than under M&A with a dominant firm.

Moreover, in hindsight, the best that anecdotal evidence suggests is that assumptions of firm growth under a standalone strategy frequently do not hold. Google, Facebook, and Twitter grew significantly following their respective refusal to sell to Excite, Yahoo!, and Facebook. But consider Friendster, Groupon, or Quicki. All of them refused to sell to Google. And all registered limited growth, if not flat out decline. Our best possible assumption in a killer acquisition scenario is that the startup operates in a market that has not yet tipped.[199] In the end, this hints at limited predictability about the startup's odds of success. This ambiguity affects the very validity of the killer acquisition conjecture.

195. Colleen Cunningham, Florian Ederer, and Song Ma, "Killer Acquisition" (2018) *SSRN Working Paper* <https://papers.ssrn.com/sol3/papers.cfm?abstract_id=3241707> accessed December 4, 2019.
196. Former EC competition Chief Economist Tommasso Valletti is reported to have said that ("6/7%—these are the things we should look into—it is not a small number"). See Jacquelyn MacLennan, Tilman Kuhn, and Thilo Wienke "Innocent Until Proven Guilty—Five Things You Need to Know About Killer Acquisitions" (*Informa Connect,* May 3, 2019) <https://informaconnect.com/innocent-until-proven-guilty-five-things-you-need-to-know-about-killer-acquisi-tions/> accessed December 18, 2019.
197. One might discuss here if the antitrust rule should allow the monopoly firm to articulate a credible business justification like the repurposing of teams and assets on other product segments.
198. Jacques Crémer, Yves-Alexandre de Montjoye, and Heike Schweitzer, "Competition Policy for the Digital Era: Final Report" (2019).
199. Assuming that it has passed the stage of product launch, which is not a given.

E. Market Definition and Market Power Analysis in Digital Markets

Our framework works on a distinction between tipped and untipped markets. Recall that the distinction was the subject of Chapter III. Untipped markets are characterized by entry, instability, and uncertainty. Tipped markets display diametrically opposite characteristics.

The distinction is key. Untipped markets constrain the market power associated with perceived monopoly positions. By contrast, in tipped markets, tech firms with observed monopoly positions can take full advantage of their market power, and optimize by extracting rents from users.

Evidence-based antitrust requires to treat the assessment of market power as an empirical question. All modern antitrust regimes follow this approach. With this in mind, market definition and market power analysis might be asked to produce findings that are likely to cast light on whether a relevant market has tipped or not.

Let us, however, be clear. The point here is not to require dispositive antitrust findings that a market is tipped or untipped. Rather, the distinction is more of a mental model, designed to help antitrust decision-makers understand idiosyncrasies of digital markets. Tipped and untipped markets might be better thought of to operate on a continuum, with markets that are more or less tipped or untipped, and more or less prone to de-tip or re-tip.

1. Contemporary Antitrust: Inferring Rivalry from Structure

What does contemporary antitrust do? US and EU doctrine do not expressly require antitrust decision-makers to assess whether a market has tipped or not. US and EU doctrine impose on agencies and courts a method that requires to (i) delineate relevant markets that comprise all rival goods or services; and/or (ii) assess market power by asking what are the possibilities of substitution of rival goods or services from the perspective of users.

To be fair, market definition and market power assessment might implicitly consider tipping. But a point might be made that, in spite of their increasing sophistication, contemporary empirical methods of market definition and market power assessment remain error prone. To start, structural analysis—still the dominant *modus operandi* in antitrust proceedings—is unlikely to sensibly distinguish between tipped and untipped markets. Durable dominant shares and high entry barriers in network effects markets do not allow inference of a tipped market, because they do not capture the set of dynamic constraints met in Chapter IV—and typical of untipped markets—like exploration, discontinuities, growth, and diversification.

More important, the market definition procedure is in every sense biased toward findings of tipped markets. Recall that market definition allows antitrust agencies and courts to define the relevant share of output on which sellers compete for users' demand. In practice, market definition starts from the largest set of substitution possibilities to users, and progressively zeroes in on substitution possibilities that are as perfect as possible. One unintended effect is to transform market definition into a *slice and dice* exercise. With eyes toward the best substitution possibilities, antitrust agencies and courts tend to discount indirect, external, and potential sources of competition informative of an untipped market. This is unfortunate because market definition was introduced in enforcement in order to simplify and objectivize the discussion of the assessment of effects between plaintiff and defendant.

Study of antitrust cases illustrates these problems. In its 2014 review of the *Facebook/WhatsApp* merger, the EC declined to fully consider whether consumer communications apps like WhatsApp were subject to the competition of SMS, and proceeded to examine the merger transaction on the basis of a "market definition limited to consumer communications apps for smartphones and excluding traditional communication services."[200] In the *Google Shopping* decision, the EC found Google guilty of exclusionary conduct against comparison shopping websites, rejecting evidence that the latter's lost market share might have been caused by participation in an untipped market comprising merchant platforms like Amazon and eBay.[201] And in the *Google Android* decision, the EC held Google dominant in a

---

200. See Commission Decision pursuant to Article 6(1)(b) of Council Regulation No 139/2004, Case No COMP/M.7217, *Facebook/WhatsApp*, C(2014) 7239 final. However, this finding was contradicted a few months later by the EC itself, when it wrote in the Proposal for a Regulation on Privacy and Electronic Communications of January 10, 2017 that "End-users increasingly replace traditional voice telephony, text messages (SMS) and electronic mail conveyance services in favour of functionally equivalent online services such as Voice over IP, messaging services and web-based e-mail services." See Proposal for a Regulation of the European Parliament and of the Council concerning the respect for private life and the protection of personal data in electronic communications and repealing Directive 2002/58/EC, [2017] COM(2017) 10 final (Regulation on Privacy and Electronic Communications), § 11.
201. See Commission Decision of 27.6.2017 relating to proceedings under Article 102 of the Treaty on the Functioning of the European Union and Article 54 of the Agreement on

market for "licensable smart operating systems," plausibly failing to consider that Android had untipped the smartphone OS market dominated by incumbent platform Apple iOS due to differences in business models.[202]

2. Improvements to Antitrust: Assessing Tipping from Pressure

What can antitrust do? Unless we are ready to tolerate an error prone method to measure market power and define markets, we may try to incrementally improve our analytical framework so as to better distinguish the properties of tipped and untipped markets. If competition law is empirical, it must acknowledge that it is empirical within a framework and set assumptions. A true commitment to empiricism requires openness to criticism and reform.

With this in mind, recall that there is more uncertainty in untipped than in tipped markets. So in addition to structural analysis, firm-level evidence of competitive pressure might improve market definition and market power evaluation.

That idea is hardly new. Across decades, major economic works on monopolies have stressed that dominant firms are subject to low pressure to change. In 1935, Sir John Hicks wrote famously "the best of all monopoly profits is a quiet life."[203] Beyond the catchphrase, Hicks suggested that monopolists being likely "people with sharply rising subjective costs" may actually "not [be] bothering to get very near the position of maximum profit," in violation of the standard profit maximization condition of economic theory.

Micro-economist Harvey Leibenstein expressed a similar idea. In his view, the real social harm of monopoly is not as much supra-competitive prices than lack of motivational efficiency. Firms subject to low competitive pressure display "inertial behavior," and occupy "non optimal effort

---

the European Economic Area [2017] C(2017) 4444 final (AT.39470—Google Search (Shopping), § 216.

202. See Commission Decision of 18 July 2018 relating to a proceeding under Article 102 of the Treaty of the Functioning of the European Union (the Treaty) and Article 54 of the EEA Agreement (2018) C(2018)4761 final (Google Android Case AT.40099).

203. Though not the only profit of monopolies. Hicks suggested that monopolists being likely "people with sharply rising subjective costs" may actually "not [be] bothering to get very near the position of maximum profit," in violation of the venerable profit maximization condition of economic theory.

positions which persist over time."[204] When competitive pressure is weak, firms do not work as hard to reduce costs, utilize or search new information.[205] Leibenstein wrote:

> In situations where competitive pressure is light, many people will trade the disutility of greater effort, of search, and the control of other peoples' activities for the utility of feeling less pressure and of better interpersonal relations. But in situations where competitive pressures are high, and hence the costs of such trades are also high, they will exchange less of the disutility of effort for the utility of freedom from pressure.[206]

And antitrust economist Franklin Fisher—later the US government economic expert in the *Microsoft* case—has discussed "dynamic constraints" on monopolies in terms of "compulsion" (or lack thereof):

> In effect, a monopolist would be someone, as in the static case, insulated from entry, from the pressures of imitators and other innovators. He might very well bring out new products, because that would be a profitable thing to do, but the crucial fact would be that he would not have to do so. As in the static case, the crucial difference between monopoly and competition is the compulsion which market forces place on the competitor and the lack of it on the monopolist.[207]

We deliberately give extant exposition to Hicks, Leibenstein, and Fisher.[208] To the economic-minded antitrust court, agency, or practitioner, all of these works are an invitation to assess a firm's "degree of effort" as a complement to structural analysis. But they are also a lot of trouble. It is indeed hard enough to delineate relevant markets and assess market power in digital

---

204. Harvey Leibenstein, "Allocative Efficiency vs 'X-Efficiency'" (1966) 56(3) *American Economic Review* 411.
205. By contrast, observation of monopoly or oligopoly positions is less informative. Competitive pressure is compatible with industry concentration, because as costs declines, "some firms are forced out and fewer firms exist." See ibid.
206. ibid 413.
207. Franklin M Fisher, "Diagnosing Monopoly" (1978) *MIT Department of Economics Working Paper No 226*, 9 (hereafter Fisher, "Diagnosis Monopoly").
208. But equal prominence should be given to business and management science studies that stress the subjectivity of competitive behavior, consistent with our findings in Chapter II. See for instance, Donald C Hambrick and Phyllis A Mason, "Upper Echelons: The Organization as a Reflection of its Top Managers" (1984) 9(2) *The Academy of Management Review* 193. Some empirical studies have confirmed the subjective nature of interfirm rivalry. Jeremy J Marcel, Pamela S Barr, and Irene M Duhaine, "The Influence of Executive Cognition on Competitive Dynamics" (2010) 32 *Strategic Management Journal* 2.

markets with nominally free goods and services, multisidedness, and rapid technological dynamism.

Nevertheless, continual improvement of empirical methods for the definition of markets and the evaluation of market power has guided, and should keep guiding, the evolution of contemporary antitrust policy.[209] By way of illustration, in the United States, the *Amex* Opinion of the Supreme Court held that, in what it called a "two-sided transaction platform," in which the platform facilitates a "simultaneous transaction between participants," the relevant market must include both sides.[210] The floor is now crowded for debate on whether the Supreme Court got it right. In the European Union, the EC in *Google Android* has attempted to overcome the difficulty of testing the price elasticity of demand in zero price markets by asking whether a substantial proportion of Google's users would switch general services in response to a "small but significant non-transitory deterioration of the quality of Google's general search service."[211]

There are reasons of principle and reasons of practicality for this. In common law systems, as *Kimble v Marvel Entertainment LLC* recalled, the US Supreme Court "has felt free to revise [its] legal analysis as economic understanding evolves and to reverse antitrust precedents that misperceived a practice's competitive consequences."[212] In other systems like the European Union, market definition and market power assessment methods have provided antitrust agencies with a practical response to make sense of ambiguous judicial standards like the concept of the "independence" of a dominant firm vis-à-vis its competitors, customers, and its consumers.[213]

---

209. See William E Kovacic and Carl Shapiro, "Antitrust Policy: A Century of Economic and Legal Thinking" (2000) 14(1) *Journal of Economic Perspectives* 43.

210. *Ohio, et al v American Express Company* [2018] 585 US __.

211. Commission Decision of 18 July 2018 relating to a proceeding under Article 102 of the Treaty of the Functioning of the European Union (the Treaty) and Article 54 of the EEA Agreement (2018) C(2018)4761 final (Google Android Case AT.40099).

212. See *Kimble v Marvel Entertainment, LLC* [2015] 576 US __.

213. *United Brands v Commission* [1978] ECLI:EU:C:1978:22 ("The dominant position referred to in article 86 relates to a position of economic strength enjoyed by an undertaking which enables it to prevent effective competition being maintained in the relevant market by giving it the power to behave to an appreciable extent independently of its competitors, customers and ultimately its consumers. In general a dominant position derives from a combination of several factors which, taken separately, are not necessarily determinative"). *Hoffmann-La Roche & Co AG v Commission of the European Communities* [1979] ECLI:EU:C:1979:36 (a dominant position "does not preclude some competition, which it does where there is a monopoly or quasi monopoly, but enables the undertaking which profits by it, if not to determine, at least to have an appreciable influence on the conditions under which that

In light of this, can we conceive of a qualitative, and if possible, quantitative test of competitive pressure that might help decision-makers to draw
a line between tipped and untipped markets in industries with network
effects, increasing returns to adoption and uncertainty? This is what we now
look at.

3. Measurement of Competitive Pressure: Methods

Several methods exist to measure competitive pressure. Hicks had stressed
the relevance of "subjective factors" to firm behavior like the willingness to
bear risks or the rate of time preference.[214] But in practice, subjective factors
are in disrepute. They are generally seen as highly gameable.

In the future, new economic learning might however improve the confidence of antitrust courts, agencies, and practitioners in subjective assessments of competitive pressure. Digital technologies have made available vast
quantities of text data. A growing amount of economic research is now
using advanced data science techniques to infer sentiment from large bodies
of corporate documents, like CEO diary data, patent applications, or 10-K
disclosure reports.[215] Of particular interest here is a 2016 article published
by Gerard Hoberg and Gordon Phillips in the Journal of Political Economy.
Hoberg and Philips provide a novel way of classifying industries based on
product descriptions in the text of company disclosures.[216] Contrary to
received industrial organization theory, they find that product competition
and rival identification cuts across industries, and are highly responsive to
external shocks. For example, Hoberg and Philips establish that the events
of September 11, 2001 redefined the boundaries of rivalry in military markets, pushing products competition toward "non-battlefield information
gathering and products intended for potential ground conflicts."[217]

competition will develop, and in any case to act largely in disregard of it so long as such conduct does not operate to its detriment"). *Michelin v Commission* [1983] ECLI:EU:C:1983:313,
para 57.

214. See John R Hicks, "The Process of Imperfect Competition" (1954) 6(1) *Oxford Economic
Papers New Series* 41, 45.

215. See Matthew Gentzkow, Bryan Kelly, and Matt Taddy, "Text as Data" (2019) 57(3) *Journal of
Economic Literature* 535.

216. See Gerard Hoberg and Gordon M Philips, "Text-Based Network Industries and Endogenous
Product Differentiation" (2016) 124(5) *Journal of Political Economy*.

217. ibid 40.

Besides, objective sources, an in particular performance measures, offer valuable information. In particular, empirical evidence of innovation expenditures might allow antitrust decision-makers to draw inferences of competitive pressure. High R&D effort can indeed plausibly be associated with the idea that a monopoly firm hustles, inconsistent with a tipped market.

But a practical reservation is that firms tend to over-report R&D in their disclosures, notably to take advantage of tax credits. We know, for example, that Microsoft has in the past reported as R&D the costs incurred to translate software for international markets.[218]

Besides these manageable anomalies, however, a greater difficulty is that R&D data is not disaggregated. This is a problem for antitrust decision-makers whose unit of analysis is a relevant product market. To say things clearly, R&D at firm level is little informative of the relative differences in competitive pressure faced by a firm in distinct markets for products A and B. This complication might be compounded when firms sell multiple products, as is often the case in digital industries.

Nevertheless, in spite of these problems, the degree of competitive pressure bearing on a firm might be illuminated by an explicit, systematic, and thorough consideration of innovation efforts in the market definition and market power assessment. Antitrust decision-makers enjoy broad fact-finding powers. Subject to adequate confidentiality, nothing prevents agencies and courts to require investigated firms to break down R&D efforts by industry, markets, or product segments. Moreover, one way to separate the wheat from the chaff in firms' disclosures consists in focusing the R&D inquiry on labor costs. Consistent with the literature, the research that we conducted under Chapter IV suggests that R&D spending in digital industries consists primarily of labor costs (attraction, remuneration, and retention of skilled workers), or of related costs like those incurred to provide facilities for employees involved in R&D.[219]

---

218. See Microsoft Corporation, Form 10-K, US SEC, 2009.
219. See Nicolas Petit, "Technology Giants, The "Moligopoly" Hypothesis and Holistic Competition: A Primer" (2016) *SSRN Working Paper* <https://papers.ssrn.com/sol3/papers.cfm?abstract_id=2856502> accessed December 4, 2019. Gary P Pisano, "Creating an R&D Strategy" Harvard Business School, *Working Paper 12-095* (2012) 5 ("[d]espite the growing use of sophisticated instrumentation, computer simulation, and laboratory automation, R&D is still a labor intensive process"); Avron Barr and Shirley Tessler, "The Globalization of Software R&D: The Search for Talent" (1996) *Council on Foreign Relations' Study Group on the Globalization of Industrial R&D*, 11 ("unlike most other engineering and product development disciplines, software has remained an art: the creative output of individuals with unique skills").

Importantly, we need not worry here that the way in which the antitrust regime draws inferences of competitive pressure will adversely influence firms' disclosure behavior. Unlike in areas like price fixing in which intrusive antitrust investigations incentivize firms to conceal evidence, asking firms to disclose more granular innovation expenditures is innocuous.

To be sure, there might be other performance indicators of competitive pressure, like marketing spending, the rate of product introduction, changes in business methods and strategy, capital allocation choices, or intrafirm divisional competition.[220] Whatever the tool, the goal is to distinguish aggregate firm-level performance measures from disaggregate market-specific competitive pressure. While the former deserves less weight in the market power assessment, the latter will allow antitrust decision-makers to address more confidently whether observed markets have tipped or not.

Beyond improvements to diagnosis accuracy (and legitimacy), additional inquiries into competitive pressure have related benefits. One might be to accommodate more heterogeneity in findings of monopoly power. Figures 5.1 and 5.2 below, for instance, give word counts of competition-related concepts in 10-Ks for Amazon and Netflix, that lend support to the idea that Amazon is subject to less pressure than Netflix.[221]

Another, more important, is that assessment of competitive pressure allows better consideration of the time dimension. To date, the market power assessment considers time by looking at whether market shares denote persistence. In digital industries, antitrust experts often infer weak competition "for the market" from the persistence of dominant market shares.[222] This has

220. For example, Titman and Wessels discuss a measure of a firm's unique products that they call uniqueness. And they provide indicators of uniqueness, namely, expenditures on research and development over sales (RD/S), selling expenses over sales (SE/S), and quit rates. See Sheridan Titman and Roberto Wessels, "The Determinants of Capital Structure Choice" (1988) 43(1) The Journal of Finance 1.
221. For obvious informational limitations, the data shown here are not disaggregated at the market specific level.
222. Jason Furman et al, "Unlocking digital Competition: Report of the Digital Competition Expert Panel" (HM Treasury 2019) §1.159, <https://www.gov.uk/government/publications/unlocking-digital-competition-report-of-the-digital-competition-expert-panel> ("a number of digital markets are dominated by one or two powerful platform companies, and that this dominance is persistent"; "Persistent dominance and market power: An important question is whether the largest incumbents of digital markets are constrained by competition 'for the market', and could be unseated by innovative entrants in the future. Although the dominant players continue to innovate and compete, there is reason to be skeptical of the notion that they face serious threats to their dominant positions in the future, unless there are changes to the current policy framework").

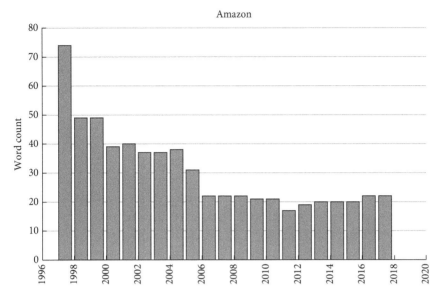

Figure 5.1 Word counts of Competition-related Concepts in 10-Ks for Amazon

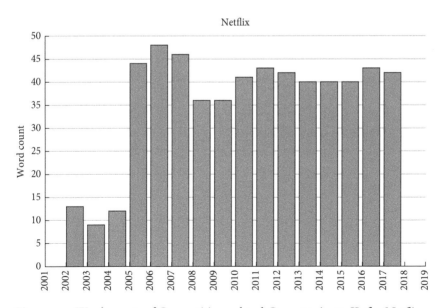

Figure 5.2 Word counts of Competition-related Concepts in 10-Ks for Netflix

led some to distinguish Google or Facebook's "bad" dominance (because persistent), from Myspace or AltaVista's "good" market power (because transient). But perhaps, the dominant market share of Google and Facebook is the result of persistent "competition seriously at work."[223] And we cannot possibly know, unless we invalidate the hypothesis of continuous competitive pressure. Often forgotten is that Schumpeter did not specify the time intervals at which "creative destruction" would hit markets, and for good reason. Schumpeter envisioned creative destruction as a "perennial gale," incessantly challenging industries, markets, and firms.[224]

Doing otherwise is falling prey to an old and well-known antitrust fallacy, namely considering that the size of greatest efficiency was reached at a relatively early stage and that further growth resulted from the employment of unfair competitive practices.[225] As we often tell students: the point that Facebook has occupied a dominant share over a decade is irrelevant. What is relevant for the market definition and market power assessment is to determine whether Facebook is the same firm today as it was in 2010.

F. Conclusion

In this chapter, we have formulated a sector-specific antitrust test for the evaluation of anticompetitive conduct in digital markets with network effects, increasing returns to adoption and uncertainty. The test works as a mental model that distinguishes tipped and untipped markets in order to overcome the crudeness of conventional rivalry assessments. It seeks to focus antitrust decision-makers' resources on the limitation of monopoly rents in tipped markets, and to allow intervention in untipped markets only in particular circumstances. The test also requires antitrust to differentiate the analytical treatment of market conduct depending on whether it takes place on one side of a platform or the other.

---

223. See Fisher, "Diagnosis Monopoly" (n 207).

224. See Joseph A Schumpeter, *Capitalism, Socialism and Democracy* (Harper and Brothers 1942) 84.

225. See Ellis W Hawley, *The New Deal and the Problem of Monopoly: A Study in Economic Ambivalence* (Fordham University Press 1995) (noting that W Wilson's antitrust policy operated under this assumption).

The principles developed in this chapter should not be thought of as strict rules of antitrust liability. They might equally work as flexible standards. What matters is this: antitrust must limit monopoly rent extraction by big tech firms in tipped markets, and promote indirect entry toward untipped markets under conditions of neutrality between established tech giants and new firms.

★

★   ★

VI

Big Tech's Novel Harms: Antitrust or Regulation?

A. Preliminary Remarks

We devote the last pages of this book to a non-technical discussion of the novel harms that are allegedly inherent to the nature of big tech firms. As previously seen, the press describes big tech as the cause of all manners of new problems leading to substantial economic and non-economic harms. Fake news, hate speech, or privacy violations are cases in point.

In this light, our proposed antitrust regime is limited. With a focus on keeping the competitive process of indirect entry open to all firms (including big tech), and indirect intervention against monopoly rents, it is more "hedgehog" than "fox."[1]

So should government adopt additional measures in relation to the tech giants? In particular, should Government address the novel harms that they are said to create? And how much of such programs should be conducted under antitrust rules?

These questions are difficult.[2] In the early twentieth century, antitrust was thought of as a program for the "simultaneous pursuit of a host of economic, social and political aims."[3] In the past fifty years, this broad conception

---

1. This remark was made by Luigi Zingales, upon reading a working paper version of what became Chapter III of this book. He referred to the Greek poet Archilochus who wrote that "the *fox* knows many things, but the *hedgehog* knows one big thing."
2. And legitimate. As Jean Tirole noted, "economists must participate in the policy debate." See Jean Tirole, "Market Failures and Public Policy" (2015) 105(6) *American Economic Review* 1665.
3. Ernest Gellhorn and William Kovacic, *Antitrust Law and Economics in a Nutshell* (4th edn, West Academic Publishing 1994). Simply put, the aim was the dispersion of economic and political power.

Big Tech and the Digital Economy. Nicolas Petit, Oxford University Press (2020). © Nicolas Petit.
DOI: 10.1093/oso/9780198837701.001.0001

has been replaced with a vision of antitrust as a law enforcement program focused on the protection of "consumer welfare." However, quite ironically, the modern diffusion of the more economic approach in antitrust enforcement has "subtly" reconfigured antitrust itself into a form of government regulation. Under this vision, the inquiry is less focused on the violation of a legal norm, and increasingly concerned with how restraints on private property might improve social welfare.[4]

This trend has been more visible in the European Union ("EU"). There, the boundary between antitrust and regulation is not subject to a clear division of labor. In Europe, the implicit view is one of antitrust as a Swiss knife for welfare optimization.[5] Antitrust operates in complementarity with regulation. Sometimes, it is used as a premise to regulation, playing a role as an *ex ante* fact-finding device.[6] Alternatively, antitrust is used as a gap filler, to correct regulatory defects *ex post*.[7] To date, this logic of cross fertilization has been mostly applied to "economic regulation," that is regulation aimed at improving the efficiency of markets.[8] But given this elusive separation, antitrust might also be used to serve adjacent social, technical, or administrative regulatory enterprises. In Europe, rule of law-minded antitrust practitioners often complain about this.

In US law, by contrast, this dynamic is less palpable. This is because an explicit theory of regulation shaped by the Supreme Court considers antitrust and economic regulation as substitutes. Antitrust is seen as a tool of law enforcement dealing with categories of bad economic conduct leading to adverse consumer welfare effects as a result of market power. When economic regulation is applied to a market, industry, or the economy, application of antitrust is excluded.[9] In turn, this limits the slippery slope of using antitrust to address non-economic regulation concerns.

---

4. Doug Melamed made this observation more than twenty years ago, and this has been a steady evolution since then. A Douglas Melamed, "Antitrust: The New Regulation" (1995) 10(1) *Antitrust* 13.
5. Cremer et al, alluding to competition law's "function as a background regime of an otherwise well-ordered marketplace." See Jacques Crémer, Yves-Alexandre de Montjoye, and Heike Schweitzer, "Competition Policy for the Digital Era: Final Report" (2019).
6. Competition cases have opened a reflection on how best to regulate roaming fees, leading to adoption of specific regulatory instruments.
7. In energy markets, competition law was used to enforce unbundling commitment in situations beyond the reach of existing regulatory frameworks.
8. For a discussion of the various categories of regulation, see OECD, "Regulatory Reform and Innovation" <https://www.oecd.org/sti/inno/2102514.pdf> accessed December 8, 2019.
9. In 2004, the Supreme Court ruled in *Verizon Communications, Inc v Law Offices of Curtis V Trinko, LLP* that a claim under Section 2 of the Sherman Act could not proceed against

As a result, the substantive question of whether policy-making, in relation to novel harms, should rely on antitrust, economic regulation, or on non-economic regulation remains intellectually relevant. In our view, one simple way to address it consists in asking ourselves a simple question: are the novel harms raised by big tech a monopoly problem? If this is the case, the concern ought to be dealt with primarily under antitrust law or economic regulation. If not, non-economic regulation might be the better instrument. Implicit in our logic is the conventional wisdom whereby a policy target requires a dedicated policy tool.[10]

As with all hard questions, logic—as well as a pinch of common sense—helps. One can conceive of a simple procedure to think about the issue under inquiry. The procedure consists in asking three sub-questions:

1. Is harm caused by monopoly power (or might harm exist in competitive markets)?
2. If monopoly power is not sole cause of harm, is harm lower under competition?
3. If harm is lower under competition, can we be confident that competition creates no other externalities?

If the answer to either or all of these questions leans toward yes, antitrust or economic regulation should probably deal with the underlying issue (or statutory reform that makes competition law stricter and broader, like a "no fault" antitrust). If the answer to either or all of these questions leans more toward no, the solution is probably some sort of non-economic regulation unencumbered by the market power threshold rules of competition law. In the latter case, a hard question is then to determine which model of regulation is appropriate.

Do not misunderstand us. We do not discuss here whether big tech firms undersupply authentic news, privacy, or civic content. The subject of our inquiry is whether we can confidently believe that the elimination of big tech monopoly positions (and the introduction of more rivalry) will increase

Verizon for violations that were more related to the Telecommunications Act of 1996 than to the antitrust laws. And in *Credit Suisse*, the Supreme Court held that even where a correctly construed antitrust claim would not actually conflict with regulation, the antitrust claim could still be barred on potential conflict grounds. See *Verizon Communications, Inc v Law Offices of Curtis V Trinko, LLP* [2004] 540 US 398 and *Credit Suisse Securities (USA) LLC v Billing* [2007] 551 US 264.

10. See Chapter I, Section C(2).

the supply of authentic news, privacy or civic content. Or put differently, we ask if a case can be made that there is a functional relationship between monopoly and the novel harms inherent to big tech, not a coincidental one.

In this chapter, we apply this simple procedure to three types of novel harms, that is privacy (B), fake news (C), and hate speech (D) and discuss models of regulation (E). The discussion is deliberately kept at a high level. We do not aspire to generate definitive answers, just to help decision-makers set out options for policy reform.

B. Privacy

There are controversial debates about the meaning of privacy.[11] In 1890, Samuel Warren and Louis Brandeis defined privacy as "the right to be let alone."[12] Initially developed to protect individuals from *intrusions* of the press, the *right* to privacy has grown to reflect evolutions in technology, business models as well as the expansion of the regulatory state. In most of the Western world, privacy is protected by law revealing a strong social choice for privacy *rights*. Besides, and regardless of legal entitlements, most people have an *interest* in protecting their privacy. Aleksandr Solzhenitsyn once declared, "Everyone is guilty of something or has something to conceal."[13]

The truth is that several tech giants use business models adverse to privacy. Google, Facebook, and perhaps to a lesser extent Microsoft and Amazon, generate substantial revenue by showing targeted advertisement ("ads") to users. Targeted ads reduce privacy at more than one level. To start, targeted ads require extraction of personal data. Then, targeted ads interfere with users' ability to make decisions, in particular when they make purchases on the Internet.[14] And because the tech giants are unavoidable platforms today, no one really enjoys "seclusion" or the right to solitude in the online world.

With this background, let us look at our first sub-question: are privacy harms caused by monopoly?

11. Herman T Tavani, "Philosophical Theories of Privacy: Implications for an Adequate Online Privacy Policy" (2007) 38(1) *Metaphilosophy* 1 (hereafter Tavani, "Philosophical Theories of Privacy").
12. Samuel D Warren and Louis D Brandeis "Right to Privacy" (1890) 4 *Harvard Law Review* 193.
13. Daniel J Solove, "I've Got Nothing to Hide and other Misunderstandings of Privacy" (2007) 44 *San Diego Law Review* 745.
14. Tavani, "Philosophical Theories of Privacy" (n 11) 6 (talking of "decisional privacy").

One intuitively attractive way to think about this question is to imagine a breakup of Google into two search advertisement companies. Can we expect a reduction of privacy harms? The likely answer is no. Adding one competing firm to the search advertisement market will lower ad prices and increase demand for ads. This, in turn, should raise search advertisement output compared to the monopoly world and decrease privacy.[15]

Granted, this conjecture is subject to implicit assumptions.[16] The important insight is that whether monopoly causes privacy losses is an empirical question. Both monopoly and competition indeed appear compatible with privacy harms. Real life observations provide anecdotal evidence that firms of all size, big, small, monopolists or startups, can and do extract personal data.

In 2017, the German competition authority, or Bundeskartellamt, held otherwise.[17] Finding against Facebook, it contented that "[i]t cannot be argued that market power will not significantly increase the scope for processing data [by Facebook] and that this scope already exists without market power." According to the Bundeskartellamt, unlike with money, "[t]here is no limited budget which would determine the consumers'" willingness to pay and force them to economize."[18] Upshot: "users are therefore less sensitive to data" than to money, and there is consequently monopoly power on the other side.

The Bundeskartellamt's economic logic is weird. When pushed to its limits, it is akin to saying that all firms that sell to wealthy people with unlimited budget constraints have market power.

Let us turn to the second sub-question. Both monopoly and competition are consistent with privacy harms. But can we expect competition to lead to a relatively lower equilibrium of data extraction?[19] It is often heard in policy circles that if competition is introduced, this will create opportunities for the

---

15. If Google is a monopolist, sales of targeted ads should take place at a supra-competitive price. True, after the breakup, each Google spin-off should incur higher average total costs due to lost economies of scale. At the same time, competition should lead to sales of targeted ads at the competitive price. Subject to specific cost and demand elasticity specifications, the second effect might dominate the first, in which case competition should lead to more targeted ads, and less privacy.
16. They are relative to costs and elasticity of demand, but they are not conservative.
17. Administrative Decision under Section 32(1) German Competition Act (GWB) [2019] 6th Decision Division, B6-22/16, 382.
18. ibid.
19. This is the standard comparative statics approach of policy analysis.

entry of firms with different business models based on data minimization. This bodes well for our earlier claim in Chapter IV that indirect entry is the rule.

One can conceive of two hypotheticals of indirect entry by horizontal differentiation. And we need not say which one is true to understand that the relationship between competition and data minimization is indeterminate. One hypothetical predicts that rivals will compete for users by supplying less extractive personal data services. Let us take the example of the B2B market for cloud computing contracts. On Microsoft's Azure, access to customer data by Microsoft is blocked by default.[20] On AWS, the standard service contract prescribes that Amazon "will not access or use [customer's] content except as necessary to maintain or provide the service offerings or as necessary to comply with the law or a binding order of a governmental body."[21] And on Google Cloud Platform, access to customer data is not excluded, subject to contractual agreement.[22]

The second hypothetical predicts that rivals will compete for extraction of personal data, subject to compensation.[23] A loose anecdotal validation might be Bing's competition against Google for users' personal data on the basis of rewards … and possibly false advertising.[24] This is a variation of the "wasteful" competition argument, whereby excessive competition leads to oversupply of socially harmful activities.[25]

---

20. See Barbara Kess et al, "Azure Customer Data Protection" (*Microsoft Azure*, June 28, 2018) <https://docs.microsoft.com/en-us/azure/security/fundamentals/protection-customer-data> accessed December 8, 2019.
21. See Article 3.2 of AWS Customer Agreement. See also, Article 8.1. ("we obtain no rights under this agreement from you (or your licensors) to Your Content").
22. See "Google Cloud Platform" <https://privacy.google.com/businesses/controls/#!?modal_active=modal-products&product_id=google-cloud-platform> accessed December 8, 2018. Google cloud platform says "We process your data only according to our agreement with your business. We do not use data you put into Google Cloud Platform for advertising." This is different from Google marketing platform where more explicit limitations seem to prevail. There, it is said, data "is never shared with any other Google product or with any other business using our services without your consent." See "Google Marketing Platform" <https://privacy.google.com/businesses/controls/#!?modal_active=modal-products&product_id=google-marketing-platform> accessed December 8, 2019.
23. This is well exposed at: Ezra Klein, "Facebook is a Capitalism Problem, not Mark Zuckerberg Problem" (*Vox,* May 10, 2019) <https://www.vox.com/recode/2019/5/10/18563895/facebook-chris-hughes-mark-zuckerberg-break-up-monopoly> accessed December 8, 2019.
24. Ian Ayres et al, "A Randomized Experiment Assessing the Accuracy of Microsoft's Bing It on Challenge" (2013) *Loyola Consumer Law Review* 26.
25. For a short exposition of the issue see Jonathan B Baker, *The Antitrust Paradigm: Restoring a Competitive Economy* (Harvard University Press 2019) 29. See also section B on "excessive competition concerns" in Frederic M Scherer (ed), *Monopoly and Competition Policy,* Vol I., The International Library of Critical Writings in Economics, Vol. 30 (Edward Elgar 1993).

Stated as is, however, the first hypothetical is a Nirvana fallacy, and the second is an inefficiency possibility theorem. What do we observe in the real world? A paper called the "Antitrust case against Facebook" from Dina Srinivasan claims that horizontal differentiation prevails under competition. The paper relies on press articles to argue that Facebook became a monopolist in 2014 following a phase of alleged intense horizontal competition on privacy terms.[26] Having driven out competing social networks in 2014, Facebook then arguably decreased privacy quality, and engaged in a pattern of false statements, misleading and deceptive representations toward users.

The paper's claim is deficient. Empirical evidence suggests that competition does not lead to horizontal differentiation manifest in privacy quality. To see this, consider Figure 6.1 below. In 2014, the growth of Facebook's ads prices (in light grey) started to decline. In other words, after 2014, Facebook's conduct was less of the monopolistic kind, and more of the competitive kind.[27] What happened to targeted ads? Impressions (in dark grey) grew faster. The implication is thus that under competition—when prices go down—it is not unreasonable to expect more targeted advertisement, and likely less privacy. This is a conservative inference. For indeed, we can see on the graph that the inverse relation between ad price and impression holds across the entire period.

In sum, when competition in social media advertising increases, privacy might be the loser.

The third question is easier. Since we cannot either infer that more competition is good for privacy, we could stop our analysis here.[28] But a brief

---

26. See Dina Srinivasan, "The Antitrust Case Against Facebook: A Monopolist's Journey Towards Pervasive Surveillance in Spite of Consumers' Preference for Privacy" (2019) 16(39) *Berkeley Business Law Journal* 81. The paper makes a qualitative before and after analysis of Facebook that compares privacy outcomes pre and post monopoly power. Srinivasan argues a sort of predatory conduct, whereby Facebook initially competed by offering superior privacy protections. Once dominant, Facebook allegedly undermined privacy to "initiate consumer surveillance to undermine for the purpose of delivering more targeted advertising, but the competitive market would not allow it." Srinivasan considers that before 2014, "privacy was a critical form of competition in a functioning market." This is a peculiar claim. Many analysts consider that Facebook's dominance owes to good timing, meticulous growth, and efficient product differentiation. In particular, Facebook required users to identify themselves, compared to Myspace. Identification hardly means more privacy (but perhaps, better user selection). See Alex Moazed and Nicholas L Johnson, *Modern Monopolies: What it Takes to Dominate the 21st Century Economy* (Saint Martin's Press 2016) 167 and 179.

27. Due possibly, to the launch of its Audience Network product in 2014, which allowed developers to place ads in their apps. This put Facebook in direct competition with Google.

28. "Final Report of the Stigler Committee on Digital Platforms" (2019) George J Stigler *Center for the Study of the Economy and the State*, 60: "The economic literature suggests that competition by itself cannot resolve the issue raised by the exploitation of behavioral biases or poor

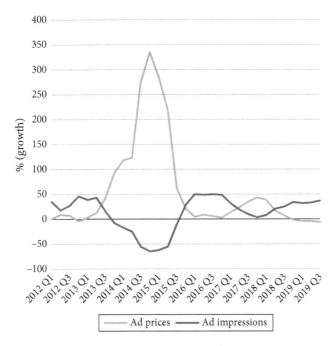

Figure 6.1 Facebook Ads—Year-over-Year Growth

discussion of additional externalities that might be created by competition will reveal why some regulation of privacy, not antitrust, is the way forward for policy.

If one thing is clear in this controversial area, it is that targeted ads do not bring undisputable consumer benefits.[29] Granted, a common belief is that people prefer targeted to non-targeted ads. But this view is not supported by the evidence (at least to the extent that targeted ads require personal data extraction). Consumer surveys find that users have low comfort levels with the use of personal data for the purpose of targeted advertisement, and that

consumer information. This is because staying profitable in a competitive environment may force firms to exploit behavioral bias to achieve maximal profitability."

29. In a survey of 2017, 26 percent of respondents found search engine advertising very annoying and 27 percent kind of annoying. And 56 percent found search advertising not helpful. See Statista, "Share of consumers who felt annoyed by advertising on search engines in the United States as of May 2017" (2017) https://www.statista.com/statistics/718462/us-consumer-opinion-search-advertising/ accessed 27 April, 2020.

search engine or social media advertisements are less trusted advertising channels than print or TV when users make purchasing decisions.[30]

Survey data thus appear to validate Sir John Hicks' view that the "expenditure upon advertisement may well be excessive, since it is determined in a way which is unrelated to its social function."[31] This categorically negative view of advertisement spending might sound shocking. Many other experts look at advertisement as a sacred cow of individual freedom, a paragon of free speech and unbridled competition. The reality is probably more nuanced. In economic literature, three theories of advertisement compete: advertisement as persuasion, advertisement as information, or advertisement as a complement.[32] Economists agree that all have distinct social value, and require different *normative* responses.

The bottom line is that competition might not promote privacy. If there is a social preference for privacy, regulation is a better approach than antitrust. In retrospect, the Court of Justice of the European Union appropriately held in *Asnef/Equifax* in 2006 holding that "any possible issues relating to the sensitivity of personal data are not, as such, a matter for competition law" and "may be resolved on the basis of the relevant provisions governing data protection."[33]

C. Fake News

Fake news are "news articles that are intentionally and verifiably false," and that mislead readers.[34] The term has become a buzzword in recent years. Claims have been made that "fake news" played a determinant role in the

30. Statista, "Adult views on targeted advertising in the U.S." (2019) <https://www.statista.com/statistics/993399/adult-opinion-targeted-ads-us/> accessed April 22, 2020 and Statista, "Most trusted advertising forms for purchasing decisions in the U.S. 2016" (2018), <https://www.statista.com/statistics/422942/most-influential-advertising-forms/> accessed April 22, 2020.
31. John Hicks, *Wealth and Welfare: Collected Essays on Economic Theory* (Harvard University Press 1981)(Preface—and a Manifesto).
32. Kyle Bagwell, "The Economic Analysis of Advertising" in Mark Armstrong and Robert Porter (eds), *Handbook of Industrial Organization* (Elsevier 2007).
33. *Asnef-Equifax, Servicios de Información sobre Solvencia y Crédito, SL v Administación del Estado Asociación de Usuarios de Servicios Bancarios (Ausbanc)* [2006] ECLI:EU:C:2006:734.
34. Hunt Allcott and Matthew Gentzkow, "Social Media and Fake News in the 2016 Election" (2017) 31(2) *Journal of Economic Perspectives* 213 (hereafter Allcott and Gentzkow, "Social Media and Fake News").

2016 US presidential elections. For example, a largely relayed fake news was that Pope Francis endorsed Republican candidate Donald Trump.

Fake news exacts substantial social costs. In particular, by decreasing news accuracy, fake news undermines the ability of the democratic process to select outcomes that correspond to the truth, and on which citizens prefer to base their decisions.[35]

The growing importance of fake news is often tied to the emergence of big tech firms in social networks and search engines. Empirical data suggests that referrals from social media account for less traffic on mainstream news sites than on fake news sites.[36]

Confronted with fake news, some have looked for a monopoly explanation.[37] As we understand it, the argument is that undisciplined by rivals search engines and social networks, Google and Facebook can freely serve fake news without fear of user, developer, or publisher dissatisfaction. Besides, firms like Google and Facebook who compete for attention with "legitimate news publishers" have ability and incentives to disfavor the latter's content, and favor other news suppliers.[38]

These facts are sufficient to guide our inquiry. To focus on social media platforms only, our first question asks whether fake news are caused by monopoly power. On close examination, the monopoly explanation does not hold. In the existing literature, the main contributive source of fake news is the intense *competition* created by social media in the market for content production, not monopoly.[39] The point is easy to make: social media has eliminated the cost of entry in the news production market, allowing small scale agents to engage in journalism without incurring the fixed cost of a newsroom.[40] The result has been entry of non-journalists— including ideology driven or profit maximizing (click baiting) agents who

---

35. ibid 219.
36. ibid 212.
37. Sally Hubard, "Fake News is a Real Antitrust Problem" (2017) 1(3) *Competition Policy International*.
38. ibid 4.
39. Previous economic studies have shown that competition in the production of news leads to slanting toward readers' biases. See Sendhil Mullainathan and Andrei Shleifer, "The Market for News" (2005) 95(4) *American Economic Review* 1031.
40. Bertin Martens et al, "The Digital Transformation of News Media and the Rise of Disinformation and Fake News" (2018) *JRC Working Papers on Digital Economy* 2, 17 (hereafter Martens et al, "The Digital Transformation of News Media").

draw advertisement revenue when users click on their site—into what was traditionally defined as journalism.[41]

True, social media technology compounds the problem of fake news. The reduced form of content on social media—snippets, newsfeeds, or short tweets read on phones—gives predominance to headlines over substance, making it difficult to assess veracity.[42] The speed of news dissemination online leaves little time for fact-checking.[43] And the "socialness" of social media ads a layer of legitimacy to "fake news" shared by aligned friends.[44] But this has nothing to do with monopoly. In reality, blaming social media platforms for fake news is like blaming supermarkets for junk food. Fake news production is the original sin.

Of course, the advent of highly efficient fake news distribution channels spurred an explosion in fake news production. But again, it is a stretch to see a monopoly problem in the distribution of bona fide or fake news by social networks. An often reported statistic suggests that 62 percent of US adults get news on social media.[45] Yet, there is a qualitative difference between news sourced from social media news and from other sources. In a seminal survey, Hunt Allcott and Matthew Gentzkow found that only 13.8 percent of respondents viewed social media as their most important news source for a US presidential election.[46] The reality is that even if 62 percent of US adults get news from social media, television remains the "dominant source" for the distribution of political news and information.[47]. It is one thing to suggest that social media platforms exacerbate the fake news problem. But it is quite another to affirm that social media monopoly is the culprit.

The second question is even easier to consider. Would competition in social media lead to a better equilibrium? As previously discussed, a possible equilibrium under competition is one of qualitative differentiation. New social media players compete by prioritizing high quality content over fake

41. Allcott and Gentzkow, "Social Media and Fake News" (n 34) 217.
42. ibid 221.
43. Martens et al, "The Digital Transformation of News Media" (n 40) 17.
44. Edson C Tandoc Jr, Zheng Wei Li, and Richard Ling, "Defining "Fake News": A Typology of scholarly definitions" (2017) 6(2) *Digital Journalism* 148; Alcott and Gentzkow, "Social Media and Fake News" (n 34) 221.
45. See Jeffrey Gottfried and Elisa Shearer "News Use across Social Media Platforms 2016" (*Pew Research Center*, May 26, 2016). <http://www. journalism.org/2016/05/26/news-use-acrosssocial-media-platforms-2016> accessed April 22, 2020.
46. Allcott and Gentzkow, "Social Media and Fake News" (n 34) 224.
47. ibid 223.

news. The other possible equilibrium is one of excess competition. As social media players compete for user attention, they prioritize addictive content over high quality content, and possibly more fake news.

The evidence available to date does not clearly tell us which equilibrium is more plausible. But we know three things. One, history suggests that competition in news distribution is highly consistent with fake news. Historian Robert Darnton writes:

> The production of fake, semi-false, and true but compromising snippets of news reached a peak in eighteenth-century London, when newspapers began to circulate among a broad public. In 1788, London had ten dailies, eight tri-weeklies, and nine weekly newspapers, and their stories usually consisted of only a paragraph. "Paragraph men" picked up gossip in coffee houses, scribbled a few sentences on a scrap of paper, and turned in the text to printer-publishers, who often set it in the next available space of a column of type on a composing stone.[48]

Two, simple economics suggest that competition in news distribution might not reduce fake news in the long term. Under competition, firms make lower profits. This, in turn, might trigger a race to the bottom. With lower profits under competition, firms have to cut down costs. They might be incentivized to focus on variable costs reductions. Laying off fact checkers might be a rational strategy under competition.[49] Alternatively, they may roll out automated fact-checking technologies like bots or cyborgs.[50] But these are fixed costs with increasing returns to scale. There is, therefore, a non-trivial possibility that due to fixed costs effects, competition might inexorably lead to consolidation in the long run.

Three, online articles can be seen by anyone. Hence, as soon as some users multi-home—that is they patronize more than one platform—there is a significant probability that fake news will spread from one social media to the others. Only in the unrealistic hypothesis that users of social media platforms single-home, can we expect (temporary) confinement of fake news on one platform, and (timely) invalidation by fact checkers.

48. Robert Darnton, "The True History of Fake News" (*The New York Review Daily*, February 13, 2017) <https://www.nybooks.com/daily/2017/02/13/the-true-history-of-fake-news/> accessed December 8, 2019.
49. Especially when fact-checkers are independent, and/or part-time, contractors who can be hired and dismissed with much flexibility.
50. David M J Lazer et al, "The Science of Fake News" (2018) 359(6380) *Science* 1094.

At this stage, it should be clear that monopoly is neither a proximate nor a distant cause of fake news. Let us look quickly at the third question. If harm is lower with competition, can we be confident that competition creates no other externalities? One way to think about this is to consider entry of a social media platform that promotes high quality news. There is reason to assume that the social media platform incurs costs to select authentic over fabricated content. And there is reason to assume that the social media service must remain free for users. Users of social media platforms are price elastic, and generally disfavor subscription-based social media.[51] Upshot? The entrant must recoup its investments in the selection of high quality content somewhere. This will be done on the money side of the platform, that is in revenue-sharing agreements with advertisers and marketers, including news publishers. This, in turn, might adversely impact the latter's ability to invest in the production of high quality content. Again, less trusted news might be the outcome.

D. Hate Speech

The case of hate speech is easier. Hate speech is speech that threatens, incites violence, inflicts severe emotional distress, harasses, defames, or silences counter speech.[52] Online intermediaries like search engines or social networks have enabled hate speech, allowing hatemongers to "propagate their rhetoric and strategies, recruit, organize and unify."[53]

By contrast to the European Union where several countries have laws prohibiting hate speech,[54] it is largely unregulated in the United States. The

---

51. Otherwise, Facebook might just have defused controversy over privacy by converting its ads-based business model into a subscription-based one.

52. Danielle Keats Citron and Helen L Norton, "Intermediaries and Hate Speech: Fostering Digital Citizenship for our Information Age" (2011) 91(4) *Boston University Law Review* 1435.

53. James Banks, "Regulating Hate Speech Online" (2010) 24(3) *International Review of Law, Computers & Technology* 234.

54. Note, though, that in the EU online intermediaries benefit from a limited liability regime for illegal users' activities provided that they do "not have actual knowledge of illegal activity." And the law prevents Member States from imposing on Internet intermediaries a general obligation to monitor the information they transmit or store or a general obligation to actively seek out facts and circumstances indicating illegal activities. See, in particular, Articles 12 to 15, Directive 2000/31/EC of the European Parliament and of the Council of 8 June 2000 on certain legal aspects of information society services, in particular electronic commerce, in the Internal Market (Directive on electronic commerce) [2000] OJ L178/1.

First Amendment only grants protection against government restrictions of free speech, leaving big tech firms full discretion over the control of online expression. Moreover, Section 230 of the Communications Decency Act limits incentives for private platforms to do so, by giving them immunity from liability on the basis of user-generated content.[55]

In the United States, some concerned with online intermediaries' large discretion over content have instrumentally analogized them to natural monopolies, and in turn called for greater government intervention.[56] Oren Bracha and Frank Pasquale have, for example, criticized search engines' excessive power over the filtering of information. President Trump has multiplied attacks against Google's alleged suppression of conservative content, and promotion of liberal content.[57]

But one can instantly see that the problem of hate speech is different. Hate speech involves passivity toward the filtering of content. In reality, no straightforward argument has been made to link hate speech with big tech firms' monopoly. And for good reason. History tells us that the correlation between monopoly and expression is more one of restriction than one of liberation. Speech monopolies have historically controlled ideas and promoted views aligned with their self-interest.[58] Hate speech by contrast is a radical form of free, uncontrolled speech.

---

55. See Communications Decency Act of 1996, 47 USC, Section 230(c)(1) provides: "No provider or user of an interactive computer service shall be treated as the publisher or speaker of any information provided by another information content provider." Note, however, that platforms might be liable for user-generated content in cases of criminal liability, IPR infringement, or when they engage in editorial scrutiny. For more, see Daphne Keller, "Toward a Clearer Conversation About Platform Liability: Response to Olivier Sylvain's essay 'Discriminatory Designs on User Data'" (2018), Knight First Amendment Institute <https://knightcolumbia.org/content/toward-clearer-conversation-about-platform-liability> accessed 1 December 8, 2019.

56. Oren Bracha and Frank Pasquale, "Federal Search Commission—Access, Fairness, and Accountability in the Law of Search" (2008) 93(6) *Cornell Law Review* 1149.

57. Adam Satariano, Daisuke Wakabayashi, and Cecilia Kang, "Trump Accuses Google of Burying Conservative News in Search Results" *The New York Times* (August 28, 2018) <https://www.nytimes.com/2018/08/28/business/media/google-trump-news-results.html?rref=collection%2Fbyline%2Fadam-satariano&action=click&contentCollection=undefined&region=stream&module=stream_unit&version=latest&contentPlacement=1&pgtype=collection> accessed December 8, 2019.

58. The concern of speech monopoly is one in which private organizations enjoy monopolistic power over ideas. Kathleen M Sullivan, "Free Speech and Unfree Markets" (1995) 42(4) *UCLA Law Review* 949. Recall the known opposition of the Church to the printing press. Or, closer to us, recall the press's opposition to radio broadcasting. On this, see Ronald H Coase, "The Market for Goods and the Market for Ideas" (1974) 64(2) *The American Economic Review* 384.

Hate speech is generally produced by individual agents or organizations operating behind information asymmetries. Antitrust is not the right remedy in this context. In fact, it might be presumably cheaper to police hate speech, and enforce laws, on a centralized Internet with a few oligopoly firms than in a more decentralized system.[59]

To date, most debates on hate speech have (rightly) started from a regulatory approach.[60] In Europe, for example, the EU Commission negotiated in 2016 a code of conduct with several firms like Google, Microsoft, Facebook, and others to combat the spread of illegal hate speech online in Europe.[61]

E. Models of Regulation

If regulation is the appropriate tool to address novel harms, what is the best model? Experts commonly discuss three types of regulatory approaches: utilities style regulation, retail distribution regulation, or consumer protection. Other models like media regulation or prudential regulation might arguably become relevant as platforms vertically integrate into specific areas like content or banking.[62] However, at this point of the conversation, we want

---

59. Edina Harbinja and Vasileios Karagiannopoulos, "Decentralized Web: What Cost a Free Internet?" *Asia Times* (March 14, 2019) <https://www.asiatimes.com/2019/03/article/decentralized-web-what-cost-a-free-internet/> accessed December 8, 2019.

60. US antitrust doctrine found that the First Amendment could limit applicability of the Sherman Act to firms' anticompetitive lobbying and advocacy activities. See *Eastern R R Presidents Conference v Noerr Motor Freight, Inc* [1961] 365 US 127 and *United Mine Workers v Pennington* [1965] 381 US 657. However, the Supreme Court refused to go as far as to exonerate exchange of information amongst competitors on the basis of the First Amendment. See *Giboney v Empire Storage & Ice Co* [1946] 336 US 490, 502.

61. European Commission Press Release, "European Commission and IT Companies Announce Code of Conduct on Illegal Online Hate Speech" (May 31, 2016) <https://ec.europa.eu/commission/presscorner/detail/en/IP_16_1937> accessed December 8, 2019.

62. Currently, most big tech firms operate as online intermediaries. They thus seem to enjoy less control over content than traditional media companies. This might have dispelled concerns of excessive concentration of ownership or threats to the diversity and the plurality of views online. This might change with big tech vertical integration in content production like movies, audio, or news. See, for a very quick reference to media regulation, Angela Daly, "Beyond 'Hipster Antitrust': A Critical Perspective on the European Commission's Google Decision" (2017) 1(3) *European Competition and Regulatory Law Review* 188. There is also an anticipation of big tech entry into banking. If this is the case, the hard policy question will be to know how a level playing field can be ensured between incumbent banking players and the tech giants. On this see Miguel de la Mano and Jorge Padilla, "Big Tech Banking" (2019) 14(4) *Journal of Competition Law & Economics* 494; Xavier Vives, "Digital Disruption in Banking" (2019) 11 Annual Review of Financial Economics 243–272.

to keep the discussion within practical bounds. We therefore focus on the three main models encountered in contemporary policy conversation. And it goes without saying that softer regulatory approaches than government regulation might be envisioned.

Let us start with utilities regulation. Under this model, regulation aims to open up to competition markets subject to natural monopolies. This is primarily done through mandatory duties of shared access to the infrastructure, access pricing rules, rate setting. Utilities regulation also occasionally tries to prevent expansion of monopoly power in related markets through line of business restrictions.

In digital markets, a version of utilities regulation that is commonly discussed consists in imposing data sharing, portability, or mobility obligations on dominant firms.[63] The underlying idea is that control of large amounts of data constitutes an "essential facility," and that shared access to large datasets promotes competitive entry. In short, the freer the data, the better. Microsoft—long-time antitrust complainant against Google—spent years unsuccessfully arguing before antitrust agencies that Google's scale in data gave it a large incumbency advantage in search. Utilities regulation would have provided a quicker remedy.

For obvious reasons, utilities-based regulation of big tech is a bad idea. The previous analysis casts doubt on the ability of market competition to supply more privacy, authentic news, or civic speech. Instead, there is a plausible chance that increased competition in digital markets will lead to a race to the bottom, in which price competition (eg, on ad markets) will be the winner, and non-price competition (eg, on privacy) will be the loser.[64] Unless one can invalidate that hypothesis, no social planner concerned with the novel harms attributed to big tech should bet on (costly) utilities regulation.[65]

---

63. Jason Furman et al, "Unlocking Digital Competition: Report of the Digital Competition Expert Panel" (*HM Treasury* 2019) <https://www.gov.uk/government/publications/unlocking-digital-competition-report-of-the-digital-competition-expert-panel>; Inge Graef, "Blurring Boundaries of Consumer Welfare: How to create Synergies between Competition, Consumer and Data Protection Law in Digital Market" in Mor Bakhoum et al (eds), *Personal Data In Competition, Consumer Protection and Intellectual Property Law* (Springer 2018).

64. We need not discuss again the losses of allocative and dynamic efficiency associated to policies that reduce concentration in markets with network effects and increasing returns to adoption.

65. A radical, and perhaps faster remedy might be government-subsidized digital platforms, that would ensure the minimal level of privacy deemed appropriate.

Additionally, to the extent that competition might produce better outcomes in relation to privacy, fake news, and hate speech, utilities regulation creates opportunities for inefficient rivals to engage in rent seeking. Appeal to public authorities and courts provides a route to reverse-engineer market outcomes. This in turn chills successful firms' incentives to innovate, and negates the very principle of competition on the merits.

The second model is retail regulation. Unlike utilities regulation, retail regulation does not seek to introduce competition, but to protect small firms. Retail regulation specifies constraints on opening hours, geographic location, marketing techniques, discount, and pricing at wholesale and retail levels, and interactions between small and large firms. To paraphrase a famous Supreme Court Opinion (albeit handed in a different context), retail regulation operates "at or near the outer boundary" of competition law.[66]

In digital markets, a concrete application of retail regulation consists in declaring big tech firms in control of a superior bargaining position (or gatekeeping position), and in turn imposing on them a gamut of non-discrimination duties, pricing moderation rules, and must carry obligation. Online music service Spotify started legal proceedings in the European Union to reduce Apple's 30 percent fee on sales made through the App Store. Retail regulation would achieve this instantly.

Retail regulation of big tech firms is clearly of no help in relation to privacy or hate speech. But it might offer a better deal to content suppliers, including news producers. At the same time, retail regulation of big tech raises two related problems. First, economic theory does not define "superior bargaining power."[67] Short of a workable threshold definition, regulatory rules based on superior bargaining power convert courts and agencies into revenue-sharing forums, to which disgruntled suppliers (or customers) can turn in order to reverse otherwise lawful contracts.

Second, by raising transaction costs, retail regulation of big tech firms promotes incentives to vertical integration or exit from markets. This means less revenue for small firms, not more. Consider the example of the EU

---

66. *Verizon Communications, Inc v Law Offices of Curtis V Trinko, LLP* [2004] 540 US 398.
67. See Benjamin Klein, Robert G Crawford and Armen A Alchian, "Vertical Integration, Appropriable Rents, and the Competitive Contracting Process" (1978) 21(2) *The Journal of Law & Economics* 297 who discuss the difficulty of distinguishing monopoly power from other types of rents at 299.

copyright directive 2019/790 on Copyright in the Digital Single Market.[68] The directive creates a special intellectual property right ("IPR") entitling EU press publishers to remuneration for online use of their press publications by information society service providers. The IPR covers press content like extracts and images. When the directive was implemented in France, Google objected that it would no longer show snippets in searches for EU press publishers unless press publishers wish otherwise—read in plain English grant Google a free license.[69] Google's exit means less revenue for smaller firms, not more.

The third model is consumer protection. Under consumer protection laws, regulation purports to empower unsophisticated consumers in the context of their dealings with sophisticated sellers. This is done by granting specific rights to consumers.

Traditionally, consumer protection has sought to improve consumer information, and to protect them from misleading advertisement, deception, and fraud. In more recent times, consumer protection laws have implemented a more expansive agenda, seeking to protect consumers against their own behavioral weaknesses. This has lent credence to concerns of institutionalized paternalism. Today, consumer protection laws cover a diverse collection of rules, including advertisement regulation, rights to mandatory contract provisions and pro-consumer interpretation, and product design obligations intended to effectuate real consumer choice.

In big tech markets, a concrete instantiation of consumer protection rules might be found in privacy regulation. In Europe, users of Internet services have a right to object to any decision-based "automated data processing," and can require "human intervention" on such decisions.[70] EU regulation foresees possible applications in relation to online credit application or e-recruiting practices without any human intervention.

---

68. Directive (EU) 2019/790 of the European Parliament and of the Council of 17 April 2019 on copyright and related rights in the Digital Single Market and amending Directives 96/9/EC and 2001/29/EC [2019] OJ L130/92.

69. Richard Gingras, "Nouvelles règles de droit d'auteur en France: notre mise en conformité avec la loi" (*Le Blog official de Google France*, September 25, 2019) <https://france.googleblog.com/2019/09/comment-nous-respectons-le-droit-dauteur.html> accessed December 8, 2019.

70. See Regulation (EU) 2016/679 of the European Parliament and of the Council of 27 April 2016 on the protection of natural persons with regard to the processing of personal data and on the free movement of such data, and repealing Directive 95/46/EC (General Data Protection Regulation) [2016] OJ L119, Article 22.

Compared with the other regulation models, consumer protection is a better framework. Privacy, fake news, and hate speech are negative externalities that all have in common to induce consumer harms.[71] Importantly, beyond its bias against sellers in B2C markets, consumer protection does not discriminate against firms on the basis of market power, business model, or technology. It is therefore neutral towards firms' choices. This feature must not be underestimated. Consumer protection laws' horizontality levels the playing field for all big tech firms, with moderate impact on incentives to innovate. Last, consumer protection is less exposed to rent seeking and revenue sharing conduct. This is because the beneficiaries of consumer protection are users. Consumer protection is therefore of limited assistance to disgruntled rivals or suppliers.

F. Conclusion

All in all, this exceedingly brief discussion suggests that novel harms allegedly inherent to big tech firms are neither causally nor consequentially related to monopoly power. Regulation appears to be the appropriate tool. More specifically, consumer protection regulation seems to be the better approach than competition spirited "utilities regulation" or revenue-sharing driven "retail regulation." Ronald Coase was right to exhort us to resist the ease of the monopoly explanation when we analyze emerging market phenomena about which we know little.[72]

★

★   ★

---

71. We use the term "consumer" in a broad meaning, but our argument applies generally to users, or even more largely, to citizens.
72. Ronald Coase, "Industrial Organization: A Proposal for Research" in Victor R Fuchs (ed), *Economic Research, Retrospect and Prospect, Volume 3: Policy Issues and Research Opportunities in Industrial Organization* (NBER Books 1972) 59–73.

Conclusion

The picture of big tech firms as monopolists is intuitively attractive, but analytically wrong. Monopoly findings based on observations of limited rivalry in the tech giants' origin market constitute a narrow view of competition. In spite of patent dominant positions, big tech firms do not live the quiet life. Their intense degree of effort is inconsistent with standard monopoly theory. A better picture is one of big tech firms as moligopolists, that is firms that coexist as monopolists and oligopolists.

The cover of this book gives the relevant allegory. It depicts a spinning top on a chess board. The spinning top represents the archetypal big tech firm. The chess pieces describe firms active in non-digital industries or in mature technology areas. Chess pieces compete by executing a series of punctuated moves informed by firm-level experience and constrained by industry norms. By contrast, spinning tops spiral in unrelenting, emergent, and unpredictable movement. When a spinning top crosses a chess piece trajectory, exit from the latter is likely. But spinning tops might also cross one another's trajectory. When this is the case, the spinning top that moves faster displays the highest survival chances.

To embrace the moligopoly framework, one is required to understand that firms can take competition from several sources, in various dimensions. Zero sum game rivalry for market share is just one of them. Technology is another. Digital industries exhibit a variety of intrinsic properties that work together to impose on firms a pressure equivalent to oligopoly competition. In particular, network externalities, increasing returns to adoption, and tipping effects produce significant discontinuities. These factors influence the direction and intensity of competition. Tech firms compete with others by a process of indirect entry, and reconfigure existing channels of competition.

Lawyers and economists may look for the lost keys under the lamppost because that is where the search is easiest. Fortunately, their problem is not

Big Tech and the Digital Economy. Nicolas Petit, Oxford University Press (2020). © Nicolas Petit.
DOI: 10.1093/oso/9780198837701.001.0001

ideological, it is methodological. Most available tools measure competition by reference to rivalry. Their focus is on analyzing the number of pieces remaining on the chess board. They do not ask whether the spinning top will then move to other games such as checkers or go. Most observers of legal and economic life make mostly static descriptions of the competitive process. That is, they attempt to provide estimation of competition when opponents' pieces are in a set position, without considering their past and future movements.

The result of this methodology is to discount two socially beneficial characteristics. The first is growth: the tech giants' diversification is a source of increasing marginal benefits to users, and in turn of allocative efficiency. The second is change: the tech giants' flexibility is a source of dynamic efficiency, that is of increases in the discounted value of users' future marginal benefits.

Legal analysis as well as economics pursue the truth, not the application of established methodologies. We should thus expect our legal and policy institutions to reject simplistic frameworks of monopoly diagnosis and embrace the complexity of moligopoly analysis.

With this said, do not misunderstand us. These pages are not a '*plaidoyer*' for big tech. A lot of heterogeneity characterizes the six tech giants. Not all of them deserve to be called moligopoly. The careful reader will probably have inferred from the previous chapters which big tech is of the good, the bad, or the ugly kind. And she will understand that the last two categories deserve an antitrust shock therapy. The point is to limit monopoly rents in tipped markets, and steer big tech firms toward competition in untipped markets.

Big tech firms' relentless growth is not without concern. Personal-data-intensive business models relying on targeted advertisement likely impose negative externalities on societies. Policy-makers are right to consider them. But again, the selection of an appropriate method matters. Looking at these predicaments through monopoly lenses is like using Facebook to get your news. It seems to do the job. But it might well be fake.

★

★   ★

Appendix 1

Full List of Firms Covered in Dataset

Firm Name	Ticker Symbol (if any)
1–800-FLOWERS.COM, Inc.	FLWS
Acer Incorporated	2353:TW
Activision Blizzard, Inc	ATVI
Acxiom	ACXM
Adobe Systems, Inc	ADBE
Advance Publications, Inc	Advance Publications, Inc
AfreecaTV Co. Ltd.	067160.KQ
Albertsons Companies, Inc	Albertsons Companies, Inc
Alibaba Group Holding, Ltd	BABA
Alphabet	GOOG.L
Altaba, Inc	AABA
Amazon.com, Inc	AMZN
AnyPerk	AnyPerk
Apache Corporation	APA
Apple, Inc.	AAPL
AppNexus, Inc	AppNexus, Inc
Apprenda	Apprenda
Archos SA	JXR.PA
Arista Network, Inc	ANET
ARRIS Group, Inc	ARRS
Asana	Asana
ASUSTEK Computer, Inc	2357.TW
AT&T	T
Atlassian	TEAM
Atos	ATO.PA
Autonation	AN
Autozone	AZO
Avid Life Media	Avid Life Media

Firm Name	Ticker Symbol (if any)
B2W Companhia Digital	BTOW3.SA
BabyAge	BabyAge
BabyCenter	BabyCenter
Baidu, Inc	BIDU
Barnes & Noble Education, Inc	BNED
Barnes & Noble, Inc	BKS
BBC Worldwide America, Inc	BBC Worldwide America, Inc
BBK Electronics Corporation	BBK Electronics Corporation
Bed Bath & Beyond	BBBY
Berkshire Hathaway Inc Class A	BRKA
Best Buy Co, Inc	BBY
Betanews	Betanews
Big Lots, Inc	BIG
Bilibili, Inc.	BILI
Blackbaud	BLKB
BlackBerry, Ltd	BB
Blockbuster, Inc	Blockbuster, Inc
Bloomberg LP	Bloomberg LP
BLOOMPIX srl	BLOOMPIX srl
Blucora, Inc	BCOR
Bluestem Group, Inc	BGRP
BMC Software, Inc	BMC Software, Inc
Booking Holdings, Inc	BKNG
Books-A-Million, Inc	Books-A-Million, Inc
Boscov's, Inc	Boscov's, Inc
Bose Corporation	Bose corporation
BOX, Inc	BOX
CA Technologies, Inc	CA
Cargurus Inc.	CARG
Casio Computer Co, Ltd	CSIOY
CBS Corporation	CBS
CDW Corporation	CDW
CenturyLink	CTL
Charter Communications	CHTR

Firm Name	Ticker Symbol (if any)
Check Point Software Technologies, Ltd	CHKP
Cisco Systems, Inc	CSCO
Citrix Systems Inc	CTXS
Cloudera, Inc.	CLDR
CloudUp	CloudUp
Clustrix	Clustrix
Cnova NV	CNV.PA
Cognizant Technology Solutions Corp.	CTSH
Comcast Corporation	CMCSA
Cookpad, Inc	CKPDY
Copart, Inc	CPRT
Corel Corporation	Corel Corporation
Costco Wholesale Corp	COST
Cox Automotive	Cox Automotive
Cox Communications	Cox Communications
Cox Enterprises, Inc	Cox Enterprises, Inc
Craigslist	Craigslist
Creative Technology, Ltd	CREAF
Criteo SA	CRTO
Criterion Theatre Trust	Criterion Theatre Trust
Cruel Design	Cruel Design
Cyworld Co, Ltd	Cyworld Co, Ltd
DataMine Lab	DataMine Lab
Decide Soluciones	Decide Soluciones
Dell Technologies Inc	DVMT
Diamondback Energy Inc	FANG
DigitalOcean	DigitalOcean
Dingus	Dingus
DirecTV Group Holdings	DTV
Discovery, Inc	DISCA
Dish Network Corporation	DISH
D-Link Corporation, Inc	2332.TW
Dollar General Corp.	DG
Dollar Tree	DLTR

Firm Name	Ticker Symbol (if any)
Dow Jones Industrial Average	^DJI
Dramatize	Dramatize
Dropbox	DBX
Dsw Inc	DSW
eBay, Inc	EBAY
eBridge Connections	eBridge Connections
EchoStar Corporation	SATS
EFFILIATION	EFFILIATION
EMC Corporation	EMC
Emusic.com, Inc	Emusic.com, Inc
Eniro AB	ENRO
Ericsson AB	ERIC
ESPN, Inc	ESPN, Inc
Eutelsat Communications SA	ETCMY
Event Zero	Event Zero
Everyday Health, Inc	Everyday Health, Inc
Express Inc.	EXPR
Facebook	FB
Family Dollar Stores	Family Dollar Stores
Fanatics, Inc	Fanatics, Inc
Fandor	Fandor
FIBERHOME TELECOM TECH CO-A	600498.SS
Fitbit, Inc	FIT
Flipkart	Flipkart
Fon	Fon
Foot Locker	FL
FORTINET INC	FTNT
Fox Entertainment Group	Fox Entertainment Group
Foxconn Industrial Internet Co, Ltd	601138.SS
Fujitsu Limited	6702.T
Fujitsu Technology Solutions (Holding) BV	Fujitsu Technology Solutions (Holding) BV
Fyndiq	Fyndiq
GameFly	GameFly

Firm Name	Ticker Symbol (if any)
Gamestop	GME
Garmin, Ltd	GRMN
Gateway, Inc	GTW
GH Capital, Inc	GHHC
Google	GOOG
Groupon Inc	GRPN
GuidePoint Media	GuidePoint Media
Gurunavi, Inc	2440.T
Harris Corporation	HRS
Hastings Entertainment	Hastings Entertainment
HBO	HBO
Hinchberger Consulting & Features	Hinchberger Consulting & Features
Honeywell	HON
Hoopniks.com	Hoopniks.com
HP, Inc	HPQ
HSN Inc (Home Shopping Network)	HSNI
HTC Corporation	2498.TW
Huawei	Huawei
Hulu	Hulu
HUYA, Inc	HUYA
IAC/InterActiveCorp	IAC
ifrs.wiley.com	ifrs.wiley.com
iKlix	iKlix
IMDB	IMDB
iN DEMAND	iN DEMAND
Indigo Books & Music, Inc	ING.DO
Infor, Inc	Infor, Inc
Insight Enterprises, Inc	NSIT
Instagram	Instagram
Intel Corporation	INTC
Intelius	Intelius
International Business Machines Corporation	IBM
Interpark Holdings Corporation	035080.KQ
iQIYI Inc.	IQ

Firm Name	Ticker Symbol (if any)
Iriver Limited	060570.KQ
iROKOtv	iROKOtv
iZSearch	iZSearch
J C Penney Corporation	JCP
Jasper	Jasper
JD.COM, Inc	JD
Jet.com	Jet.com
Jitterbit	Jitterbit
Jumia	Jumia
Juniper Networks, Inc	JNPR
Just Dial Ltd.	JUSTDIAL.NS
KAYAK Software Corporation	KAYAK Software Corporation
Kering	KER.PA
Kobo	Kobo
Koninklijke Philips NV	PHG
Koudai Gouwu	Koudai Gouwu
KYOCERA Corporation	KYOCY
L-3 Communications Holdings, Inc	LLL
Lazada	Lazada
Lenovo Group Ltd	LNVGY
Level 3	Level 3
Lexmark	Lexmark
LG Electronics	066570.KS
Liberty Interactive Corporation	QRTEA
LINE CORP	LN
LinkedIn Corporation	LNKD.N
Linksys	Linksys
Livesense, Inc	Livesense, Inc
LOVEFiLM UK Ltd	LOVEFiLM UK Ltd.
Lowe's Companies	LOW
Lycos	Lycos
Macy's	M
Media Matrix Worldwide Ltd	MMWL.BO
Media Networks	Media Networks

Firm Name	Ticker Symbol (if any)
Medianet Digital	Medianet Digital
MERCADOLIBRE INC	MELI
Metao	Metao
Micro Focus Software Inc	MFGP
Microsoft Corporation	MSFT
Microsoft Network (MSN)	Microsoft Networks MSN
mixi, Inc	2121.T
MobileVideo.TV	MobileVideo.TV
Molotov	Molotov
MOMO, Inc	MOMO
Monoprice	Monoprice
Monster Worldwide, Inc	MWW
MontaVista Software LLC	MontaVista Software LLC
Motorola Mobility LLC	Motorola Mobility LLC
Motorola Solutions, Inc	MSI
Mozilla Foundation	Mozilla Foundation
MTV Networks Company	MTV Networks Company
MUBI	MUBI
MySpace	MySpace
N-able Technologies	N-able Technologies
NAVER Corporation	035420.KS
NBCUniversal	NBCUniversal
Nebula	Nebula
NEC Corporation	6701.T
NetEase Inc	NTES
Netflix	NFLX
NETGEAR, Inc	NTGR
NetSuite, Inc	NetSuite, Inc
New York Times	NYT
Newegg, Inc	Newegg, Inc
News Corporation	NWSA
NHN BUGS Corporation	104200.KQ
Nintendo Co., Ltd	7974.T
Nokia Corporation	NOK

Firm Name	Ticker Symbol (if any)
Noon Pacific	Noon Pacific
Novell	Novell
Nuance Communications, Inc	NUAN
Oath, Inc	Oath, Inc
Office Depot	ODP
Okta, Inc	OKTA
One97 Communications	One97 Communications
Open Office	Open Office
Open Web Social Sourcing	Open Web Social Sourcing
OpenPeak	OpenPeak
Oracle Corporation	ORCL
Otello Corporation Asa	OPESY
Overstock.com, Inc	OSTK
PALO ALTO NETWORKS INC	PANW
Panasonic Corporation	PCRFY
Pandora Media Inc	P
Paypal Holdings, Inc	PYPL
PCCW	PCCWY
PCWorld Communications	PCWorld Communications
Peach	Peach
Peapod	Peapod
PeerStream, Inc	PEER
Pinterest	Pinterest
Quickflix	Quickflix
Quidsi	Quidsi
QVC, Inc	QVC, Inc
Rackspace Hosting, Inc	RAX
Rakuten, Inc	RKUNNY
Ravello Systems	Ravello Systems
RealNetworks, Inc	RNWK
REALWORLD Inc.	3691.T
Red Hat, Inc	RHT
Redbox Automated Retail, LLC	Redbox Automated Retail, LLC
Renren, Inc	RENN

Firm Name	Ticker Symbol (if any)
RhythmOne plc	RTHM.L
RLabs	RLabs
ROKU INC	ROKU
RunSignUp	RunSignUp
Ryze	Ryze
S&P 500 Index	^GSPC
Safeway	Safeway
Salesforce.com, Inc	CRM
Salon Media Group, Inc	SLNM
Samsung Electronics Co, Ltd	005930.KS
Samsung SDS Co Ltd	018260.KS
SanDisk Corporation	SanDisk Corporation
Sanyo Electric Co, Ltd	Sanyo Electric Co, Ltd
SAP SE	SAP
SAS (Statistical Analysis System) Institute	SAS
Scribd, Inc	Scribd, Inc
Seagate Technology plc	STX
Sears Holding Corporation	SHLD
SERVICENOW INC	NOW
SGI-Suggs Group, Inc	SGI-Suggs Group, Inc
Sharp Electronics Corporation	Sharp Electronics Corporation
Shoe Carnival	SCVL
ShopRunner	ShopRunner
Showtime Networks, Inc	Showtime Networks, Inc
Siemens AG	SIE
Siemens Healthineers AG	SHL.f
SINA Corporation	SINA
Skype	Skype
Slack Technologies	Slack Technologies
Smashrun	Smashrun
Smyth	Smyth
Snap Inc	SNAP
Snapdeal	Snapdeal
Software Engineering Professionals	Software Engineering Professionals

Firm Name	Ticker Symbol (if any)
Sogou, Inc	SOGO
Sohu.com Ltd.	SOHU
Sony Corp	6758.T
Sony Mobile Communications, Inc	Sony Mobile Communications, Inc
Spark Networks, Inc.	LOV
Splunk, Inc	SPLK
Spotify Technology SA	SPOT
Sprouts Farmers Market	SFM
Staples	Staples
Starz	Starz
Studio SBV, Inc	Studio SBV, Inc
Suitable Technologies	Suitable Technologies
Sun Microsystems, Inc	Sun Microsystems, Inc
Symantec Corp	SYMC
sys-con.com	sys-con.com
Tagged	Tagged
Talkin' Cloud	Talkin' Cloud
Target Corporation	TGT
Tencent Holdings Ltd	0700.HK
Tesla, Inc	TSLA
The finish line	The finish line
The gap	GPS
The Home Depot	HD
The Hut Group	The Hut Group
The J.M. Smucker Company	SJM
The Kroger Co	KR
The Meet Group Inc.	MEET
The Michaels Companies	MIK
The Saga Group plc	SAGA.L
The TJX Companies	TJX
Thomson Reuters Corporation	TRI
Time Warner Inc	TWX
Toshiba Corporation	TOSBF
Toys	Toys

Firm Name	Ticker Symbol (if any)
Traders Joe's Company	Traders Joe's Company
Trip4Real	Trip4Real
TripAdvisor Inc	TRIP
Tucows Inc.	TCX
Tumblr	Tumblr
Turner Broadcasting System	Turner Broadcasting System
TWENTY-FIRST CENTURY FOX	FOX
Twitch Interactive	Twitch Interactive
Twitter, Inc	TWTR
United Parcel Service	UPS
United Technologies Corporation	UTX
VentureBeat	VentureBeat
Verisign	VRSN
Veritone, Inc	VERI
Verizon Communications, Inc	VZ
VIACOM, INC	VIAB
Viki	Viki
Vipshop Holdings Ltd.	VIPS
VMware, Inc	VMW
VUDU, Inc	VUDU, Inc
Walmart, Inc	WMT
Walt Disney Company (The)	DIS
Wayfair LLC	W
WebMD Health Corporation	WebMD Health Corporation
Weibo Corporation	WB
Western Digital Corporation	WDC
Workday, Inc	WDAY
Xiaomi	1810.HK
Xtraice	Xtraice
Yahoo!, Inc	YHOO
Yandex NV	YNDX
Yelp, Inc	YELP
Youku Tudou	Youku Tudou
YouTube	YouTube

Firm Name	Ticker Symbol (if any)
YY Inc.	YY
Zappos.com, Inc	Zappos.com, Inc
ZTE CORP	ZTECOF
Zynga, Inc	ZNGA

Appendix 2

Firm Level Accounting Data: MB, MC, and MP

Firm	Year	Output (Q)	Price (P) ie R/Q or Marginal Benefit	Marginal Cost ie "Cost of Revenue"/Q	Marginal Profit
AMZN	1997	1,500,000	$98.51	$79.30	$19.21
	1998	6,200,000	$98.39	$76.80	$21.59
	1999	14,000,000	$117.13	$96.37	$20.76
	2000	20,000,000	$138.10	$105.31	$32.79
	2001	25,000,000	$124.90	$92.96	$31,94
	2002	n/a	n/a	n/a	n/a
	2003	40,000,000	$131.59	$100.16	$31.43
	2004	n/a	n/a	n/a	n/a
	2005	n/a	n/a	n/a	n/a
	2006	n/a	n/a	n/a	n/a
	2007	76,000,000	$195.20	$151.08	$44.12
	2008	88,000,000	$217.80	$169.27	$48.52
	2009	105,000,000	$233.42	$180.74	$52.68
	2010	130,000,000	$263.11	$204.32	$58.79
	2011	164,000,000	$293.15	$227.37	$65.79
	2012	200,000,000	$305.47	$229.86	$75.61
	2013	237,000,000	$314.14	$228.61	$85.53
	2014	270,000,000	$312.39	$232.41	$79.97
	2015	304,000,000	$326.27	$235.69	$90.58

Firm	Year	Output (Q)	Price (P) ie R/Q or Marginal Benefit	Marginal Cost ie "Cost of Revenue"/Q	Marginal Profit
GOOG	2008	27,880,000,000	$0.38	$0.15	$0.23
	2009	35,940,000,000	$0.31	$0.12	$0.19
	2010	41,250,000,000	$0.34	$0.12	$0.22
	2011	45,260,000,000	$0.39	$0.13	$0.25
	2012	46,760,000,000	$0.49	$0.17	$0.32
	2013	52,630,000,000	$0.51	$0.19	$0.32
	2014	50,520,000,000	$0.56	$0.22	$0.34
	2015	46,890,000,000	$0.74	$0.28	$0.46
	2016	40,920,000,000	$1.04	$0.40	$0.63
NFLX	2012	99,600,000	$36.24	$26.63	$9.61
	2013	123,490,000	$35.42	$25.24	$10.18
	2014	148,240,000	$37.13	$25.32	$11.82
	2015	171,620,000	$39.50	$26.75	$12.75
	2016	191,030,000	$46.23	$31.57	$14.66
	2017	210,290,000	$55.60	$36.42	$19.18
FB	2012	2,280,000,000	$2.23	$0.60	$1.63
	2013	2,849,000,000	$2.76	$0.66	$2.10
	2014	3,385,000,000	$3.68	$0.64	$3.05
	2015	3,949,000,000	$4.54	$0.73	$3.81
	2016	4,624,000,000	$5.98	$0.82	$5.16
	2017	5,378,000,000	$7.56	$1.01	$6.54

Appendix 3

Accounting Data: Alternative Allocation for Google

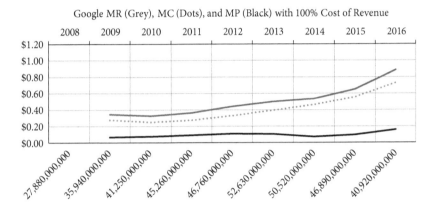

Google MR (Grey), MC (Dots), and MP (Black) with 100% Cost of Revenue

Appendix 4

Discontinuous Demand Curve in Network Effects Market

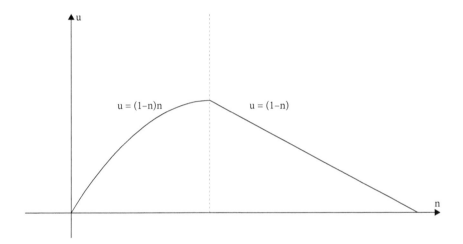

Author Index

Subject Index